Colonel the Hon. H. Mentz, D.T.D., Minister of Defence.

THE

UNION OF SOUTH AFRICA

AND

THE GREAT WAR

1914–1918

OFFICIAL HISTORY

The Naval & Military Press Ltd

in association with

The Imperial War Museum
Department of Printed Books

Published jointly by
The Naval & Military Press Ltd
Unit 10 Ridgewood Industrial Park,
Uckfield, East Sussex,
TN22 5QE England
Tel: +44 (0) 1825 749494
Fax: +44 (0) 1825 765701
www.naval-military-press.com
www.military-genealogy.com
www.militarymaproom.com

and

The Imperial War Museum, London
Department of Printed Books
www.iwm.org.uk

Printed and bound in Great Britain by
CPI Antony Rowe, Chippenham and Eastbourne

PREFACE.

AN attempt to write the history of South Africa's participation in the Great War of 1914 to 1918 presents problems the difficulties of which are not so apparent until their solution is undertaken.

While the efforts of the other Dominions were comparatively homogeneous and centralized, circumstances directed the South African activities into divergent channels that had little relation to each other.

Operations commenced for the purpose of obtaining certain objectives in German South-West Africa. These had suddenly to be suspended and attention diverted to something entirely different—the rebellion within the Union. When this concluded, the first objective was returned to, but along different lines and with differently organized means. There are thus two campaigns here—or even three—closely related, and at the same time so different as not to admit of simultaneous treatment.

The rebellion period has been broadly sketched, sufficient only to form an idea of its magnitude and relation to the South-West operations.

The actual German South-West campaign, which may be taken as having commenced after the Union Government had restored order within the Union—that is from 1915—is one of the most clear-cut and ideal campaigns of history. The chief concern here would be not to obscure and involve what was simple and successful.

After the South-West campaign the efforts of the Union of South Africa became divergent and are not easy to connect.

An Infantry Brigade is raised which is intended to represent the Union in France, but it finds its way to Egypt. Later, this Brigade returns to France, is practically annihilated, and reconstructed more than once. Heavy Artillery, to the extent of two brigades, also go from South Africa to France, but they serve far away from the Infantry Brigade.

A Signal Company that is sent to France becomes an Army Corps Signal Company, but is no more associated with the Artillery or Infantry Brigades than it is with the Railway Company, Auxiliary Horse Transport Company, or South African Labour Corps that are also in France.

In the meantime the East African campaign has been undertaken by South Africa. Large forces are sent there, and South Africa breaks the German resistance so far as to huddle his forces into the south-east corner of the colony; then to a large extent withdraws to partly take the matter up again later.

A Brigade of Field Artillery goes to Egypt and Palestine, and is followed by the Cape Corps. Recruiting for the Royal Air Force draws many South Africans into that service, while large numbers had gone overseas at their own initiative and are serving in Imperial units. The late German South-West Colony has to be garrisoned by occupation troops, and these have a successful little native campaign of their own. All the time the South African work behind the front to maintain all these enterprises has to continue.

To write a narrative that will do full justice to all these detached undertakings is difficult if, at the same time, each event is to be kept in its correct position of relative historical importance. The Battery or Battalion will sometimes demand more letter-space than can be given to a Division or Brigade in an equally important episode elsewhere, while on many notable achievements this work must remain silent for lack of space or because the incident was unconnected with the main success.

In general, the conflicting claims to importance are difficult to decide; judged from the view point of results, the rebellion and South-West campaigns must come first. For the reasons previously stated, not much is written about the rebellion, but an idea of the difficulties that had to be surmounted may be obtained by comparing this campaign to the later stages of the Anglo-Boer War, with this difference, that the irregular troops now were not so exhausted, and to some extent, at least, had the support of a great European Power.

But if South Africa had in these two campaigns shown that by rapid and well-directed action she could obtain great results inexpensively, in France and East Africa she had been found no less ready to pay a high price, and had shown that the South African soldier had also the great military virtue of knowing how to die.

This work does not attempt to assess and record what different units had achieved individually. That must be left to the unit historian, of which we have already had two very-well-written forerunners—"The South African Brigade in France" and "The History of the Cape Corps." And least of all does this claim to be a popular biography or "Who is Who." The main purpose kept in view has been to record the effort and achievement of South Africa as a whole, bearing in mind the old adage "too many trees and one fails to see the wood."

CONTENTS.

PAGE

PREFACE 3

PART I.—MILITARY OPERATIONS DURING 1914—THE REBELLION AND SOUTH-WEST AFRICA 9

PART II.—GERMAN SOUTH-WEST AFRICA 27

PART III.—GERMAN EAST AFRICAN CAMPAIGN 61

PART IV.—GERMAN EAST AFRICAN CAMPAIGN—SECOND PHASE 89

PART V.—THE SOUTH AFRICAN INFANTRY BRIGADE IN EGYPT 95

PART VI.—THE SOUTH AFRICAN INFANTRY BRIGADE IN FRANCE 99

PART VII.—OTHER SOUTH AFRICAN UNITS IN FRANCE 185

PART VIII.—ADMINISTRATION 211

APPENDIX I.—VICTORIA CROSSES WON BY SOUTH AFRICANS DURING THE WAR 225

APPENDIX II.—CASUALTIES 229

UNION OF SOUTH AFRICA AND THE GREAT WAR 1914-18.

OFFICIAL HISTORY.

ERRATUM.

Part I, Chapter V, Page 13.

"5th Mounted Regt. Permanent Force (S.A.M.R.)" should read "5 Mounted Regts. Permanent Force (S.A.M.R.)."

PART I.

MILITARY OPERATIONS DURING 1914: THE REBELLION AND SOUTH-WEST AFRICA.

PAGE.

I.—South Africa's Internal Conditions and External Relations at the Outbreak of War in 1914 ... 9

II.—General Summary of Opening Events of the War in South Africa 10

III.—South-West Africa—Nature of the Country 10

IV.—Enemy Resources 12

V.—Operations in 1914 against German South-West Africa and the Rebellion 13

I.

SOUTH AFRICA'S INTERNAL CONDITIONS AND EXTERNAL RELATIONS AT THE OUTBREAK OF WAR IN 1914.

BEFORE the South African military operations of 1914 can be correctly appreciated, it is necessary to have a clear conception of the internal conditions of South Africa and the external relations to other countries and people that were involved in the war.

A mere chronicle of events that have happened does not satisfy the sense of historical analysis, and gives no help towards gauging the importance or magnitude of events. All historical events are also matters of dispute to some extent, and, to minimize the probability of forming unjust or incorrect conclusions, we cannot be too careful in reconstructing the environment of the event.

South Africa, even if it presents no other advantages, is an indispensable post on the ocean line of communication between Europe and Asia. The Suez Canal may be barred by hostile land operations in its neighbourhood.

In addition to its strategic value, South Africa produces the largest part of the world's gold, sufficient coal for the requirements of the ocean line of communication, and considerable quantities of wool and maize, all of which are important items in war resources.

Even apparently insignificant events like strikes or labour unrest on the South African railways or mines may seriously interfere with the coal supply and impede ocean communication.

That the enemy was fully aware of these possibilities must be conceded, and that he had a very favourable field for enterprise in this direction must also be admitted.

The Dutch population of two of the Provinces of the Union of South Africa had, as citizens of independent republics, been engaged in a bitter war—which extended to the two other Provinces—with Great Britain twelve years previously, and the feeling then inflamed had not cooled down as much as it might have done if party politics in South Africa were entirely disassociated from racial questions.

A German Imperial Colony bordered immediately on Union territory, and, during the native war a few years previously, many South Africans had entered into closer relations with the German Government there.

The mission work among South African natives was very largely under German control. German communities had their own schools in South Africa, and that in these a certain amount of pan-Germanic propaganda was fostered was but natural. In trade and industry Germany was very well represented either by unnaturalized German subjects or British-born persons of German descent.

In view of all these circumstances it will have to be admitted that Germany had a more favourable field of influence in South Africa than anywhere else. To assume that she was not aware of these circumstances, or made no effort to derive advantage from them, would be doing an injustice to her intelligence and enterprise, and would presume an oversight on her part that is inconceivable to the average imagination.

II.

GENERAL SUMMARY OF OPENING EVENTS OF THE WAR IN SOUTH AFRICA.

Although it was fully realized by the Union Government that the ultimate fate of the German colonies would be decided on the battlefields of Europe, it was at the same time necessary to take immediate measures to obtain control of the south-west seaboard and harbours, so as to deny the enemy the advantage of a friendly coast on the flank of the European-Oriental line of ocean communication. Von Spee's Asiatic Squadron was at large in the South Atlantic; there were long-range wireless stations at Swakop and Luderitz harbours; and if the enemy could establish submarine or other raiding bases there, it would considerably inconvenience the European-South African line, and in the event of the Suez Canal closure the entire European-Oriental line of ocean communication would be affected, whether from a trade or military point of view.

The Union Government considered that Luderitz Bay presented better possibilities to the enemy than Swakopmund, which is an unsheltered roadstead, so it was decided only to occupy Luderitz Bay, while the wireless station and landing equipment at Swakopmund were destroyed by naval bombardment.

To take pressure from the Luderitz Bay expeditionary force, a Union force was landed at Port Nolloth to operate against the enemy's southern frontier, while another force was concentrated at Upington to threaten his eastern border.

These operations were, however, viewed with the greatest disfavour by a large section in South Africa, and although the operations could at that stage scarcely be considered of an offensive nature, being from the numbers employed as compared with those of the enemy more correctly considered as defensive demonstrations, the party in the Union which had been against the Government's action emphasized their disapproval by taking up arms in rebellion.

For the time being all attention had to be diverted to the rebel forces in the Cape, Free State, and Transvaal Provinces of the Union, and any defensive or offensive schemes against German South-West Africa had to be subordinated to the task of regaining control within the Union. By December, 1914, this object was attained, and the Union was free to consider a campaign against South-West Africa.

III.

NATURE OF THE COUNTRY—SOUTH-WEST AFRICA.

The largest part of South-West Africa is a plateau at an average altitude of 3,500 feet above sea-level. It has a very limited humidity and rainfall, and great variations of temperature. Along the railway from Windhoek over Karibib northwards is a narrow belt that receives more rain. This belt broadens out northwards, spreading as far as Outjo and Grootfontein.

Owing to the want of moisture the decomposition of surface is imperfect, forming a coarse sand unable to sustain any but the coarser forms of vegetation. The country is sandy where it is not rough, and the vegetation, although sufficiently dense to present obstacles to deployment and movement, is of no value as a source of supplies except for fuel.

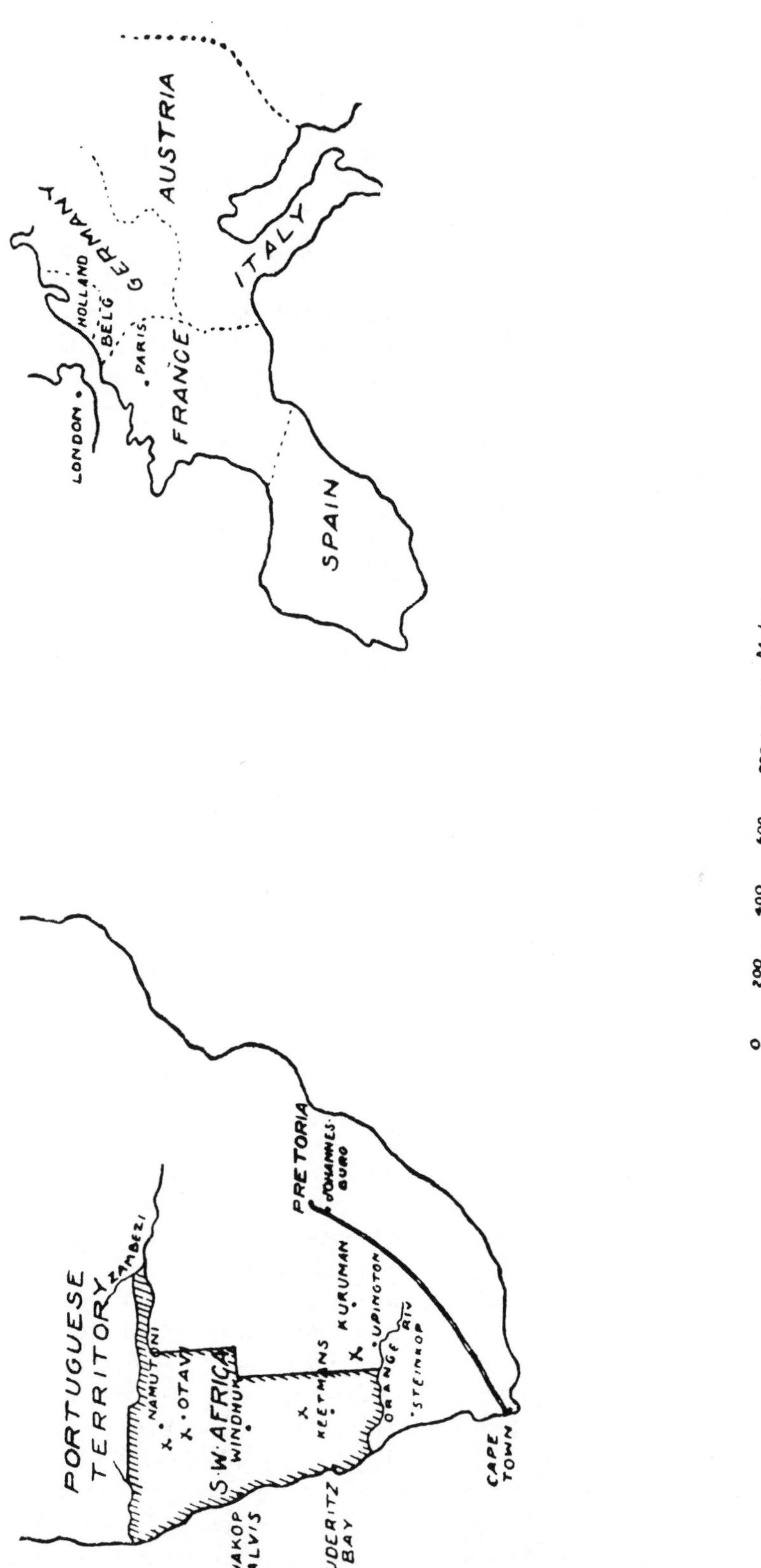

DIAGRAM No. 1.

For the Comparison of Areas and Distances.

To the west the plateau falls rapidly to sea-level, forming a coastal belt from 40 to 100 miles wide. This part is absolutely barren and waterless, and for the greater part covered with sand dunes. Improved roads do not exist, and the going for all arms may be classed as difficult over the whole of the country.

The railway system (see Diagram No. 2) was on two different gauges—a 3 ft. 6 in. gauge from Luderitz Bay over Keetmanshoop to Karibib over Windhoek, and having an extension from Seeheim near Keetmanshoop to Kalkfontein. From Swakopmund, the only other part of the colony, a 2 ft. 6 in. gauge went to Karibib, and from there northwards to Tsumeb and Grootfontein.

The climate is dry and healthy. The limited rainfall occurs chiefly in January and February. The country has no permanent running streams anywhere near any possible line of advance; the water-supply had to be derived from digging in river beds or making use of wells where they existed.

Supplies, with the exception of meat, were before the war never sufficiently raised in the territory to supply its own needs.

The Union territory where it adjoins South-West Africa presents similar features, forming a barren and difficult belt at least 200 miles wide, which any overland advance would have to cross before reaching the South-West border (*vide* Diagram No. 2).

Statistical Information—

Area of South-West Africa ...	322,450 sq. miles.
Population, 1912	14,816 Europeans.
Adult European males in 1912 ...	9,046
Native population in 1912 ...	80,900
Miles of broad gauge railway ...	800
Miles of narrow gauge railway ...	420
Coastal belt rainfall, per year ...	0·4 inch.
Inland belt rainfall, per year ...	4 to 12 inches.

IV.

ENEMY RESOURCES.

The peace establishment of the German forces in South-West Africa at the outbreak of war was 140 officers and 2,000 other ranks, organized in mounted companies and batteries. These were all specially picked men for colonial service. There were further known to be about 7,000 adult European males, most of whom had military service, besides several hundred South African rebels who had joined the German forces. In munitions the enemy was well supplied, large stores having remained in the country from the last native campaign.

At the beginning of 1915 the hostile forces were organized in eight regiments and nine separate companies, together with reserve and depot companies.

The food resources of the country were placed under rigorous control at the outbreak of hostilities, and considerable attention was devoted to agriculture—from all information obtained it was clear that the enemy would be able to subsist for a considerable time.

Although numerically weak and cut off from his home supplies, the enemy had natural advantages which, in his own estimation, rendered his position secure. The want of water and road laid down the Union lines of advance within very definite and narrow boundaries; any advance could be easily foreseen and the area mined, water "destroyed," and such dispositions made that the head of the attacking column could always be met by superior force. The broken nature of the country was in a high degree suitable for defensive tactics, and the enemy could dispute the advance at places where he held the water, and where the attacking force would have to deploy on very inconvenient ground after a 40 miles march from the last water. Any serious check under these circumstances would have resulted in absolute disaster, as the troops could not have held out long or undertaken a retirement without water. Besides this, the enemy had the advantage of acting on interior lines along a well-appointed railway system, which, as far as it gradually fell into our hands, would have to be repaired with material brought from oversea.

The enemy had several aircraft and an advantage over the Union resources in having an efficient camel corps—his information would presumably thus be so effective as to minimize any element of surprise.

V.

OPERATIONS IN 1914 AGAINST GERMAN SOUTH-WEST AFRICA AND IN CONNECTION WITH THE REBELLION.

On the outbreak of the war it became, in the first instance, necessary to secure the South African European line of ocean communication by denying the enemy any friendly seaports on the flank of this line. Formidable hostile naval forces were in the South Atlantic, to which the two ports, Swakopmund and Luderitz Bay in German South-West Africa, might have been of use. The first of these ports is dependent on artificial landing arrangements, the destruction of which by a British naval bombardment had neutralized the value of the place to the enemy.

Luderitz Bay was, however, more a natural harbour, and required occupation to deny it to the enemy, the wide desert-belt from the port inland rendered it strong against an attack from the land side, while the hills around the bay would give cover against bombardment from the sea. A Union force there would thus probably survive a combined land and sea attack, and once established could be expected to hold out for some time.

The importance of Luderitz Bay was, however, not appreciated by the German command, and no resistance was offered to Colonel P. S. Beves when, on the 18th of September, 1914, he landed there with—

The 7th Citizen Batt. Field Artillery (six guns).

One Squadron 5th Mounted Rifles (Imperial Light Horse).

8th Infantry (Transvaal Scottish).

11th Infantry (Rand Rifles).

One Section Engineers.

A total of 1,824, all ranks.

But the establishment of a diminutive force like the above in an important and hostile town and harbour, to which the enemy had railroad communication, could not have succeeded without the enemy's attention being pinned down elsewhere.

For this purpose Brig.-General Lukin had landed at Port Nolloth on the 1st September, and was moving towards and threatening the drifts over the Orange River into German territory. His force consisted of:—

2nd and 4th Permanent and 8th Citizen Batteries Field Artillery (each four guns).

Ammunition Column.

5th Mounted Regt. Permanent Force (S.A.M.R.).

10th Infantry (Wit. Rifles).

One Section Engineers.

A total of 2,420, all ranks.

At the same time there was a Union force of about 1,000 Mounted Rifles without Artillery, under Colonel Maritz, at Upington, on the Orange River.

The Union of South Africa had therefore a force of 5,324, all ranks, mobilized in three widely separated bodies far from their bases. It was known that the enemy had at the least a numerical equality and a great preponderance in artillery, besides he could act on interior lines and was not far from his base. The difficult intervening desert ground made it unlikely, however, that the enemy could deal a crushing blow to either of the three Union forces, and the situation may be looked on as well balanced for the object in view, which was the gaining of control of Luderitz Bay.

These satisfactory dispositions were suddenly and gravely deranged by the Government obtaining information that the force under Maritz was on the verge of deserting to join the enemy. Instead of being a component in the outward acting force directed against the enemy, it had swung round in a menacing way and was threatening to detonate inwards and ignite other dangerous elements in the Union.

We may now compare the situation to three cables that had been arranged to sustain a heavy weight, when, with little warning, one of the cables broke high up and, falling on the weight, added to what the remaining two had to sustain. That the situation now held possibilities of confusion, and even disaster, will be conceded. While the Government was as rapidly as possible mobilizing other forces, the force under General Lukin on the Orange River had chiefly to bear the additional strain, and, to take pressure off Colonel Beves at Luderitz Bay, Headquarters had to request high-pressure to the verge of self-sacrifice on the part of General Lukin, to which he most loyally responded. An incident of this period was the unfavourable action at Sandfontein. It has frequently been advanced that the tactical handling of troops at this action was unsound in getting committed to an action with very greatly superior numbers, or in not disengaging and retiring while it was still possible. Let us in justice to the officers concerned analyse their mental attitude at the time. When they left Capetown there were those vague rumours that always precede important events—to the effect that something was wrong with Maritz and his officers. Later on these vague rumours had gained substance, and although Maritz had not yet openly joined the enemy, the question of his strange conduct—news travels fast on the veld—was the subject of conversation in the Officers' Messes of General Lukin's force. They knew that of the two forces under the eyes of South Africa as supporting Colonel Beves at Luderitz Bay, the one under Maritz was attracting attention which in its kindliest form amounted to a question of the courage of Maritz and his officers to advance. Can we not condone General Lukin's officers for having gone to the other extreme rather than have the slightest trace of a shadow cast on their loyalty or courage.

On the 26th September a detachment of General Lukin's force, consisting of 190 rifles, two machine-guns, and two 13-pounder field guns, under Colonel Grant, came into contact at Sandfontein with a German force under the personal direction of Von Heydebreck, the German Commander-in-Chief, and his Chief of Staff. Von Weck. The German force consisted of the two detachments of Von Rappart and Ritter with Francke's detachment in reserve as follows:—

Major Von Rappart's Column—
- 3rd Regular Battery (four guns).
- 2nd Reserve Battery (four guns).
- 3rd Regular Mounted Company.
- 4th Regular Mounted Company.
- 5th Regular Mounted Company.

Major Ritter's Column—
- 2nd Regular Battery (four guns).
- 8th Regular Mounted Company.
- 4th Reserve Mounted Company.

Major Francke's Column—
- 1st Regular Battery (four guns).
- 2nd Regular Mounted Company.
- 6th Regular Mounted Company.
- 1st Reserve Mounted Company.

The small detachment of General Lukin's force under Colonel Grant had marched all through the night from Ramans Drift on the Orange River. Their route lay over heavy sandy ground without water, and when they the next morning discovered at Sandfontein that a

Infantry on the March, South-West Africa.

Armoured Cars—South-West Africa—which took part in the Action at Trekkop.

strong German force was advancing on them, there was no possibility of saving their two guns by retirement, as the teams were exhausted. The unequal contest lasted from 7.45 in the morning until 6 p.m. that night, when Colonel Grant, who was severely wounded earlier in the day, surrendered to avoid a hand to hand struggle in the dark, which could only be expected to have one termination, considering the superiority of the enemy numbers. Colonel Grant's casualties were 16 killed and 51 wounded, while the German losses were 23 killed, including Major Von Rappart, the one Column Commander. The German War Diaries of the units engaged, which were obtained after the final surrender of the German forces in South-West Africa, testified to the stubborn resistance of Colonel Grant's little force to a superiority of eight times the number of guns, and at least ten times the number of rifles.

The next event of the period was on the 22nd of October, when Maritz, who had now openly joined hands with the enemy, and had been reinforced by them and supplied with artillery, attacked a small detachment, which defeated him, at Keimoes. He had, by a system of weeding out and substitution, surrounded himself with officers who were open to his propaganda of sedition, rebellion, and desertion. On the 9th October, at Van Roois Vlei, he had disarmed and betrayed to the enemy the few officers and men of his force who had refused to join him. From Van Roois Vlei he moved over Keimoes to Kakamas, from where he attacked Keimoes on the 22nd of October. At 5 a.m. on the morning of that date he deployed his force of 1,200 rifles and a German 6-gun battery of field artillery against Captain Ross, who occupied Keimoes with 96 rifles of the Imperial Light Horse, and was without artillery or machine-guns. By 9.30 a.m. Ross was still holding the attack and Maritz was severely wounded. Reinforcements arriving about 10 a.m., Maritz's force retired back to Kakamas, leaving four prisoners and two killed, who were all Germans.

The Government had in the meantime mobilized troops under trustworthy and reliable officers. Brig.-General Mackenzie had arrived at Luderitz Bay on the 3rd of October with reinforcements, Colonel Brits at Upington on the 5th of October, also with reinforcements, and Colonel J. van Deventer at Calvinia on the 15th of October, where he was mobilizing the surrounding districts in support of General Lukin's force.

Colonel Brits endeavoured to attack Maritz at Kakamas on the 24th October, but Maritz retired to Schuit Drift, further west on the Orange River, while rebel forces raised at Maritz's instigation in the Carnarvon and Kenhardt Districts surrendered without severe resistance to Colonel Van Deventer on the 24th October.

By the 25th of October the energetic action of the Union Government had thus not only restored the equilibrium of forces around the German colony, but had further secured and reinforced its position there, while consolidating its coast objective at Luderitz Bay.

The Union Government was thus ready to meet the storm that was going to burst nearer home. It is not necessary here to recount details of the activities of the certain officers before they turned their arms against the Government. These will be found fully set out in the Government's Report on the Outbreak of the Rebellion, of 2nd February, 1915, the Report of the Select Parliamentary Committee on the Rebellion, April, 1915, and the Report of the Judicial Commission of Inquiry into the Rebellion, December, 1916.

On the 15th of September, 1914, General C. F. Beyers, the Commandant-General of the Citizen Forces, had tendered his resignation, which was accepted by the Government on the 19th September. On the same day the resignation of Kemp, who was Major and District Staff Officer in charge of No. 7

Military District (Potchefstroom), was also accepted.

Beyers left Damhoek with his commando on the 25th October, and on the afternoon of the following day General Botha, in command of a force mainly composed of commandos from the eastern Transvaal, left Pretoria by train, arriving on the morning of the 27th at Rustenburg, where the force detrained.

In the meantime events had occurred which gave evidence of determination on the part of those who had rebelled to persist in hostile action.

A rebel commando under N. W. Serfontein, M.L.A., demonstrated at Reitz, a centre of disaffection in the north-eastern Free State, and seized a train load of rifles and ammunition.

Heilbron was occupied by a rebel force and the Magistrate of the place imprisoned, while, on the 25th October, Kopjes, in the Orange Free State, was raided by a party of rebels under Hans Meyer and horses, rifles, and ammunition, as well as £500 cash from the local bank, stolen.

Telegraph lines were cut in several places in the Orange Free State. Parys was occupied by a rebel commando under Hans Meyer on the 27th October, and the first shot in the rebellion in the Orange Free State was fired outside that town at Commandant Van der Merwe, M.L.A.

Vredefort was seized on the same date by a detachment of the same rebel commando.

In the Transvaal, rebels under Muller conducted a forcible recruiting campaign and seized the police station at Bronkhorstspruit, near Pretoria.

It was quite apparent that the greatest difficulty would be experienced in bringing any substantial rebel force to an engagement, and that at first a considerable amount of immunity would be enjoyed by small raiding bands which it was obviously waste of time and resources to pursue.

Large concentrations under important leaders were therefore the first objects of attack by the Government, and the force under Beyers was the first to gain dimensions, which made its defeat or capture an object upon which effort might be profitably expended.

General Botha Defeats Beyers at Commissie Drift.

General Botha having detrained his force at Rustenburg in the early morning of the 27th October, and having obtained, locally and by means of his scouts, information as to the whereabouts of the rebel force, moved without delay towards Commissie Drift, a few miles south-east of the town. In the course of the afternoon touch was established with the rebel force, which thereupon, without even a perfunctory show of resistance, bolted headlong from the field, closely pursued by Government troops, of which a portion under Commandant Dirk van Deventer succeeded in bringing a party of rebels to a short engagement at Rooiwal. Here the first shot in the rebellion in the Transvaal was fired by a rebel, who wounded one Koster, of Commandant Van Deventer's force.

Beyers and his force reached Steenbokfontein that evening, and General Botha and his commandos, after resting at Commissie Drift, moved off in pursuit the same night in a south-westerly direction towards Koster, on the Zeerust-Johannesburg railway line.

Beyond some skirmishes the pursuit failed to bring any rebel force to action, and from Koster Station General Botha, having disposed several commandos to maintain order in the districts through which he had passed, returned by rail with the bulk of his force to Pretoria.

The operations, though they had produced little, if any, material result, had the immense value of establishing the *moral* of the Government troops and clearly showing their military superiority. This sense of superiority never left the Government forces throughout the two months' campaigning which was to ensue, and the ignominous flight of the rebel forces discouraged their supporters at the outset of their enterprise.

The rapid and effective movements of General Botha were thus of incalculable value at this early stage.

Early Operations in the Transvaal.

To deal with the different bands of rebels which were springing up throughout the disaffected areas, local commandants and commandoes of proved loyalty and experience were charged with the duty of attending to the rebels of their own districts.

A series of independent operations was thus early in train, and of these operations the most important at this time were those undertaken by Colonel J. J. Alberts, who was entrusted with the task of settling with the rebel forces in the western Transvaal under Wolmarans and Claasen, who had been the instigators of the mutiny at Treurfontein on the occasion of mobilization.

On the 29th October Colonel Alberts arrived at Treurfontein Station and, observing rebel patrols, pushed out reconnaissances, with the result that a rebel attack immediately developed and was signally defeated with heavy loss to the attackers who fled and were vigorously pursued for 20 miles. The toll of rebels killed and wounded was comparatively heavy and 240 were captured. Among the latter, and wounded, was Claasen, the first instigator of the local movement.

The sole loss on the Government side was Captain Nolte, who was brutally shot when conducting negotiations under a flag of truce.

Colonel Albert's victory was a heavy blow to rebellion in the western Transvaal and, combined with General Botha's success of two days earlier, effectually decided a large number of waverers to save their skins and abstain from active disloyalty.

Kakamas in the north-west Cape was reoccupied by Colonel Brits' troops on the 26th October.

De Wet entered Vrede on the 28th and insulted and maltreated the local magistrate, thus publishing his intention to resist the Government.

On the day of the fight at Treurfontein a rebel force occupied Wolmaransstad.

The Government on the same day advised all commanders of their forces that, if rebels would surrender their arms and go home quietly, no harm would be done to them and that the conditions applied to all rebels, leaders and rank and file alike.

Some resentment was expressed by the loyal burghers of Albert's force at this leniency, considerable bitterness having evidently been engendered by the rebels' shameful conduct in the case of Captain Nolte.

Events of the Closing Days of October.

Minor episodes during the last days of October were the rebellion of a large number of burghers at Senekal, the rebel occupation of Frankfort, and an attack on rebels under Fourie and Pienaar by Commandants Van Heerden and Klopper at Zoutpansdrift, in the Rustenburg District, when the Government force was compelled to retire.

Great efforts were being made about this time by General Hertzog to induce De Wet to go to Bloemfontein and see President Steyn, and all Union troops were instructed on the 1st November to desist from operations against the rebels till further instructions. A similar request was made by President Steyn to De Wet for reciprocal action towards the Union forces, but without effect, and it soon became apparent that De Wet had no intention of listening to reason or advice, and hostilities were resumed by the Government troops.

Situation in November.

After the action at Treurfontein, Beyers and Kemp collected their scattered forces and effected a large concentration at Vleeskraal, in the District of Bloemhof.

On the 2nd November Beyers left Vleeskraal with a force southwards towards the Vaal, and Kemp, who had joined Beyers at Vleeskraal a few days earlier, left with a large rebel force "to meet Maritz on the German border."

At the beginning of November therefore the situation to be dealt with by the Government was as follows:—

Beyers with a large force, having suffered defeat with a consequent set-back to the cause of rebellion in the Transvaal, was on his way to the north-western Free State, where a rebel leader, Conroy, was meeting with some measure of success in inducing burghers to join his commando.

De Wet, with gathering forces, was moving in the north-eastern Free State where the countryside was ripe for rebellion and the prestige of his name was a potent influence.

Kemp, with strong commandos, was rapidly heading for the north-western Cape Province, intent upon junction with Maritz.

For the rest, small isolated bands were causing some anxiety and damage in the Transvaal and Free State.

Pursuing the policy, already mentioned, of leaving small rebel bands to be dealt with in their districts by the locally raised forces, the three large forces, under the three chief leaders mentioned, were obviously the correct objectives for the Government's main military efforts.

Steps taken to deal with the Three Main Rebel Forces under Beyers, De Wet, and Kemp, at the beginning of November, 1914.

To deal with Beyers' force, which, though partially unarmed and indifferently organized, was of considerable strength, a force of Active Citizen Force units under Colonel Celliers was brought down from the north-western Cape Province, where it had been operating, to Kimberley, and had arrived there by the 8th November, and another strong burgher force under the command of Colonel Lemmer was concentrated at Maquassi.

General Botha personally assumed command of the operations at this stage against De Wet, whose influence and successful propaganda in the north-eastern Free State had become the most pressing menace at the moment. For the purpose of the operations which were to ensue, General Botha had on the evening of 10th November effected at Theunissen a strong concentration of Transvaal commandos under Colonels Myburgh and T. Smuts and others, while also at his disposal were a Free State force under Colonel Brand, the S.A.M.R. Brigade under General Lukin, and another strong Transvaal burgher force under Colonel Brits who had been summoned from the north-western Cape, having handed over command at Upington to Colonel Bouwer.

Local troops were raised in the districts through which it seemed obvious Kemp was likely to travel, and a commando (later to be reorganized for the German South-West African campaign as the Kalahari Horse) under Colonel Van Zyl, assisted by Captain Frylinck, was conspicuous in keeping touch with Kemp's forces, which were successfully engaged several times in their passage through the Kuruman District. Steps were taken to strengthen Colonel Bouwer's forces at Upington, and this officer was instructed from Defence Headquarters to find out the best places to meet and defeat Kemp before he should actually reach the Orange River.

General Botha's Operations Against De Wet.

General Botha, having completed his arrangements for his own concentration at Theunissen, left Pretoria by train on the afternoon of the 9th November, and after interviewing his chief officers at Vereeniging and Colonel Brand on the train, arrived at Theunissen on the afternoon of the following day.

De Wet, who had been at Lindley on the 3rd November and had refused finally to meet President Steyn, was known to have occupied Winburg on the 9th with a large force and to have allowed violence and insult. He himself assaulted the Mayor. The death of his son in action at Doornberg on the previous day no doubt contributed to his temporary loss of self-control.

General Botha accordingly marched with his force on the night of the 10th-11th November for Winburg and occupied that town without opposition early on the following morning.

After a day's halt, and in the light of information, the force left Winburg early in the evening of the 11th for Mushroom Valley to the south-east.

To this point of tactical concentration had been directed the force of Colonel Brand from the west and those of General Lukin and Colonel Brits from the south-west.

Daybreak brought to the main force the sounds of a heavy engagement close at hand in the direction of Hoenderkop, at Mushroom Valley, which was reached very shortly and where contact was at once established with the rear and right flank of a force which proved to be heavily engaged with Colonel Brand advancing from the west. After a brisk engagement the enemy, who sustained heavy casualties, succeeded in making good his escape through a nek to the south, which General Botha had issued orders should be blocked. Unfortunately these orders miscarried and De Wet, with the whole of his force, was thus enabled to escape what would otherwise have meant certain capture.

The Hoenderkop engagement practically sealed the fate of the rebellion, and the wholesale defection of De Wet's followers which followed, decided their former chief in trying to make good his escape to Kemp and Maritz, after joining hands with Beyers and Conroy in the north-western Free State. This intention, as a matter of fact, coincided with the purpose of the Government, and all efforts by the Government forces were at this time ordered to be directed to driving all rebel bodies westwards with the object of compelling as large an enemy concentration as possible.

General Botha, after marching through the adjacent districts, where resistance had completely died down, by way of Barletta, reached Clocolan on the 15th November, and when he had arranged for the disposal of adequate forces—which included the S.A.M.R. Brigade—to maintain the re-established order, entrained there with the bulk of his forces for Kimberley with the object of being able to march from there in any direction which circumstances might indicate as desirable.

De Wet, with a somewhat reduced following, and that shaken in *moral*, crossed the main line heading westward on the 16th November at Virginia, where a small force of 180 all ranks of the Active Citizen Force not only held their own but inflicted heavy damage on the stronger rebel force and prevented a number (reported by the Government officer, Lieut.-Colonel Badenhorst, as 1,500) from crossing the line at all. It may well be however, that little persuasion in the way of force was needed to suggest to the more faint-hearted of the enemy that the game was no longer worth the candle.

At this stage General Botha abandoned giving any further special attention to De Wet and turned his mind to the situation which was maturing as a consequence of Kemp's approach to Upington.

Colonels Celliers' and Lemmers' Operations in the North-Western Free State against Beyers and Conroy.

Beyers moving south from Katbosfontein, in the Wolmaransstad District, where Mr. Meintjes had interviewed him on behalf of the Government, crossed the Johannesburg-Fourteen Streams railway line, near Kingswood Station, on the 5th

November. His force was here fired upon by troops under Commandant Swartz, who pursued the enemy to the Vaal River. Beyers' force crossed and encamped some two or three miles to the south in the Free State.

On the 7th November Colonel Lemmer, who had started in pursuit of Beyers after receiving information from Commandant Swartz, having rapidly detrained his troops for the purpose, came into touch with Beyers' force at Verlatenkraal Drift, nine miles north-west of Hoopstad, and defeated it heavily, inflicting loss and capturing 400 prisoners.

Colonel Lemmer was thereupon instructed so to dispose his units along the railway line—with his own headquarters at Maquassi—as to be "ready to be moved by train any moment in order to meet Beyers and De Wet when they move west."

On the 10th November Beyers had reached Bultfontein and left under safe conduct to see President Steyn at Bloemfontein. A safe conduct for Beyers to visit De Wet having been refused by the Government, the former returned to Bultfontein on the 12th, the day of the latter's severe defeat at the hands of General Botha.

On the same day Colonel Celliers arrived at Boshof, his whole force reaching that place on the same evening.

Four days later, in consequence of information received from Colonel Lemmer to the effect that he was leaving for Aaronslaagte, where Beyers and Conroy had been located, Colonel Celliers left Boshof with his force and on the following day, 17th November, encountered the enemy on Verhelslaagte, twelve miles west of Bultfontein. The engagement which began, and continued for some time, with brisk fighting, became a sharp running fight over a line of from six to eight miles, and upon a general advance by the Government troops, at once developed into a rebel rout, during which a pursuit of eighteen miles was sustained, being broken off in consequence of the exhaustion of the horses of the pursuing force.

In addition to some loss in killed and wounded, 487 rebels were captured, 259 voluntarily surrendered, and some 300 rifles, together with to 30 to 40 vehicles, were taken.

As in the case of De Wet's force after the Hoenderkop fight, so in this instance the evidence of determination on the part of the Government caused a wholesale disappearance of Beyers' supporters, many of whom were in entire ignorance that their effort was isolated and by no means met with the approval of the bulk of their own countrymen.

The commandos of Colonels Celliers and Lemmer so effectively hustled the remaining portions of the forces of Beyers and De Wet, which were now vainly endeavouring to unite, that by the 26th November Colonel Celliers was able to report that De Wet had escaped over the Vaal River with only six men, hundreds of his supporters having doubled back and left him after Beyers' defeat on the 17th.

Beyers, having escaped with a small following, fled in the direction of Reitz, where Wessel Wessels and Serfontein were directing the assemblage of large rebel forces which eventually, as the last remaining formed rebel body in the Union, were to be dealt with by General Botha.

Operations against Kemp during his Journey to, and until his junction with, Maritz.

Kemp, as has been stated, left Vleeskraal on the 2nd November with the object of effecting a junction with Maritz on the German border.

Moving rapidly with a strong force of some 2,000 men he was at Schweizer Reneke on the 3rd and reached the vicinity of Kuruman five days later on the 8th November when, after a skirmish with the Government forces outside the town, he attacked the place without success.

General Botha watching the Action at Riet.

General Botha and Staff with the German Burgermaster at Windhoek.

He encamped some three miles from the town and sent an ultimatum to the local authorities demanding the surrender of all Government property which was stored in the town in comparatively large quantities.

After a meeting with the Government officials in the afternoon, Kemp succeeded in inducing the townspeople and police to give up their rifles.

He was, however, less successful in his negotiations with Captain Frylinck, commanding the detachment of Van Zyl's commando on the spot, who declined to listen to any proposition of surrender, and moved out of the town with his small force of 75 men, 200 rifles, and some wagons and stores, and took up a position some four miles from the town, and was shortly afterwards surrounded by the rebels during an armistice which had been arranged to extend from the 8th to the 10th November.

A patrol sent by Frylinck to advise Van Zyl, then a hundred miles distant, of the situation was captured by Kemp's men but sent back with their arms and unmolested.

Kemp upon this terminated the armistice, but refrained from attacking or interfering with the Government troops and, after obtaining supplies from Kuruman, moved off on his journey westward in the afternoon of the 9th.

Captain Frylinck immediately followed him and before long joined hands with Colonel Van Zyl who had 125 men with him.

In the course of the pursuit by Van Zyl an engagement took place at Mamaghodi on the 13th November, with the result that Kemp was diverted from the Hay District and forced into the desert beyond the Langeberg.

Three days later Van Zyl again attacked Kemp at Witzand, a water-hole, with some success, but was there compelled to give up the pursuit.

Kemp endeavoured to cross the Orange River at Kheis Drift on the 18th November but, having been checked here by a force under Colonel Royston, was compelled to follow a route to the north of the river in dry country.

For the next week Kemp's force was constantly in touch with patrols from Colonel Bouwer's force at Upington and was eventually brought to a running engagement by a considerable Government force at Rooidam. An unexpected fall of rain filled the temporary water-holes and lent invaluable aid to the now practically exhausted rebel forces.

The latter eluded capture at Rooidam (where General Botha, who had just arrived at Upington, witnessed the operations), and, with the exception of those who were too worn out to go further, were received by a detachment of the German Vrij Korps under Schoeman at Zwart Modder on the 26th November. Another patrol under Piet de Wet came to their assistance at Grond Neus, from which point Kemp's force was taken over the border and joined Maritz at Ukamas, in enemy territory.

Kemp's march was a fine example of the Boer mobility and was carried out with an energy and a rapidity of which the large numbers of overridden and worn-out horses left in the veld to the north of Upington furnished striking evidence.

For some time after its arrival in German territory Kemp's force was engaged in re-equipping, reorganizing, and resting after its strenuous experiences.

The Situation in December, 1914.

The month of November had been full of activity and had seen the dispersal of the forces under De Wet and Beyers, each of whom was at the beginning of December in flight accompanied by a small band of adherents. Their imposing forces of a few weeks earlier had entirely disappeared.

On the 27th November De Wet crossed the Bechuanaland railway line north of Vryburg with 100 men, pursued by Colonel Brits, to whom had been assigned the task of rounding up the Free State rebel leader, and fifty of his followers were captured three days later.

As we have seen, Kemp had succeeded in bringing a strong accession of strength to Maritz, and the only really dangerous concentration of rebels left was that which the latter and Kemp now controlled to the north of Upington.

Colonels Mentz and Pretorius, together with Commandants Dirk van Deventer and Geyser, had been dealing with various rebel leaders in the Transvaal in the vicinity of Pretoria, and to the north a severe engagement had taken place between the Government forces and rebels under " Jopie " Fourie and Pienaar at Rondefontein, near Haman's Kraal, with indeterminate result.

Colonel Mentz had defeated Muller at Molutzekop and Wolmarans at Vleeschkraal.

Muller was severely wounded at Molutzekop and captured a few days later, and this entirely cleared up the position to the East of Pretoria.

The position in the Transvaal was well in hand, Fourie being the only rebel of any determination remaining there.

For some time past however, the north-eastern Free State had been the scene of widespread rebellion fostered by Wessel Wessels, N. W. Serfontein, and Van Coller.

Senekal, Bethlehem, Vrede, Heilbron, Lindley, Frankfort, and Harrismith Districts were all the scenes of rebel excess and the unrest in the north-eastern Free State had focussed at the town of Reitz, which had become the headquarters of ambitious rebel military activity.

General Botha's Operations against Wessel Wessels and other Rebel Leaders near Reitz, 1st to 8th December, 1914.

To this rebel concentration, formidable in strength, and for the time being in moral effect, though, as was speedily to be shown, of little military account, General Botha now directed his energies.

The temporary immobility of the rebels under Maritz and Kemp, together with the presence of strong forces in the north-west Cape District under Colonel J. van Deventer, who had relieved Colonel Bouwer in command at Upington, gave cause for anticipating nothing serious in that quarter for the moment.

Leaving Upington by train on the 29th November, General Botha arrived at Kroonstad late on the evening of the 30th and there had consultation that night with General Smuts, who had come from Pretoria for the purpose.

On the following day General Botha left for Bethlehem, where in the afternoon he interviewed the various commanders who had been summoned to take part in the forthcoming operations.

Among these were General Lukin and Colonel T. Smuts, who, it will be remembered, had been left to deal with the situation after the Mushroom Valley operations of a fortnight earlier. Commandant Dirk van Deventer and Colonels Manie Botha and Fouche, from the Free State, were also in the vicinity with strong forces.

The rebel concentration had been carried out at, and in the close vicinity of, Reitz, where a week earlier Wessel Wessels had issued several " proclamations " clearly indicating an intention to fight. The second " proclamation " bore witness to considerable miscalculation on the part of its author as to the proportion of his fellow countrymen who supported rebellion.

An effort by Wessels, on the 16th November, to enlist the sympathies of Basutos, and in certain eventualities (e.g. " in case the British arm the coolies ") their armed co-operation, had miscarried, the letter having been intercepted by the Basutoland Police.

However, a very considerable proportion of the male population of the adjoining districts was in revolt, and on the assumption that resistance was intended, a strong concentration of Government troops was essential.

At Bethlehem General Botha received the news of De Wet's capture. He had been overtaken the same day, 2nd December, at Waterbury, in the Kuruman District, by a detachment of Brits' force under Lieut.-Colonel Jordaan.

At daybreak on the 2nd December the Government forces were put in motion and trekked in column all day in driving rain to a point just north of Haaksch Siding, on the Bethlehem-Frankfort railway.

That evening General Botha disposed his forces on a broad front and on the following morning, after a night of torrential rain, the advance on Reitz was carried out.

Reitz was occupied during the morning, the forces of Colonels Botha and Fouche being the first to enter the place, which was evacuated by the rebels without a semblance of resistance.

The operations resulted in the capture of a considerable number of prisoners, which received numerous additions in the following two days, during which operations were pressed against the rebel forces in the adjoining broken country.

After some negotiations which were begun by a communication on the 5th December from Wessels to General Botha, which contained a request that De Wet—of whose capture Wessels was ignorant—should be consulted and which, as far as the rebels were concerned, were mainly directed so as to avoid unconditional surrender, Wessel Wessels, Serfontein, and Van Coller surrendered unconditionally to General Botha with some 1,200 men at Tiger River on the 8th December.

In the meantime Beyers had emerged from his concealment with a small party of followers and crossed the main Free State railway line near Ventersburg, and on the same day that the surrender at Tiger River was effected, the 8th December, came in contact with a small party of Government troops under Field Cornet De Necker in the Hoopstad District.

Attacked and pursued by this party to Greylings Request the rebels, some 23 in number, surrendered after an engagement lasting for a quarter of an hour.

During the fight Beyers, accompanied by a man named Pieterse, entered the Vaal River at an old drift and attempted to cross, but, the river being full, both were drowned, their bodies being recovered two days later.

With these events the rebellion in the Union proper may be regarded as having come to an end.

The Capture of " Jopie " Fourie.

There remained to be reckoned with only the forces under Maritz and Kemp and a small but determined band of which " Jopie " Fourie was the motive power and which had been giving considerable trouble near Pretoria, in the direction of Haman's Kraal.

On the 15th December a mounted force under the command of Lieut.-Colonel N. J. Pretorius moved out of Pretoria for the purpose of dealing with Fourie's party, and in the afternoon of the following day came up with it entrenched in a donga on the farm Nooitgedacht.

A hot engagement ensued for the next two and a half hours, and when darkness fell Fourie and his band, with a few exceptions who escaped, had been defeated and captured.

The engagement was severe and the Government casualty list, 12 killed and 24 wounded, was a reflex of the determined character of the rebel leader, who as an officer of the Union Defence Force, taken in arms against the Government, paid the extreme penalty for his actions a few days later after trial by court martial.

With the end of the year came peace in the Union and the end of active rebellion within its borders.

Concluding phase of the Rebellion, terminating with Kemp's Surrender at Upington.

Since the arrival of Kemp's worn-out commando at the end of November little of importance had occurred in the north-western Cape area controlled by Colonel J. van Deventer while the rebellion was dying out in the Union, and the first sign of renewed activity on the part of Maritz was the capture by some of his forces of a patrol of Government troops under Commandant Du Plessis near Schuitdrift on the 10th December.

On the 22nd a far more severe blow was struck when Maritz attacked Nous and, evidently having surprised the garrison there, captured the place in circumstances reflecting small credit to the Union troops concerned.

Maritz and Kemp had joined forces on the 20th December at Schuitdrift.

After their successful coup at Nous Maritz and Kemp withdrew again with their troops to the German border, and military operations until the 23rd January were confined once more to skirmishes of varying dimensions.

On the 23rd January, however, Maritz, having learned of the state of affairs in the Union and of the complete collapse of the rebellion there, and, quite possibly, further influenced by an intimation from the German authorities that he must not fall back on German territory as there was no food there for his troops, sent a parlementaire to Colonel Van Deventer asking for terms of surrender. The detention of the parlementaire, pending the receipt of telegraphic instructions on the situation from Pretoria, either annoyed Maritz or made him suspicious, and on the following day, the 24th January, Maritz and Kemp launched an attack on Upington which contained a garrison of 2,000 troops and had been prepared for defence.

After six hours' fighting 70 rebels were captured and the remainder retired.

On the same evening Maritz addressed a letter to Colonel Van Deventer to the effect that as " the strife appeared hopeless " he was disposed to surrender his commandos, but wished to discuss certain points.

Colonel Van Deventer replied on the following day, having been instructed by the Government, that unconditional surrender only could be considered, subject to the undertaking that burghers should remain in arrest to be dealt with as Parliament should determine, and that the leaders should stand their trial before the Courts of Justice, and after sentence the Government would consider whether in the circumstances of each sentence any reduction or mitigation was possible.

On the 26th Maritz replied that it was essential that there should be an interview and that if " we discuss the matter personally we shall be able to clear it up and find a solution." He added he would do his utmost to encourage those with him to lay down their arms.

Finally, at a meeting held on the 30th January, an agreement was drawn up and signed providing for the unconditional surrender of the commandos under Maritz, Kemp, Bezuidenhout, and De Villiers, and the surrender took place at Upington on the 2nd and 3rd February, 1915.

Maritz and Piet de Villiers, with some 50 companions, did not surrender but left for German South-West Africa.

The number included in the surrender was 1,230 all told.

The threat to Upington had necessitated the despatch of Brits' Mounted Brigade from Capetown, where it was mobilized for embarkation for Walvis Bay, to the north, but the altered circumstances allowed of one wing of it being turned back at De Aar, though its place on board the transports had to be taken by another (Alberts') Mounted Brigade, and its departure for German South-West Africa was correspondingly deferred. The other wing reached Upington, where it remained until after the surrender.

The surrender of the 2nd and 3rd February marked the conclusion of the entire rebellion, which had lasted from the 9th October, when Maritz disarmed his loyal troops and led the remainder into revolt.

Though it may be accepted that if the rebellion had been conducted with more acumen by its leaders some addition to the ranks of the rebels might have occurred, nevertheless the strictly limited portion of the population which took up arms against the Government may be regarded as practically all those who were willing at this time to go to the length of armed resistance to the Government.

The number of rebels was out of all proportion to the damage which they caused, the bitterness which was engendered by their conduct, and the actual cost to the State of the suppression of the revolt.

The total number of persons who went into rebellion was 11,472, made up as follows: —

Orange Free State	7,123
Transvaal	2,998
*Cape Province...	1,251

* Including 1,059 with Maritz.

To restore order violated by this handful of the population of the State, 30,000 troops (of which 20,000 were of Dutch descent) were employed at a cost of £5,100,000: a casualty list of 132 killed and died of wounds of the Government Forces was sustained, and 242 of the loyal troops were wounded; and 190 rebels paid the penalty of their lives for their leaders' insensate action, and from 300 to 350 were wounded.

General Botha left Pretoria early in January, 1915, and proceeded to Capetown, there to superintend the embarkation of the first of the troops who were to accompany him to the successful conclusion of his campaign in German South-West Africa.

The Government, freed of anxiety as to conditions within the Union, was able to resume the conduct of the operations against the enemy on its border, which had been so effectually interrupted by the sudden outbreak of the rebellion.

General the Rt. Hon. L. Botha, P.C., D.T.D.

PART II.

GERMAN SOUTH-WEST AFRICA.

PAGE.

I.—COMMENCEMENT OF THE CAMPAIGN 29

II.—STRATEGIC OPERATIONS 29

III.—ORGANIZATION OF TROOPS 34

IV.—TACTICAL OPERATIONS 38

V.—NAVAL OPERATIONS 55

VI.—TRANSPORT—LINES OF COMMUNICATION AND SUPPLIES ... 56

VII.—INTELLIGENCE 58

VIII.—ENGINEERING 59

IX.—COMMUNICATIONS 59

X.—MEDICAL SERVICE 59

XI.—SUMMARY OF TROOPS IN THE FIELD, MARCH, 1915... ... 60

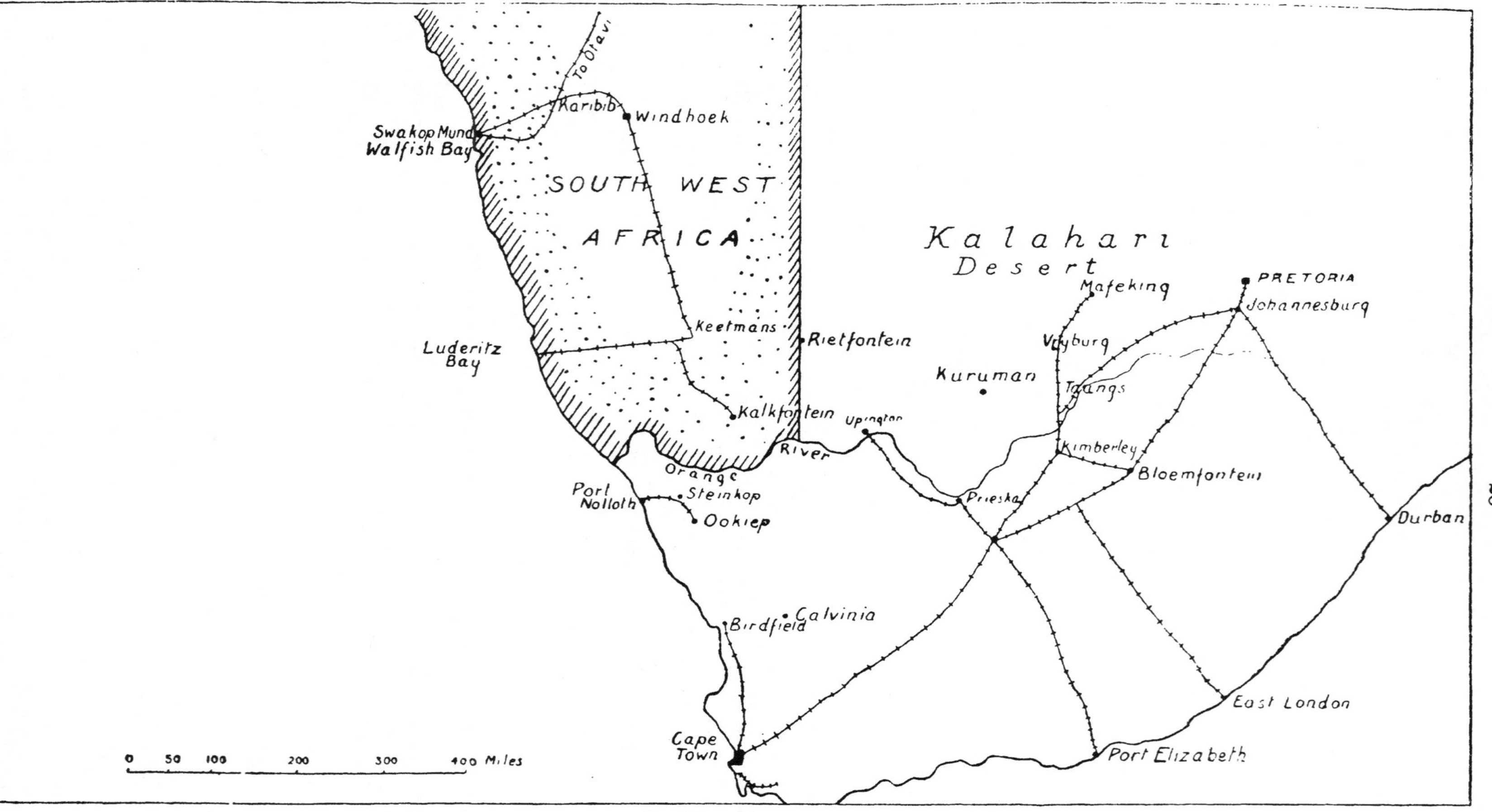

DIAGRAM No. 2.

Showing the strategic relation of South-West Africa to the Union of South Africa.

The shaded dotted portions represent desert or semi-desert country.

The railway (shown) from Prieska to Upington, and later from Upington to Kalkfontein, was laid down after hostilities commenced.

Capetown was the point of strategic concentration for the deployment on Swakop–Walfish Bay and Luderitz Bay. Upington and Steinkop were for the Southern Forces, and Kuruman was the concentration point for the Eastern Force.

THE GERMAN SOUTH-WEST CAMPAIGN.

I. Commencement of the Campaign.

AS the Union Government was engaged to the end of 1914 in dealing with the rebellion within the Union, the suppression of which was unconditionally necessary to the prosecution of a successful campaign in South-West Africa, the date of the commencement of this campaign should be taken as early in January, 1915. The operations that had previous to that date taken place should be considered as military expedients to meet various emergencies as they arose, and not as forming part of any co-ordinated plan of campaign against South-West Africa. Any plans that were formed in August, 1914, to meet the request of the Imperial Government for control of the South-West wireless stations, which was considered of great importance by the Admiralty, had to be abandoned or modified suddenly to meet the grave menace which had unexpectedly arisen within the Union, and which, from its insidious nature and the numbers engaged, presented a far more formidable undertaking than an expedition against South-West Africa.

II. Strategic Operations.

On a superficial consideration of this campaign it may be thought that the numerical superiority of the Union Forces eliminated all questions of strategy except those of the steam-roller. It must, however, be remembered that the wide and formidable strategic obstacle of the desert—*vide* Diagram No. 2—effectually attenuated any force committed to it, however numerically strong, and that the long lines of communication also absorbed large numbers. How this intervening desert was crossed will be considered elsewhere. But the question of where its penetration would be most inconvenient to the enemy was a strategic problem of some importance. It was known that the enemy derived most of his supplies from the area north of the Karibib-Windhoek railway line, and that if he intended to prolong the campaign by ultimately leading it into a guerilla phase, he had practically the whole Central African continent at his back door. The strong expedition pushed beyond his northern frontiers in December, 1914, was perhaps not so much with the object of pilfering in Portuguese police posts as to get experience of operating in that area and to impress the native mind.

The strategic objective, in the first instance, was thus to secure a jumping-off place beyond the desert, situated so as best to facilitate the realization of the next and final objective which was the enemy's fighting force in the field, and their destruction before they could initiate a guerilla campaign. A glance at a map will be sufficient to establish the claims of Karibib as the first strategic objective; its fall decides the fate of Windhoek and all the country to the south. The first indication of its being seriously threatened caused the enemy to concentrate for the defence of this area, but owing to the rapidity of the Union operations the defensive concentration was so hurried and imperfect that the enemy declined to risk a decisive action and retired northwards. The first objective was gained. and the difficulties of the second could now be more clearly realized. The destruction of the enemy's living forces will always remain the grandest aim of strategy, also the most difficult, and what accentuated the normal difficulties in this case was the fact that the scarcity of water and supplies would compel the employment of isolated forces for the wide turning movements out of communication with each other or with the Commander-in-Chief, and each considerably weaker than the concentrated body of the enemy. A textbook advance would always have enabled the enemy to disengage and escape under cover of a rearguard action until the time arrived for him to adopt guerilla methods. The strategic operations in connection with the second objective are remarkable for two reasons, the departure from traditional methods—launching comparatively weak, isolated forces, out of communication for days—and the complete success that resulted from these innovations. In military history, Cannae and Sedan have always been looked upon as the two classical examples of a realization of the highest strategic ideal; strictly speaking, this is open to question. Cannae was more of a tactical envelopment, while Sedan was the destruction of only a portion of the French Army in the field. The South-West campaign, however, presents what appears to be a unique instance of strategical operations culminating in an envelopment that completely destroyed the enemy as a fighting force in the entire theatre of operations. How this result was attained may be seen best by means of the Diagrams Nos. 2, 3, 4, 5, 5A, and 6.

Diagram No. 2 presents the problem: The enemy area entirely surrounded by a wide strategic obstacle. His railway lines leading to the weaker links in his armour, and thus not presenting any possibility of being turned.

Diagram No. 3 represents the dispositions on 1st January, 1915. Up to this time the Union Government had been engaged in suppressing the rebellion in the Union, and it was necessary in the first place to prevent the enemy assisting the rebels or the latter escaping into enemy territory. The dispositions up to this date are thus not the result of a strategy exclusively directed against South-West Africa.

Diagram No. 4 shows some advance towards the first objective. A bad part of the desert had been penetrated, the enemy had been defeated at Riet, and it was clear to him that his communication with the north—from where his supplies came and where he hoped to prolong the campaign—was being seriously threatened.

Diagram No. 5 shows the first objective gained. In the course of this an interesting problem presented itself, the solution of which is recorded on Diagram No. 5A. On the 26th of April, 1915, when the advance began that resulted in the drill-book like dispositions of the 6th of May shown on Diagram No. 5A, it was not quite clear what the enemy intentions and dispositions were. The intelligence of the Union northern force was to the effect that most of the enemy force was concentrated at or north of Karibib, a view which was strengthened by the enemy attack on Trekkoppies the same day. But on the following day, 27th of April, the enemy had also offered stiff resistance to General MacKenzie at Gibeon (*vide* Diagram No. 5). The possibilities that had to be considered by General Botha were thus either that the main force of the enemy was somewhere near Karibib or that the general retirement had been delayed too long, and that the enemy would be found at Windhoek or any place between Windhoek and Karibib. The dense bush and vastness of the country, which on several occasions had rendered it impossible for the Air Force to locate our own brigades, even when their position was known approximately, prevented the situation being cleared up by these means. The advance had therefore to be so arranged that, while in the main directed against Karibib and the railway eastwards, it kept the possibility in view that the enemy might be in force anywhere in the area Windhoek-Otjimbingue, Karibib, and then along the railway to Windhoek. The

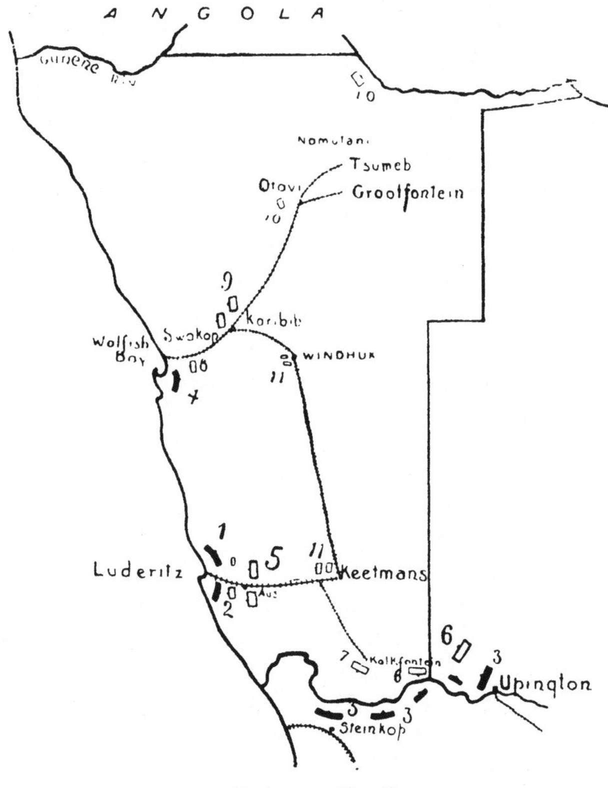

DIAGRAM NO. 3.

Strategic Situation on 1st January, 1915.

Union Forces ... ▬
German Forces ... ▭
Railways ... ...

Disposition Notes.

Nos. 1 and 2.—Central Force (Brigadier-General Mackenzie)—2 Batteries (6-gun) Field Artillery, 2 Batteries (4-gun) Heavy, 4 Mounted Regiments, 7 Infantry Battalions (landed in two detachments, 18th September and 3rd October, 1914).

No. 3.—Colonel Van Deventer's Southern Force—About 29 Commando Units (approximately 5,000 all Ranks) and 1 Battery Field Artillery.

No. 4.—Northern Force (Colonel Skinner)—2 Infantry (3-Regiment) Brigades, 2 Batteries (4-gun) Heavy Artillery, 1 Mounted Regiment (landed December 25th, 1914).

No. 5.—Enemy Main Force (Major Bausus)—3 Batteries Field Artillery, 4 Mounted Companies, 2 Infantry Companies.

No. 6.—Rebels under Maritz and Kemp—1 Battery Field Artillery (German) and about 900 rifles.

No. 7.—Major Van Ritter—1 Battery Field Artillery, 3 Mounted Companies.

No. 8.—Major Wahle—1 Battery Field Artillery, 2 Mounted Companies.

Nos. 9 and 10.—Portuguese Punitive Expedition, returning German Commander-in-Chief, Colonel Francke—3 Batteries Field Artillery, 5 Mounted Companies.

No. 11.—Depot and Reserve Troops.

Diagram No. 5A perhaps conveys a clearer idea of the strategy than may be obtained by any further written explanation. It can be seen there that the strategic direction of pressure was at first in the direction Otjimbingue-Okahandja by the 5th, 3rd, and 2nd Mounted Brigades, the 1st Mounted Brigade and the 4th Infantry Brigade following up with pressure in the direction Kubas, Karibib. When about half-way between Otjimbingue and Okahandja, the 5th and 3rd Mounted Brigades suddenly doubled north-west and got astride the railway at Willemsthal. Up to this point it could not have been clear to the enemy what their intentions were—Willemsthal, Okahandja, or Windhoek—as they were on the only possible line of advance from Otjimbingue to Windhoek up to the point from where they deviated north-westwards, and they were at any time most favourably disposed to hold an attack from either Windhoek, Okahandja, or Willemsthal until reinforcements arrived, while they were always available should an attack on the 1st and 4th Brigades develop from Karibib. As it was, the enemy had barely escaped being partially cut off and was in no condition to risk a serious engagement, but took up the position shown in the diagram.

Diagram No. 6 shows the strategic operations that resulted in realizing the final objective of destroying the enemy as a fighting force in the field and preventing him from prolonging the operations by a guerilla campaign. After the first objective had been gained, as shown in Diagram No. 5A, there was a six-weeks' period of refitting and reorganization (see chapter on Organization), and then the final operations were commenced, which within eighteen days enveloped the enemy and compelled his surrender a few days later. The surrender of Windhoek, the capital, on 12th May was an inevitable result of the first objective being gained, and has no further strategic interest. The strategic advance began on 18th June. The diagram shows a convergence of the lines of march on Kalkveld, where it was considered that the enemy would attempt the determined rearguard action that might be expected in a long strategic pursuit. He did not, however, take advantage of the possibilities offered by this place for that purpose, and as it was known that the country was less suitable further north up to Otavi, the strategic directions were not again deviated from for this reason. The convergence shown towards Otjiwarongo was for water and supplies for the 1st Mounted Brigade.

It was known that the enemy had prepared a line of retirement from Tsumeb over Namutoni and then northwards. Of the depots established on this line, Namutoni was by far the most important from the supplies collected there. The objective of the 1st Mounted Brigade under Brig.-General Brits was to get astride this line of retirement at Namutoni. To do this he would be entirely out of communication for some time and also out of reach of assistance, a strategic risk which cannot be taken without the absolute confidence of Headquarters in the tactical superiority of the detached force in marching, and the ability to disengage itself from an unprofitable action.

The 2nd and the right wing of the 3rd Mounted Brigade, under Brig.-General Myburgh, had a somewhat similar task as regards the want of communication and possibility of support—they were, as can be seen on the diagram, to envelop from the eastward. The 5th Mounted Brigade, under Brig.-General M. Botha, acted as the advance guard to the main body; 6th Mounted Brigade, Brig.-General Lukin, and 1st Infantry Brigade, Brig.-General Beves, marching along the railway. This Brigade, in the most brilliant tactical operation of the campaign, on 1st July at Elephants Neck, Osib, and Otavifontein (see chapter Tactical Operations) secured the water and high ground at Otavi. This was a condition on which the whole strategical scheme hinged—there is no water between Otavi and

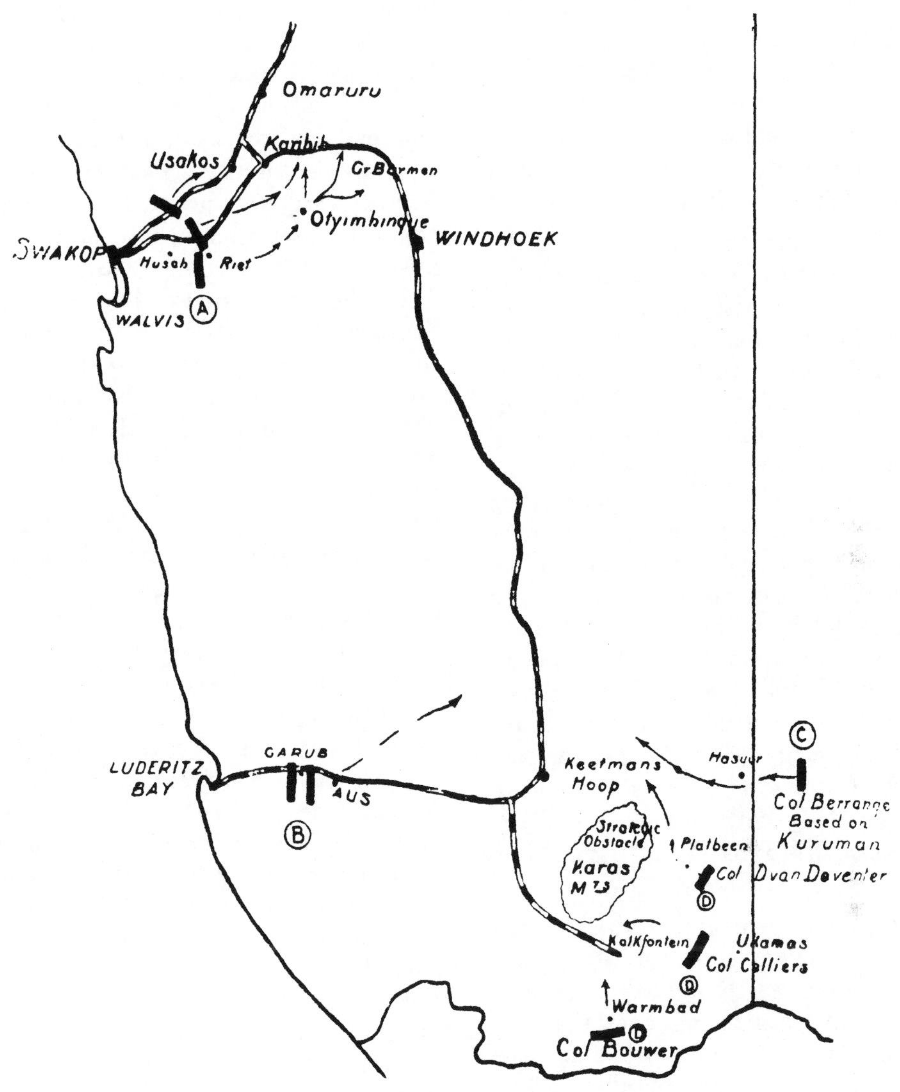

DIAGRAM NO. 4.

Strategic Objectives and Situation, 20th March, 1915.

(A) Northern Force (Right Hon. General L. Botha)—2 Batteries Field Artillery, 2 Batteries Mountain Artillery, 2 Mounted Brigades, and 3 Infantry Brigades.

(B) Central Force (Brigadier-General Sir Duncan Mackenzie)—2 Batteries Field Artillery, 2 Batteries Heavy Artillery, 1 Infantry Battalion, 4 Mounted Regiments.

(C) Eastern Force (Colonel Berrange)—1 Battery Field Artillery, 4 Mounted Regiments.

(D) Southern Force (Colonel J. van Deventer)—1 Battery Field Artillery and about 5,000 Mounted Rifles.

Okaputa, and a check at Otavi would have given the enemy opportunity to throw himself in superior numbers on the isolated forces in his rear. But the confidence of the Commander-in-Chief in the tactical superiority of his troops again enabled him to realize a strategy which, without this tactical superiority, would have been hazardous in the extreme.

On the 1st July the main body of the Union Force was in occupation of the water and strong positions at Otavi, the enemy main body was at Korab (about 15 miles from Otavi) with detachments at Tsumeb and Namutoni, while the force under Brig.-General Myburgh was a little way north of Grootfontein, and the force under Brig.-General Brits nearing Namutoni. The enemy could retire over Tsumeb or direct to Namutoni only to be met in either case by a force strong enough to delay it until the main body came up. In a few days these places were occupied, their garrisons surrendering after slight resistance, and the main body of the enemy acknowledged the success of the Union strategy by surrendering on the 9th July with 204 officers, 3,166 other ranks, 37 guns, and 22 machine-guns.

Although no opportunity to add to the records of elegantly solved strategical problems presented itself to the forces in the southern theatre of operations, a study of the direct strategy employed there is far from unprofitable. The march of the Eastern Force under Brig.-General (then Colonel) Berrange, for instance, will remain a fine example of the difficulties that may be overcome in a strategic advance across a desert. The rapid rate of building the strategic railway from Prieska into the enemy's country—three miles per day—is also an instance of what may be done with limited resources in a desert when strategy demands it.

On a consideration of Diagrams Nos. 3, 4, and 5 it may be asked why this great strategic pressure in the south, when obviously a thrust at the enemy vitals at Karibib would attract all his resistance there. The reason, as previously pointed out, is that up to January, 1915, the Union had to reckon with the rebellion in territory adjoining that of the enemy, and had to prevent a junction of rebel and enemy forces. That the Southern Forces were not superfluous is evident from the fact that one rebel force succeeded in joining hands with the enemy. After the suppression of the rebellion the Southern Forces were established on long lines of communication that had been laboriously created, and it would have been unwise to abandon these before the Northern Force had definitely gained its first objective. In strategy, as in other matters, nothing but uncertainty is certain, and there may have been serious checks in the north before the first objective was attained; the Southern Forces then would have served to minimize the pressure on the Northern Army. Their strategic object therefore all through was to exert a converging pressure on the most suitable point, which, from Diagram No. 5, is seen to be situated somewhere north of Keetmanshoop. That the strategic movements were well co-ordinated, taking into account the long and diverging lines of communication, can be seen from the diagrams. The timing of the Eastern Force under Colonel Berrange especially draws attention in Diagram No. 4, and more so when it is remembered that his bases are Kimberley and Kuruman (see Diagram No. 2).

III. Organization of Troops.

The Union Forces were organized in a Southern, a Central, an Eastern, and a Northern Force.

Great modifications in the sub-organization of these four strategic units were occasioned from time to time by the varying circumstances. The Central Force field troops were, for instance, at one time entirely composed of mounted units, while previously they had almost entirely been formed of infantry battalions.

The military traditions of South Africa have been very largely influenced by the so-called commando system, which for more than a century has been the organization basis of many military operations and also influenced the evolution of South African tactics. The principle of the commando system is to organize a tactical unit so as to retain the cohesion that exists among the individuals inhabiting the same locality or district. It has no fixed numerical establishment, the recruits from one area or district being organized into one commando, it follows that thinly populated areas furnish small commandos and vice versa, there always, however, remaining an automatic check on overheavy commandos in the civil sub-division of districts when the population increases.

It is not the purpose here to investigate the advantages and weak points of the commando system, but as this system had got a firm hold on the South African military mind, a few characteristics must be briefly sketched to throw light on the tactics and organization of this campaign.

In the sub-sections of the commando, the men probably knew each other and their officers since boyhood. The commandant and the officers are generally men of considerable individuality and influence and are the natural leaders of the men, even in civil life. The result is great internal cohesion and a somewhat refractory external attitude with reference to other units. As a minor tactical unit the commando is an ideal organization, in grand tactics it requires very careful handling. The relations between the men and officers in peace-time make routine discipline rather difficult, but the subtle influence of the officers over the men enables them to get more out of the latter in a forced march or a "hot corner" than is possible in a regular unit. The tactical initiative of the commando is thus a joy to the staff just as their behaviour in combined operations is always a source of considerable concern. Without the commando influence, many mistakes in this campaign may possibly not have occurred, but then also several tactical achievements would certainly not be on record to-day. The South African Defence Force in the eighteen months of its life before the war had done much by inspiration, organization, and training to develop the wider coherence required for combined operations. Brigade organization was aimed at, and this was also the organization of the four strategic forces in the campaign. The spirit of the commando system is, however, perceptible everywhere; the Mounted Brigades were of two types; some being on regular lines with regimental establishment, while others were modified to make more use of the commando principle. These last were formed of two wings, right and left, each under a Colonel-Commandant, the wings being of three commandos, each about 300 rifles strong. The whole Mounted Brigade of from 1,800 to 2,400 rifles was at first under the command of a Colonel but the rank was later advanced to that of a Brigadier-General.

The Southern Force.

This force which had experienced organization changes demanded by the rebellion operations previous to January, 1915, from which date we are considering the campaign, was composed of one battery Field Artillery and 29 mounted commandos, together about 5,000 rifles, under the command of Lieut.-General Sir J. van Deventer, then Colonel Van Deventer. It operated in five and later in four columns. This force was on the 24th April combined with the Eastern Force to form the 2nd Division of the Southern Army, which latter was demobilized on the 5th of May as the enemy had evacuated the southern theatre of operations.

Central Force.

On the 18th of September, 1914, this force landed at Luderitz Bay and was reinforced from time to time so that in January, 1915, it comprised:—

2 six-gun batteries Field Artillery.

2 four-gun batteries Heavy Artillery.

2 Mounted Brigades of two regiments each.
7 Infantry Battalions organized in two Brigades.
The necessary Engineering, Medical, and Communication Services.

In March, 1915, this was reinforced with another Mounted Brigade of two regiments. In April, 1915, it formed the 1st Division of the Southern Army.

Eastern Force.

This consisted of four mounted regiments and a section of 12-pounder Heavy Artillery together with a special Motor Transport and Water Supply Service. On establishing contact with the Southern Force in March, 1915, it was combined with the latter to form the 2nd Division of the Southern Army.

Northern Force.

On the 1st of January, 1915, this stood organized in two three-battalion Infantry Brigades which had, together with seven guns of the Artillery Brigade and one mounted regiment landed at Walvis Bay on 25th December, 1914. In March, 1915, the mounted troops had been reinforced and the organization had to provide for Field, Line of Communication, and Special Troops to protect the railway reconstruction, as the railway did not coincide with either the Line of Communication or the intended direction of advance (see Diagram No. 4).

The Force was thus organized as follows:—

Field Troops—

2 four-gun batteries of Field Artillery.
2 Mounted Brigades (modified commando system).
1 three-battalion Infantry Brigade.
Engineering, Medical, and Communication Services.
(Each of the Mounted Brigades had one of the above batteries attached.)

Railway Construction Protective Troops—

1 section Heavy Artillery.
1 Mounted Regiment.
1 three-battalion Infantry Brigade.
Medical and Communication Services.
(The actual reconstruction work of native labour under direction of the S.A. Engineer Corps, see chapter Engineering.)

Line of Communication Troops—

1 Battery Heavy Artillery (four guns).
1 Armoured Car Division.
2 Infantry Battalions.
Medical and Communication Services.

In April the Field Troops were increased by two additional Mounted Brigades, each with a four-gun battery Field Artillery, and the organization then remained as described until after the occupation of Karibib. As the nature of strategic objective had then changed (see Strategic Operations) a reorganization of the Northern Force was necessary and the other three forces which had previously been combined into an army of two divisions were demobilized.

The new organization had to provide Field, Lines of Communication, and Garrison Troops.

The Field Troops were—

5 batteries Field Artillery (four guns).
2 batteries Heavy Artillery (four guns).
4 Mounted Brigades, less one wing (modified commando type).
1 Mounted Brigade (five regular-establishment regiments).
1 Infantry Brigade (five battalions).
1 squadron Armoured Cars.
South African Aviation Corps (six planes).
Transport, Engineering, Medical, and Communication Services.

The distribution of artillery was one battery Field Artillery per Mounted

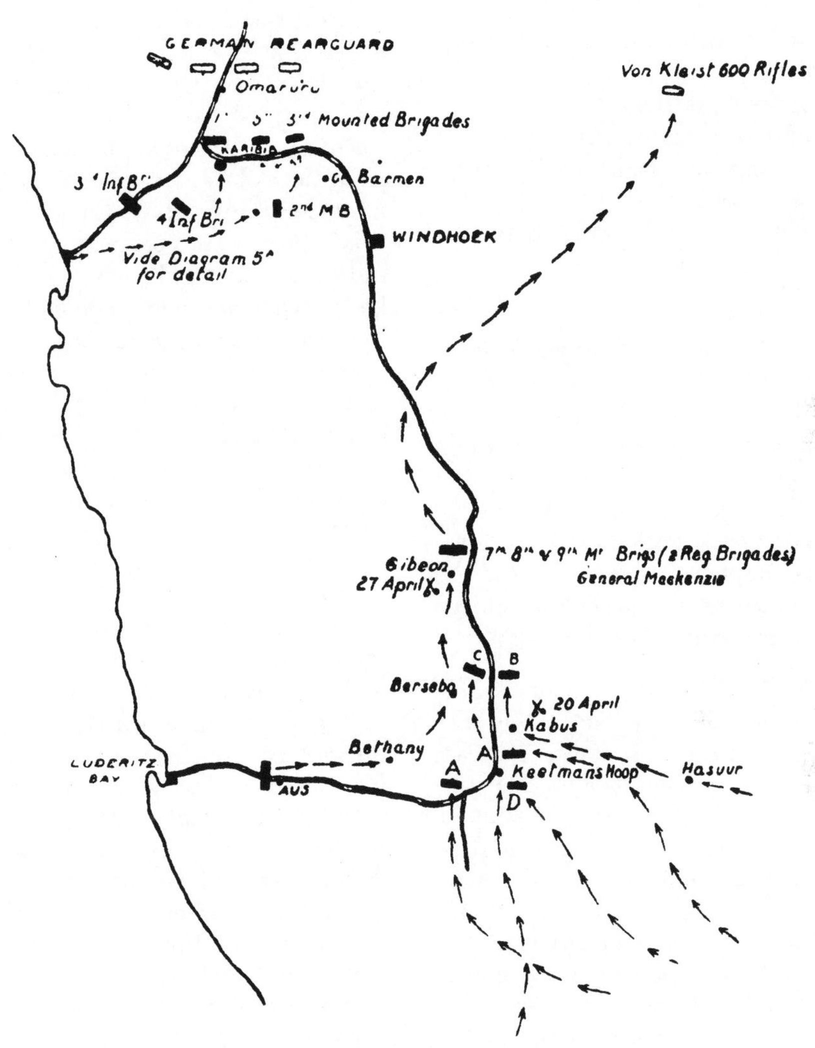

DIAGRAM No. 5.

Strategic Situation, 6th May, 1915.

A.—Colonels Celliers and Bouwer—Southern Force.
B.—Colonel Berrange—Eastern Force.
C.—Colonel D. van Deventer—Southern Force.
D.—Remainder of Southern Force.

Brigade, the detached Mounted Brigade wing having a section of 12-pounder Heavy Artillery while the two Heavy Artillery batteries were attached to the Infantry Brigade.

Lines of Communication Troops—

- 2 Infantry Brigades of three battalions.
- 2 Infantry Battalions.
- 2 squadrons Mounted Infantry.
- Engineering and Railway Construction Service.
- Transport, Medical, and Communication Services.

Garrison Troops—

- 1 section 12-pounder Heavy Artillery.
- 1 Mounted Brigade, less one wing detached for Field Troops.
- 1 Mounted Regiment (commando type).

NOTE.—For organization of Engineering, Railway Construction, Medical, etc., Services see chapters under these heads.

This organization sufficed for the object in view and terminated the campaign.

IV. Tactical Operations.

Before recounting the tactical operations, a brief review of South African tactics as they had been developed in the past, by operations under the commando system, may help to a better understanding of the incidents in this campaign.

In the past, the life and environment of the South African had fully developed every possibility presented by the horse and rifle. In later years opportunity for this was restricted, but the tradition was there, and certain standards of riding and shooting are maintained and live as an ideal in the minds of the younger generation, who eagerly avail themselves of the facilities offered by the Defence Force to realize this ideal of individual development as a marksman and rider. The tactical result of this is a soldier who can deliver quick, sure, and economical fire, while availing himself of every scrap of cover as he works forward, who can ride over almost any ground and who uses his horse to rush the fire position from where he will have the best advantage over his opponent. But his traditions lean towards independent action; fire control is difficult; and manœuvre control would have been impossible were it not for the commando influence. In the chapter on Organization of Troops it was pointed out that the result of forming the commando out of recruits from the same area was cohesion and good understanding within the unit. Besides this, there are commando traditions, individual and collective. The recruit knows what his commando had done when his father was a member of it; he knows further what is generally done on commando and what not, and therefore has a general knowledge of elementary tactics.

These factors, and the intercourse between officers and men, produce the curious phenomena that tactically the commando operates more by instinct than on command. Like a herd of antelope, moving off or wheeling simultaneously, the commando performs many operations without command and with a spontaniety that gives them a whirlwind character. On getting fire unexpectedly the head of the column will extend automatically and with inconceivable rapidity, and will further almost invariably do what a skilled tactician would have commanded under the circumstances—either by making use of the ground on which deployed or by charging forward or backwards to a better fire position.

Every trooper of a commando knows nearly as much about the general situation as the Commanding Officer. The information of the scouting patrols had been discussed the night before, the Commandant had told his friend what the General's opinion was, and the family spirit of the unit, after having digested all the information available, seems to suggest the best course for all concerned when the time for action comes.

What may be called the herd instinct—not unkindly, but appreciative of all its

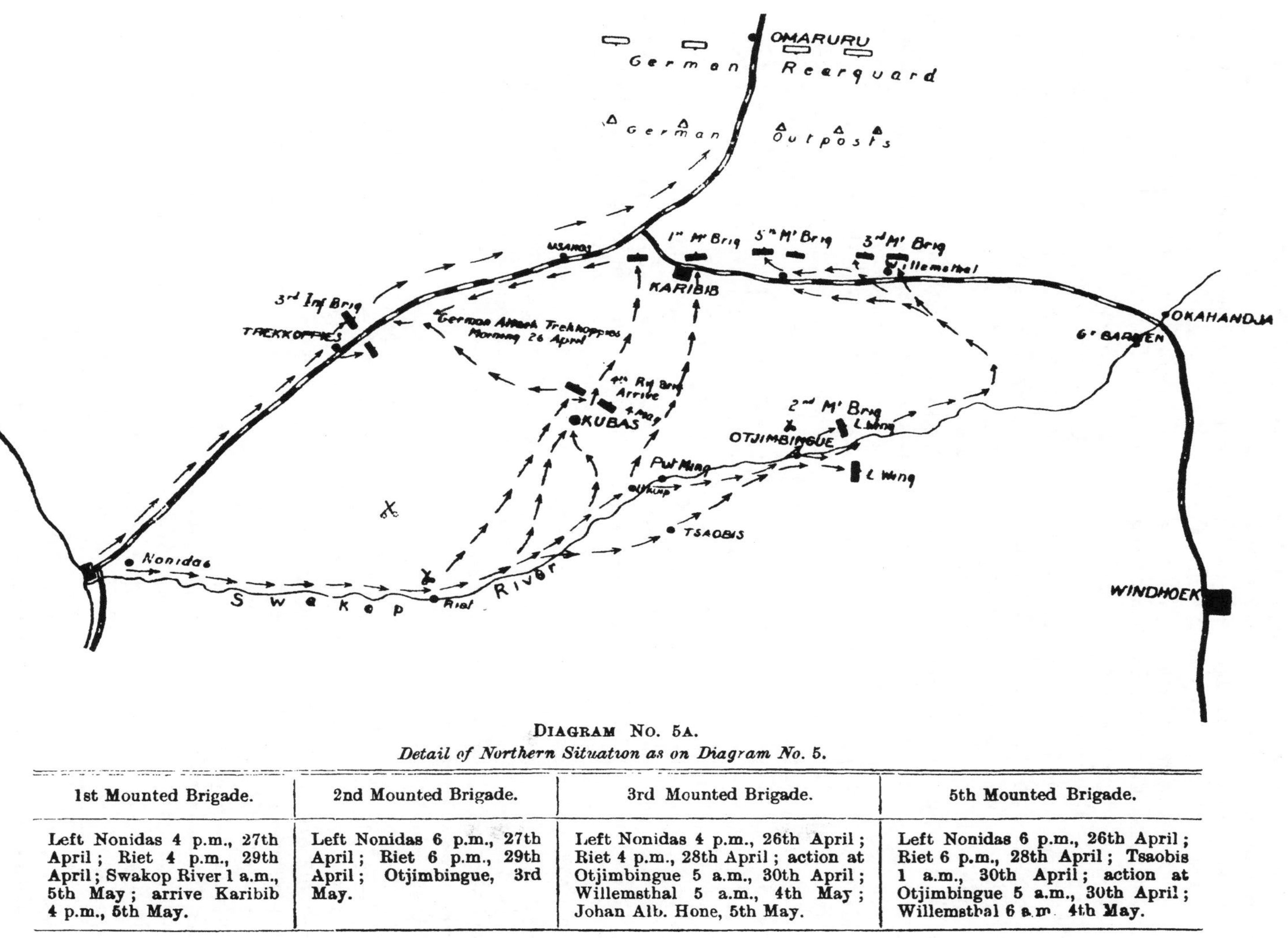

DIAGRAM NO. 5A.

Detail of Northern Situation as on Diagram No. 5.

1st Mounted Brigade.	2nd Mounted Brigade.	3rd Mounted Brigade.	5th Mounted Brigade.
Left Nonidas 4 p.m., 27th April; Riet 4 p.m., 29th April; Swakop River 1 a.m., 5th May; arrive Karibib 4 p.m., 5th May.	Left Nonidas 6 p.m., 27th April; Riet 6 p.m., 29th April; Otjimbingue, 3rd May.	Left Nonidas 4 p.m., 26th April; Riet 4 p.m., 28th April; action at Otjimbingue 5 a.m., 30th April; Willemsthal 5 a.m., 4th May; Johan Alb. Hone, 5th May.	Left Nonidas 6 p.m., 26th April; Riet 6 p.m., 28th April; Tsaobis 1 a.m., 30th April; action at Otjimbingue 5 a.m., 30th April; Willemsthal 6 a.m. 4th May.

qualities that have contributed to the success of this campaign—is also to be seen on the march. No orders (and no disorders) in the early morning or midnight march off. The men wake, saddle, and move off at the appointed time, the only discoverable intimation of which may have been a remark by the Commandant the previous night on the bad luck of again having to march at 1 o'clock.

The operations of a commando are thus spontaneous and natural, while those of a regular unit appear artificial and restrained in comparison. But while the high qualities of initiative, cohesion, individual efficiency, and the rapid appreciation of a situation are very valuable, the inclination to independent action is always a danger.

The ultimate tactical value of a commando unit depends on how far the officers realized this fact; some officers increased the tactical efficiency of their commandos by wisely not interfering with what was good, and, by using the powers conferred by the Defence Act, instilled discipline and training and thereby obtained better co-operation with other units.

In general, the troops had the good qualities associated with the commando, while Defence Force training had developed the ability to operate brigaded.

The Northern Force.

The scarcity of water anywhere within striking distance of Walvis Bay or Swakop probably accounts for the fact that the enemy did not dispute the landing of Colonel Skinner with seven guns of the Artillery Brigade, one Mounted Regiment, and two Infantry Brigades at Walvis Bay on Christmas Day, 1914. A few days later Colonel Skinner advanced on and occupied the port and town of Swakop, the enemy outposts retiring after inflicting light casualties by sniping and exploding several observation mines laid in places where the advancing troops had to pass in close formation. The occupation of these two places was consolidated, and the construction of a railway from Walvis Bay to Swakop was commenced. On the 23rd February an advance in force was made to clear the country in the vicinity of the Swakop River and the railway to Karibib. General Botha had arrived in February, and the Northern Force had been increased by a battery of Field Artillery and a Mounted Brigade. The enemy retired before this advance with a loss of twelve prisoners, and the country was cleared for a distance of 20 miles inland as far as Rossing and Heigamchab.

The reconstruction of the railway line could now proceed, and advance depots were established for the next forward move. On the 18th of March another advance was made, which the enemy determinedly but unsuccessfully disputed on the 20th of March at Riet, Pforte and Jackhalswater, retiring on the night of the 20th with considerable loss.

On the 26th of April the enemy attacked the railway protective troops under Colonel Skinner at Trekkoppies (see Diagram No. 5A). The attack, which was with the object of covering the enemy retirement northwards from the Karibib area, was repulsed with considerable loss to the enemy. Preparations were now completed for the advance on Karibib (see Strategic Operations and Diagram No. 5A), and the advance, which commenced on the 27th April, ended at Karibib on 5th May, after slight enemy resistance at Otjimbingue.

Windhoek was occupied on the 12th of May, and on the 18th of June the advance northwards was commenced (see Diagram No. 6). The 5th Mounted Brigade under Brig.-General M. Botha had an important and successful action at Osib, Elephants Neck, and Otavifontein on 1st July.

The 1st Mounted Brigade under Brig.-General Brits captured the Namutoni garrison after slight resistance on the 6th of July, and the 2nd Mounted Brigade and right wing of 3rd Mounted Brigade, under Brig.-General Myburgh, drove the enemy from Chaub on the 4th of July and captured the Tsumeb garrison after slight resistance on 6th July.

Besides numerous advance guard, patrol, and outpost encounters, the Northern Force thus had one defensive action (Trekkoppies) and seven offensive actions, of which the Riet-Pforte, Trekkoppies, and the Elephants Neck-Otavi will now be described with more detail.

The Riet-Pforte Action.

From Diagram No. 7 it can be seen that the topography of the Riet-Pforte area is in a high degree suitable for defence towards the west from where the Union advance would come. The "Langer Heinrich," or Riet Berg, a bare, open sloped hill more than 2,000 feet above the river bed, extends for many miles eastward along the south bank of the Swakop River and cannot be turned. The Pforte range also extends from the Swakop River for 20 miles to the Geisib Berg north-eastwards, having only a few narrow gaps.

The old railway line from Karibib to Swakop passes through one of these gaps. This line, which had been taken up before the war on completion of the northern better-graded line, was relaid by the enemy from Karibib over Jackhalswater to Pforte. From Jackhalswater a branch line, not shown on Diagram No. 7, was laid over Modderfontein nearly to Riet. The enemy was thus able to have railway transport from his base almost into the fire position.

The nearest water to the west is at Husab, where the Union Force had established their furthermost advanced depot.

The Pforte position was known to be occupied by at least two mounted companies (German company 175 to 200 rifles) and a section field artillery. The Riet position by at least four mounted companies and a battery of field artillery, while a general reserve of two batteries and four or five companies was at Jackhalswater and Modderfontein.

On the 18th of March the Union Force of—

- Transvaal Horse Artillery Battery (4 guns) and 1st Brigade under Colonel (later Brig.-General) Brits;
- 4th Permanent Battery (4 guns) and 2nd Mounted Brigade under Colonel Alberts;

left the camp at Nonidas and arrived at Husab on the morning of the 19th, after a 30-mile waterless march. On the evening of the same day they left Husab, the force under Colonel Brits being ordered to march south of and along the Swakop River, with the enemy positions at Riet Berg as the objective to be attacked the next morning at daybreak. On the maps then available the Riet or Langer Heinrich Mountain was shown isolated from the mountains to the east, and with a road passing through the gap. The force under Colonel Brits was therefore instructed to detach the Bloemhof Commando of 300 rifles to make a detour southwards until they got on the road shown, and to attack the rear of the Riet position. This, however, was a topographical error on the map, the Riet Mountain being connected by very formidable hill features which did not even present a bridle path, so that this detachment had to return. The force under Colonel Alberts was ordered to advance with the Battery of Artillery and the right wing of the Brigade under Colonel-Commandant Badenhorst direct against the Pforte position, while the left wing under Colonel-Commandant Collins was to make a detour to the north and advance from the north-west on Jackhalswater, detaching a force to cut the railway north-east of Jackhalswater to prevent the enemy training reinforcements down from Karibib. The force under Colonel Brits got in action with the enemy at 5.30 on the morning of the 20th, finding them holding the Riet Berg from the highest peak downwards along a spur to the bed of the Swakop River. (See Diagram No. 7.) Colonel Brits' attack developed towards his left, but was held up, the country being very rough and offering no possibility of getting round that flank. In the afternoon he developed an attack from his right, direct on the enemy left position. This attack had made considerable progress by nightfall, having nearly carried the highest peak from where the whole enemy position could be rolled up, when the enemy retired under cover of the darkness. The situation with the right wing of the 2nd Mounted Brigade under the Brigade Commander Colonel Alberts and Colonel-Commandant Badenhorst, the wing commander, was as follows:—

At 6.30 in the morning the Ermelo and Standerton B Commandos were a few miles ahead with instructions to attack the Pforte gap area. When at point H on diagram they received heavy artillery fire from the enemy section at D; as the ground was quite open, affording no cover whatever, they were forced to deviate considerably before getting to their objective. At the same time Swarts' Scouts were in action at the gap marked F. This was lightly held by the enemy, but was heavily mined with contact mines, which, however, failed to explode or were discovered in time. On getting through this gap the Scout Corps made a wide detour and got into action at L, near the railway, at 7 a.m. Here we have an instance of rapidity of commando tactics; a force attacks and carries a position, and within about thirty minutes has travelled at least 8 miles and is in action again. A mounted body of the enemy, marked at E on Diagram No. 7, moved as on the diagram to intercept the Scouts, while at the same time the enemy artillery was withdrawn from position D to the new position shown on the diagram. The main body of the right wing then cleared the ridge on either side of gap D and poured through the gap, taking up the positions K and L shown on the diagram, a manœuvre which was also performed at full gallop.

The country on which the operations now took place was more undulating and afforded cover. On the diagram the features are not shown, as they will obscure what is already a somewhat complicated diagram; also the distances between troops are exaggerated for the sake of clearness, the positions L being much nearer the enemy than shown.

By the time the positions K and L were taken up, the two commandos shown at H had got into action at their objective, soon getting a high point of the ridge in their possession. From the diagram it will be seen that the situation was now likely to confuse the unit commanders; the air was dense with the fine dust raised by the racing troops, and the heat mirage, which becomes troublesome very early, also helped to obscure vision.

Commandant Piet Botha, from the point he had gained on the ridge, saw artillery almost immediately below him firing eastwards, while he had to deal with the enemy still holding the ridge close to him. He personally descended the ridge to find out what artillery this was, and so dense was the dust that he was right up to the enemy section before he could distinguish them. On the pretext of having come to demand their surrender, he interviewed the commanding officer and returned to the ridge, from where the rifle fire of his troops soon became inconvenient to the officer he had interviewed. By about 8.30 the section of artillery was captured, as also 9 officers and 200 other ranks of the enemy force in this particular area, the broken ground and dust haze, however, making escape easy. A small body of enemy held out till 3 p.m., when they surrendered on the point of the ridge marked G. This, and the spent condition of the horses prevented the troops from operating further towards the enemy at Jackhalswater on that day.

The left wing of the 2nd Mounted Brigade, which had to cut the railway east of the junction of the branch to Riet, arrived at the place marked M on the diagram about 5 a.m. Discovering that the guides had led them too far westwards,

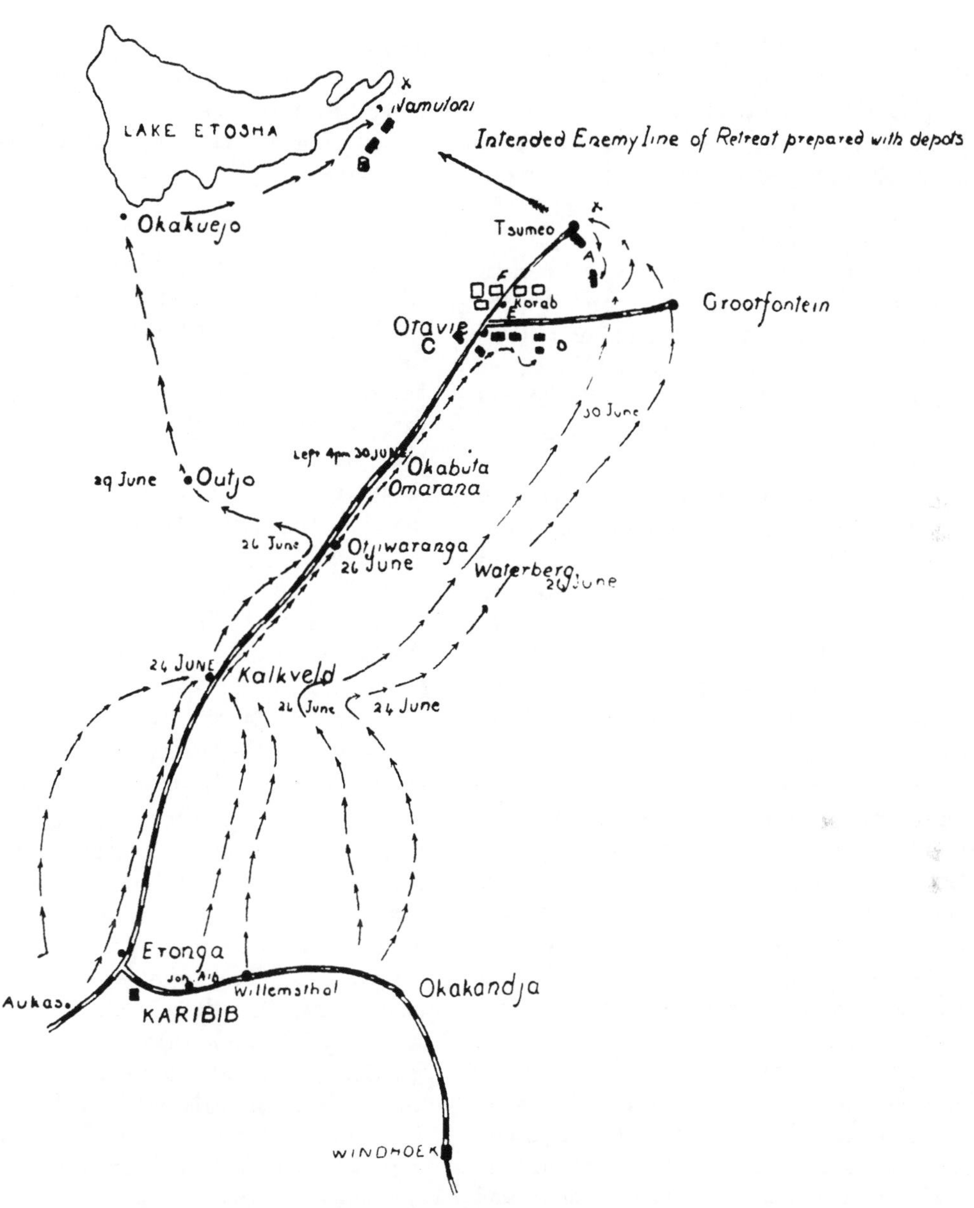

DIAGRAM No. 6.

Strategic Situation on 7th July, 1915.

A.—2nd Mounted Brigade, Right Wing 3rd Mounted Brigade (Brigadier-General Myburgh).
B.—1st Mounted Brigade (Brigadier-General Brits).
C.—1st Infantry Brigade (Brigadier-General Beves).
D.—5th Mounted Brigade (Brigadier-General M. Botha).
E.—Headquarters (General Louis Botha) and 6th Mounted Brigade (Brigadier-General Lukin)
F.—Entire German Force in the Field.

one detachment was sent to cut and hold the railway at N, while another detachment occupied the Jackhalswater station.

The enemy general reserve attacked them at 6.30, and, as they had no artillery and were unfavourably disposed in three detachments, they had to retire at about 10 a.m. with the loss of 43 men, taken prisoners in consequence of their horses being killed.

This force, although unable to realize the whole of their mission, which was to block the enemy line of retreat as well as divert his general reserve and intercept his reinforcements from Karibib (of the latter they captured one troop train with infantry, which, however, had to be abandoned when retiring), contributed considerably to the success of the operations. If the strong general reserve of the enemy, which at all cost had to keep their line of retreat open, had been free to devote their attention to the Pforte situation, the position of the troops shown at L on Diagram No. 7 would have been extremely uncomfortable.

The sincerity of the left wing's endeavour is clear from the fact that the German general reserve was in no condition to interfere to their left or rear after the left wing of the 2nd Mounted Brigade had retired, but were satisfied to remain at Jackhalswater holding the positions which covered the general retirement that night.

The enemy losses on this day were:—

Two field-guns, 9 officers, and 275 other ranks prisoners, while 4 officers and 12 other ranks killed were left on the field, together with 1 officer and 20 other ranks wounded.

The Union casualties were:—

2 officers and 11 other ranks killed.
5 officers and 36 other ranks wounded.
43 men captured at Jackhalswater.

The result of the day's operations was that the pick of the German troops had, with considerable loss, in one day been turned out of strong and carefully prepared positions which topographically were ideal for their purpose. They had every advantage, interior lines, local knowledge of the intricate terrain, water, and railway transport nearly to their fire positions.

The reasons of their subsequent reluctance to try tactical conclusions with the Union troops are thus not difficult to conjecture.

The Action at Trekkoppies.

While the strategic direction of advance was along the Swakop River the Northern Force had also to reconstruct the railway to Karibib (see Diagram No. 5A) so as to have no delay in achieving the final strategic objective after the first was obtained. Colonel (now Major-General) C. P. B. Skinner was in command of the troops protecting this reconstruction.

On the 26th of April his force, consisting of 2nd Transvaal Scottish, 1st Rhodesian, and 2nd Kimberley Battalions were at Trekkoppies while General Skinner personally was about eighteen miles in advance with his mounted troops (Imperial Light Horse, three squadrons).

At 1 a.m. on the 26th April these mounted troops located an enemy column marching south and later on one going south-west. Leaving two troops to observe the enemy General Skinner returned to Trekkoppies to await the enemy attack. The section of Heavy Artillery had been withdrawn a few days previously, to take part in the advance on Karibib, so this force had only one 15-pounder Armstrong Field Gun converted into an anti-aircraft gun. At 5.45 the enemy blew up the railway to the north of the camp by mistake instead of to the south. At 7.40 the action began by the enemy shelling with two batteries of Field Artillery from a range of hills that extended parallel to the railway line to the north-west. The range was about 5,000 yards. Under cover of this fire the enemy dismounted attack developed from the north and mainly from the west where better cover was available for an advance.

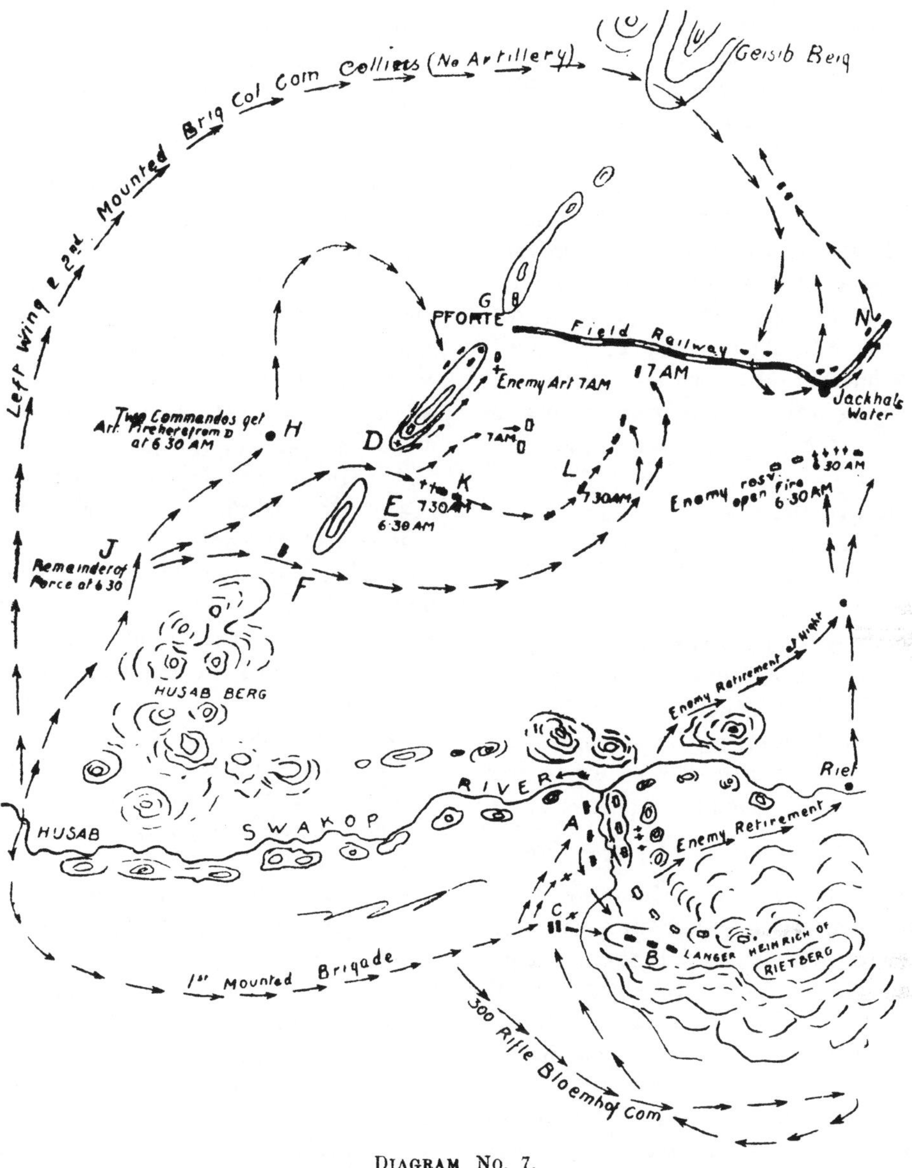

DIAGRAM No. 7.

Tactical Operations at Pforte and Riet on 20th March, 1915.

A.—First attack of Colonel Brits's Brigade, commenced about 6 a.m.

B.—Second attack developing in afternoon.

C.—Headquarters and General Officer Commanding-in-Chief and General Reserve.

▬ Union Troops.

▭ Enemy Troops.

—+— Sections of Field Artillery.

J.—Colonel Alberts with Right Wing 2nd Mounted Brigade and 4th Battery.

H.—Ermelo and Standerton B Commandos of the Right Wing at 6.30, deviated by artillery fire.

D.—Enemy artillery, first position direct fire.

F.—Swarts' Scouts at 6.30 a.m.

E.—Enemy Local Reserve at 6.30 a.m.

K.—4th Permanent Battery and Local Reserve at 7.30 a.m. (Heidelberg B Commando).

L.—Swarts' Scouts, Heidelberg A and Standerton B Commandos at 7 a.m.

At 10.30 this attack had spent itself, and the Kimberley Battalion—which had borne the brunt of the attack—together with the Transvaal Scottish and the Imperial Light Horse Regiment counter-attacked towards the enemy right. The counter-attack without artillery support could, however, not make much progress in the face of the enemy artillery fire which now increased in intensity to cover his retirement. At 11.30 the enemy artillery withdrew and the action terminated. The Section Armoured Cars effectively co-operated although the ground was most unfavourable.

Union casualties:—

3 officers, 6 other ranks killed.

2 officers, 30 other ranks wounded.

Enemy left:—

2 officers and 5 other ranks killed.

2 officers and 12 other ranks wounded, also 13 prisoners.

The attack was repulsed before the reinforcements that had been sent could take part in the action.

Actions at Elephants Neck and Otavi.

On the 30th June, 1915, General Botha, the Commander-in-Chief, was at Omarassa with the centre of the strategic advance, consisting of the 5th and 6th Mounted Brigades; the 1st Infantry Brigade being two days march in the rear.

The enemy was known to hold the Elephants Ridge—Diagram No. 8—in strength with his camps and depots at Otavi and Otavifontein. It was known that the enemy had heavily mined the gaps and flanks of the Elephants Ridge from where he had a good view and command of the flat plain below. There was no water between Okaputa and Otavifontein.

The 5th Mounted Brigade under General M. Botha was ordered to march that night from Okaputa at 6 p.m. on to Otjikurume, while the 6th Mounted Brigade under Brig.-General Lukin had to march from Omarassa half an hour later, the intention of the Commander-in-Chief being to have the 5th Brigade as his right and the 6th as his left in the attack on the Elephants Ridge the next day.

The 5th Mounted Brigade got into contact with the enemy outposts—see Diagram No. 8—while it was still dark and rushed them at such a rate that they had no time to let off the rockets and light signals prearranged to warn the main body. Brig.-General M. Botha, who appreciated the possibility of the situation, pursued the outposts with his whole Brigade in the hope of surprising the main body instead of continuing his march to Otjikurume as ordered. His initiative in accepting the responsibility of such a deviation from his orders was rewarded by there being a considerable element of surprise in his attack on the western flank of the Ridge at about 6.30 a.m.

Owing to the want of water near the Ridge, the enemy did not hold it in full strength but relied on timely warning—which failed—to garrison it from the main body at Otavi and Otavifontein. By about 7 a.m. the western flank was turned and other enemy troops further east on the Ridge had retired. Advancing a few miles the 5th again got into action with what was probably belated reinforcements from Otavi. This action, which was the most severe of the day, was fought on the flat, dense bush country, the enemy right still clinging to the hill west of the railway line, Diagram No. 8. After a few hours the enemy retired to the western flank of the Otavi range and the 5th again got into action about 12 noon, driving the enemy further north on to the Khorab Hills, where the final surrender took place eight days later.

About 9.30 a.m. the Commander-in-Chief, General L. Botha, and Brig.-General J. J. Collyer, the Chief of Staff, met Brig.-General M. Botha near the west flank of the Elephants Ridge. The Brigade Commander of the 5th then explained his reasons for departing from his orders and also his action in engaging his whole Brigade without retaining a reserve. A portion of his Brigade once committed to a running fight in close country densely covered with bush, became difficult to direct or recall. What has been said previously in this chapter about the commando psychology may now help to illuminate the situation in which Brig.-General M. Botha found himself. He is one of those officers who perfectly realize the strength and limitations of the commando spirit, so he decided to push the attack and bring all his force into action in support of the portion committed. The result of his rapid decision and action was that the enemy, who hoped, for once at least, to have his own way tactically, only succeeded in bringing a small portion of his force into action, the remainder having rapidly to retire under cover of rearguard actions at C and D on Diagram No. 8.

General M. Botha's command numbered 4 guns and 1,958 officers and other ranks. The German strength at Otavi and Elephants Neck was 36 guns, 22 machine-guns, and 3,372 officers and other ranks.

A study of Diagram No. 8 will show that there is a great deal of truth in the Chief of the German Staff's declaration a few days later, at the armistice interview, that if they only had one hour's time to occupy their carefully selected positions General Louis Botha with his two Brigades would never have got back to Okaputa. In numbers, General Louis Botha's force of two Mounted Brigades was about equal to the German force, which latter, however, in artillery, outnumbered the Union guns by more than four to one, besides having the advantage of an ideal position as can be seen from the diagram. Had the Union troops been checked and held up for one day they would have been forced to return the forty miles to Okaputa for water: that the German troops with fresh horses would then have become an inconvenient factor, can be imagined.

The 5th Brigade, in the running fight, captured men from the 1st, 2nd, and 5th Regular Companies and from the 2nd, 3rd, and 4th Reserve Companies, so it cannot be said that the German outpost line was weakly held.

The Union casualties were 4 killed and 12 wounded.

General Botha's First Operation Order.

Before concluding the history of the tactical operations of the Northern Force, it may not be out of place to give a copy of the first Operation Order issued by the Commander-in-Chief, General Louis Botha. The document is not only of historical interest by being the first to direct the operations of the Northern Force, but instructive as to the general conditions and difficulties. The Order was in connection with the advance on Heigamchab and Goanikontes which were not seriously resisted by the enemy:—

Operation Order No. 1, by General the Right Honourable Louis Botha, Commanding-in-Chief the Union Forces in the Field.

General Headquarters,
Swakopmund,
22nd February, 1915.

Reference to Map S.1, issued herewith.

1. The following information as to the enemy's dispositions is mainly based upon intercepted wireless telegraph messages and has *not* been verified by actual observation.

The information should, therefore, be regarded as the best obtainable but as based mainly on assumption.

Our position at Swakopmund has since the arrival of our troops been under close observation by the enemy who occupies a position in contact with our outposts on the east of the town. The strength of the forces occupying this position is unknown, but as far as can be ascertained no troops other than the 2nd Reserve Company have been in the position. The peace strength of a mounted company is 120 men, which may have been increased to 150 or even more.

At Goanikontes there are apparently the headquarters of the 2nd Reserve (Captain Schultetus) and whatever strength of that company is not at any time immediately before Swakopmund; the 5th Reserve Company (Captain Ohlenschlager); half a battery of mounted artillery and six machine-guns.

Unless therefore other troops happen to arrive at a time when an attack is made on Goanikontes, a liberal estimate of the force of the enemy to be expected there would be 300 mounted men, 2 mountain guns, and six machine-guns.

No information is to hand of the existence of any hostile force at Heigamchab.

There is, however, a force of the enemy at Jakalswater and it is reasonable to assume that some connecting force may be at Heigamchab. The presence of such a force should, therefore, be calculated with and steps should be taken to guard against its sudden arrival. Nothing is known about the strength at Jakalswater, but from indications it would seem that about 500 mounted troops, a battery of field artillery, and a mountain battery may perhaps be there. This is, however, merely assumption on meagre data. In any case no reinforcement from Jakhalswater could probably reach Goanikontes in less than five hours.

2. It is the intention of the General Officer Commanding-in-Chief simultaneously to attack the enemy in his positions immediately east of Swakopmund and at Goanikontes early on the morning of Tuesday, the 23rd instant.

For this purpose the forces disposable will be divided into three forces and a general reserve, and a special task will be assigned to the 1st Imperial Light Horse. " A " Force will be under the command of Colonel P. C. B. Skinner, and will consist of:—

4th Permanent Field Battery.

" D " and " F " Batteries Heavy Artillery.

3rd Infantry Brigade.

" B " Force will be under the command of Colonel J. J. Alberts, and will consist of:—

The right wing, 2nd Mounted Brigade.

Two mounted sections machine-guns, to be detailed by Major Giles, who will accompany " B " Force.

" C " Force will be under the command of Colonel Commandant W. R. Collins, and will consist of:—

The left wing, 2nd Mounted Brigade, less such portion of that wing as is detached for the general reserve.

One mounted section machine-guns, to be detailed by Major Giles.

The General Reserve will consist of:—

That portion of the left wing, 2nd Mounted Brigade, of which the horses are judged to be unfit for the duty assigned to " C " Force, under the command of Colonel Commandant L. J. Badenhorst, Rand Rifles.

1 mounted section (I.L.H.) machine-guns.

The General Reserve will be under the direct command of the General Officer Commanding-in-Chief, who will exercise general control over the whole operations.

3. The attack on the enemy's positions immediately east of Swakopmund will be carried out by " A " Force under the command of Colonel P. C. B. Skinner, to whom the hour of the commencement of the attack will be communicated.

" B " Force (under the command of Colonel J. J. Alberts) will move on Goanikontes from Swakopmund at an hour and under instructions which will be communicated to Colonel Alberts.

" C " Force (under the command of Colonel-Commandant W. R. Collins) will move on Goanikontes from Swakopmund at an hour and under instructions which will be communicated to Colonel-Commandant Collins.

The 1st Imperial Light Horse, under the command of Major H. G. L. Panchaud, will move from Swakopmund at the same time and in company with " C " Force, leaving that force at a

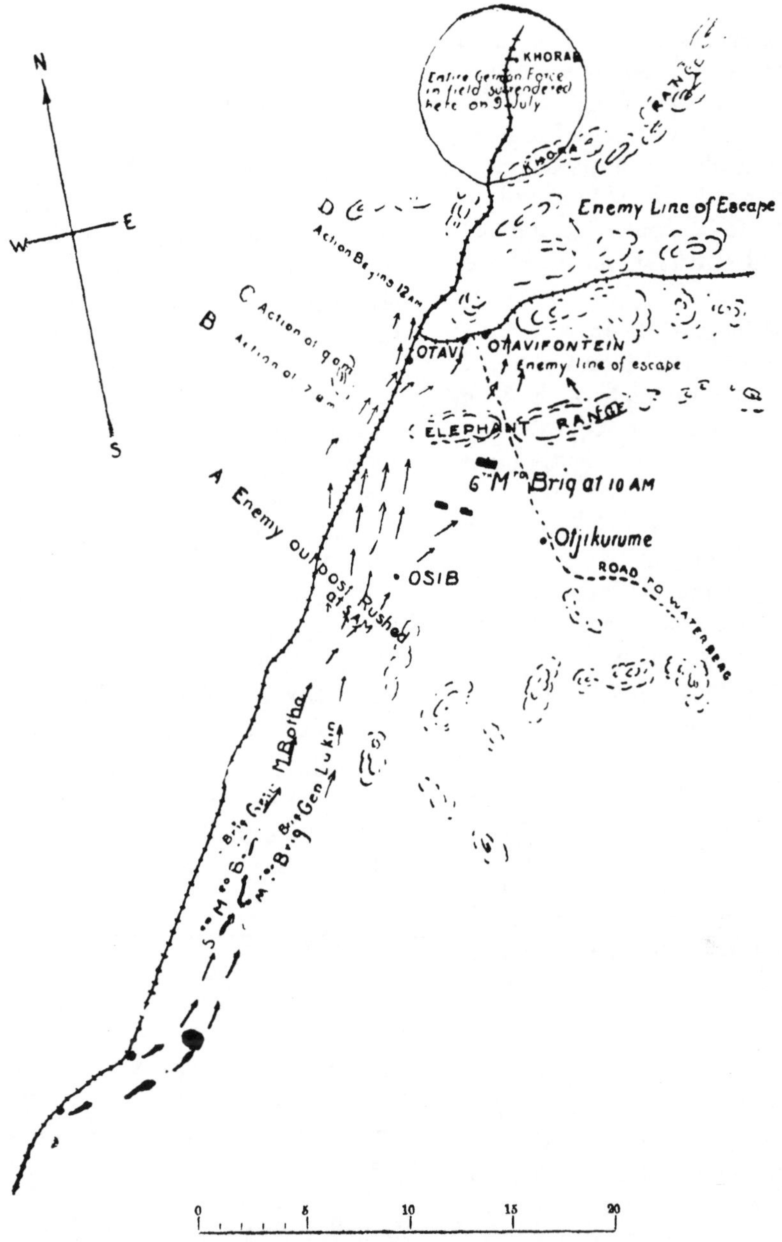

DIAGRAM NO. 8.

Tactical Operations at Otavi on 1st July.

Country densely bush covered, level plains with hills 500 to 1,000 feet above level of plains. No water between Otavi and Okaputa.

5th Mounted Brigade left Okaputa 6 p.m., 30th June... ... ... 6th Mounted Brigade left Omurassa 6.30 p.m., 30th June	To attack the enemy holding the Elephants Range in force with his camp at Otavifontein.

A.—5th Brigade after 28 miles night march rushes enemy outposts at 5 a.m., 1st July.

B.—5th Brigade after 36 miles march in action at 7 a.m. Enemy Artillery (1 Battery) at F. Union 2nd Permanent Battery at E.

C.—5th Brigade in action at 9 a.m. Enemy two Batteries at H.

D.—5th Brigade after 44 miles march and three actions, in action again 12 noon to 3 p m Enemy Artillery at K. Union two Batteries near H.

point and under special instructions which will be communicated to Major Panchaud.

The mounted troops from the 2nd Mounted Brigade for the General Reserve, and the Rand Rifles, will parade at a point and at an hour which will be communicated to Colonel-Commandant Badenhorst and Lieut.-Colonel Purcell respectively.

4. The line of defence hitherto occupied at night by infantry of the 3rd Infantry Brigade will be taken over on the night of the 22nd-23rd instant, at 8 p.m., by the South African Irish, under the command of Lieut.-Colonel F. H. Brennan, V.D.

The Officer Commanding, 3rd Infantry Brigade, will indicate the line of defence to be occupied to Lieut.-Colonel Brennan who, immediately the line has been occupied by the regiment under his command, will report in writing to that effect to the Chief Staff Officer at General Headquarters.

5. The Staff Officer, Signalling, will make arrangements for communication between the forces in agreement with the plan of operations, which will be communicated to him, and will especially ensure as rapid and effective communication as possible between Goanikontes and General Headquarters.

The Staff Officer, Signalling, will not later than 6 p.m. to-day acquaint all commanders of forces and detached units with the details of the scheme of intercommunication (including the strength of personnel and nature of means of communication allotted to each force of unit), and will report to the Chief Staff Officer in writing that this has been done when all acknowledgments of these details have been received from the commanders referred to.

6. Medical units are allotted as under:

To Force " A "—

" B " Section, 2nd Mounted Brigade Field Ambulance.

To Force " B "—

" B " Section, 9th Mounted Brigade Field Ambulance.

To Force " C "—

" A " Section, 9th Mounted Brigade Field Ambulance.

Sick and wounded will be evacuated to Swakopmund.

7. An officer from each of the following units will report at General Headquarters at 10 minutes to 6 o'clock this evening to take the official time in agreement with which all movements will take place:—

S.O. Signalling, Headquarter Staff.
" A " Force.
" B " Force.
" C " Force.
4th Permanent Field Battery.
Heavy Artillery Brigade.
1st Imperial Light Horse.
Portion of 2nd Mounted Brigade in General Reserve.
Rand Rifles.
2nd Mounted Brigade Field Ambulance.
9th Mounted Brigade Field Ambulance.

Commanding officers of the units remainder of the troops mentioned in this time being made known in their commands after receiving it from General Headquarters.

8. Two days' rations will be carried by " B " Force and one day's rations by the referred to will arrange for the correct Order.

Commanding officers will make the best possible arrangements to carry as substantial feed as possible for the horses in the nosebags.

9. Every commander of a force or detached unit will be held responsible for assuring himself that every unit attached to his command reports at the proper hour and *moves off with his force.*

10. Hand-flags for officers will be issued for the purpose of identifying bodies of our own troops.

11. The General Officer Commanding-in-Chief will be at the trenches now occupied by the Transvaal Scottish, east of the Lazaretto.

(Sgd.) J. J. COLLYER, Colonel,
Chief Staff Officer.

Brig.-General J. J. Collyer, C.B., C.M.G., D.S.O.

By Orderly at 7 a.m. to:—

Officer Commanding " A " Force.
Officer Commanding " B " Force.
Officer Commanding " C " Force.
Officer Commanding 1st I.L.H.
Staff Officer, Field Artillery.
Staff Officer, Signalling.
Assistant Director of Medical Services.
Officer Commanding 4th Permanent Field Battery.
Officer Commanding Heavy Artillery Brigade.
Officer Commanding Mounted Troops, General Reserve.
Officer Commanding South African Irish.
Officer Commanding Machine-Gun Brigade.
Officer Commanding Bodyguard.

By Orderly at 11 *a.m. to A.Q.M.G.; and by Orderly at* 12 *noon to*:—

Officer Commanding Rand Rifles.

The Central Force.

The enemy did not resist the landing of the first Union troops under Colonel, later Brig.-General P. S. Beves, at Luderitz Bay on the 18th of September, 1914. The reasons for not doing so were probably also the want of water anywhere within striking distance, but out of range of the escorting cruiser's guns. The Union troops were reinforced later (see chapter on Organization) and commanded by Brig.-General Sir Duncan MacKenzie, the opposing enemy force being commanded by Major Von Bauzus.

The Central Force had a long period of defensive waiting until the Union Government had its hands free from the incubus of the rebellion and could prosecute the South-West campaign vigorously. Then the Central Force co-operated by exerting strategic pressure inwards until it came before Aus, where the strong positions of the enemy and the want of water for the Union troops made a direct attack inadvisable before strategic pressure from the other Union Forces had influenced the situation. This pressure caused the enemy to evacuate Aus and retire northwards, General MacKenzie following up with his three Mounted Brigades. In addition to a number of patrol, outpost, and advance-guard encounters, the Central Force had one important tactical operation near Gibeon.

The Action at Gibeon.

Brig.-General MacKenzie left Aus on the 16th of April with one 6-gun battery of Field Artillery and three Mounted Brigades. After a march of 160 miles he was near the point C (on Diagram No. 9) at 6 p.m. on the 26th April. Here he received intelligence that an enemy force under Major Von Kleist with two guns was at Gibeon Station. There was also a train with steam up at the station.

Brig.-General MacKenzie then pushed on with the intention of capturing this body of the enemy. When at point B on Diagram No. 9 he detached Colonel Royston with one Brigade and one regiment, and instructed him to make a detour to the east, get astride the railway north of Gibeon, and co-operate in the attack on the enemy next day at dawn. General MacKenzie, with the remaining half of the force, marched on and bivouacked at point K.

Colonel Royston got on to the railway at A about 1 p.m. the next morning. He had disposed his force unfavourably, and when attacked by the enemy had to retire with the loss of 3 officers and 21 other ranks killed, 49 wounded, and 72 missing. This was about 3 a.m. on the 27th of April. At 5 a.m. on the 27th April Brig.-General MacKenzie advanced from his bivouac at K on the enemy at Gibeon.

The enemy was disposed at H, about 2½ miles north of Gibeon Station, from where they were driven to the second position D on the diagram. About 8 a.m. they were driven from the second position D with the loss of their two guns; the 72 prisoners captured early that morning from Colonel Royston at A were also recovered here.

Brig.-General MacKenzie in this operation under his personal conduct lost 3 killed and 13 wounded, the enemy leaving 11 killed, 30 wounded, and 188 prisoners on the field.

The Southern Force.

This force of about 5,000 rifles and one battery of artillery was, on the 1st of January, 1915, disposed as on Diagram No. 3, previous to that date having had the task of resisting any German advance into the Union or preventing any rebel bodies from escaping into enemy territory. The enemy force immediately opposed to it was under Major Ritter, and was based on Keetmanshoop. Ritter's force comprised a battery of artillery and four mounted companies, together with a body of rebels, numbering about 800, under Maritz and Kemp. This latter body, which acted independently, had been reinforced by the Germans with a mounted company and a battery of four field-guns and two pom-poms.

Besides a number of patrol, outpost, and advance guard encounters, the Southern Force had three defensive actions and three offensive engagements in the course of its work of exerting strategic pressure from the south and south-east.

Defensive Action at Nydasputs.

About 400 rifles of the Southern Force were camped at Nydasputs, 45 miles north-west of Upington, and were attacked there at daybreak on the 18th January by about 800 enemy and the artillery under Maritz and Kemp. They were compelled to retire with the loss of 9 killed, 20 wounded, and 170 prisoners. The enemy loss could not be ascertained. The experienced enemy troops, of the same tactical quality as the Union troops and superior by two to one, besides having artillery, availed themselves of all the advantages derived from an intimate knowledge of the methods and weak points of the Union commandos, and it required very dexterous handling to extricate the somewhat rawer Union troops without greater casualty.

Defensive Action at Upington

On the 24th January the same enemy force under Maritz and Kemp, but reinforced by 300 German rifles under Schoeman, attacked Colonel J. van Deventer at Upington. The Union Force—12 commando units, about 2,400 rifles, and a 6-gun battery of artillery—were attacked at dawn, the attack lasting until about 12 noon, when it had spent itself. Colonel Van Deventer then counter-attacked and pursued the enemy for some distance.

Union casualties: 7 killed, 24 wounded. Enemy casualties: 18 killed, 23 wounded, 85 prisoners.

The result of this action was that Kemp surrendered unconditionally with nearly the entire force a few days later, Maritz and Schoeman, with a few followers and the artillery, retiring on the enemy troops under Major Ritter.

Defensive Action at Kakamas.

Kakamas was occupied by five commando units (about 1,600 rifles), disposed on both sides of the Orange River, which was in flood. This unfavourable disposition was due to the fact that as late as 22nd December the enemy had attacked Nous, 17 miles south of the river, at Schuit Drift. As there were interests to be protected on both banks of the river at Kakamas, the disposition remained similar to that in force at the time the place was threatened from both sides. On the morning of the 4th February Major Ritter, with a force of four guns and about 400 rifles, attacked the Union troops on the north bank of the river. By about 11 a.m. the attack was beaten off, the enemy leaving 12 killed and 12 prisoners on the field, but removing his wounded.

Offensive Action at Nabas.

During the advance of the Southern Force towards Keetmanshoop Major Smith was instructed to attack Nabas, about 10 miles north of Ukamas (Diagram No. 4). His force numbered 270 rifles, and the enemy was about 160 rifles strong. On the morning of the 8th of March Major Smith surprised the enemy

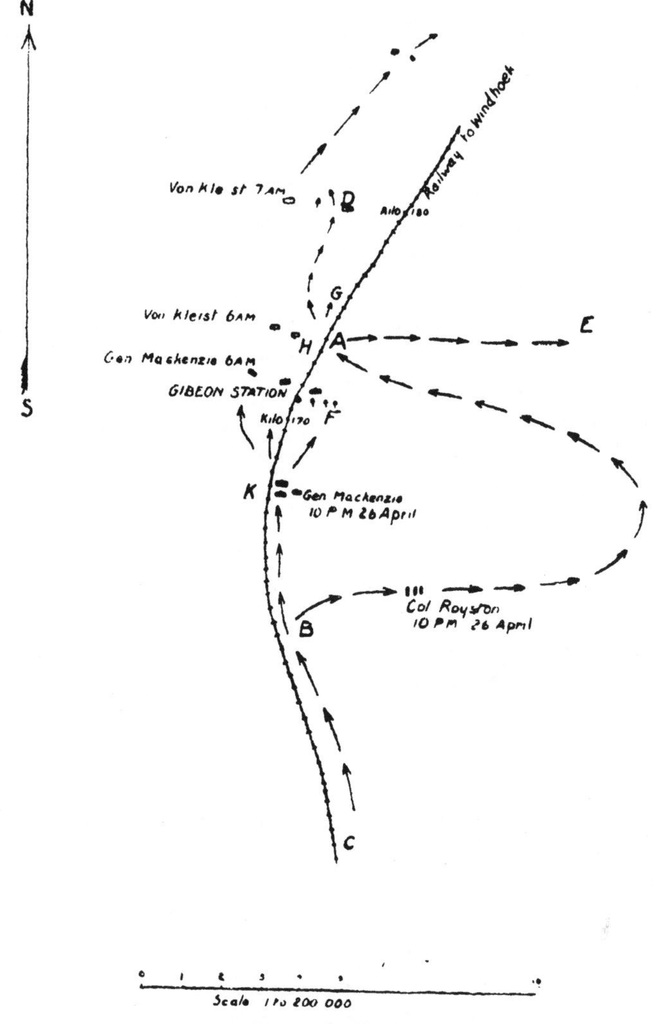

Diagram No. 9.

Tactical Operations at Gibeon, 27th April.

C.—Position of General Mackenzie's Force of 1 6-gun Battery Field Artillery and 3 Brigades (2 Regiments each) of Mounted Troops, at 6 p.m., 26th April, when ascertained that Major Von Kleist at Gibeon Station with 1 Section Field Artillery and about 600 rifles.

B.—Colonel Royston with half the force, less the artillery, detours to east and gets astride the railway at A. He is attacked by the enemy and driven off in direction of E at 3 a.m.

K.—General Mackenzie advanced from here at 5 a.m., 27th April, and attacks Von Kleist just as day dawns, defeating him with the loss of two guns.

F.—First position of Union Artillery, about 6 a.m.

G.—Second position of Union Artillery, about 7.30 a.m.

H.—Von Kleist's first position.

D.—Von Kleist's second position. (His two guns were taken and the 72 prisoners captured from Colonel Royston at A were released here.)

■ Union Regiments.

▭ German Troops.

and compelled them to retire with the loss of all their transport and supplies and 1 killed and 3 wounded.

Offensive Action at Platbeen.

In the course of the further advance towards Keetmanshoop, Colonel D. van Deventer, with about 300 rifles of his Brigade, attacked the enemy, numbering about 200 rifles, at Platbeen on the morning of 27th March. Colonel Van Deventer compelled the enemy to retire with the loss of their transport and supplies, 14 prisoners, and 6 wounded.

Offensive Action at Kabus.

On the 20th April Colonel D. van Deventer, with about 1,400 rifles of his Brigade, attacked the enemy, numbering two guns and about 300 rifles at Kabus. He was later on reinforced by 300 rifles from Colonel Berrange's Eastern Force, and the enemy then retired with the loss of 2 killed and 16 wounded, the Union casualties being 10 wounded.

Operations of the Eastern Force.

This force was constantly engaged in advance guard and patrol affairs. It had no defensive actions of any magnitude, and had four offensive engagements.

Offensive Action at Rietfontein.

On the 19th March Captain Van Vuuren, of this force, with one squadron (about 100 rifles), attacked about 200 enemy rifles at Rietfontein. The enemy retired with the loss of their transport and supplies, and left 4 killed, 20 wounded, and 2 captured on the field. The Union casualties were 1 killed and 2 wounded.

In view of the importance of the water at Rietfontein and the enemy superiority in numbers, Captain Van Vuuren may be considered as having operated in a highly creditable manner.

Offensive Action at Koes.

On the 5th of April Colonel Van Zyl, with two commando squadrons, attacked the enemy at Koes. With a loss of one man wounded, Colonel Van Zyl captured one prisoner and several hundred head of cattle.

Offensive Action at Kiries West.

On the 16th April the enemy, with two guns and about 300 rifles, was attacked at Kiries West by Colonel Berrange, who had one regular regiment (5th Regiment, South African Mounted Riflemen) and two commando regiments. The enemy retired with a loss of 4 killed, 1 wounded, and 8 captured. The Union loss was 1 killed and 1 wounded.

Offensive Action at Kabus.

On the 20th April Colonel D. van Deventer, of the Southern Force, had commenced an attack on Kabus at dawn (see Operations, Southern Force, action at Kabus). Later in the day he was reinforced by 300 rifles from Colonel Berrange's Eastern Force. This reinforcement largely assisted in the success of the operations on that day, the enemy retiring with a loss of 2 killed and 16 wounded, the Union casualties being 10 wounded.

MARCHING RECORD OF FIELD TROOPS.

Number of Miles Marched,

By.	In Enemy Territory.	From Base.
	Miles.	Miles.
Northern Force, 2nd Mounted Brigade	480	480
Northern Force, 3rd Mounted Brigade (Right Wing) ...	480	480
Northern Force, 1st Mounted Brigade	460	460
Northern Force, 5th Mounted Brigade	420	420
Northern Force, 6th Mounted Brigade	350	350
Northern Force, 1st Infantry Brigade	330	330
Central Force, 7th, 8th, and 9th Mounted Brigade ...	290	290
Central Force, Infantry	65	65
Southern Force, Right-hand Column...	240	340
Southern Force, Middle Column	220	320
Southern Force, Left of Steinkopf Column...	190	240
Eastern Force	200	500

Note.—Distances measured along actual route and do not include return of troops.

LONGEST SUSTAINED ADVANCES.

Force.	Unit.	From.	To.	Miles.	Days.	Average Miles Per Day.
Northern	1st Mounted Brigade	Aukas ...	Namitoni ...	340	20	17
Northern	2nd and Right Wing, 3rd Mounted Brigade	Willemsthal	Tsumeb ...	280	20	14
Northern	5th and 6th Mounted Brigades	Karibib ...	Otavi ...	230	13	17·7
Northern	1st INFANTRY Brigade	Karibib ...	Otavi ...	230	16	14·4
Central	7th, 8th, and 9th Brigades	Aus... ...	Gibeon ...	200	12	16·7
Southern	Central Column	Karus ...	Warmbakkies	100	10	10
Eastern	Entire Force	Hazuur ...	Kabus ...	120	18	6·6

BEST FORCED MARCHES (Including Halts and Delays).

Force.	Unit.	From.	To.	Miles.	Hours.
Northern	Left Wing, 2nd Mounted Brigade ...	Husab ...	Jackhalswater and back to Husab	76	22
Northern	5th Mounted Brigade	Okaputa ...	Kilo 500... ...	44	18
Northern	6th Mounted Brigade	Omarassa ...	Elephants Neck...	36	15
Northern	3rd and 5th Mounted Brigades ...	Riet... ...	Otjimbingue ...	70	37
Central	7th, 8th, and 9th Brigades	Berseba ...	Gibeon	70	72
Southern	Col. Dirk van Deventer's Column ...	Neu Khais ...	Kabus	120	144

The record march of the campaign was by the 2nd Mounted Brigade, Left Wing, which after a 40-mile march in 14 hours, marched 76 miles in 22 hours, the diary being as follows:—

Left Swakop 6 p.m. 18th March, arrive Husab 8 a.m. 19th March (40 miles in 14 hours); left Husab 8 p.m. 19th March, arrive Jackhalswater 5 a.m. 20th March; in action 3 hours and return for water, arriving Husab same day.

V. *Naval Operations.*

In an attempt to record the assistance rendered by the Navy in this campaign we are faced by the same difficulties which present themselves in considering the Union's military operations before 1915. The Navy had in 1914 to perform operations like the bombardment and destruction of the Swakop harbour works, which in no way directly assisted in the conquest of South-West Africa but were necessitated by events far removed from the South-West coast. As with the Union military enterprise, it will be best to recount only those operations which were performed after the situation had been so far cleared up that attention could be exclusively directed to South-West.

When the Union Government had its hands free to deal with the South-West campaign, the first work of the Navy was to examine and sweep the waters of Luderitz, Swakop, and Walvis Bay and remove the mines. Such craft as was anchored in these harbours was secured for use of the Union Forces: the enemy had grounded some of the large vessels and the smaller craft—one launch and about a dozen lighters—had been placed on railway trucks and removed inland to Otavi, where they were captured by the 5th and 6th Mounted Brigades on the 1st of July, 1915.

The work of escorting, conveying, and disembarking the Union Forces from Capetown to Luderitz, Swakop, and Walvis was conducted by the Navy without the loss of a single life or vessel, and in January, 1915, before the railway from Walvis to Swakop was completed, the troops in Swakop were entirely dependent on the daily sea transport service between these two places for their supplies.

In addition to the dull but indispensable work of maintaining the ocean line of communication and overcoming the daily vagaries of tide and weather in disembarking the thousands of troops, animals, heavy railway and other stores—an operation which was accomplished with the loss of but one locomotive tender, subsequently salved—the Navy also assisted in the military operations inland with a squadron of armoured motor-cars. These cars did very excellent work at the "Trekkopjes" action (see Tactical Operations) and they accompanied the final advance of the Northern Force without however getting a further opportunity of action. From subsequent conversations with members of the German General Staff it appears that the presence of these cars—the tactical value of which may even have been overrated by the enemy—prevented many a proposed minor enterprise, such as small raids or sniping expeditions, and kept the hostile reconnaissance patrols at a respectful distance.

VI. Transport, Lines of Communication, and Supplies.

General.

From Diagrams Nos. 1 and 2 the probability may be gathered that formidable transport problems would be presented to the four Union Forces which were to operate on exterior lines.

The ocean transport from Capetown to Walvis Bay was 850 miles and from Capetown to Luderitz Bay 550 miles.

In the enemy territory the existing railway line of 1,040 miles was repaired and used while 340 miles of new line were laid, partly in Union and partly in enemy territory.

Supplies, with the exception of meat, were unobtainable in the country, and the great scarcity of water presented obstacles the elimination of which will be considered in the chapter on Engineering.

The Northern Force.

The base of this Force was Capetown, where dock and embarking facilities were to be had. Walvis Bay, the disembarking end of the 850-mile sea transport line, is sheltered and calm but ships have to anchor about two thousand yards from shore and there are no harbour works. The men, horses, and other material, including entire locomotives, were landed on pontoons with from 10 to 50 ton load capacity. The landing jetties were of various type to allow for tide differences (see chapter Engineering).

A 3 ft. 6 in. gauge railway was constructed to Swakopmund and the relaying on a 3 ft. 6 in. basis of the German 2 ft. gauge line from Swakop to Karibib was commenced.

The transport problem of urgent interest, however, was how to maintain the far-advanced and rapidly operating mounted field troops, there being absolutely no grazing of any description until Karibib was reached.

After General Botha had cleared the country as far as Goanikontes and Heigamchab (see Tactical Operations) depots were established at these places and at Husab, which was in "No man's land" between the outpost lines at first but later was incorporated under an infantry garrison. By motor lorry and mule-wagon trains, these intermediate depots were stocked and supplied, so that the Mounted Brigades could rapidly cross the intervening country without transport. Transport was necessary from Husab, where a five-days' supply had been accumulated. After the occupation of Riet, the same method was followed for the advance on Karibib.

This rather novel way of supplying an army in the field by withdrawing the majority of the troops to the base, establishing intermediate depots, and a well-stocked advanced depot near the outpost line, and then rushing the troops without transport, to be maintained by the intermediate "catering establishments," to the advanced depot, where they pick up transport with supplies for several days, is not without tactical interest. On a first consideration it may even be regarded as a twisting of Fortune's caudal appendage that met with more success than it deserved. The probability of enemy interference was, however, constantly kept in view, and the picked infantry garrisons were well aware of their responsibility of

THE UNION G.O.C. AND STAFF DISCUSSING OPERATIONS IN THE FIELD.

GENERAL BOTHA AND COLONEL FRANKE, THE GERMAN COMMANDER.

holding an enemy attack until reinforcements could be rushed up. The absence of enemy interference does not constitute any lack of enterprise; he had to consider similar transport difficulties imposed by the desert, and preferred to keep his troops fresh for disputing well-selected localities, to frittering them away on missions the best success of which would merely delay the Union advance. As with the strategical innovations connected with the final objective, the best argument as to the propriety of the methods employed, was their success and the consciousness that no other alternative presented a hope of attaining the desired result.

At the time of the advance on Karibib from Riet, a birdseye view of the Transport and Lines of Communication situation would have shown (Diagram No. 5A) two diverging lines of communication from the base Swakop. The one going to Riet as advanced depot and having intermediate depots to feed large bodies of passing troops, and the other along the railway to Trekkoppies. This last being prepared in advance to serve as the main line of communication to Karibib.

On the occupation of Karibib, there was an acute shortage of supplies as the transport had to be switched from the one line of communication on to the other. The advanced base of supplies was made at Usakos (Diagram No. 5A), the railway being completed to a few miles beyond Trekkoppies, from where about fifty miles of rough, sandy country, very unsuitable for motor transport, intervened to Karibib, where the field troops now had to be supplied. The light railway laid by the enemy from Karibib to Pforte could not be made of much service for want of rolling stock, and all efforts were directed to continuing the 3 ft. 6 in. line from Trekkoppies to Karibib. This railway was completed to Usakos on the 14th May, but the scarcity of rolling stock, especially locomotives, caused considerable delay before sufficient supplies were accumulated for the final advance.

For this advance (see Diagram No. 6) one hundred wagons (twelve mules each) were allotted to each Brigade, Brigade Commanders being made responsible for the supply of their own units and the protection of their trains; the line of communication for each detached force being more or less directly behind its own advance. The main line of communication from Walvis to Karibib, under Brig.-General Skinner as General Officer Commanding Lines of Communication, was to extend northwards along the railway as rapidly as the enemy demolitions could be repaired and shorten the independent lines of communication established by the Brigade Commanders. Only mealie meal, coffee, tea, sugar, salt, biscuits, soap, tobacco, and matches were to be carried; meat was to be procured from the country covered in the advance, and the horses and transport mules were to depend on grazing. It was, however, later found possible to provide the animals with a small grain ration. The railway from Karibib northwards was on a 2 ft. gauge, and considerable delay would have resulted for want of rolling stock if once the advance was seriously checked and the supply carried by each Brigade on its hundred wagons exhausted. This danger was only removed when Brig.-General Myburgh's troops captured the entire rolling stock of this line intact at Tsumeb, where all the locomotives stood ready charged and primed for demolition.

Eastern Force.

This Force, with its base at Kimberley, had a Line of Communication more than 500 miles long with waterless stretches of more than a hundred miles. The transport was by motor vehicles and mule-wagons. On the long waterless stretches tank stations were established that were filled by motor-cars carrying 60 gallons each; these cars, of which about forty were allotted to each tank station, worked in pairs, the drivers having to fill and empty the drums themselves.

Central Force.

The transport of this Force was by sea from Capetown to Luderitz Bay, where there were better disembarking facilities than at Walvis Bay as the jetties and cranes of the port were soon repaired. Water was, however, very scarce and had to be condensed from sea-water (see chapter Engineering). The 3 ft. 6 in. gauge railway to Keetmanshoop was repaired as far as Aus, where General MacKenzie began to build up a supply depot for his further advance; he had about a hundred wagons available and with these he commenced the advance on Gibeon. This wagon train sufficed for the supply of his troops near Gibeon until the railway was repaired.

Southern Force.

This was partly based on Upington, to which place a railway had been constructed from Prieska, and partly on Steinkoff. The troops at Steinkoff were supplied by an ocean line from Capetown to Port Nolloth and thence by the Cape Copper Company's railway to Steinkoff. The railway from Prieska to Upington was extended behind the advancing troops until it joined the enemy railway system at Kalkfontein. The field troops being supplied from railhead by mule-wagon supply columns.

VII. Intelligence.

On a consideration of the facts that the enemy was operating in country well known to him, that he had the extra advantage of an Air Service and Camel Corps, had carefully interned all enemy and suspicious subjects, and that in the Union he had sympathy that went to the extent of armed rebellion, it will perhaps be readily conceded that he had a great advantage in the matter of procuring information. It is not of much interest to investigate the extent to which he had availed himself of these advantages, but it is instructive from a point of future application to note some inconceivable oversights of the enemy that enabled the Union General Staff to obtain their information. There was no—or a very perfunctory—internal censorship over newspapers, letters, telegrams, and wireless messages; these almost invariably disclosed dispositions or intended movements; wireless messages especially were a never-failing source of information. When a wireless station had for days been ordering so many kilo butter for the 4th Battery, cut-grass for the 3rd Company, boot-laces for another company, and so on, it was in a few days possible not only to have a complete marching state of the troops to which the wireless station was attached, but also to have considerable information as to the interior economy of the units and the character—or want of it—of the officers. If, then, certain things were urgently ordered to be delivered by a certain date, a move by the units concerned could with every degree of probability be speculated on, generally in a direction and to a destination that could be anticipated from the indiscretions of the previous messages. When eventually the official marching orders in cypher were transmitted from Headquarters, it did not take the Union Staff long to discover the keyword used, as a very close guess of the contents of the message could be made and the enemy were obliging enough frequently to give part of a message in cypher only and the rest in clear.

Reconnaissance by aeroplane was only available as far as the Northern Force was concerned after the occupation of Karibib—the Central, Southern, and Eastern Forces never had the benefit of air information. The enemy, however, almost daily photographed and bombed the dispositions of the Central Force, and also made air reconnaissances over the northern dispositions.

Another point of interest in the Intelligence work of this campaign that must be noted for future guidance was the futility of depending on persons with alleged local knowledge of the country. Of the numerous guides engaged, it was

General Botha and the German Governor of South-West Africa discussing the Terms of Surrender.

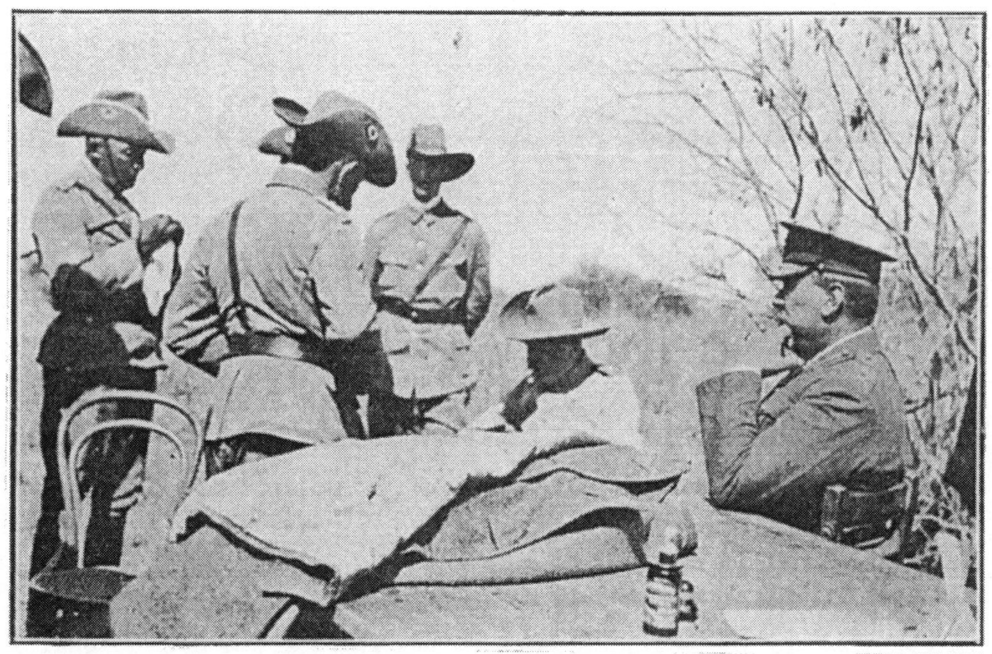

The German Governor of South-West Africa imparting to his Officers the Terms of Surrender, in the presence of General Botha.

with few exceptions found that they invariably had complete knowledge of the entire country except just that particular portion on which information or column guiding was immediately required. The best of these guides went entirely wrong when leading a column in the first advance from Swakop to Goanikontes. Fortunately the Brigade Major had checked the line of march by prismatic compass, and when he discovered how far they were deviating from the objective he took over the guiding and marched by compass. As a result, valuable time was lost and the column arrived too late to intercept the enemy. The left wing of the 2nd Brigade also went wrong on the night march to Jackhalswater through trusting entirely to guides with local knowledge, and it is known that one German column in the attack on Trekkoppies never reached its objective for the same reason, although they had a much better knowledge of the country. It therefore appears safe to assume that reliance should in these cases be placed more on mathematical direction.

VIII. Engineering.

The South African Engineer Corps, under the command of Lieut.-Colonel Collins, was responsible for the construction, repairs, and operations of railways; provision of landing and disembarking facilities at Walvis, Swakopmund, and Luderitz Bay; the removal of mines laid by the enemy on the line of advance; provision, conservation, and distribution of water; and the construction of blockhouses along the lines of communication.

Of these, the most important duty was the provision of drinking water. From Luderitz Bay to Garub every gallon of water had either to be carried from Capetown or condensed from sea-water, and for the Eastern Force every gallon had at certain stages of the march to be provided by motor-car from wells or bore-holes sunk by the Engineers in the desert. For the Northern Force wells had to be dug in the Swakop River bed, pumping machinery provided, and troughs erected to water the thousands of horses and transport animals.

In connection with the technical details of the engineering work a valuable paper has been prepared by Major Beaton on Railway Construction during the Campaign, 1914-15 (Transactions of the South African Society of Civil Engineers, July, 1916), which also records the other work besides railway construction.

IX. Communications.

Communications were established by line and wireless telegraph, telephone, visual signals, dispatch carrying by patrols, mounted orderlies, motor-car, and cycle, and message-dropping from aeroplane.

In spite of all efforts the nature of the country and the great distances to be traversed frequently caused a want of communication at critical times. The 1st Mounted Brigade, the 2nd and Right Wing 3rd Brigades (see Diagram No. 6) were out of communication for several days before reaching their objectives. In these cases dispatch carrying by motor-car proved to be the best means of restoring communication. The field wireless sets which were attached to the outflanking columns were of the pack pattern, and very liable to break down. Although the enemy wireless sets, both permanent and mobile, were of much greater power than the Union sets, defects or want of adjustment of their receiving apparatus gave them considerable trouble. It was no unusual occurrence for two enemy stations to be asking for repetition of the message long after the Union operator—twice as far away as the enemy stations were from each other—had taken down the message complete, in spite of its being in a language foreign to him.

X. Medical Service.

As the country was very healthy and the casualties small, no great demands were made on the medical service. The provision, however, to meet heavy casualties at any time was there, and the Mounted Brigade Field Ambulances kept up and sustained the same marching records as the Brigade to which they were attached.

Well-built hospitals were found in Swakop, Luderitz Bay, Karibib, and Windhoek, from which places casualties were evacuated to Capetown by train and hospital ship.

XI. Summary of Troops in the Field on 15*th March*, 1915.

Force.	Artillery.	Mounted.	Infantry.	Administrative.	Total.
Northern	741	12,773	5,864	1,491	20,869
Central	575	3,858	5,583	855	10,871
Southern	117	8,438	—	631	9,186
Eastern	40	2,016	—	420	2,476
TOTAL	1,473	27,085	11,447	3,397	43,402

The above figures represent about the largest number actually in the field at any time. Early in May the Central, Southern, and Eastern Forces were returned and demobilized, while the Northern Force was also slightly reduced.

Signing the Terms of Surrender, South-West Africa.

The German Governor bidding farewell to General Botha after the Surrender of South-West Africa.

PART III.

THE GERMAN EAST AFRICAN CAMPAIGN.

(SEE ALSO PART IV.)

PAGE.

I.—Introduction 63

II.—The Assumption by General Smuts of the Chief Command in East Africa and the Kilimanjaro Campaign 66

III.—Reorganization of Forces 70

IV.—Occupation of Kondoa Irangi 71

V.—Advance on the East to the Central Railway ... 74

VI.—Resumption of Advance from Kondoa Irangi to Central Railway 76

VII.—Resumption of Advance on the East from Msiha to Morogoro 77

VIII.—Advance of 2nd Division along Central Railway ... 78

IX.—Occupation of Morogoro 80

X.—The Pursuit to the Southern Extremity of the Uluguru Mountains 80

XI.—The Reorganization towards latter part of 1916 ... 82

XII.—Events in Other Portions of East Africa during August and September, 1916 82

XIII.—Operations Generally pending the Resumption of Advance of Main Force 83

XIV.—The General Advance Resumed—Movements of the Main Force at Mgeta and Kissaki 84

LIEUT.-GENERAL THE RT. HON. J. C. SMUTS, P.C., C.H., D.T.D.

I.

THE CAMPAIGN IN EAST AFRICA.

Introductory.

THE campaign in German West Africa, though its original main objectives were indicated by the Imperial Government to the Union Government, was as regards its plan, cost, and conduct the sole concern of the latter.

The responsibility for the cost and method of prosecution of the campaign in East Africa rested solely with the Imperial Government, though at different times two South African officers exercised the chief command, being answerable to the British War Office.

In the East African campaign therefore, just as overseas, the share of the Union was to assist the plans of the British military authorities but to assume no further responsibility.

The account which follows only deals with those periods of the campaign during which South African personnel was engaged.

A short summary of what occurred prior to the despatch of aid from the Union is however essential to a clear comprehension of the circumstances in which that aid was offered, accepted, and extended, and it is accordingly necessary first shortly to recapitulate the early events of the campaign.

Short Statement of the Military Position in German and British East Africa on the Outbreak of War.

On the declaration of war in August, 1914, the German authorities in East Africa were prepared, as far as their resources allowed, for the local contest which it was evident would occur in the event of Great Britain and Germany engaging in hostilities against each other.

German East Africa had been the scene of comparatively recent activity in slave-dealing, of which one result—which had an important military bearing—was a clear division of the natives into warlike and non-warlike categories.

The non-warlike—and far more numerous—portion of the aboriginal population furnished the source of the slave supply, whereas the warlike tribe was employed by the Arab slave-dealers to coerce and generally to maltreat their fellow natives with the object of their enslavement.

One consequence of this state of affairs was that, when in 1886, by the terms of a convention between Great Britain and Germany, the possessions of the Sultan of Zanzibar were defined and the British and German spheres of influence in the hinterland were determined, the German Government gained in a portion of its native population magnificent material for the formation of a native army.

The potential military value of this material had been brought home very plainly to the local military authorities as a consequence of their experiences in the native wars which had engaged attention from time to time since the establishment of the colony.

The fact that the tribes from which military recruits were drawn consisted of natives who were arrogant and overbearing and had for long been accustomed to bully the bulk of their fellow countrymen, in no way detracted from their value in the eyes of their new employers, who took all care to inculcate in their Askari the Prussian view of the military caste as altogether superior to, and apart from, the inferior civilian population.

The native army of German East Africa had by 1914 reached a high pitch of military efficiency and boasted of a degree of discipline which might well be envied by some military organizations with European personnel.

Though at the first successful, the long series of defeats and retirements under the pressure of superior numbers which the German forces were compelled to undergo never really shook the *moral* of their native soldiers, who to the last responded unfailingly to the call of their commander, and made any opponent who was the least incautious or inefficient, pay dearly for any shortcoming.

Add to these valuable advantages the fact that the endemic diseases of the country, to which Europeans and Indians fell ready victims by the thousand, had practically no effect on the Askari; that the British forces advanced with a steadily and daily diminishing force which was often hardly superior in numbers to the enemy when, after heavy marching, contact had been established; that the German forces practically lost only such men as became casualties in action; that the British forces invariably moved hundreds of miles away from their bases of supply, whereas the enemy always fell back on his own supplies, and the fact that the country had always been previously reconnoitred before action by the retreating enemy, whose country it was, whereas the advantage of anything like reliable tactical reconnaissance was consistently denied to his opponent, and it will be realized that the Germans possessed incalculable advantages which went far to counterbalance the superiority in numbers and convenience of supply of material and other necessaries enjoyed by their antagonists. Climatic conditions also aided the defence enormously.

These facts must never be ignored by the fair critic when the length and cost of the campaign in East Africa are the objects of scrutiny and comment.

The forces at the disposal of the enemy were approximately as follows (the figures given are those recorded by General Von Lettow Vorbeck, the German commander, in his account of the campaign*): —

Protective Force, 216 Europeans; and 2,540 Askari.

Police Force, 45 Europeans and 2,154 Askari.

Crew of "Konigsberg," 322 Europeans.

Crew of "Moewe," 102 Europeans.

The total number enrolled during the war were approximately 3,000 Europeans and 11,000 Askari.

In August, 1914, two light British cruisers, "Astraea" and "Pegasus," and some guardships were on the station of East Africa. These cruisers bombarded Dar-es-Salaam on the 8th August and sank the floating dock and a survey ship, the "Möwe."

On the departure of "Astraea" for Capetown, the enemy cruiser "Konigsberg" appeared on the scene and sank "Pegasus" and two guardships at Zanzibar.

The military forces in British East Africa at the outbreak of war consisted only of the normal peace establishment of the King's African Rifles, which was barely enough to maintain order in the territory without any complications introduced by war conditions.

The enemy at the outset was thus infinitely better prepared in every respect for the struggle.

The Course of the Campaign prior to the Despatch of Assistance from the Union.

The very slender force in British East Africa at the outbreak of war precluded all idea of an immediate offensive. The number of troops available was insufficient even for an effective defence.

---

* See "My Reminiscences of East Africa,' by General Von Lettow Vorbeck, p. 19.

The superiority of the German commander induced him at once to assume the offensive, and within the first fourteen days a German force occupied Taveta, on British soil, thus threatening alike the Uganda railway, between Nairobi and the sea, and the port of Mombasa.

Taveta was held by the enemy for almost two years.

The position at Longido, to the west, was also held by an enemy force for the protection of the communications and line of retirement of the force at Taveta.

A movement on Mombasa from Tanga, along the coast, was frustrated by the timely arrival at the former place of a Brigade of Infantry from India.

Constant raids on the railway and water supplies were carried out by the enemy, until, on the 2nd November, 1914, 6,000 troops in transports arrived off Tanga, from India, under the command of Major-General Aitken.

This force disembarked and attacked the town of Tanga, but the attack was heavily repulsed with a loss of 800 all ranks. The force was then withdrawn to its transports and sailed to Mombasa.

A simultaneous offensive against the enemy position at Longido likewise failed.

When in April, 1915, the command in East Africa was transferred to Brig.-General Tighe, all enemy offensive action on a large scale had ceased, though his position at Taveta remained intact and constituted a severe menace to the British East Africa Protectorate.

An enemy invasion of Uganda attempted in September, 1914, had failed, and the British position in that region had been secured by the destruction of the German base at Bukoba, on Lake Victoria Nyanza.

On the outbreak of hostilities all forces available in Nyasaland had been mobilized and concentrated at Koranga, south of the south-western boundary of enemy territory.

The enemy attempted an invasion of Nyasaland by a force concentrated at Neu Langenburg; this however was severely defeated and forced to retire.

By a series of brilliantly conceived plans executed in wonderful fashion—which included the transport overland and by water of two motor-launches through the Belgian Congo—the enemy's shipping on the inland lakes was soon totally destroyed.

In Northern Rhodesia an enemy force, having crossed the border in July, 1915, attacked the garrison (470 Rhodesian native police), but after investing and attacking the place for six days and nights withdrew, leaving the post intact.

Early in 1916 the only real danger from the enemy was that caused by the continued presence of his main force at Longido and Taveta, threatening the railway communication between Mombasa and the interior.

At this juncture the command in East Africa had been accepted by General Sir Horace Smith-Dorrien, who, however, became seriously ill on the voyage from England and after a short stay at Capetown returned to England without taking up the command.

The Initiation of Measures of Assistance from the Union.

In consequence of the satisfactory progress of the campaign in German South-West Africa, Lord Buxton, the Governor-General of the Union, had in April, 1915, mooted the subject of further aid from the Union to other theatres.

The Secretary for State for the Colonies cabled on the 11th May, 1915, that the British Government would gladly take any troops South Africa could send, and accordingly the 1st Infantry Brigade was formed and sent to Europe.

The East African Command, which was within easy reach of South Africa through the Union port of Durban, had made occasional inquiries as to the supply of material of various kinds for the prosecution of the campaign, and it soon became apparent that the Union could give practical and substantial assistance to the East African military authorities. The probable scope of this assistance seemed to be large and, accordingly, on the 9th September, 1915, Ministers addressed a minute to the Governor-General of the Union asking whether, "in view of the constant requests that have been received and may be anticipated for assistance in personnel and material from the Union for the operations in East Africa," the Union Government might send two or three military officers of its own service in East Africa "for the purpose of making themselves familiar with and reporting upon the circumstances and requirements of the military operations in those parts."

Experienced officers who had been through the campaign in German South-West Africa were to be sent.

To this request the British Government cordially acceded and two officers left Durban for East Africa on the 14th October, 1915.

They returned and submitted a full report of their experiences and views on the 26th November, 1915.

At this time the following troops had been promised by the Union Government—

- 5 (4-gun 13-pounder Q.F.) Batteries Field Artillery;
- 1 Mounted Brigade;
- 1 Infantry Brigade;
- 1 Battalion Cape Corps (coloured);

and a variety of smaller departmental units.

An additional unbrigaded mounted regiment was added shortly afterwards and was raised in the urban area of Johannesburg. The other mounted units, including those of the 2nd Mounted Brigade, furnished later, were recruited from country areas.

By December, 1915, it had been decided to add another Infantry Brigade for East Africa and accordingly the 3rd Infantry Brigade was formed. The 1st Infantry Brigade was sent to France, the 2nd and 3rd Infantry Brigades served in East Africa. Brig.-Generals Beves and Berrange were posted to the command of the 2nd and 3rd Brigades respectively.

The main units went forward from Durban as follows:—

- The 1st Mounted Brigade, less one regiment, 24th December, 1915.
- Remaining regiment of the 1st Mounted Brigade, 31st December, 1915.
- The unbrigaded mounted regiment (4th S.A. Horse), 28th January, 1916.
- 5th and 6th S.A. Infantry (of the 2nd S.A. Infantry Brigade), 9th January, 1916.
- 7th and 8th S.A. Infantry (completing 2nd S.A. Infantry Brigade), 15th and 16th January, 1916.
- 3rd S.A. Infantry Brigade (comprising 9th, 10th, 11th, and 12th S.A. Infantry), 7th, 12th, 15th, and 28th February, 1916.
- The S.A. Field Artillery, 15th January, 1916.
- The 2nd S.A. General Hospital, 20th January, 1916.
- Cape Corps Battalion, 9th February, 1916.

In addition, a constant stream of smaller units, supplies, animals, and material was being maintained.

II. The Assumption by General Smuts of the Chief Command in East Africa and the Kilimanjaro Campaign.

The illness of General Sir Horace Smith-Dorrien, as has already been stated, necessitated that officer's abandonment of the Chief Command in East Africa and return to England early in 1916, when the vacant command was offered to and accepted by General Smuts.

General Smuts left Durban on the evening of the 12th February and reached Mombasa on the morning of the 19th February, 1916.

He was met on his arrival by General Tighe, from whom he took over the command, and at once went to the Taveta front whence, after an inspection and reconnaissance, he proceeded to the Longido front, and, after similar investigations there, went to General Headquarters, at Nairobi, where he arrived on the morning of 23rd February.

On the 12th February, prior to the arrival of General Smuts, the action of Ol Dorobo or Salaita Hill took place (the former is the word used in German and the latter in British accounts) and this was the first engagement of any magnitude in East Africa in which a South African formation participated.

The 2nd S.A. Infantry Brigade formed a portion of the troops that attacked Salaita Hill. The scheme of attack, involving as it did a flank movement by the South Africans in view of and within the fire zone of the enemy front, cannot be considered tactically sound. The attack was repulsed with severe casualties.

The urgent necessity of re-establishing the general moral of the troops and achieving some strategical advantage before the wet season set in, decided General Smuts on a general offensive, with the terminus of the Tanga railway at Moshi—and as far down as Kahe—as the strategic objective. The general situation was as follows:—South-east of the formidable Kilimanjaro, the highest mountain in Africa, which, being nearly 80 miles in diameter, forms as complete a strategical barrier as can be imagined, lay the Pare Mountains, forming, with the Usambara Mountains, nearly a continuous barrier to the coast. Behind these insurmountable natural fortifications was the railway from Tanga, on the coast, to Moshi, at the base of the Kilimanjaro, which was of considerable importance to the enemy. To get at this railway there were three gaps in the barrier; the first was between the Kilimanjaro and the North Pare, and this was well covered by Salaita Hill in front and Lake Jipe on the south-east flank, and in addition (as General Von Lettow says on page 104 in his book) any advance by this gap would be cramped by the Kilimanjaro, on which the enemy had troops; the other two gaps south-east were less suitable.

The main enemy force lay at Taveta, with a force at some distance up the Kilimanjaro slope at Rhombo, while the other two gaps were also held and the rear protected by a force at Longido. The troops for the offensive were concentrated at Mbuyuni, which was General Smuts' headquarters. This concentration included the transfer of Brig.-General Van Deventer's Mounted Brigade from the 1st Division under Major-General Stewart near Longido to this front, where it came under the direct command of the Commander-in-Chief.

General Smuts' general offensive began to materialize on the evening of the 7th March, 1916, when his troops marched off from the Mbuyuni camp. By daylight the next morning Van Deventer's Mounted Brigade was miles to the rear of Salaita Hill, surprising and sweeping the enemy off Chala Hill through Taveta on to the Latema and Reata Hills. Early the same morning the Commander-in-Chief, with the Force Reserve, had reached the Lumi River, near to Chala Hill, and had an engagement with a body of the enemy posted higher up the Lumi. These troops, being now cut off, were endeavouring to rejoin their main body. Owing to the dense bush they were enabled to escape through the gap between Van Deventer's troops and the Force Reserve.

The following day, the 9th of March, and also on the 10th, fighting continued on the slopes of the Latema-Reata position. Van Deventer's mounted troops were here at a disadvantage on the steep, sloping, dense bush-covered ground.

During the 10th the Force Reserve and the 2nd Division had arrived at Taveta and relieved the Mounted Brigade, which could now be employed to make a wide flanking movement and threaten the rear of the Latema-Reata position. The frontal attack on the position was commenced on the 11th, and in the evening two frontal assaults were delivered—one at 5.30 p.m. and the last at 9 p.m. These attacks were defeated by the enemy, and in the last assault, which was a bayonet affair by the 5th and 7th Infantry of the 2nd S.A. Infantry Brigade, the two regiments sustained severe casualties.

About 170 rifles of the 7th, under Lieut.-Colonel Freeth and Major Thompson, had, however, during the last bayonet charge, penetrated clean through the enemy position and consolidated thenselves in the rear of the enemy. This, coupled with Van Deventer's flank movement, the development of which was apparent at sundown, compelled the enemy to retire from the well-chosen positions he had defended so energetically. Lieut.-Colonel Freeth and Major Thompson were decorated on the spot for their share in the operations.

The result of General Smuts' five days offensive was that the enemy was driven out of the positions covering the gaps in the line of mountain barrier—the strategic objective was gained, the railway terminus and the road into the interior secured, and the enemy driven out of a most fertile region which had furnished him with plentiful supplies. Henceforth the operations could not be confined to a few cramped valleys, where defensive measures could be prepared long in advance.

To get a little more elbow room by pushing the enemy further south-west, operations were resumed on the 18th of March. General Headquarters had been established on the Himo River, near the Taveta-New Moshi road, while the 2nd and 3rd South African Infantry Brigades and the 4th South African Horse were camped on either bank of the river, Van Deventer's Mounted Brigade being at Moshi and New Moshi.

The line the enemy now held extended from the swamps near the northern base of the Nord Pare Mountain, where his right flank was very strong and unturnable, to Kahe Station, and thence 4 miles southwards to Kahe Hill. The enemy line of position was across the Himo, the Defu, and the Rau Rivers, while he had the Ruwu River behind his line, and his left at Kahe Station in the corner between the Ruwu and Pangani Rivers. His front was thus intersected by these rivers and his left was isolated, weakly held, and cut off from Kahe Station by the Pangani River.

These particulars deserve special mention and consideration from the fact that General Von Lettow in his book states that he retired from this position on receiving a false report that the enemy was already at Kissangire. There was not the least necessity, however, to occupy Kissangire to make Von Lettow's position untenable once Kahe Hill slipped out of his hands.

To Von Lettow the loss of Kahe Hill was of far greater consequence than the occupation of Kissangire, as once his enemy was established at Kahe Hill he could not remain in the cramped and river-intersected positions a day longer without avoiding serious disaster.

General Von Lettow's statement that he evacuated the Latema-Reata position on erroneous reports that the enemy was far in his rear will be allowed to pass, although, even there, the full development of the Mounted Brigade flank movement would twelve hours later have placed him in an intensely uncomfortable position.

To the military reader the probability of a commander continuing to take the most momentous decisions on information which had previously proved unreliable, and which, being considered with relation to the distances involved, must have appeared improbable, seems so unlikely that further comment is unnecessary. But for the benefit of the lay reader it may be of interest to somewhat labour the point. The East African campaign is by superficial critics classed as an unrelieved series of blunders. The operations on either side will be freely criticized in this history and the reader left to judge for himself. The operations at Tanga and Jasin were regrettable incidents with which the Union of South Africa had nothing whatever to do. The attack on Salaita was by a force partly South

African, but was directed and disposed of by the East African Command of that time.

From the day that General Smuts took over command and commenced his offensive the operations are not easy to criticize. The key was inserted into the lock of the barrier door the moment Chala Hill was captured by surprise, and with little casualty, on the morning of the 8th of March. The key was turned and the door opened by the Reata-Latema actions. Here all that the most exacting critic may advance is that the frontal attack on the position should have been delayed a little longer, until the out-flanking move by the Mounted Brigade had fully developed. But in a dense forested, unknown, and mountainous country the timing of operations to occur simultaneously is no easy matter, and if Van Deventer's horses were still glissading on the mud slopes below the perpetual glaciers of Kilimanjaro when they should have been 10 miles further, their record will not suffer by admitting the fact. The door was now open and the window had to be opened to let in fresh air; that is, the enemy had to be pushed further south-west from the position he had taken up after retiring (as the result of information which, although it proved false, must always be recollected with gratitude by General Von Lettow).

Strong reconnaissance infantry operations thus began against the enemy front on the 18th of March. By the 20th these had developed into a holding action on the enemy front, while the time had now come to attack his left and threaten his rear. While the infantry were engaged in this holding action the enemy severely counter-attacked in several places along his front, inflicting heavy casualty on the 3rd S.A. Infantry and 1st East African Brigades.

On the evening of the 20th of March General Van Deventer's Mounted Brigade, with two S.A. Field Artillery Batteries, began its 25 miles' night march from Moshi, through the bush, for the enemy's left and rear at Kahe Station and Kahe Hill.

Early the next morning the Mounted Brigade deployed against Kahe Hill under the fire of the German 4-inch naval gun, the indirect fire of which was directed from the hill. At about 8 a.m. the hill was taken and the attack directed towards the strong body of hostile troops at Kahe Station. By 11 a.m. these troops were driven across the Pangani River, blowing up the Kahe railway bridge and also the road bridge behind them. The hill had been taken by a small number with the best horses, getting across the swamp-bordered, crocodile-infested Pangani under the heavy rifle and artillery fire of the enemy. To, however, act effectively in cutting off the enemy's retirement, the entire Brigade with its artillery would have to cross this river. The troops had marched all night and fought till nearly noon. That they were not all across the river and actively attacking Von Lettow in the rear that afternoon, and cutting off his only line of retreat through the narrow plain between the Pangani River and the Pare Mountains, was no guarantee that they would not be about this business the first thing next morning. If General Von Lettow had not realized this at the time, and had only acted on the incorrect information that the enemy were 17 miles in his rear at Kissangire, as he states on page 123 of his book, then we can only hope that the source of this incorrect information was, with feelings of the kindliest gratitude, suitably rewarded as having been the means of preventing a general disaster.

General Von Lettow states on the previous page that he had expected this move to work round his left and to be cut off from his communications. "I had therefore posted a strong reserve of eight companies in readiness at Kahe Station, but as I thought it necessary during the action to remain at Kahe Village, I was unable to exercise rapid and direct control over the reserves at Kahe Railway Station. The dense vegetation prevented any distant observation. The control of the reserve at Kahe had to be left to the initiative of the commander on the spot and his subordinates. The latter had observed that hostile troops had advanced through the bush and occupied a hill (Kahe Hill) south-west of Kahe Railway Station. One company had, on its own initiative, attacked this force, but the advance had broken down under shrapnel fire. Thereupon our 4-inch gun opened fire on these light guns and drove them off."

General Von Lettow's own words (see page 122 of his book) are quoted here, because it is intended to prove that he was completely defeated at this place, and could not have retired for any other reason, as he endeavours to make out.

Let us analyse his statements:—He was not, as is usual, with the reserve at Kahe Station, and was unable to exercise rapid and direct control over them. He was at Kahe Village, a short 3 miles away from them, presumably in telephonic communication, as this reserve was certainly on the railway telephone, and it would have been a matter of no great difficulty to have arranged communication by native runner from the nearest point on the line. Failing this, direct runner communication between the village and the station 3 miles away would be only a matter of 30 minutes. It is apparent therefore that they were by no means so "out of touch" as his statement leads one to infer. But we will imagine that his reserve of eight companies are acting entirely on their own at Kahe Station. They see the enemy occupy the hill, which is of vital importance to them, three miles in their rear. One of the eight companies "on its own initiative" attacks. The remaining seven companies, we are asked to believe, remained at the station twiddling their thumbs. This is somewhat difficult to believe of troops trained under the patronage of the Prussian Army, and only the fact that the seven companies were very profoundly busy with something else at Kahe Station can account for what otherwise would have been a very serious situation.

In the meantime, "thereupon our 4-inch gun opened fire on these light guns and drove them off." Now, this gun is at Kahe Village (see page 116), where General Von Lettow is, and (see page 121) there are "elevated sites affording a good view."

This shows that the German Headquarters must have known very well what was happening at Kahe Station, and that the reserve there was not thrown on its own initiative as we are asked to believe.

After we are told that the fire of the 4-inch gun had succeeded in "driving off" the two batteries of the Mounted Brigade a discreet silence is maintained as to what further happened on that day. With a long jump we are taken, late that night, to Kissangire, to which place General Von Lettow had proceeded "as the result of erroneous reports."

III. Reorganization of Forces.

The capture of the Kahe-Ruwu position successfully terminated the first offensive. The rains were now on hand and there would not be time for another general forward move before these set in, a reorganization on the following lines was then effected:—

General Headquarters at Old Moshi.

The 1st East African Division, Major-General Hoskins, had its East African Mounted Brigade, its 1st East African Infantry Brigade, and Divisional troops at Mbuyuni, while part of the 2nd East African Brigade was at New Moshi and the remainder at Kahe.

The Army troops, consisting of Artillery, Royal Engineers, Air Service, Belfield's Scouts were at Moshi and Himo. The South African Mounted Brigade and the South African Infantry Brigade, Brig.-General Berrange, were organized as the 2nd Division. As it would be some considerable time before Brig.-General M. Botha, who had been appointed to command the Mounted Brigade, could arrive from South Africa, Major-General J. van Deventer continued to command the Mounted Brigade while at the same time commanding the Division.

IV. The Southward Movement of the 2nd Division and the Occupation of Kondoa Irangi.

By the success of the offensive the enemy had been pushed to one side, being at Kissangire. The road into the heart of the country lay open and the enemy could not prevent, or interfere, with penetration in this direction without going a very roundabout way.

A forward move in this direction commenced on the night of the 3rd of April when the Mounted Brigade moved off from Arusha to Lol-Kisale, an isolated granite hill in the Massai Plain, where a body of the enemy had been located.

At daylight the next morning after a 35-mile night march—in, however, fairly open country—the enemy was attacked and soon afterwards the crest of the mountain was taken, and the enemy surrounded near the only water, at the foot of the hill. The next day the South African Rifles worked closer so that by nightfall they were in places as near as thirty yards to the enemy.

On the morning after, that is on the 6th, the German force of about 500 surrendered. There was no place in the rear from which erroneous reports could come this time, and General Von Lettow certainly does his commander an injustice by stating that the situation was not properly appreciated. The second in command had fought gallantly for two days after Captain Rothert (who was not so severely wounded as to be incapacitated from travelling soon after the first shots were fired) had undertaken the long journey to Kondoa, together with those Askari who are cited, on page 126 of General Von Lettow's book, as samples of sound military education because they refused to surrender. It is quite true that they refused to surrender, but they had arrived at this decision very soon after the two days' action started, and while there was still time to realize the prudent resolution. Moving on, the Mounted Brigade had a two days' action at Ufiome and then continued to Kondoa Irangi. On the 16th of April the enemy was attacked before Kondoa Irangi. The Mounted Brigade which, at Lolkisale had a paper strength of seven hundred rifles, could now hardly bring three hundred rifles into the firing line. Operations in continuous rain, with practically nothing to eat, had sadly thinned the ranks in this malaria-infested area.

Fighting continued on the next day, the 17th. Towards nightfall, General Van Deventer, who with his staff and an escort of twelve men, was making a personal reconnaissance forward on his left flank, came accidentally on several enemy companies with their carriers marching round to his rear, probably for a combined attack the next day.

Allowing these, in close marching order, to come quite near, he opened rapid fire from the twelve rifles of his escort. This completely surprised and disorganized these companies, which broke in wild disorder, so that General Van Deventer retained the initiative for the next day. Fighting recommenced early the next morning, and by 2 p.m. a hill commanding the German positions from the left flank was occupied. One of the two batteries was now brought up to this hill with the result that the enemy position below was under the cross-fire of the two batteries firing at right angles to one another and at about 3,000 yards range. The enemy was soon in full retreat on Kondoa Irangi, three miles away, suffering considerable casualty in the retirement over the open cultivated ground.

The following day, the 19th, the enemy could be seen evacuating Kondoa Irangi; dense columns of Askari and porters passing over the open, just out of artillery range, beyond the town, where the bigger buildings were in flames. Struggling forward, with the gun-teams in places chest-deep in the mud, every endeavour was made to get within range. The incessant rains had transformed the whole country-side into a bog, and progress was so slow that it was only until about 10 a.m. that gun-fire could be brought to bear on the town, where the rearguard had taken position. By 5 p.m. this had been driven out and away from the hills beyond the town and Kondoa was in Van Deventer's hands. All the supply and store buildings had, however, been burnt, and the food, which was so urgently required, had vanished in smoke. The whole district was cleaned up by the enemy after the last harvest, and the produce had been concentrated in the town, so there were no supplies obtainable until a porter transport had been arranged to forage far afield. In the meantime the troops had to live on green guavas, paw-paws, or ground-nuts, when they could get them.

Some days later, Berrange's Infantry Brigade, which had been steadily pushing through the mud in the wake of the Mounted Brigade, began to arrive at Kondoa Irangi. The last of this Brigade did not, however, arrive until the 9th May, the day on which General Von Lettow attacked Kondoa Irangi with the strong forces he had brought up. In connection with this action, we again take General Von Lettow's book and analyse some of the statements and also the general impression he conveys. He has been first in the field of publication, his work has been translated into English and widely read, and without an attempt to reflect a more correct light on some of the events of this period, this work cannot rank as a true historical record. The general impression formed by reading General Von Lettow's version, from page 126 to 142, is that he decided merely to occupy the station in the Kilimanjaro country, and to direct his main force against the hostile group which had meanwhile pushed forward to near Kondoa Irangi (page 127), and after practically his entire force had been switched round over the many hundred miles to this front, a small number of rifles of his force—about four hundred—accidentally got into touch with Van Deventer's troops on the night of the 9th of May, "contrary to all our expectations" (page 136) and that after this episode nothing of any importance was further undertaken by him. Page 137 states "On the whole, the enemy in Kondoa did not seem to be in great strength as yet."

General Von Lettow thus comes all the way, finds the enemy in no great strength, but refrains from a general attack and instead decides to while away the time by a series of "minor enterprises"; so much for the general impression. Let us now examine details to decide for ourselves whether there was a general and well-planned attack on the 9th of May or not. General Von Lettow states, on page 136 of his book, that the "stiff fight" which was noticed by him at 11 p.m. was caused by some of his companies running up against the entrenched position.

Now, if the time was 8 p.m., or even 9 p.m., we would perforce have had to give the benefit of the doubt to General Von Lettow. But 11 at night is too late for organized companies to be prowling about an enemy front for any other purpose than attack. Before dark they are stated to have been near their destination and preparing "to settle down for the night," while a little further on the same page, 136, we are told "Our companies had indeed found the high ground, which had been examined by the patrols, to be clear of the enemy; but immediately in rear of it was another rise, and on this was the enemy which our companies ran up against." His companies were thus at 11 p.m. beyond the ground examined by the patrols, presumably merely enjoying a moonlight stroll.

We may now leave General Von Lettow's version for what it is worth and return to the events that actually happened.

The distant patrols had as early as the 2nd of May located hostile bodies advancing along the Dodoma road. Owing to the dense bush no correct idea as to their strength could be obtained either by patrols or air reconnaissance. On the 8th of May there was, however, no doubt that a strong hostile force was advancing. At about noon on the 9th of May, General Van Deventer's outposts were all driven in and the enemy occupied the high hills about 14,000 yards south-east of Kondoa. At 4 p.m. the enemy commenced to shell the town and camps with 4-inch howitzers and naval guns. This strong artillery was the only element of surprise in the operations. The bombardment continued till sundown when there also came a cessation of the skirmishing on Van Deventer's left flank, between squadrons of the Mounted Brigade and enemy bodies attempting to work round the flank: on the front they were allowed to come in. When it was quite dark the action commenced along the middle of the front where General Berrange's Infantry Brigade, the last of which had only arrived that morning, hurriedly entrenched as soon as the shelling commenced. Towards sundown there had been a general cessation; the enemy, which had advanced on the front, appeared to turn back. Shortly afterwards a very large number of camp fires, rather conspicuously sited, lit up the enemy position on the nearer slopes of the hills. These raised suspicions which were very soon fully justified; the enemy, who had pretended to go back at sundown, had again advanced when it was sufficiently dark, and had, under cover of the standing maize crops, crept quite close to the lines before assaulting. The infantry, however, was not caught napping; from then on, fighting was continuous until 3 a.m. the next morning. Very determined and heavy assaults were delivered at 9 p.m., 10 p.m., and 11 p.m., and again about 12.30 a.m.

These were all driven off with heavy losses to the enemy, including some of his best officers.

The enemy had, however, not yet lost the initiative and the next day commenced to test Van Deventer's left flank while threatening a hill on the right which commanded the infantry positions. The left flank operations continued to extend from day to day until there was a front of nearly ten miles. Weakened by fever as General Van Deventer's two Brigades were, he could never aspire to more than limited local counter-strokes against the greatly superior numerical force of the enemy main body. Early in June the heavy artillery arrived, and he could now minimize the enemy daily bombardment. This hostile bombardment was chiefly directed at the transport lines, supply depots, and hospitals. General Van Deventer's Headquarters were in a prominent house about a hundred yards from which was a church used as a hospital. As a large Union Jack was always flying over the Headquarters it was generally the first object on which the enemy artillery directed attention; for some unaccountable reason they never hit the building, although closely bracketed, nor the hospital-church. The patients had, however, to be carried out into the dug-outs every morning before daylight; this was rather trying to the severely wounded—some of whom were Von Lettow's Europeans who made unkind remarks about their countrymen with the guns. The hospital was eventually shifted one mile to the rear into a large mission school-room. The next morning, the German gunners seeing the Red Cross flag transferred, had a shot at the new premises and put a four-inch shell into the main ward. This curiously did no damage in the closely packed ward beyond overturning some beds and causing some corrosive comments, especially from the German patients; but a splinter which penetrated the wall killed the cook who was outside. The hospital was then shifted into the open under shelter of a river bank. Von Lettow's forces remained before Kondoa from the 9th of May to the end of June.

The rains were now over and the advance was resumed down the Tanga line. The German force thereupon left Kondoa to resist this advance.

V. *The Advance on the East to the Central Railway, as far as Msiha River.*

It is not proposed in this record to deal in any detail with operations other than those in which the South African units took an important part, and consequently a short statement of the share of South African units in General Northey's operations in the south-west will be for the present deferred, while the general advance along the Pangani River and from Handeni to Morogoro is described.

The forces under the immediate command of the Commander-in-Chief had reached quarters for the rainy season, as indicated earlier, and from the beginning of April until towards the end of May, 1916, action on the Kahe front had been limited to reconnaissance, mainly by air, and watching the enemy in front.

Preparations for the coming movement southwards were pushed on to the limit allowed by the torrential rains.

The rains came to an end during the first half of May, and the advance began on the 18th May, 1916, when troops of the 1st Division (the 3rd K.A.R.) were moved from Mbuyuni to Ngulu Gap in the north Pare Mountains.

Four days later, on the 22nd May, the general advance began. Hannyngton's Brigade of the 1st Division moved from Ruwu along the railway line, while Sheppard's Brigade, of the same Division, together with the 2nd S.A. Infantry Brigade, marched southwards along the Pangani River.

The 2nd Mounted Brigade had not yet reached the country, and the 2nd S.A. Infantry Brigade was accordingly at this time the only combatant South African formation among the forces which accompanied the Commander-in-Chief.

As stated in the dispatch from the Commander-in-Chief, published in the *London Gazette* of the 17th January (from which a full idea of the Commander's views and intentions may be gathered), "the general conception was to move eastward along these mountains (i.e. Pare and Usumbara), and at a point opposite Handeni to swing south and march towards the central railway in a movement parallel to that of Van Deventer."

The main column, with which was Beves' 2nd S.A. Infantry Brigade, was to proceed as the right of the advance down the left bank of the Pangani River (i.e. that nearer to the mountain ranges mentioned), while a smaller column in the centre followed the railway line, and a third small column (the 3rd K.A.R., which has been mentioned as having left Mbuyuni on the 18th May) on the left moved through the Ngulu Gap from the east of the Pare Mountains, and eventually rejoined its own Brigade (the 2nd E.A.) at Same Pass, between the Middle and South Pares. The 2nd E.A. Brigade (less the 3rd K.A.R.) formed the centre force moving along the railway.

The enemy's first position was reported at Lembeni, but, in consequence of the movement by the Ngulu Gap, it was evacuated, and the enemy fell back gradually in front of the advance, until the 29th May, when the advance troops of the main force came in contact with the enemy troops at Mikotscheni, where the Pangani River rejoins the Usambara railway close to the mountains. Mikotscheni is a little more than 100 miles from the original starting point at Moschi.

An engagement ensued, but, as a consequence of a wide turning movement by way of the mountains against the enemy's right, he evacuated the position during the night of the 30th-31st May, and Buiko Station was occupied by the main force on the following day, 31st May.

The Rhodesian Regiment was the unit which delivered the frontal attack at Mikotscheni while the turning movement described above was in progress.

A short halt was called at Buiko, as the troops needed rest and the bridging of the Pangani was essential. The main force was now to advance on the right bank of the Pangani, and shortly to leave the river with its magnificent water supply altogether.

The 2nd Mounted Brigade had by this time arrived in the country, and General Brits came to Buiko on the 31st May, and, after receiving instructions as to the movements of the Brigade, returned on the 2nd June to Mbuyuni, where his headquarters were for the time located.

The Commander-in-Chief now took advantage of the pause to visit General Van Deventer at Kondoa Irangi, and leaving Buiko on the 2nd June reached Kondoa Irangi on the 5th.

On the Commander-in-Chief's return on the 10th June to the main force at Mkalamo, on the Pangani, the following was the disposition of the different units:—

At Mkalamo (which had been occupied that morning after an engagement with the enemy on the previous afternoon), the 1st E.A. and 2nd S.A. Infantry Brigades. (A detachment of the 1st E.A. Brigade was some miles in advance of the main force.)

2nd E.A. Brigade at Mombo on the railway.

From Mombo the occupation of Wilhelmstal was effected, only women and children having been left there by the enemy.

On the 11th the advance was continued; the main body and 2nd E.A. Brigade meeting with opposition.

The 2nd S.A. Infantry Brigade continued to move behind and in support of the 1st E.A. Brigade.

On the morning of the 15th June Korogwe, an important station on the Usambara railway, was occupied by the 2nd E.A. Brigade.

On this date the main force had reached Mbagui, where the 1st E.A. Brigade was thrown out in front towards Handeni, before which place the enemy held a strongly entrenched position.

It was accordingly decided to send the S.A. Infantry Brigade by a wide movement to the west to Ssangeni, where good water was procurable and whence the interception of the southward retreat of the enemy before the 1st E.A. Brigade seemed to be a feasible project.

Ssangeni was reached by the S.A. Infantry on the 17th June, and the next day the enemy's retreat along the Handeni-Morogoro road to the south was considerably interfered with, and substantial losses were inflicted.

Some retaliation was, however, dealt to the 5th S.A. Infantry by the retreating enemy on the evening of the 20th, when he ambushed the unit at Kangata, to the south on the Morogoro road, and inflicted numerous casualties.

The natural eagerness inspired by the success of the last few days had resulted in too impetuous an attack by the South Africans, who came unawares against a strongly prepared rear-guard position.

The S.A. Infantry held their own, however, though they had 96 casualties, and the following morning the enemy had continued his retirement.

The 2nd E.A. Brigade had been instructed, after leaving a garrison at Korogwe, to rejoin its Division (the 1st), and reached Handeni on the 20th June.

Just south of Kangata, the scene of the 5th S.A. Infantry's fight, the force came into the first made-road encountered since leaving Kahe, i.e. the main south road from Handeni to Morogoro; this was excellently suited for motor transport until badly cut up by continuous traffic.

The advance was pressed until the 24th June, when contact was again established with the enemy at the Lukigura River.

Intelligence of the enemy's intention to stand at this place had been received, and while the main force advanced along the motor road, General Hoskins, with a specially composed force (comprising two South African Infantry battalions and a battalion of Kashmir Imperial Service

Infantry, together with the 25th Royal Fusiliers) had moved on the evening of the 23rd towards the enemy's left to a point on the Lukigura River with the object of getting astride the main road south and in rear of the enemy's position.

The movements were entirely successful and resulted in the infliction of casualties on the enemy, who, however, effected his retirement in the dense bush.

This engagement saw the termination of the first advance in the direction of the Central Railway, and a halt for rest and reorganization of the lines of communication now became a matter of paramount necessity.

A large standing camp was accordingly formed on the Msiha River, 8 miles south of the Lukigura, and preparations for the next movements were commenced.

The troops at Msiha remained at that place and were subjected to heavy and effective shelling by the enemy, who held the mountains and thus had the only means there were available of observing artillery fire in the bush * until the beginning of August.

During this pause the coastal towns of Tanga, Pangani, Sadani Bay, and Bagamoyo were occupied, but no South African troops took part in these operations—the Navy combining for the purpose with a column of Indian Army troops.

Guerrilla ventures by the enemy against the lines of communication north of Msiha were brought to an end by the occupation of the coastal area.

Important operations were also undertaken in the Western Lake area, and resulted in the occupation of Kigali, Ukerewe Island with its large rice supplies, and the important port of Mwansa at the south of Lake Victoria.

Though no South African troops took part in these operations, the British forces engaged were commanded by a South African officer, Brig.-General the Honourable Sir Charles Crewe.

VI. The Resumption of the Advance by the 2nd Division from Kondoa Irangi to the Central Railway.

As explained by the Commander-in-Chief in his dispatch, it was necessary for the execution of his plans that the 2nd (Van Deventer's) Division should advance before he resumed his own movement.

Accordingly, on the day upon which the advance along the Handeni-Morogoro road came to an end in the east, the 2nd Division attacked all enemy positions outside Kondoa Irangi, and succeeded in occupying them with comparatively little loss.

Indications of enemy withdrawals from this front had been apparent for some time. This transfer of forces is described by General Von Lettow, who observes: "The English were informed of this movement down to the smallest details."

The Commander of the Division was directed "to clear its right flank towards Ssingida, to move a small column along the Saranda road towards Kilimatinde, and to move his main force towards Dodoma and further east on the road to Mpapua."

An infantry battalion, accompanied by a mounted squadron and a section of artillery, was therefore sent to Ssingida, which was occupied on the 2nd August, and leaving a detachment as garrison at Ssingida, the column moved south to Kilimatinde.

A similarly composed column was sent to Saranda, and on the way had a sharp engagement at Mpondi, which was taken. Saranda was occupied on the following day, 31st July.

The main advance of the Division to the railway was meanwhile proceeding.

After some sharp fighting Tissa-Kwa-Meda, Naju, and Membe were occupied by the 1st Mounted Brigade, which reached Kikombo Station on the 30th July, and troops from the 3rd S.A. Infantry Brigade occupied Dodoma on the Central Railway on the 31st July.

---

* See "My Reminiscences of East Africa," by General Von Lettow Vorbeck, p. 144.

The Division was now concentrated during the following week at Njangalo, on the main road to Mpangua.

VII. The Resumption of the Advance on the East from Msiha to Morogoro.

The following summary, given by the Commander-in-Chief in his dispatch, published in the *London Gazette* of the 17th January, 1917, shortly explains the general situation at this time:—

"Van Deventer had occupied the Central Railway from Kilimatinde to Dodoma. In the Lake area the British and Belgian forces were well south of Lake Victoria, and preparing for a combined move towards Tabora. Further west a Belgian force had crossed Lake Tanganyika and occupied Ujiji and Kigoma, the terminus of the Central Railway. In the south-west General Northey's force had occupied Malangali after a brilliant little action, and was prepared to move towards Iringa, 70 miles further north-east. All coast towns as far as Sadani had been occupied, and a small column was working its way southward to the Wami River and clearing the country between Nguru Mountains and the coast. The time had therefore come to resume the advance to the Central Railway. Hannyngton's (the 2nd E.A.) Brigade had rejoined the 1st and Enslin's (2nd S.A.) Mounted Brigade had joined the 3rd Division at Lukigura."

The enemy was occupying a very strong and carefully prepared position astride the main road some 8 to 10 miles south of Msiha camp, and accordingly a wide turning movement—to assist the advance along the main road—was to be undertaken by the 3rd (S.A.) Division through the mountains, while another movement by the 2nd E.A. Brigade was to be carried out between the mountains and the main road along the Mdsonga Valley.

The task of feinting against the strong enemy positions on the main road, while the two movements described above were executed, was assigned to the 1st E.A. Brigade.

In pursuance of this plan—for a proper appreciation of which the clear description of the terrain, which is given in the Commander-in-Chief's dispatch, should be read—on the 5th August the 2nd Mounted Brigade moved from Lukigura, via Kimbe, well to the west of the Mdjonga Valley and entered the Nguru Mountains.

On the following day the remainder of the 3rd Division, viz., the 2nd S.A. Infantry Brigade, followed the route taken by the Mounted Brigade, and the 2nd E.A. Brigade marched up the Mdjonga Valley on Mahassi.

The last to move, on the 7th August, was the 1st E.A. Brigade, to which the advance along the main road had been assigned.

General Enslin, with the Mounted Brigade, moved rapidly through the mountains, which were found to be quite impracticable for wheels of any description, and, after passing through Mhonda Gap, seized positions on the 8th barring the enemy's retreat. One of his regiments, having lost its way earlier in the movement, came out of the Nguru Mountains at Matomondo and attached itself to the force in the Mdjonga Valley.

The enemy, realizing the importance of this movement, concentrated on the 2nd Mounted Brigade and drove it back off the line of retreat to Mhonda Mission, where, though it remained, it ceased to be an immediate obstacle to an enemy retirement. However, the threat which the Brigade in its position constituted to the enemy's lines of communication compelled the German commander to effect an immediate withdrawal of his whole force to the south.

Strong opposition was being encountered during the advance of the 2nd E.A. Brigade down the Mdjonga Valley, and accordingly the 2nd S.A. Infantry Brigade was brought eastward from the mountains into the valley to reinforce the East African unit.

Heavy fighting ensued at Matamondo in the valley on the 10th and 11th August, and the enemy there were driven south with heavy loss. The stubborn resistance of the enemy was of course dictated to him by the circumstances in which he was compelled to extricate his forces for the general retirement which at once followed.

Resistance by the enemy for the same reason had been encountered by the 1st E.A. Brigade opposite the Ruhungu position on the main road, but on the 11th the enemy retired here also; and Turiani, the late General Headquarters of the enemy, was occupied on the 12th August.

The next point where the enemy were encountered in force was at Dakawa, on the Wami River.

A flanking movement was initiated against Dakawa from Kwedihumbo.

The 1st E.A. Brigade moved by the left, and, crossing the Wami at Kipera, proceeded along the south bank of the river westwards towards Dakawa.

In the meantime the remainder of the force, less the 2nd E.A. Brigade (which was detached to follow the Kilossa road) had been directed by the road to Dakawa, and on the 16th August the 2nd Mounted Brigade reached the Wami River at that place, and came immediately in contact with the enemy strongly posted in force on the opposite side of the river.

The 1st E.A. Brigade, working upstream towards Dakawa, had in the meantime been checked by the enemy, who also prevented the South African mounted troops opposite from crossing.

On the following day, however, the mounted troops negotiated a passage higher up the river, and the enemy immediately retired.

The engagement of the 16th had been severe, and the losses on the British side amounted to 120.

The Dakawa crossing was occupied on the 18th August, and bridging operations began without delay. The bridge had been as usual destroyed by the enemy.

The route from Lukigura is intersected frequently by deep rivers, and the consistent destruction of the bridges had given the enemy valuable breathing time the whole way.

General Von Lettow's account of the operations, which have just been described, is of much interest and will be found on pp. 145-147 of his reminiscences.

He allows that the conduct of the action at Matamondo was "very skilful," and gives credit for good work done by some of the Indian troops.

VIII. Advance of the 2nd Division along the Central Railway and its Establishment of Contact with the Main Force under the Commander-in-Chief.

Meanwhile substantial progress had been made by the 2nd Division to the west under Van Deventer, whose force, after reaching the Central Railway, had been concentrated at Njangalo, towards Mpapua.

On the 9th August the 2nd Division resumed its advance, and contact was effected with the enemy at Tschunjo late on the 11th.

The march to Tschunjo had been carried out over a waterless tract of country, and the action which ensued was entered upon without any rest.

After fighting all night and the following morning the enemy retired, and was pursued to Mpapua, where he was again defeated on the evening of the 12th August.

The advance had been maintained continuously for 42 miles.

The country along the railway, being mountainous and densely bushy, was dangerous for fast advance, but the pressure was kept up until the 22nd August, when Kilossa and Kimamba were occupied, the day before the main body resumed its advance from the Wami River on Morogoro.

Major Kraut, the enemy commander opposing the 2nd Division, now moved south from the railway line and took up a position on the road to Mahenge.

The description of the 2nd Divisional Commander, Major-General Van Deventer, perhaps gives the best picture of the task with which his command was faced on leaving Kondoa Irangi.

He reported as follows:—

"The railway from Kidete to Kilossa for a distance of 25 miles follows a narrow defile cut through the Usugara Mountains by the Mkondokwa River; every yard of advance was stubbornly resisted by the enemy. Of the more important engagements, those on the 19th at Msagara, on the 21st before Kilossa, should be mentioned. In all the actions on this advance the fighting consisted of the enemy receiving our advance guard with one or several ambushes, then falling back on a well-prepared position, and retiring from that on to further well-selected ambush places and positions. All the time our less-advanced troops were subjected to vigorous shelling by means of long-range naval guns.

"Since leaving Kondoa Irangi the troops who have reached Kilossa by the shortest route have done at least 220 miles. Those troops who have gone via Kilimatinde and other places have done many more miles. Owing to bad roads, shortage of transport, and the rapidity of advance, the adequate rationing of the troops was not possible. The under-feeding and overworking are sadly reflected in their state of health. Regarding the animals of my Division, the advance from Mpapua to Kilossa was through one continual fly-belt, where practically all the animals were infected.

"After the occupation of Kilossa it was ascertained that the enemy held Uleia, 20 miles south, in force, and was being reinforced by troops from the Southern Command, who had opposed General Northey's advance. As my Division was now weakened by the absence of the 1st Mounted Brigade (less one regiment), which had gone to Mlali on 25th August to co-operate with the 2nd Mounted Brigade, and as my infantry was in an exhausted condition, the Commander-in-Chief's wire of 26th August, asking for an advance on Kidodi and Kidatu, imposed a task which I had not intended to ask from my troops before they had had some rest. The advance was, however, ordered in accordance with the request of the Commander-in-Chief, the enemy being driven out of Uleia on 26th August and out of Kidodi on 10th September.

"From Uleia to Kidodi the country consists of high mountain ridges running across the road for several miles. These had all been entrenched by the enemy some time ago, so that in the various actions his troops could fall back from one entrenched position to the next a mile or so in rear. The operations thus called for an extraordinary amount of mountain climbing and constant fighting.

"The slight casualties sustained in the various engagements over an enormous track of country, bristling with dongas and difficulties at every point, were mainly due to the advance being carried out by avoiding as far as possible frontal attacks. Dispositions were made with a view to carry out flanking movements, while holding the enemy to the position occupied by him, but this the enemy carefully avoided, and under cover of darkness the engagement was usually broken off and a retreat effected.

"The success with which the whole movement from Kondoa Irangi to the Central Railway, thence to Kilossa and on to the Ruaha River, was carried out is due to the loyal co-operation and splendid spirit displayed by all units under my command.

"It is difficult to express my high appreciation of the conduct and spirit of the troops, who all worked with determination and zeal. Their endurance and hardships during long marches through dry and waterless stretches on scanty rations form an achievement worthy of South African troops."

IX. Occupation of Morogoro by Main Force and Re-establishment of Direct Touch with 2nd Division.

While waiting at the Wami the Commander-in-Chief became aware that the bulk of the enemy forces had retired to Morogoro, and an effort was accordingly made to bring them to a decisive action at that place.

With this object the 2nd (S.A.) Mounted Brigade, which had occupied Mkata Station on the Central Railway on the 23rd August, was directed on Mlali, 15 miles south-west of Morogoro, on the road to Kissaki, by the route west of the Uluguru Mountains. Mlali was occupied on the 24th. The 2nd Mounted Brigade was joined a day or two later by the 1st (S.A.) Mounted Brigade, which had been called for from the 2nd Division, and on the 27th August the two Brigades had pursued an enemy force from Morogoro into the Uluguru Mountains, having headed it off from the road round the west of the mountains to Kissaki.

On the morning of the 23rd August the main force moved from the Wami, crossing the river by the bridge, which the force had been halted to prepare.

The direct route to Morogoro was not followed, but a most exhausting and arduous forced march was executed to the Ngerengere River to the east, whence, on the 24th August, Msungulu, on the same river, about 18 miles north-east of Morogoro, was reached.

Small advanced detachments of South African mounted troops had been pushed forward to seize an important eminence, Mkugua Hill, and reached their objective early on the 24th.

The severe conditions of the movements of the 23rd now imposed a necessary halt, and the 25th was spent in reconnaissance, but the following day, 26th August, saw the occupation of Mikesse Station and Morogoro.

It was now found that the enemy had retired along three routes—by the east and by the west of the Uluguru range, and by a pathway due south from Morogoro through the mountains.

The careful reconnaissance of the southward mountain track by the enemy Commander-in-Chief is described in his book on page 146. The existence of this track, which General Von Lettow had personally tested on foot to Kissaki, was unknown to his pursuers until after Morogoro had been occupied.

X. The Pursuit to the Southern Extremity of the Uluguru Mountains.

The 1st Division was sent after the retreating enemy along the road to the east of the Uluguru Mountains, and from the 26th August until the 13th December, a long series of stubbornly contested rearguard actions was the chief feature of the retirement and pursuit in country admirably adapted to the defence and calculated to impress upon the pursuer the need for wariness and caution in the offence.

On the 10th September Tulo was occupied, and after some days heavy fighting Duthumi was captured on the 13th; the enemy retreating across the Mgeta River.

The South Africans during this time had been engaged in the centre, in the heart of the mountains, and to the west, on the Mlali-Kissaki route.

On the 29th August the Commander-in-Chief personally visited General Brits at Mlali and entrusted the latter with the task of reaching Kissaki by the route to the west of the Uluguru Mountains.

For the purpose of this operation the 1st Mounted Brigade, under Nussey, came under orders of General Brits.

The two Infantry Battalions under General Beves completed the 3rd Division.

It should here be observed that the 2nd Infantry Brigade, throughout the existence of the 3rd Division, never consisted of more than two battalions.

The 7th and 8th Infantry had been sent to Van Deventer just after the Taveta campaign and had never rejoined.

All reference to the 2nd S.A. Infantry Brigade while it continued to serve with the 3rd Division must be understood to be to the Brigade as it was at the time constituted, viz., the 5th and 6th S.A. Infantry.

Judging from General Von Lettow's account of his solution of the problem as to where he should direct his retreat, he had come to the conclusion that a general retirement to the fertile Mahenge District was the best course to adopt (see page 141, "My Reminiscences of East Africa," by General Von Lettow Vorbeck).

The impression, as recorded in the despatches of the British Commander-in-Chief, that the enemy would stand at Morogoro or in the Uluguru Mountains seems to have been at variance with the enemy's real plan.

However this may be, the position was such as to decide the Commander-in-Chief to push the pursuit of the enemy by each route which the latter had followed, and, accordingly, while the 3rd Division pressed round the west of the mountains, the pursuit through the heart of the range was allotted to the 1st Mounted Brigade, temporarily detached, as has been explained, from the 2nd Division.

The combined movements of this Brigade and the 3rd Division were placed under the command of General Brits and Kissaki was defined as the common objective of the two forces.

The capture of Morogoro had proved an important event and in the next few weeks over 1,000 enemy Askari surrendered in the mountains and vicinity of the recent operations.

The importance of Morogoro is fully appreciable from General Von Lettow's book (page 152), in which an account of the surrenders just referred to is given.

The soundness of the decision to continue the pursuit may be gauged by the enemy commander's own account of the many difficulties which at this time beset him.

The 3rd Division whose journey round the mountains was devoid of important incidents, but bristled with difficulties in connection with transport, reached the vicinity of Kissaki on the 5th September. On this date the eastern advance of the 1st Division was as far as the Ruwu River and the 1st Mounted Brigade had occupied Kikeo, in the mountains, after a rearguard action. For some days later communication was lost with the last-named force in consequence of the roughness of the country and damage to the wireless equipment.

This led to an unfortunate want of timing and co-operation which enabled the enemy—who never failed to profit by such an opportunity—to take a good chance of defeating the attack in detail.

General Brits decided to attack Kissaki on the 7th September without waiting for the arrival of the 1st Mounted Brigade from the mountains, and on this date the 2nd S.A. Infantry Brigade advanced against the enemy position on the right bank of the Mgeta River while the 2nd Mounted Brigade, moving well by the right, attempted a flank attack.

A clear description of the enemy's *modus operandi* on this occasion is given by General Von Lettow and is as follows:—

"The hope of being able to defeat one or more of these columns (he refers to the 1st and the 2nd Mounted and the 2nd Infantry Brigades as 'three Brigade columns') was fulfilled beyond expectation. . . . The turning movement which the enemy was making round the left wing of Otto's detachment was allowed to continue until the outflanking detachment had got right round in rear near Boma of Kissaki. . . . Reserves were now loosed upon him."

The result was a check and retirement to a position below Little Whigu Hill, six miles from Kissaki.

On the following day the 1st Mounted Brigade emerged from the mountains, and, in ignorance of the previous day's happenings, proceeded to attack.

Faced by superior numbers of the concentrated enemy the Brigade maintained a fight till the evening of the 8th, when

General Brits' instructions to retire to the position at Little Whigu reached General Nussey and were complied with.

As General Von Lettow says, in stating his view that an attack would be launched by all three Brigades simultaneously, " General Brits did hold this perfectly sound idea; but the execution failed."

The capture of Dutumi by the 1st E.A. Brigade mentioned earlier was the deciding factor in the enemy's eventual decision to retreat, which he did on the 15th September when the 3rd Division occupied Kissaki.

The forces pursuing the enemy, who had made good his escape towards the Rufiji, had reached the limit of their endurance, the transport was in a serious condition of disrepair and had become very short, illness was rife, and complete reorganization was essential.

In these circumstances entrenched positions were prepared along the Mgeta River, of which the main points were Tulo, Dutumi, Kwa-Hongo, Dakawa, and Kissaki.

This line was held from the 15th September until the 1st January, 1917, in close daily touch with the enemy similarly entrenched opposite the Mgeta River.

XI. The Reorganization Towards the Latter Part of 1916 *in its Relation to the South African Units.*

The health of the white personnel as well as that of the Indian troops of the Expeditionary Force had by this time become gravely undermined and a wholesale weeding out of those who, from repeated attacks of fever and dysentery, had practically become physical wrecks, was an urgent necessity, as was a substantial increase to the force in the way of reinforcements from outside.

The abolition of the 3rd Division was therefore decided upon and all mounted South African troops fit for service were posted to one Brigade. All white troops declared by medical boards to be medically unfit were returned to the country of their origin.

Under these arrangements, approximately 12,000 white troops left East Africa between the middle of October and the end of December, 1916.

The South African formations which remained with the Commander-in-Chief after this reorganization were the 2nd Division, which was to continue to sustain its independent role, and the 2nd S.A. Infantry Brigade, which formed a reserve under the immediate control of the Chief Command.

XII. Events in Other Portions of East Africa during August and September, 1916.

Bagamoyo had been occupied by the Royal Navy on the 15th August, 1916, as already described, and at this place a force of some 1,800 rifles was collected for the operations against Dar-es-Salaam.

The Navy appeared before Dar-es-Salaam on the 3rd September when the place surrendered and was occupied by the force from Bagamoyo on the following day, 4th September.

The enemy forces had previously evacuated the town.

The assistance of the Navy was now enlisted for the purpose of occupying the entire enemy coast line and forces were conveyed by sea. Between the 7th and 16th September the ports of Mikindandi, Ssudi Bay, Lindi, Kilwa, Kissiwani, Kilwa Kivinge, and Kiswere were occupied.

Strong forces were collected at Kilwa for offensive operations inland.

In the south-west the Nyasaland force under Brig.-General Northey had occupied Lupembe and Iringa on the 19th and 29th August respectively, as well as Ssongea in the south-west corner.

In the north-west the British forces under Sir Charles Crewe and Belgian columns from the west had occupied Igalulu, on the railway, and Tabora on the 26th and 19th September respectively.

A Portuguese force had crossed the Ruvuma and occupied positions in the extreme southern portion of enemy territory.

XIII. Operations Generally Pending the Resumption of the Advance by the Main Force.

As has been stated, strong forces were landed in September, 1916, with a view to operations inland based on Kilwa.

No South African units were in these forces, and only a very brief account of their activities during September, October, and November, 1916, will be given.

During these months the main force lay in the centre, opposite to and in constant touch with the enemy main force at Mgeta River, at the southern extremity of the Uluguru Mountains.

A detachment was pushed to the north from Kilwa, and occupied a position at Kibata, and this soon drew an attack.

Mpotora, on the Kilwa-Liwale road, was occupied on the 7th November and on the 2nd December Ngarambi was taken.

An attack was delivered on the garrison at Kibata on the 6th December and heavy fighting continued until the 21st December, when the enemy abandoned the offensive.

The Kilwa force was then held in readiness to assist the general plan when the main advance was resumed.

In the west, on the Ruaha River, and southwards towards Mahenge, the South African troops under General Van Deventer had frequent engagements with the enemy during the period between the occupation of Morogoro and the advance to the Rufiji from the Mgeta front.

The enemy force, which had been facing the Belgians and Crewe's force from the lake, had, after the occupation of Tabora, moved south-east towards Mahenge and was marching, apparently without much definite plan or purpose, southwards.

To deal with this force General Van Deventer sent the 7th South African Infantry (which it will be remembered was one of the two battalions that had been taken from the 2nd S.A. Infantry Brigade at Arusha in April) and a cyclist battalion; both units being placed under the command of Lieut.-Colonel Fairweather, of the cyclists.

On the 23rd and 24th October this force reached Iringa, where it joined a detachment from Northey's force.

The comparatively small number of troops which it was possible to maintain with supplies in the west, south of the Central Railway, prevented a full measure of success being obtained against the enemy retiring from Tabora.

On the 25th October this portion of the enemy forces broke through between Alt-Iringa and Ngominji. At the same time attacks in superior force were being delivered against Northey's forces on the Ruhudje River to the south.

General Van Deventer at this time was placed in charge of all operations at Iringa and vicinity.

A variety of minor encounters, some of which were of a severe nature, occurred at the end of October and the beginning of November between the enemy and the lines of opposing British forces, until the former had effected a passage through the lines to the south, and in these affairs the South African troops were constantly engaged. Several senior officers, among whom was Lieut.-Colonel Fairweather, lost their lives in these wearing and difficult operations. Captain Clark, a South African officer, was killed in a determined resistance at Ngominji, and his troops were eventually compelled to surrender to very superior enemy forces on the 29th October.

Several signal successes were obtained by Brig.-General Northey at this time, notably the capture of Lieut.-Colonel Heubener's force of 54 Europeans and 249 Askari with a howitzer and 3 machine-guns by a Rhodesian force under Lieut.-Colonel Murray, on the 24th November at Ilembule.

By the end of November, after many weeks of confused and indefinite fighting, the enemy from Tabora had extricated his forces and disposed of them on a line running from north-east to south-west, covering Mahenge.

The passage through the lines of British troops had cost the enemy in killed and captured between 700 and 800 fighting troops, European and native.

On the 25th November the Commander-in-Chief visited General Van Deventer at Dodoma and proceeded to the Ruaha and there investigated the country. On the 29th November General Van Deventer was instructed to retake Muhanga and then to move a force eastward to Infanara and on to Luwegu. General Northey was to co-operate in a general movement from the west, eastward, by advancing to the Ruhudje River and Mponda against the left of the enemy line at Mfirika and Ssongea.

Constant patrol fighting now ensued in this quarter.

Heavy rain now complicated the already trying problem of supply, and as a consequence the South African force at Iringa was reduced to three infantry battalions and a squadron of mounted troops; the remainder of the 2nd Division returning to the Central Railway.

Preparations on this front were now made to combine with the general advance, timed to begin about Christmas Day.

XIV. The General Advance Resumed—Movements of the Main Force at Mgeta and Kissaki.

On the occupation of Dar-es-Salaam the enemy force from that place (or some considerable portion of it) had retired to the country, west of the coast line, lying between the Central Railway and the Rufiji River and occupied a strong position at Kissangire. During November and December some fighting occurred in this area, but South African troops were not engaged, although, after an unsuccessful attack on the enemy position at Kissangire, a South African officer, Lieut.-Colonel Burne, was appointed to the command of the area.

At Christmas, 1916, the disposition of the main British force on the Mgeta front was as follows:—

In front line, facing the enemy position, the 1st E.A. Brigade.

On the road between Ruwu and Tulo, the 2nd S.A. Infantry Brigade, en route for Dakawa.

The Nigerian Brigade, recently arrived from the West Coast, concentrating at Ruwu, to assemble at Tulo.

The 1st Division, reorganized with another Brigade in place of the 1st E.A. Brigade, about Kibata and in the Kilwa area.

The columns in Mssanga-Kissangire area (i.e. south-west of Dar-es-Salaam and north of the Rufiji River) were waiting the order to advance.

The positions of Van Deventer and Northey in the west have already been indicated.

The advance on the Mgeta front, timed for the 26th December, was postponed on account of heavy rains until the 1st January, 1917.

The object of the coming operations was two-fold; i.e. the seizure of a crossing over the Rufiji and the capture, or destruction if possible, of the opposing enemy force.

It was decided, for the first purpose, to detach a force widely to the west (right) to capture and hold a bridgehead near Mkalinso on the Rufiji River, 20 miles south-west of Kibambawe. The main force was to advance and attack the enemy in front, north of the Rufiji.

The highly important task of seizing Mkalinso, after a long detour, was entrusted to the 2nd S.A. Infantry Brigade under General Beves, whose two regiments were augmented by the attachment of the Cape Corps.

The remainder of the troops engaged were not South Africans, so the venture of the latter will first be described.

It was carried out without a hitch, and was probably the most outstanding of many wonderful marches performed by the Brigade in the campaign, and was executed in tremendous tropical heat.

On the 31st December the Brigade reached Kirengwe, 10 miles east of Kissaki, and sent on a picked body of scouts towards the Rufiji, followed on the 1st January by engineers and pioneers together with half a battalion of infantry.

A crossing was to be effected over the Rufiji, below its junction with the Ruaha, before daybreak on the 4th, in Berthon boats.

The remainder of the Brigade followed one march in rear of the advanced troops.

The enemy was to be kept to his positions by a general attack by the main body, which began on the 1st January.

The advanced troops of the Brigade reached the Rufiji a few miles south of Mkalinso at 6.30 a.m. on the 3rd January, crossed the river and entrenched on the right bank.

The task assigned to the force had been executed with wonderful rapidity twenty-four hours earlier than had been ordered.

The general advance had in the meantime proceeded on the following plan:—

A frontal attack supported by artillery, designed to hold the enemy to his positions, was delivered by the Nigerian Brigade, while two forces were directed by turning movements against the enemy's flanks, one by way of Kiruru, 12 miles east of Duthumi, under Colonel Lyall, against the enemy's right and the other against the enemy's left by way of Wiransi, west of the Dakawa road, under General Sheppard.

The two forces were to establish contact with each other behind and south of the enemy position at Dakawa, at, or about Kiderengwa.

The advance proceeded according to plan, and after some heavy fighting by a portion of Sheppard's force on the Wiransi road, soon after the general advance began, on the 1st January, and a severe engagement between Lyall's force and the enemy in the evening of the same day, near Tshimbe, on the road to Kiderengwa, a general retirement of the enemy took place.

Beho Beho, further south towards the Rufiji, was known to be an enemy position and a further effort to encircle him there was made.

In the course of the next forward movement Lyall's force come in contact with the enemy, just north of Beho Beho, late in the afternoon of the 3rd, and a sharp engagement continued until dusk.

Another turning movement round the enemy's left, west of Beho Beho, was executed by Sheppard's force during the night of the 3rd-4th January, and the force reached the Beho Beho-Kibambawe road on the morning of the 4th just as the enemy was retiring from Beho Beho past the point of its arrival. The enemy sustained some severe punishment but made good his retreat.

It was during this engagement that that gallant old South African, Captain F. C. Selous, was instantaneously killed by machine-gun fire on reaching the open road.

Air reconnaissance now revealed the enemy hard at work at Kibambawe, repairing the damage, caused by flood, to the bridge over the Rufiji. On the 4th the work was almost completed.

On the 5th January the 1st E.A. Brigade reached the left branch of the Rufiji, at Kibambawe, and found the enemy holding the opposite bank after having removed all the roadway of the bridge.

The crossing of the Rufiji was ordered to be undertaken by the 1st E.A. Brigade during the night of the 5th-6th January and by the morning of the 6th one double company and two machine-guns had crossed unobserved by the enemy and lay concealed on the right bank during the day.

Crossing continued at night, in spite of severe difficulties, until enough troops were on the right bank to maintain themselves against the enemy.

An enemy force now appeared at Mkalinso and entrenched itself there but retired again after an engagement with a force from the 2nd Infantry Brigade sent to turn it out.

Further advance by this Brigade was now suspended in consequence of its exhausted condition, and its detachment was withdrawn from Mkalinso and concentrated entrenched at the bridgehead on the right bank of the Rufiji, at its original crossing.

On the 20th January, 1917, General Smuts, summoned to London for the Imperial Conference, handed over the chief command in East Africa to General Hoskins.

On General Smuts' departure the position was as follows:—

The main force under his immediate command had crossed the Rufiji at Kibambawe and Mkalinso and held the right bank strongly at each place.

Immediately to the west, between Dar-es-Salaam and the Rufiji, the force under Colonel Burne had occupied Koge towards the Rufiji, while troops of the 1st Division south of the Rufiji had reached Mohoro from the direction of Kibata.

PART IV.

THE GERMAN EAST AFRICAN CAMPAIGN.

SECOND PHASE.

PAGE.

I.—Irregular Operations 89

II.—Operations to the end of 1917 90

III.—The Final Operations 91

I.

IRREGULAR OPERATIONS.

WHEN armed forces no longer have bases, depots, and permanent lines of communication in secure and uninvaded parts of their country, but move freely about and live on what they can find, then entirely different principles of warfare are required in dealing with them.

While an enemy is still regularly established on his bases and depots, the principle applied to him is that of the wedge, of splitting up and chipping off. He is bound to certain places, locality plays an important part, and he cannot avoid the wedge but must resist it. Once however he has lost all places and localities of value, the loss is to a certain extent compensated for by his increased freedom and ability to avoid the wedge. The principle that then has to be applied is that of compression; he has to be rounded up and concentrated before he can be crushed. There are thus, in irregular warfare, two distinct operations: first the concentration and then the subjugation; and if the first fails the second can never succeed.

For this reason all the irregular or guerrilla operations of history have been largely in favour of the irregulars. Given a country and conditions under which irregular warfare is at all possible, it can be considered a foregone conclusion, that however poor in quality the irregulars may be, it will take a long time and considerable expenditure to subdue them. Now the German troops in East Africa were certainly not poor in quality, while the area they had to operate in seems to have been created for no other purpose than the conduct of guerrilla warfare. As a theatre for favourable irregular war, East Africa must take first place; densely forested, mountainous, and river-intersected, large forces can hide themselves or move close to an enemy without being perceived; food can always be found unless it has purposely been removed, and for half the year operations are practically impossible owing to the rains, so that the pursued has a respite, can grow crops, and train recruits, and generally recuperate his forces.

After General Smuts left, Lieut.-General Hoskins directed operations until Lieut.-General Sir J. L. van Deventer, who had formerly commanded the 2nd Division, took over command at the end of May, 1917.

The enemy forces were still holding an uninvaded area around Mahenge and from there to near Kilwa, so that strictly speaking, the phase of irregular warfare had not yet commenced.

The disposition of the enemy force was about 3,000 men around Mahenge, commanded by Major Tafel, while the main force, under General Von Lettow himself, was disposed in the coastal area near Kilwa and Lindi; it numbered 4,000 to 5,000 all ranks. In addition there were two detachments which had already commenced irregular action. One was that of Captain Nauman, who had broken northwards and was operating in the area between Tabora and Arusha, with a strength of about 500 rifles. The other detachment under Captain Von Steumer, consisting of about 300 rifles, had gone south and invaded Portuguese territory in the Mwembe District.

The troops at General Van Deventer's disposal were:—

At Lindi, one Brigade under General O'Grady.

Between Kilwa and Mohoro, two columns under General Hannyngton.

On the Rufiji River, at Kibambawe, the Nigerian Brigade (less one battalion) under General Gunliffe.

Pursuing Nauman was the equivalent of one Brigade, with a similar number of Belgian troops.

Two battalions were at Iringa and a small central reserve at Morogoro.

General Northey's Force, which held a line from Ubena to Songea, numbered about the strength of a Brigade.

General Van Deventer's force consisted of a cosmopolitan collection of races, so that it is difficult to disentangle the part that South Africans played. There were Belgian and Portuguese troops, Pathans and Cashmiries, West Indian and Nigerian units, Imperial European Regulars, and South Africans.

All that can be done is briefly to sketch the remainder of the campaign. The South Africans at the time in the field were:—

North of the Rufidje:
- 3rd Battery, S.A. Field Artillery.
- The South African Mounted Regiment.
- De Jager's Scouts.
- 7th and 8th S.A. Infantry.
- The 1st Cape Corps.

With General Northey to the south:
- South African Motor-cycle Corps.
- 1st and 2nd South African Rifles.
- 5th South African Infantry.
- B.S.A. Police.
- 2nd Cape Corps.
- North Rhodesian Police.
- 1st Rhodesian Native Regiment.

The Mechanical Transport and other services had many South Africans, and towards the end of 1917 all European units were evacuated and the operations continued by King's African Rifle regiments locally recruited; these were to a great extent officered by South Africans.

II.

OPERATIONS TO THE END OF 1917.

General Van Deventer decided to make his main advance from Kilwa and Lindi, also to operate against the Mahenge area from Dodoma and Kilossa, and to capture Nauman's force which was raiding in the north, as soon as possible.

Early in October Nauman's raiding detachment had been accounted for. After weary marching and counter-marching for many months, he was at last surrounded and captured, an operation in which the 10th South African Horse and the 1st Cape Corps took a prominent part. This raid had started under Wintgens, the previous commander, from near Songea, in the beginning of February, 1917. New Langenburg and Bismarkburg were threatened in turn; the force then turned north, passed through Itunda (at which place Wintgens became sick and Nauman assumed the command) crossed the Central Railway near Tabora, engaged the Belgians at Ikoma, and made for Lake Magadi and Kondoa Irangi. After passing near Moshi, Nauman with his force was captured in the vicinity of Geiro, on the Luita Hill.

The several wedges which General Van Deventer (still on the principle of regular warfare) forced into the enemy's uninvaded area, were beginning to have their splitting effect.

After continuous and severe fighting, of which the four days' action at Nyangao in October was perhaps the most intense, the area was penetrated and the enemy force split into two main bodies. The one under Tafel was so crippled by the severe fighting that it surrendered on the 28th November with 19 officers, 92 European N.C.O.'s, and 3,400 native troops. Von Lettow with the remaining body of troops escaped over the Rovuma River into Portuguese East Africa.

The regular phase of the campaign was now at an end; the enemy in future would not have depots or bases, except such as he could establish during the six months' respite of the rainy season. His force which still numbered about 50 officers, 250 Europeans, and 2,300 Askaris, with 2 guns and 30 machine-guns, had offered a resistance to the invasion of German East Africa that was only conquered after nine-tenths of the European and native personnel had been killed or captured.

Nauman's raid had shown what could be done in the way of irregular operations, and General Von Lettow now had the advantage of the fertile and well-stocked Portuguese territory, where the natives were hostile to the Portuguese and more or less pro-German. During the six months of operations General Van Deventer's casualties had been close on 6,000, against which must be set 1,618 Germans and 5,482 Askari killed or captured during that period. Fourteen guns, 77 machine-guns, and several thousand rifles had also been captured.

III.

THE FINAL OPERATIONS.

After General Von Lettow had crossed the Rovuma into Portuguese territory in the last week of November, 1917, he captured Ngomano after a sharp engagement, during which the Portuguese commander was killed.

The rainy season set in soon after, but as the enemy had no lines of communication to maintain or transport to arrange he was able to move south rapidly, living on the land as he went. By the 14th of December he occupied Medo and was threatening Port Amelia.

On the 11th of April, 1918, General Edwards attacked and drove the enemy from Medo westwards, and followed them to Koronue, where, after a brisk engagement on the 1st of May they were driven further west. During these and the lesser engagements General Von Lettow had lost rather heavily and was being driven into bad country. He therefore broke through to the south again and got down far enough to seriously threaten the port of Quelimane.

Converging forces again pressed the enemy, which, after severe fighting at Anguros, broke northwards and crossed the Rovuma back into its old haunts of the last days of September. Here Von Lettow found the country improved, for the rest it had enjoyed, and was again able to supply his foraging parties with ease.

The operations in Portuguese territory had lasted ten months. The pursued and pursuers had in this time covered immense distances and fought many sharp engagements, but on the whole the operations only went to show the extreme difficulty of rounding up a mobile force which is independent of the usual encumbrances of regular troops. On the 2nd of November General Von Lettow was again out of East Africa, unsuccessfully attacking Fife, and by the 8th of the same month his advanced troops had reached Kasama, about 100 miles due south of Abercorn, in Northern Rhodesia.

On the 14th November the Armistice terminated operations which were remarkable and in many ways unique. It was the first occasion on which extensive operations with modern arms had taken place in tropical Africa. Diverse as are the features of the East African theatre of operations, ranging from high mountainous country to flat coastal swamps, the predominating feature of dense forest and bush never changes; this enormously increases the difficulty of co-ordinating movements and magnifies the obscurity that at the best of times veils an enemy's intentions. Two considerable forces might be a mile from one another and yet be totally unaware of each other's presence. Instances are on record where portions of the pursuing force over-marched the enemy and were then encountered in their rear by the enemy advance guard. The distances covered by hostile as well as our own troops, especially in the later stages of the campaign, would have been remarkable even in a temperate climate and with a good supply system; but carried out in the heart of Africa under a blazing sun or in torrential rain on indifferent rations, they must rank as wonderful feats of endurance.

Though few engagements in the East African campaign rose to the dignity of battle, yet the fighting was often continuous as well as severe; the theatre of operations was perhaps the most difficult in which any large body of troops ever fought. The wild impenetrable nature of the country, its vastness, the deadly diseases, and the difficulty of supply, greatly increased the hardships inseparable from any form of campaigning.

General Von Lettow had, at the beginning of 1916, 2,700 Europeans and 12,000 Askari. The force that laid down its arms at Abercorn on the 25th of November, 1918, in terms of Clause 17 of the Armistice, numbered 155 Europeans and 1,168 Askari. In a civilized or more open country, the life of such a force would have been short indeed, but with the extraordinary advantages that the country presented for irregular operations, it is possible that the operations might have been prolonged for a considerable time. General Von Lettow and his officers had contributed a brilliant chapter to the Military History of Irregular Operations, and they were allowed to retain their arms in recognition of their gallant and prolonged resistance.

PART V.

THE SOUTH AFRICAN INFANTRY BRIGADE IN EGYPT

PAGE.

I.—The Brigade and the Situation in Egypt 95

II.—General Lukin's Operations 95

I.

THE BRIGADE AND THE SITUATION IN EGYPT.

AFTER the German South-West campaign had successfully terminated the Union of South Africa raised an Infantry Brigade to represent South Africa on the French front. This Brigade of four battalions, under the command of Brig.-General H. T. Lukin, was recruited as follows:—

- The 1st S.A.I. (the Cape Province).
- The 2nd S.A.I. (Natal and the Orange Free State).
- The 3rd S.A.I. (Transvaal and Rhodesia).
- The 4th S.A.I. (the Scottish Regiment in South Africa).

The Brigade, numbering 160 officers and 5,648 other ranks, had arrived in England early in November, 1915, and commenced their training for France, when it became desirable to employ them in Egypt on work for which they were thought to be specially fitted.

The situation in Egypt was that the Suez Canal was threatened by the Turks from their Syrian bases on the east, while on the western frontier the Senussi tribes had been stirred up and threatened to overrun Egypt from the west.

The Senussi had been well armed from Constantinople and were commanded by Gaafer Pasha. The British posts were drawn in to Mersa Matruh. On the 13th December Major-General Wallace, who commanded the Western Egyptian Force, had severe losses in dispersing some 1,200 enemy near Beit Hussein. Towards the end of December some 5,000 enemy under Gaafer Pasha himself were dispersed by General Wallace 8 miles south-west of Matruh, but early in January they again appeared in force near Matruh.

The South African Brigade disembarked at Alexandria early in January, 1916, and the 2nd South African Infantry at once went forward to reinforce General Wallace for his attack on the hostile concentration south-west of Matruh.

The 2nd S.A.I., together with the 1st Battalion New Zealand Rifles and the 15th Sikhs, formed the infantry of General Wallace's force, which attacked the Senussi at Hazalin on the 23rd January. The enemy was dispersed and his camp taken, but the casualties were somewhat severe and no pursuit could be undertaken.

After this action the Egyptian Western Frontier Force was reorganized, and Major-General W. E. Peyton took over the command from Major-General Wallace, whose health had given way. The Sikhs and New Zealanders were withdrawn, the South African Brigade and the Royal Scots being the only infantry formations in the force.

II.

GENERAL LUKIN'S OPERATIONS.

Early in February, 1916, the Senussi forces were mainly concentrated at Barrani and Sollum; the Western Frontier Force at Mersa Matruh. All thus at coast ports. As the entrances to the hostile harbours were mined, and would require some time to sweep, an overland advance was decided on. An advance depot was established at Unjeila, and it was decided to keep as close to the coast as possible during the march as scorching winds, a glaring sun, and want of water would make the march arduous, and some relief could be obtained by sea-bathing at halting places.

We now come to General Lukin's part in the Egyptian operations. On the 22nd of February, 1916, he marched out of the advanced depot, Unjeila, with a column consisting of the—

Notts Battery R.H.A.
1st South African Infantry.
3rd South African Infantry.
1/6th Royal Scots.
Dorset Yeomanry.
One squadron Royal Bucks Hussars.

The Senussi had been located at Agagia, 14 miles south-east of Barrani, and it was known that Gaafer Pasha was with them. General Lukin's intention was to make a night attack, but on the afternoon of the 25th the enemy anticipated this intention by shelling General Lukin's camp. The next day an air reconnaissance disclosed that Gaafer Pasha had gone back to his Agagia positions, so General Lukin began an advance at 9.30 a.m., leaving 300 Royal Scots to guard the camp.

The action, which commenced at 11 a.m. on the 26th February, can be looked on as a model of a successful desert action. In the centre, the 3rd S.A.I. under Lieut.-Colonel Thackeray, advanced on a front of about 1,700 yards, with Yeomanry and armoured cars on either flank, the 1st S.A.I. being kept in reserve. On the enemy trying to envelop General Lukin's left flank, one company of the 1st S.A.I., in reserve, was sent there to restore the balance. This company of Colonel Dawson's battalion soon broke into the enemy line, to be immediately followed by the 3rd S.A.I. all along the line. The mounted troops under Colonel Souter now got their turn. They waited until the enemy was well on the move in retreat, extended for about a mile with a depth of 300 to 400 yards. Moving parallel to this retreating force, the Dorset Regiment charged about 3 p.m., galloping in two lines under a severe machine-gun and rifle fire. The cavalry charge completely broke and dispersed the enemy; many prisoners were captured, including the Commander-in-Chief, Gaafer Pasha, and his staff. This very complete success, not gained without severe loss, especially among the cavalry and 3rd S.A.I., was due to the perfect co-ordination of infantry and cavalry and General Lukin's prompt and correct decision after the action had begun.

This action sealed the fate of Egypt's enemies on her western frontier. Barrani and Sollum were occupied without any resistance, there being no further fighting, beyond two brilliant affairs by the ten armoured-cars under the command of the Duke of Westminster, who pursued the enemy to Bir Asia and relieved the prisoners which the Senussi had at a camp deep in the interior. By the 15th of April the South African Brigade was in France.

PART VI.

*THE SOUTH AFRICAN INFANTRY BRIGADE IN FRANCE.

PAGE.

I.—Battle of Somme: Delville Wood... 99

II.—Battle of Somme: Butte de Warlencourt 111

III.—Battle of Arras 120

IV.—Third Battle of Ypres 129

V.—The Eve of the Great German Attack, November, 1917–March, 1918 138

VI.—The Somme Retreat—Gauche and Marrières Woods 143

VII.—Battle of the Lys 155

VIII.—The Summer of 1918 164

IX.—The Advance to Victory 169

* Adapted from Colonel Buchan's story of "The South Africans in France," by permission and arrangements with the holders of the Copyright.

CHAPTER I.

THE BATTLE OF THE SOMME: DELVILLE WOOD.

(APRIL—JULY, 1916.)

THE South African Brigade disembarked at Marseilles on the 20th April. Owing to a case of contagious sickness on board the *Oriana*, the 4th S.A.I. and part of the 1st were placed in quarantine, while the remainder of the troops entrained at once for Flanders. Steenwerck was reached on the morning of the 23rd, and the 2nd and 3rd S.A.I. marched to their billeting area along roads wholly under water. Headquarters were established at Bailleul, and the Brigade was attached to the 9th (Scottish) Division, under Major-General W. T. Furse. For three weeks detachments of the two battalions took their place in the trenches for instruction, and on 11th May the 4th S.A.I. and the rest of the 1st arrived from their quarantine at Marseilles. On 14th May the 28th Brigade of the 9th Division disappeared, being absorbed in other divisions, and the South African Brigade took its place.*

The April of 1916 was a critical month in the Western campaign. On the 9th the first and deadliest stage of the German assault on Verdun had closed with the failure of the attackers. General Pétain's thin lines had held their ground; the little city was still inviolate; and, though France had lost terribly, she had wrecked the plans of her enemy, inflicting upon him irreparable loss, and by her heroism won that quiet confidence which is the surest guarantee of victory. When the Imperial Crown Prince opened the battle, one part of his purpose had been to induce a British counter-offensive. That counter-offensive did not come, for General Joffre did not desire it. He preferred to wait until Germany had spent her strength, and to use the armies of France and Britain in a great movement against a weakened foe. Our task, therefore, during the first months of 1916 had been to wait. The duty had been costly, for on our front the average daily toll of loss in trench fighting was not far from 1,000. It was a difficult time, for there was no great objective to quicken the spirit, and those indeterminate months imposed a heavy strain upon the *moral* of our troops. Yet the apparent stagnation was not without its advantage, for it gave the new British Commander-in-Chief time to complete his field army and perfect its education. When Sir Douglas Haig took over the supreme command he set himself to the work of training his men for a new kind of warfare, and the whole British front became one vast seminary.

Moreover, during these months of waiting our strength in munitionment had grown beyond belief. The Allied offensives of 1915 had failed largely because there was not sufficient weight of shells and guns behind them. But by June of 1916 Britain was manufacturing and issuing to the Western front weekly as much as her whole pre-war stock of land service munitions. In heavy guns the output in the year had increased six-fold. The weekly production of machine-guns had increased fourteen-fold, and of rifles

---

* The 9th Division was now composed of the 26th Infantry Brigade, comprising the 8th Black Watch, the 7th Seaforths, the 5th Camerons, and the 10th Argyll and Sutherland Highlanders; the 27th Infantry Brigade, comprising the 11th Royal Scots, the 12th Royal Scots, the 6th K.O.S.B., and the 9th Scottish Rifles and the South African Infantry Brigade. The Pioneer Battalion was the 9th Seaforths.

three-fold. In small-arm ammunition the output was three times as great, and large reserve stocks had been accumulated. The production of high explosives was sixty-six times what it had been in the beginning of 1915, and the supply of bombs for trench warfare had been multiplied by thirty-three.

The South African Brigade was inspected on 29th April by Sir Douglas Haig, and on 4th May by Sir Herbert Plumer. The next two months were devoted to its initiation in the methods of trench warfare, which were wholly new to it. During May it held a portion of the front line, and on 4th June the whole Brigade and the Field Ambulance moved into the Steenbecque and Morbecque training area. Battalion training was followed by Brigade training until 14th June, when orders were received for the Division to move to the Somme. The Brigade was quartered in the neighbourhood of Ailly-sur-Somme, whence parties of officers and N.C.O.'s visited the front line in the Maricourt region. Meantime the 2nd and 3rd S.A.I. were attached to the 30th Division, to assist in the work of preparation for the coming attack.

On 23rd June the Brigade moved to Corbie and Sailly-le-Sec, where it was within a few miles of the line. Next morning, Saturday, the 24th, in grey, cloudy weather with flying showers of rain, the main bombardment opened.

The story of the Battle of the Somme belongs to history written on a larger scale than this, for here we are concerned with only a part of it. But to understand that part it is necessary to grasp the purpose of the whole action. The enemy was suffering from a lack of immediate reserves, and the depression of *moral* due to his failure at Verdun and the recent successes of Brussilov in Galicia. He had boasted so loudly of his "war map," and the amount of conquered territory which he held, that he dared not resort to the expedient of shortening his long line. He trusted to the great natural and artificial strength of his positions in the West to repel the Allies, whatever weight of men and guns might be brought against him. In no part of the Western front were these positions stronger than between Arras and the Somme, where he held in the main the higher ground, and had in the rear many fortified woods and villages which could be linked together into reserve lines.

The Allies had learned the lesson of the futile offensives of 1915, and of the long-drawn contest at Verdun. They no longer dreamed of breaking the enemy's front by a sudden bound, for they realized the depth of his fortified zone. They had accepted the principle that an attack should proceed by stages, with, as a preliminary to each, an elaborate artillery "preparation"; and they realized, too, that, since the struggle must be protracted, fresh troops must be used for each stage. Their new plan was simply attrition on a colossal scale. Their method was that of "limited objectives," with new troops and a new bombardment for each phase. This method of attrition presupposed the continuance of the war on two fronts. When Russia fell out of line the situation was utterly changed, and the plan became futile against an enemy with a large new reservoir of recruitment. But at the time of its inception, uninspired and expensive as it was, it was a sound plan.

Our aim was to crumble the enemy's defences on the Bapaume Ridge so completely that he could not find an alternate position of equal strength, and would be slowly forced into open warfare. The British front of attack was from Gommecourt in the north to Maricourt in the south, whence the French carried the battle across the Somme to a point opposite the village of Fay. It was Sir Douglas Haig's intention to make his main attack between the Ancre and Maricourt, and it is clear from his dispatch that he regarded the movement of his left wing as a subsidiary operation. The effort of the British left on the first day failed, and thereafter the battle became a stubborn frontal attack up the slopes from the west. The enemy's fortress was assaulted on its most formidable side, and when after six months he admitted defeat and fell back, he yielded not to any strategical brilliance in our plan, but to the incomparable valour and tenacity of the Allied troops.

On 30th June, the day before the battle began, the South African Brigade, comprising the four infantry battalions, the 64th Field Company R.E., the 28th Brigade M.G. Company, and the South African Brigade Trench Mortar Battery, moved to Grove Town, a large dump on the outskirts of Bray, the 9th Division being in general reserve to the XIII Corps. That night the weather suddenly cleared to a blue midsummer evening. Next morning, Saturday, 1st July, at half-past seven, under a cloudless and windless sky, the Allied infantry went over the parapets, and the battle began.

The result of that day was that the German first line was carried almost everywhere from the Ancre southward. In no part of the field was the success more notable than in the area of the XIII Corps, which took Montauban, and came to the edge of Bernafay Wood. For the next few days, while our centre was struggling for Ovillers and Contalmaison, the XIII Corps, on the British right wing, working in co-operation with the French, was endeavouring to clear the woods of Trônes and Bernafay, which intervened between the first and second German positions. Bernafay soon fell; but Trônes Wood, being commanded from the south by the Maltzhorn Ridge and from the north by the German position at Longueval, was a hard nut to crack, and though we took most of it, we could not hold it. That was the position by the 13th of July, when the capture of Contalmaison allowed Sir Douglas Haig to begin the second stage of the action.

Meantime the South African Brigade had entered the fringes of the battle. On the night of 2nd July the Brigade moved forward to Billon Valley to relieve the 27th Brigade, which was advancing into the line. On 4th July General Furse ordered the South African Brigade to relieve the 21st Brigade in divisional reserve and the 89th Brigade in the Glatz sector of the front.* This relief was completed by 3.15 a.m. on the morning of 5th July. The position now was that the 1st and 4th S.A.I. held the line from the junction with the French to Briqueterie Trench east of Montauban, the 2nd S.A.I. were in divisional reserve at Talus Boise, and the 3rd S.A.I. were in support in the old British and German front-line trenches immediately to the north-west of Maricourt.

The 27th Brigade had cleared Bernafay Wood on the night of the 4th, and during the following days the French 39th Division of the famous XX Corps was assiduously attacking towards Maltzhorn Farm, while the British right division, the 30th, was labouring to secure the wood of Trônes. On the afternoon of the 7th the relief began of the 1st S.A.I. by the 18th Manchesters of the 21st Brigade. That evening came the preliminary orders from General Headquarters for the second stage of the battle, which for the 9th Division was an attack upon the German line at Longueval.

At dawn on the 8th the only South Africans in the line were the 4th S.A.I., holding the Briqueterie Trench and the section from Dublin Trench to Dublin Redoubt. The 2nd S.A.I., which had been in reserve at Talus Boise, was ordered to relieve the 12th Royal Scots and the 6th K.O.S.B. of the 27th Brigade, which were holding a portion of Bernafay Wood. "A" and "C" Companies were detailed for the task, and the following day they were joined by "D" Company. During the 10th these companies of the 2nd S.A.I. were replaced by two

* Both these brigades belonged to the 30th Division.

companies of the 4th. The 2nd during its short time in the line was most severely shelled, and incurred some 200 casualties.

The 4th S.A.I., now the only part of the Brigade in the line, was about to be drawn into the fight for Trônes Wood, where the 30th Division had made a lodgment on Saturday, the 8th. There were heavy counter-attacks all through the Sunday, and on Monday, the 10th, an attack was ordered to clear the place. At 11 p.m. on the 9th, "A" Company of the 4th was sent to support the 90th Brigade, a platoon was dispatched to the garrison of the Briqueterie, and the 3rd S.A.I. was held in reserve at the disposal of the 30th Division. At dawn on the 10th came the attack, and troops of the 30th Division, together with "A" Company of the 4th S.A.I., advanced through the southern half of the wood, and reported it clear of the enemy. But it could not be held. The half-moon of German artillery positions around it made communication with our rear too perilous, and the denseness of the covert, cut only by the railway clearings and the German communication trenches, rendered organized movement impossible within it. In the afternoon a German counter-attack lost us most of our gains.

On the 11th the fighting in Trônes continued, and the 4th S.A.I., whose "A" and "C" Companies were in the neighbourhood of Glatz Redoubt, and whose headquarters and "B" and "D" Companies were in Bernafay Wood, came under the barrage with which the enemy prepared his counter-attacks. That day the Brigade suffered a grievous loss in the death from a shell-splinter of Lieut.-Colonel F. A. Jones, D.S.O., the commanding officer of the 4th S.A.I. The command of the 4th S.A.I. now passed to Major D. M. MacLeod.

On the 13th orders were issued for the attack on the German second line, and the 4th S.A.I. was relieved by the 2nd Royal West Surreys and the 7th Middlesex of the 55th Brigade in the 18th Division. That evening the whole South African Brigade was concentrated at Talus Boise as the reserve brigade of the 9th Division. Its week in the front line had been costly. In the 1st S.A.I. there were 50 casualties, in the 2nd 205, in the 3rd 91, and in the 4th 191, and these included 7 officers killed and 9 wounded.

At dawn on Friday, the 14th of July, the attack against a section of the German second position—the four miles of front from a point south-east of Pozières to Longueval and Delville Wood was launched. It was the business of the XIII Corps to takke Bazentin-le-Grand, Longueval, and Delville Wood, and to clear Trônes Wood and form a defensive flank. The result of the day was that we carried all our objectives from Bazentin-le-Petit to Longueval, a front of over three miles, and at one moment had all but penetrated the enemy third position at High Wood. Here we are concerned only with the British right flank, the attack of the 9th Division against Longueval, and of the 18th Division, under Major-General Ivor Maxse, on its right at Trônes Wood.

This section was beyond doubt the most difficult in the battle-front. To begin with, we were fighting in a salient, and our attack was under fire from three sides. This enabled the enemy to embarrass seriously our communications during the action. In the second place, the actual ground of attack presented an intricate problem. The land sloped upwards from Bernafay and Trônes Wood to Longueval village, which was shaped like an inverted fan, broad at the south end, where the houses clustered about the junction of two roads, and straggling out to the north-east along the highway to Flers. Scattered among the dwellings were many little enclosed gardens and orchards. To the east and north-east of the hamlet stretched the wood of Delville, in the shape of a blunt equilateral triangle, with an apex pointing northward. The place, like most French woods, had been seamed with grassy rides, partly obscured by

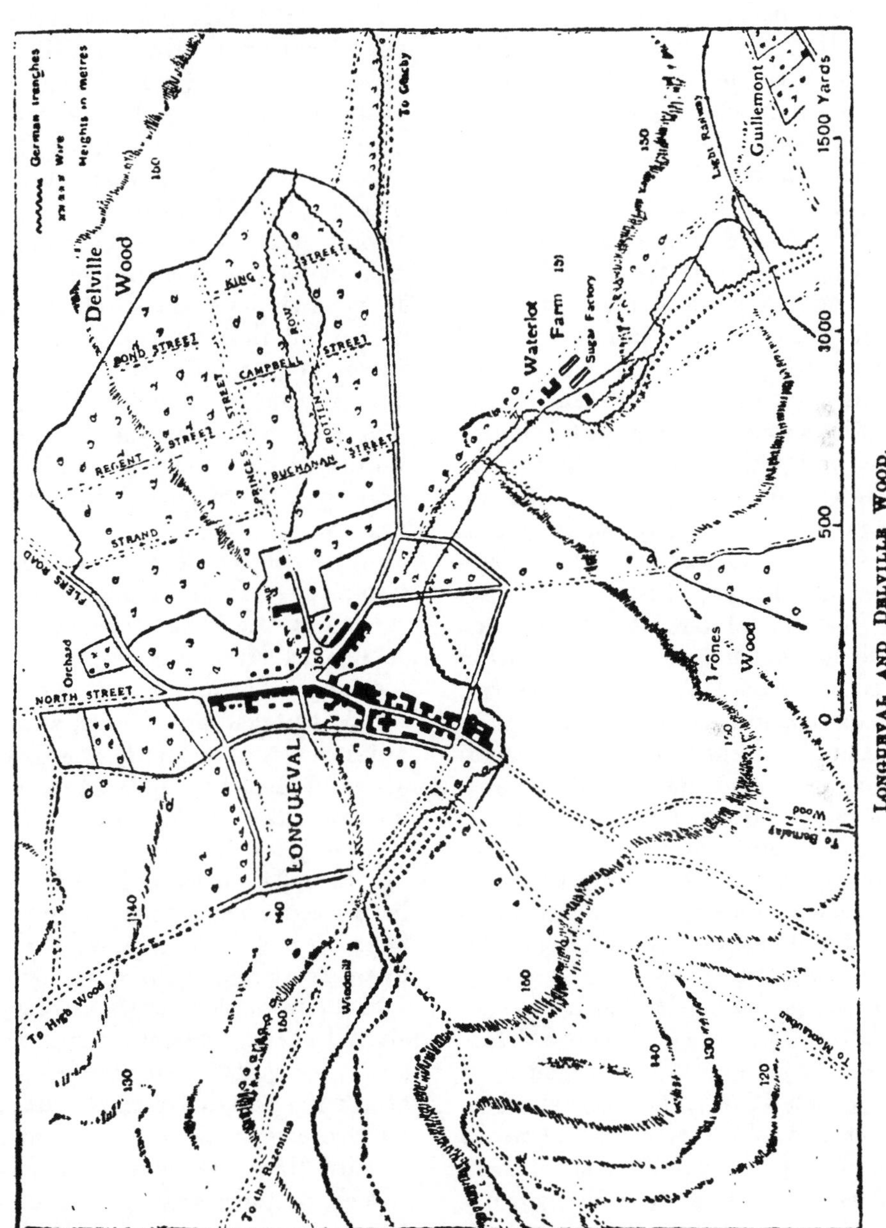

LONGUEVAL AND DELVILLE WOOD.

scrub, and the Germans had dug lines of trenches along and athwart them. The main German positions were to the north, north-east, and south-east, at a distance of from 50 to 200 yards from its perimeter, where they had strong entrenchments manned by machine-guns. It was Sir Douglas Haig's aim to carry Longueval, and make it the flanking buttress of his new line, from which a defensive flank could be formed running south-east to the junction with the French. But it was obvious that the whole of Longueval could not be held unless Delville were also taken, for the northern part, where the road climbed towards Flers, was commanded by the wood. Nothing short of the whole village would make an adequate pivot; and, with the wood still in German hands, there would be no good leaping-off ground from which to press outward in the direction of Ginchy and Guillemont.

The attack on Longueval on the morning of the 14th was entrusted to the 26th Brigade of the 9th Division—the 8th Black Watch and the 10th Argyll and Sutherlands leading, the 9th Seaforths in support, and the 5th Camerons in reserve. The 27th Brigade moved behind them to "clean up," and the intention of General Congreve was that day to make good Longueval and also Delville Wood, if the latter should prove practicable—a heavy task for two Brigades. Shortly after dawn General Lukin received orders to put a battalion at the disposal of the 27th Brigade to assist in clearing the Longueval streets, and the 1st S.A.I. was sent forward for the purpose. The 3rd S.A.I. was also allotted to the 26th Brigade, but this order was subsequently cancelled.

The assault of the Highlanders was a most gallant performance. They rushed the trenches outside the village and entered the streets, where desperate hand-to-hand fighting took place among the houses, for the enemy made a resolute defence. Before noon all the west and south-west part of Longueval was in our hands; but it had become clear that the place in its entirety could not be held, even if won, until Delville Wood was cleared. At 1 p.m. General Furse informed General Lukin that, as soon as the other two Brigades had taken Longueval, the South African Brigade was to capture and consolidate the outer edge of Delville Wood. For this purpose the whole of the Brigade was available with the exception of the 1st S.A.I. General Lukin thereupon drew up his orders for the operation. The first hour suggested for the attack was 5 p.m. that afternoon; the time was later changed to 7 p.m., and then to 7.30 p.m.; the several changes in the time had had to be made owing to the fact that the village was not entirely captured, which at that time was considered a necessary prelude to launching the further attack on Delville Wood.

A staff officer of the Brigade, Lieutenant Roseby, was sent to ascertain the exact position of our troops in Longueval village.

At a conference with the Divisional Commander at Montauban that evening it was arranged that the attack should take place at 5 a.m. on the following morning. The orders were that the wood was to be taken at all costs, and that the advance was to proceed, even if the 26th and 27th Brigades failed to capture the northern part of the village.

Meantime during that day the 1st S.A.I., under Lieut.-Colonel Dawson, had been heavily engaged in Longueval. At 2 p.m. it had deployed along the line held by the two Scottish Brigades, having been brought through a severe artillery fire in eight lines of sections in file without a single casualty. Its business was to attack the remainder of the village, and its leading companies, "A" and "B," reached their first objectives about four o'clock, but were unable to advance owing to the machine-gun fire from front and flank. During the night three parties were sent out to capture the enemy posts which were checking the advance, and found that the whole village in its northern part was a nest of machine-guns. On the morning of the 15th, after the other three battalions had started for Delville Wood, the 1st S.A.I. rejoined the Brigade.

Two hours before dawn the 2nd and 3rd S.A.I. left Montauban for Delville Wood, followed by the 4th S.A.I., which was to support the attack. The exact position of our troops in Longueval was still unknown as Lieutenant Roseby had not then returned from his difficult reconnaissance, and the probable impossibility of executing the existing order was still a difficulty. In the circumstances, the officer commanding the attack, Lieut.-Colonel Tanner, was instructed by General Lukin to ascertain the position of affairs in Longueval and to base the plan of attack upon the result of his reconnaissance.

It was a cloudy morning, but as the sun rose the sky lightened above the Bapaume Ridge. On the right front lay the shadow which was Delville Wood and the jumbled masonry, now spouting like a volcano, which had been the hamlet of Longueval. On the way orders came from the division to put two companies at the disposal of the 26th Brigade in Longueval, and accordingly "B" and "C" companies of the supporting battalion, the 4th, were instructed to report to the officer commanding the 5th Camerons there. The rest of the Brigade moved over the broken ground under heavy fire till they were close on the southern edge of the village.

It was Lieut.-Colonel Tanner's first business to find out the situation. He visited the commanding officers of the battalions of the 26th Infantry Brigade, and found that the northern part of Longueval and all wood adjoining the streets were still strongly held by the Germans, but the position in the greater part of the wood was obscure. Also it was ascertained that a company of the 5th Camerons had during the early hours of the morning occupied and dug themselves in along the line of Buchanan Street, in the south-west corner of the wood.

The position of this company offered a covered approach to the wood which would otherwise have proved a difficult undertaking; therefore it was decided to attack from a position of deployment along the line of Buchanan Street.

The O.C. 5th Camerons supplied a guide, and the troops were skilfully conducted, in single file, from the junction of the Montauban and Bazentine roads through a portion of the south end of Longueval, thence across the fields to Buchanan Street Trench, which was reached by the leading battalion, the 3rd S.A.I., at 6 a.m.

As the coming action was fought in a narrow area, where the smallest landmark had its importance, it is necessary to understand the nature of the place. From the road junction in Longueval there ran nearly due east a long ride which our men called Princes Street. Subsidiary rides branched off it to the north and south extending to the perimeter; these were in order from west to east, on the north side the Strand, Regent Street, and Bond Street; and on the south side Buchanan Street, Campbell Street, and King Street—an odd mixture of the nomenclature of London and Glasgow. Another ride, parallel to Princes Street and about half-way between it and the southern edge, ran from Buchanan Street to the eastern perimeter, and was named Rotten Row. Lieut.-Colonel Tanner decided to occupy the wood by first clearing the southern part—that is, the area south of Princes Street—and then pushing north from Princes Street, and occupying the Strand and the perimeter from its northern end round to the south-west corner. This would give him the whole of Delville except the north-west corner, which abutted on the uncaptured part of Longueval village.

At first the attack moved swiftly. By 7 o'clock the 3rd S.A.I., supported by one company of the 2nd, held everything south of Princes Street. Thereupon Lieut.-Colonel Tanner sent the remaining three companies of the 2nd to occupy the Strand and the northern perimeter. This proved to be a heavy undertaking. The three weak companies reached their objective, and found themselves compelled to hold a front of some 1,300 yards on which it was almost impossible to maintain connection. They were well supplied with shovels, and did their best to dig themselves in and wire the ground they had won; but as soon as they reached the edge the whole wood was violently shelled by the enemy, while machine-gun and rifle fire broke out from the strong German lines around the perimeter. Meantime, in the southern and eastern part, two patrols of the 3rd S.A.I., under the command of Captains Medlicott and Tomlinson, had managed to get to close quarters with the enemy, and had captured three officers, 135 other ranks, and a machine-gun.

At 2.40 p.m. Lieut.-Colonel Tanner reported to General Lukin that he had won the whole wood with the exception of strong-points in the north-west abutting on Longueval and the northern orchards. He had succeeded brilliantly in the first part of his task, but the problem of Delville was far less to carry the wood than to hold it. General Lukin's plan had been to thin out the troops in the wood as soon as the perimeter was reached, leaving it to be held by small infantry detachments with machine-guns. But now came the enemy's counter-attack, which made this plan impossible, for every available man was needed to resist the German pressure. About 3 o'clock elements of the 6th Bavarian Regiment of the 10th Bavarian Division attacked in force from the east, but were driven back by rifle-fire. At 4.40 p.m. Lieut.-Colonel Tanner reported that the enemy was also massing for an attack at the northern end, and at 6.30 he again reported an enemy concentration to the north and north-east. He informed General Lukin that his casualties had been heavy, one company of the 2nd S.A.I. having virtually been destroyed, and he asked for reinforcements. He had already received a company of the 4th S.A.I., and another company of that regiment was sent forward to reinforce the 3rd S.A.I. The 1st S.A.I. had now returned to General Lukin's command, and one of its companies was dispatched to reinforce the 2nd. At 7 p.m. General Lukin sent a staff officer to obtain full details of the position in the wood. The officers commanding the 2nd and 3rd S.A.I. were urged to see that their battalions, in spite of their fatigue, dug themselves in, since heavy shell-fire might be expected on the morrow. This had already been done. The officer commanding the 1st S.A.I. was ordered to detail special carrying platoons to keep up the supply of ammunition, and to put up a Vickers and a Lewis gun at the south-west corner of the wood to command the southern edge.

As the sun went down the activity of the enemy's guns increased, and the darkness of night was turned by shells and liquid fire into a feverish and blazing noon. The German rate of fire was often as high as 400 shells a minute. The position that evening was as follows:—The north-west corner of the wood was in the enemy's hands. The north-east corner was held from left to right by one and a half companies of the 2nd S.A.I., with one company of the 1st in support, and by one company of the 3rd S.A.I., with one company of the 4th in support. The south-east corner was held by two companies of the 3rd S.A.I. The southern face from left to right was held by one company of the 2nd S.A.I. and by one company of the 3rd, with one company of the 4th in support. A half company of the 2nd S.A.I. held the western third of Princes Street, with two companies of the 1st forming a defensive flank on the side of the village. The headquarters of the 2nd and 3rd S.A.I. were at the junction of Buchanan Street and Princes Street. Machine-guns were in position round the perimeter—four at the northern apex, four at the eastern end of the north-eastern face, and two in the eastern half of the southern face. It will be seen that twelve companies of infantry, now gravely weakened, were holding a wood little less than a mile square with a long, rambling perimeter—a wood on which every German battery was accurately ranged, and which was commanded at close quarters by a semi-circle of German trenches. Moreover, since the enemy held the north-west corner, he had a covered way of approach into the place. The only reserves of the South African Brigade were one company of the 1st S.A.I. and the two companies of the 4th, which had been lent to the 26th Brigade, and were due to return the following morning.

To complete the story of the day, we must record the doings of these two companies. On the 14th the 18th Division had cleared Trônes Wood and established their line up to Maltzhorn Farm. They joined hands with the 9th Division just west of Waterlot Farm, where, in the ruined sugar factory, the enemy had a position of great strength. On the morning of the 15th the 5th Camerons were attacking this point, and the two companies of the South African Scottish were to be used as troops to follow and consolidate. Major Hunt, who was in charge of the companies, sent a platoon from each to occupy the trenches close to the farm, which they did under heavy fire from the concealed posts to the south and east. The farm was not taken till the following day, and the work of the South Africans was therefore less that of consolidation than of protecting the skirts of the Camerons attack under a heavy German barrage. About six in the evening an enemy force was detected coming from Guillemont, but this was checked by our artillery barrage. An hour later the two companies were ordered to fall back and construct a strong point, and at 2.30 on the morning of the 16th they were relieved by the Camerons and withdrawn to the sunken road behind Longueval.

All through the furious night of the 15th-16th the troops in Delville Wood were working for dear life at entrenchments. No soldiers ever worked harder with the spade, but their task was nearly impossible. In that hard soil, coagulated by incessant shell-fire, and cumbered with a twisted mass of roots, wire, and tree trunks, the spade could make little way. Nevertheless, when the Sunday morning dawned, a good deal of cover had been provided.

At 2.35 a.m. General Lukin received orders from the Division that at all costs the northern entrance into Longueval must be blocked, and that for this purpose his Brigade must complete the capture of the northern perimeter of the wood and advance westward till they joined hands with the 27th Brigade. There was a lane called North Street, which was a continuation of the main street of Longueval from the point where the Flers road branched off to the north-east. Between these roads lay an orchard, the tactical importance of which will be obvious from the map. The plan was for the 27th Brigade to push north through the village and capture that orchard and the other enclosure east of North Street, and to join hands with the South Africans on the Flers road. This was to be the work of the 11th Royal Scots, while two companies of the 1st S.A.I. (those which, as has been already explained, had formed a defensive flank at the south-west corner of the wood) were to push north from the Princes Street line. The situation did not allow of a previous artillery bombardment, but it was arranged that a "preparation" by trench mortars should precede the infantry attack.

The advance was made at ten on the Sunday morning and failed completely, since the Royal Scots were held up in their area by a strongly wired stone redoubt, and the South Africans by machine-gun fire from the ominous orchard between the two roads. It was then that Private W. F. Faulds, of the 1st S.A.I., won the first Victoria Cross which fell to the lot of the Brigade. Lieutenant Craig had attempted to reach a German trench with a bombing section, and had fallen severely wounded half-way between the lines. He was rescued by Private Faulds, who, along with Privates Baker and Estment, crossed the parapet in broad daylight under a drenching machine-gun and rifle fire.

After this failure the attacking troops fell back to the trenches midway in the wood, and for the rest of the day had to endure a steady concentrated fire to which they had no means of effective reply. It was hot, dusty weather, and the enemy's curtain of shells made it almost impossible to bring up food and water or to remove the many casualties. That afternoon Lieut.-Colonel Dawson, commanding the 1st Regiment, met General Lukin in Longueval, and reported that his men were greatly exhausted. He asked for an early relief, but General Lukin could only repeat his divisional commander's instructions that at all costs the wood must be held. At the same time he was so impressed with the signs of strain and fatigue on the faces of the men that he submitted the matter to General Furse. The situation, indeed, was becoming desperate. Longueval and Delville had proved to be far too strongly held to be overrun at the first attack by one division. At the same time, until they were taken, the objectives of the battle of the 14th had not been achieved, and the stability of the whole right wing of our new front was endangered. Fresh troops could not yet be spared for the work, and the thing must be attempted again by the same weary and depleted battalions. It was a vicious circle. Longueval could not be won and held without Delville; Delville could not be won and held without Longueval; so what strength remained to the 9th Division had perforce to be divided between two simultaneous objectives.

That Sunday evening it was decided to make another effort against the north-west corner next morning. At 10.30 p.m. orders were received to withdraw all the infantry in Longueval village to a line south of Princes Street, and all infantry in the wood to the area east of the Strand, in order that the north-west corner of Delville and the north end of Longueval might be bombarded. The bombardment was to cease at 2 a.m. on the morning of Monday, the 17th, when the 27th Brigade and two companies of the 1st S.A.I. were to repeat their attack of the Sunday. Lieut.-Colonel Tanner, commanding in the wood, was instructed to order the men of the 2nd S.A.I., who were now holding the Strand, to move slowly forward so as to narrow the front of the 1st S.A.I. attacking from Princes Street.

The attack was made shortly before dawn, and did not succeed. Once again machine-gun fire from the fatal enclosures blocked any advance from east or south. The enemy, too, was in force just inside the angle of the wood. The 2nd S.A.I., moving west from the Strand according to plan, met with a stubborn resistance, and were forced to fall back to their original position.

That morning General Lukin visited Delville and discussed the position with his commanding officers. He had now no troops which had not been in action for at least forty-eight hours. It was the most wearing kind of battle, for there was rarely a chance of getting to close quarters with the enemy. Now and then the brilliant marksmanship of the South Africans was given its opportunity, but for the most part they had to wait under a continuous machine-gun and artillery fire, contending with a distant and impalpable foe. Their general was gravely concerned both at the fatigue of the men and the impossibility of making the wood anything but a death-trap. On his return to Brigade Headquarters he discussed the situation on the telephone with General Furse, but could get no hope of relief or reinforcements. General Congreve's instructions stood that Delville must be held at any cost.

There was no change in the situation during the Monday afternoon. Lieutenant Roseby, the Brigade Intelligence Officer, was sent forward to get information,

Portion of Delville Wood from corner of Longueval.

and was mortally wounded. During the evening Lieut.-Colonel Tanner was hit, and Lieut.-Colonel Thackeray, commanding the 3rd S.A.I., succeeded him in charge of the troops in the wood. That afternoon the news came that the 9th Division was drawing in its left flank, and that the 3rd Division, under Major-General Aylmer Haldane, was to attack Longueval that night from the west. About half-past seven General Lukin received orders to take before the next dawn the enemy trench parallel to and 200 yards distant from the south-east edge of the wood. The perimeter facing this trench was held by two companies of the 3rd S.A.I., and their commanding officer reported that the enemy trench before them was very strongly manned and contained several machine-guns. He added that he could not furnish more than 200 men for the attack without endangering the whole position. On receiving this news General Furse cancelled the operation. At half-past ten that night the Corps informed General Lukin that as soon as the 3rd Division completed the occupation of the village they would establish machine-guns on the north-west edge of the wood to protect his men. The attack was to take place at 3.45 a.m. on the 18th, and was to advance as far east as the Strand.

During the night all available reinforcements were pushed up to the perimeter, where they had to face a strong enemy attack. In the southern area the Germans advanced as far as Buchanan Street and Princes Street, and drove the South Africans out of some of their new trenches. A counter-attack cleared the ground, but only at the cost of heavy casualties. At a quarter to four the 76th Brigade of the 3rd Division succeeded in obtaining a footing in the orchard between Flers road and North Street. At eight in the morning Lieut.-Colonel Thackeray was ordered to send up patrols to get in touch with this Brigade, and directed the company of the 1st S.A.I., then occupying the Strand and the western part of Princes Street, to move forward for the purpose. They were not seriously opposed, and presently they joined hands with the 1st Gordons just west of the orchard.

On that morning, the fourth of the battle, came the crisis for the defenders of Delville. The arrival of the company of the 1st S.A.I. at the outskirts of the wood was the signal for the enemy to open a bombardment of unprecedented fury. Every part of the area was searched and smothered by shells, but the fire was most intense around the perimeter and down the Strand. At the same time the 76th Brigade was driven in, and the Germans began to enter the wood on the exposed left flank of the South Africans. About 9 o'clock an officer and fifty other ranks were dispatched as reinforcements. All through the morning the wearied handful, now rapidly thinning, held out as best they could. Their one relief was when the enemy came on to reap the fruits of his shelling, for then their admirable rifle-fire took heavy toll of him.

About half-past two in the afternoon the position had become desperate. Lieut.-Colonel Dawson was ordered to take forward as reliefs all the men available under his command—a total of 150 from the 1st S.A.I. These men had just been withdrawn after having been continuously in action for four days; they had had no rest. On arriving at Longueval Lieut.-Colonel Dawson placed his men in a trench at the south-east corner of the village, and went into the wood to find Lieut.-Colonel Thackeray. At the same time the men of the Trench Mortar Battery, numbering three officers and some eighty other ranks, under Lieutenant Phillips, were brought up from Montauban and placed at Lieut.-Colonel Dawson's disposal. Lieut.-Colonel Dawson found Lieut.-Colonel Thackeray in serious straits. In many parts of the wood the garrisons had been utterly destroyed, and everywhere north of Princes Street the few survivors had been forced back. Lieut.-Colonel Thackeray was now holding only the south-west corner, defined by Buchanan Street and the western part of Princes Street. The wounded filled the trenches, for it was impossible to remove them, since all the stretcher-bearers were casualties, and no men could be spared to take their places. Lieut.-Colonel Dawson, acting under General Lukin's instructions, did his best to cope with the situation. He sent Lieutenant Phillips and the Trench Mortar Battery men to reinforce Lieut.-Colonel Thackeray, and through the division procured additional stretcher-bearers from the cavalry, in addition to those from the 1st S.A.I.

At 6.5 p.m. that evening came the welcome intelligence that that night the South African Brigade would be relieved by the 26th Brigade. But a relief under such conditions was a slow and intricate business. By midnight the work had been partially carried out, and portions of the two companies of the 1st S.A.I. and the two companies of the 4th were withdrawn.

The enemy had brought up a new division—the 8th of the 4th (Magdeburg) Corps—and made repeated attacks against the Buchanan Street line. For two days and two nights the little remnant under Lieut.-Colonel Thackeray clung to the south-west corner of the wood against impossible odds, and did not break. The German method of assault was to push forward bombers and snipers, and then to advance in massed formation simultaneously from the north, north-east, and north-west. The three attacks on the night of the 18th-19th were repelled with heavy losses to the enemy; but in the last of them the South Africans were assaulted on three sides. All through the 19th the gallant handful suffered incessant shelling and sniping, the latter now from very close quarters. It was the same on the 20th, but still relief tarried. At last, at 6 o'clock that evening, troops of the 76th Brigade in the 3rd Division were able to take over what was left to us of Longueval and the little segment of Delville Wood. Lieut.-Colonel Thackeray marched out with two officers, both of whom were wounded, and 140 other ranks, made up of details from all the battalions of the Brigade. He spent the night at Talus Boise, and next day joined the rest at Happy Valley.

It is not easy to reproduce the circumstances of a battle so that a true impression may be made upon the minds of those who have not for themselves seen the reality of modern war. The six days and five nights during which the South African Brigade held the most difficult post on the British front—a corner of death on which the enemy fire was concentrated at all hours from three sides, and into which fresh German troops, vastly superior in numbers to the defence, made periodic incursions only to be broken and driven back—constitute an epoch of terror and glory scarcely equalled in the campaign. There were positions as difficult, but they were not held so long; there were cases of as protracted a defence, but the assault was not so violent and continuous. The closest parallel is to be found, perhaps, in some of the incidents at Verdun, and in the resistance of units of the old British regulars at the point of the Ypres salient in 1914; but even there we shall scarcely find an equal feat of tenacity, and certainly none superior. Delville Wood was not finally taken till the 25th of August, a month later, when the 14th Light Division cleared it for good. The high value set upon it by the enemy is proved by the fact that he used his best troops against it—successively the 10th Bavarian Division, the 8th Division of the 4th Corps, and the 5th of the 3rd Corps. The South Africans measured their strength against the flower of the German army, and did not draw back from the challenge. As a feat of human daring and fortitude the fight is worthy of eternal remembrance by South Africa and Britain, but no historian's pen can give that memory the sharp outline and the glowing colour which it deserves.

At midnight on 14th July, when General Lukin received his orders, the Brigade numbered 121 officers and 3,032 men. When Lieut.-Colonel Thackeray marched out on the 20th he had a remnant of 143, and the total ultimately assembled in Happy Valley was about 750. The casualties were—for the 1st S.A.I., 558; for the 2nd, 482; for the 3rd, 771; and for the 4th, 509. These figures included 23 officers who were killed, 7 who died of wounds, 47 who were wounded, and 15 who were prisoners or missing. All the commissioned ranks of the 2nd and 3rd S.A.I. who were in the wood became casualties, as did all the officers of the Machine-Gun Company attached to the Brigade.

If we take the casualties from the 1st July, the total is 2,815—made up of 502 killed, 1,735 wounded, and 578 missing.

There is no more solemn moment in war than the parade of men after battle. The few hundred haggard survivors of the Brigade in the bright sunshine in Happy Valley were too weary and broken to realize how great a thing they had done. Tributes had come to them from high quarters. Sir Douglas Haig had sent his congratulations. The commander of the Fourth Army, Sir Henry Rawlinson, had written that "in the capture of Delville Wood the gallantry, perseverance, and determination of the South African Brigade deserves the highest commendation." They had earned the praise of their own intrepid commanding officers, who had gone through the worst side by side with their men. "Each individual," said Lieut.-Colonel Tanner's report "was firm in the knowledge of his confidence in his comrades, and was, therefore, able to fight with that power which good discipline alone can produce. A finer record of this spirit could not be found than the line of silent bodies along the Strand over which the enemy had not dared to tread." But the most impressive tribute was that of their Brigadier. When the remnant of his Brigade paraded before him, General Lukin took the salute with uncovered head and eyes not free from tears.

CHAPTER II.

THE BATTLE OF THE SOMME: THE BUTTE DE WARLENCOURT.

(July—December, 1916.)

After the fight at Longueval and Delville Wood the 9th Division left the Somme and was transferred from the XIII Corps in the Fourth Army to the IV Corps, under Lieut.-General Sir Henry Wilson, in the First Army. The South African Brigade marched to Maricourt on 23rd July, where it entrained for Hengest, and on the 27th arrived in the Frévillers area, north of the main road between Arras and St. Pol.

Here its first task was reorganization. Drafts to the number of 40 officers and 2,826 other ranks had been sent from Bordon during July, and their training had to be completed before they could be absorbed into the different regiments.* On 5th August, the Army Commander, Sir Charles Monro, inspected the Brigade, which at the moment showed a parade strength of 62 officers and 2,523 men. By the third week in the month the Brigade

---

* Lieutenant-Colonel Tanner was wounded on 17th July and his second in command, Major Gee, took over the 2nd Regiment. Major Gee was killed almost at once, and as there were no senior officers of the 2nd left Major Heal, of the 1st, took over command. This he held till the arrival from England at the end of August of Lieutenant-Colonel Christian, who took command of the 2nd Regiment. After the death of Lieutenant-Colonel Jones the 4th Regiment was under Major D. M. MacLeod. He was wounded on the 17th July, after which Major D. R. Hunt took over, and continued in command till 31st December, 1916.

was sufficiently rested and reconstituted to take its place once again in the front line, and on 23rd August it took over from the 26th Brigade the Berthonval and Carency sections of the Vimy area.

Vimy was a quiet area, for the great battle on the Somme continued, and this stage was for the Brigade almost barren of incident. The exception was a raid into the enemy's trenches on the night of the 13th September, carried out by parties from "B" and "D" Companies of the 2nd S.A.I., under the command of Lieutenants Lilburn and Walsh. There was a bright moon occasionally obscured by passing clouds; but the raiding parties managed to reach the enemy's side of our wire without being observed. Our artillery put down a barrage, and under its cover the men doubled across No Man's Land and jumped into the German trenches, the barrage lifting as they arrived there. Prisoners were secured, dug-outs were bombed, and at a pre-arranged signal the raiders returned to their lines before the German barrage began. Their casualties were only two, though one was so severely wounded that he could not be moved from the German lines.

On 23rd September the Brigade was relieved, and on the 25th it moved to a new training area, that of the Third Army. On 5th October the 9th Division was restored to the Fourth Army, and on the 7th the South African Brigade marched southward to the Somme. Next day, in heavy rain, they relieved the 141st Brigade of the 47th Division in Mametz Wood, and on the 9th moved to High Wood, where they took over from the 142nd Brigade.

Since the 20th of July much had happened on the Somme. The advance of 1st July had carried the first enemy position on a broad front, but the failure of the attack north of the Ancre had made the breach eight miles less than the original plan. The advance of 14th July gave us the second enemy position on a still narrower front—from Bazentin-le-Petit to Longueval. The danger now was that any further movement might result in the formation of a sharp and precarious salient; so the Commander-in-Chief broadened the breach by striking out to left and right, taking first Pozières and the high ground at Mouquet Farm, and then on the other flank Guillemont and Ginchy. This made the gap in the second enemy line seven miles wide, and brought us in most places to the highest ground, from which direct observation could be had over the slopes and pockets to the east. On 3rd September the Allies everywhere between Thiepval and Estrées were facing the German third line. At the outset of the battle this third position had been only in embryo, but before the assault of 14th July it had been for the most part completed, and by the beginning of September it had been elaborately fortified, and a fourth position prepared behind it. The third line was based on a string of fortified villages which lay on the reverse slopes of the main ridge—Courcelette, Martinpuich, Flers, Lesbœufs, and Morval. Behind it was an intermediate line, with Le Sars, Eaucourt l'Abbaye, and Gueudecourt as strong points in it. Further back lay the newly made fourth line, just west of the Bapaume-Péronne road, covering the villages of Sailly-Saillisel and Le Transloy. This was the line protecting Bapaume, and at the moment the final German prepared position.

On Friday, 15th September, the Commander-in-Chief struck from a point south-east of Thiepval to Ginchy, with a force the larger part of which, such as the Guards, the Canadians, and the New Zealanders, was fresh to the Somme area. He used for the first time the new British tanks, and in one day advanced to an average depth of a mile on a front of more than six, taking Courcelette, Martinpuich, and Flers. Only on the right was there any serious check. On 25th September he struck again between Combles and Martinpuich, and for the second time advanced one mile on a front of six, and took Morval, Lesbœufs, and Gueudecourt, while on the 26th the right wing of the Fifth Army carried Thiepval and the whole of that crest. That evening the Allied fortunes in the West had never looked brighter. The enemy was now back in his fourth line, and had lost all the advantages of the higher ground. His *moral* was seriously shaken, and it appeared as if his great machine was getting out of gear.

The guns were scarcely silent after the attack of the 26th when the weather broke, and October was one succession of tempestuous gales and drenching rains. Now appeared the supreme difficulty of trench warfare. For three months the Allies had been slowly advancing, blasting their way forward with their guns before each infantry attack, and the result was that the fifty square miles of old battleground which lay behind their front lines had been tortured out of recognition. The little country roads had been wholly destroyed, and, since they never had much of a bottom, the road-menders had nothing to build upon. New roads were hard to make, for the chalky soil had been so churned up by shelling that it had lost all cohesion. In all the area there were but two good highways, and by the third month of the battle even these showed signs of wear. The consequence was that there were now two No Man's Lands—one between the front lines and one between the old enemy front and the front we had won. The second was the bigger problem, for across it must be brought the supplies of a great army. It was a war of motor transport, and we were running the equivalent of steam engines not on prepared tracks but on highroads, running them day and night in endless relays. The problem was difficult enough in fine weather, but when the rain came it turned the whole land into a morass. Every road became a watercourse, and in the hollows the mud was as deep as a man's thighs. The army must be fed, troops must be relieved, guns must be supplied, so there could be no slackening of the traffic. Off the roads the ground was one vast bog, dug-outs crumbled in, and communication trenches ceased to be. It was into such miserable warfare, under persistent rain in a decomposing land, that the South African Brigade was now flung.

The line of the Fourth Army from a point north-east of Courcelette ran southward for the most part along the foot of the slopes which culminated in High Wood, and which were known to us as the Thiepval-Morval ridge. But a special topographical feature must be noted, for on it depended the fighting in October. From that ridge a series of spurs descended eastward into the hollow, one of which specially concerns us—the hammer-headed spur immediately west of Flers, at the end of which stood the odd tumulus called the Butte de Warlencourt. Below the eastern edge of this spur lay the German fourth position. It was a position on reverse slopes, and thus screened from direct observation, though our command on the high ground to the west gave us a view of its hinterland. Our own possession of the heights, great though the advantages were, had this drawback, that our communications had to descend the reverse slopes, and were thus partly exposed to the enemy's observation and long-range fire. The task of the Fourth Army in this sector was, therefore, to carry the spurs, and so get within assaulting distance of the German fourth line. The spurs were not part of the German main front, but were held as intermediate positions, every advantage being taken of sunken roads, of ruins, and of the undulations of the country. Till they were carried no general assault on the main front could be undertaken.

At first things went well. From Flers north-westward, in front of Eaucourt l'Abbaye and Le Sars, ran a very strong trench system which we called the Flers Line, and which was virtually a switch connecting the old German third line, now in our hands, with the intermediate positions on the spurs. The capture of

Flers gave us the south-eastern part of this line, and during the last days of September and the beginning of October the rest of it was won. On the 1st of October the 50th and 47th Divisions carried the Flers Line north of Destremont Farm, and the ruined abbey of Eaucourt, though in the latter remnants of the 6th Bavarian Division made for some days a stout resistance. On 7th October the 23rd Division took the village of Le Sars, on the Albert-Bapaume road; but the 47th Division, on their right, failed to reach the Butte de Warlencourt. These two divisions were now relieved, and the 15th and the 9th took their places, with orders to carry the Butte and the German intermediate line.

During the day of 9th October the 2nd S.A.I., under Lieut.-Colonel Christian, to the strength of 20 officers and 578 other ranks, took over the portion of the front line to be held by the Brigade. The relief, with the exception of two posts, was complete by 1.25 a.m. on the 10th and shortly before daybreak the missing posts were discovered.

The boundary of the 9th Division on the left was the road from the Butte de Warlencourt to Martinpuich, where it ran along the depression of the ground west of Eaucourt. The South African Brigade was on the left of the division, and its brigade boundary ran through the ruins of Eaucourt l'Abbaye, beyond which the 26th Brigade held the front. The 27th Brigade was in divisional reserve. "B" and "C" Companies of the 2nd S.A.I. held the front line, as shown in the map, together with two strong posts, Nos. 58 and 77, on their left and right fronts respectively. "A" and "D" Companies were in the support trenches of the old Flers Line running along the south-west side of Eaucourt l'Abbaye. The German front trenches, known to us as Snag and Tail, lay about 1,000 yards from our front line, and conformed roughly to its shape. Beyond them, running through the Butte de Warlencourt, was the enemy main intermediate position, cutting the Albert-Bapaume road beyond Le Sars. The confused fighting of the past weeks and the constant rains had made the whole front on both sides indeterminate. Odd lengths of fantastically named trenches abounded, and at any one moment it was doubtful which were held by the Germans and which could be claimed by the British.

On the left of the South African front, and under their control, stood the ruins of a mill. The first instructions of the 2nd S.A.I. were to link up the posts 58 and 77 with the mill; but owing to the slowness of the relief this could not be done till the second night, when some 600 yards of trench were dug. During the whole of the 10th and the 11th the 2nd S.A.I. was heavily shelled; but their casualties were not large. On the 11th General Furse issued orders for an attack during daylight on the 12th in conjunction with the 26th Brigade on their right, and the 44th Brigade of the 15th Division on their left. The enemy's trenches were accordingly reconnoitred, and a certain number of machine-guns located. So far as could be judged, there was no wire in the immediate vicinity. Orders were issued to push out a post to the point marked 93, and to link it up with the mill, but this instruction was presently cancelled. A new communication trench was dug between Flers Trench and the front line.

The attack on the 12th was fixed for 2.5 in the afternoon. The assault was to be carried out on a one-battalion front by the 2nd and 4th S.A.I., the 2nd S.A.I. leading, with the 3rd and 1st in reserve. There were two objectives; the first the enemy trenches called Snag and Tail, and the second the main intermediate line through the Butte de Warlencourt. The cloudy morning dissolved after midday in a drizzle of rain. At 2.5, after a well-arranged barrage, the 2nd S.A.I. crossed the parapets, closely followed by the 4th, under Major Hunt. One minute after zero an enemy barrage of exceptional

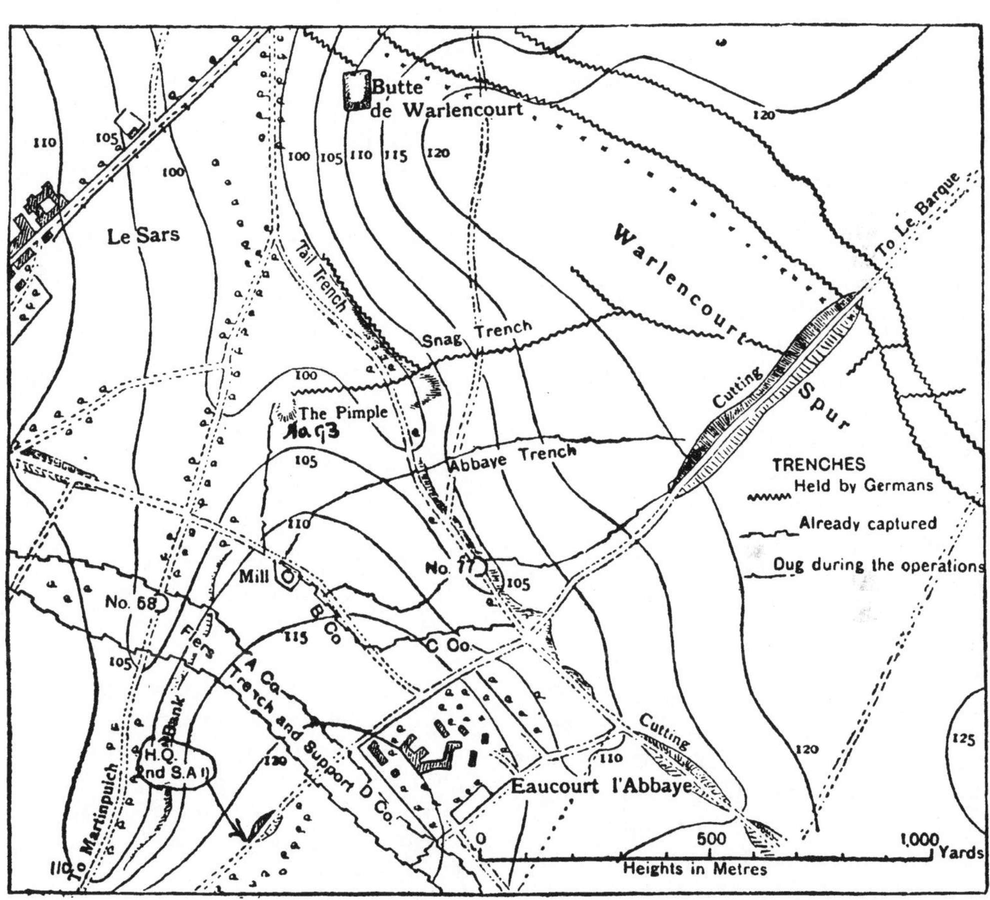

THE FIGHTING BEFORE THE BUTTE DE WARLENCOURT: BATTLE OF THE SOMME.

violence began, with the result that in a quarter of an hour the telephone wires to the front line were cut, and no reports were received for some time. In the misty weather it was impossible to see any distance, and the difficulty was increased owing to a smoke barrage, which we had laid down around the Butte, drifting in our direction. Presently it appeared that the enemy was following a new practice. The ground over which we were attacking was a gentle slope, perfectly suited to machine-gun fire. He had his machine-guns placed well back in prepared positions, and caught our attack at long range. Under this blast no troops could live, and presently the impetus of the assault died away, long before the first objective had been obtained.

At 4 p.m. General Lukin received a message from Captain Ross of the 4th S.A.I. that he, with some details of the 2nd, was holding a line of shell-holes and a shallow trench half-way between our old front line and the first objective, and that in front of him, near the first objective, was a company of the 4th, while a part of the 2nd seemed to be farther forward. General Lukin had already sent forward a company of the 3rd S.A.I. to hold the old front line, and he now ordered two officers' patrols from this company to clear up the situation. They reported that the Brigade had nowhere reached its first objective. A message was received from Lieutenant Pearse, 2nd S.A.I., that he, with about 60 men, had dug themselves in about 150 yards south of point 93. As the attacking battalions had suffered heavily, and were now more or less disorganized, General Lukin ordered the 3rd S.A.I. to relieve them, while the 1st was moved up in support. The relief was no light task, owing to the congested state of the communication trenches, and the difficulty of obtaining reliable guides; and it was not till after dawn on the 13th that the 2nd and 4th S.A.I. were brought back to High Wood.

On the 13th Lieut.-Colonel Thackeray, commanding the 3rd S.A.I., withdrew Lieutenant Pearse's party during the evening. Meantime much work had been done in digging trenches and consolidating the ground won.

Orders were received from the Division at 6.15 p.m. to reconnoitre the strong-point 93, with the object of occupying it. A patrol reached it with little opposition, and found there many signs of German occupation, including a field and two machine gun emplacements and a deep dug-out. This place, a little mound some 60 feet long, 12 feet wide, and from 12 to 15 feet high, afterwards became known as the Pimple. The patrol did not return till daybreak, so it was impossible to occupy the Pimple that night. On the afternoon of the 14th the officer commanding the 3rd S.A.I. was instructed to occupy the Pimple after dark that evening and join it up with the front line at the mill. "B" Company of the 3rd S.A.I., under Captain Sprenger, was detailed for the work. Lieutenant Mallett led the advance for 400 yards and reached the mound, which was thereafter garrisoned by a party under Lieutenant Medlicott. Lieutenant Mallett then entered the trench running from the Pimple towards the enemy position in Snag and Tail Trenches, and bombed the enemy out of a portion of this till he was driven back by machine-gun fire. Another party, however, under Lieutenants Harris and Estill, continued the work, and succeeded in taking and holding a considerable part of this section of the old German communications. That night the place was heavily bombed by Germans moving along the trenches. The garrison of "B" Company continued to hold the Pimple and the captured trenches until relieved by "A" Company of the 3rd on the night of the 15th-16th. The casualties during the operation amounted to 3 officers and 35 other ranks. It was one of the most gallant exploits during this stage of the battle.

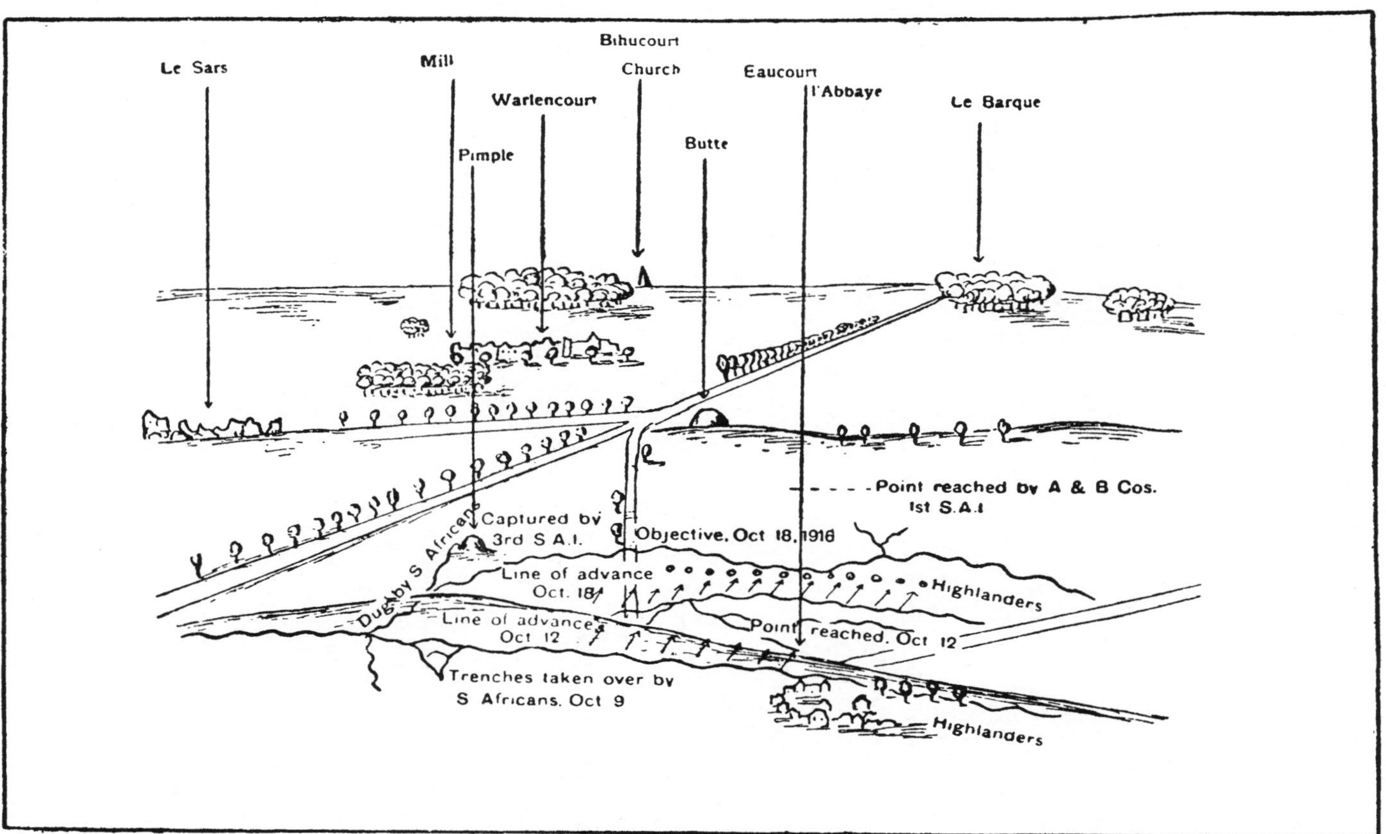

SCENE OF SOUTH AFRICAN BRIGADE'S ADVANCE AGAINST THE BUTTE DE WARLENCOURT POSITION.

On the night of the 16th-17th the 3rd S.A.I. was withdrawn to the support line, and their place in the front trenches was taken by the 1st, under Lieut.-Colonel Dawson. Meantime, large working parties had been employed in widening and deepening the communication trench between the Pimple and our front line and back to Flers Switch. On the 17th orders came from the division for an assault in the early morning of the 18th against the same objectives which had been attacked without success on the 12th.

All that evening and for most of the night heavy rain fell, so that the trenches and parapets were mere undulations in a quagmire. The front-line trench being deep and narrow with few fire-steps, it was difficult for the men to leave it, and realizing this, the company commanders began getting their troops out more than an hour before the time fixed for the attack. Zero hour was at 3.40 a.m. on the 18th, and when it came the three assaulting companies of the 1st S.A.I. were already formed up in No Man's Land.

Keeping as close as they dared to their barrage, the 1st S.A.I. advanced, with "C" Company on the left, "B" Company in the centre, and "A" on the right. They disappeared into the rain, and for several hours were unheard of. When news came it was news of failure. "C" Company passed the communication trench leading south from the Pimple, and came to that junction of Tail and Snag Trenches called the Nose of the Switch. Here they were held up by wire at the foot of a steep bank in front of the German line, and were also heavily bombed from the trenches themselves. The leading platoon was almost entirely shot down, and though an officer and six men of the following platoon managed to get into the German trench, they, too, immediately fell. The only officer left was Captain Jenkins, who was himself wounded; and, seeing that the enemy line was so strongly held, and that there was no hope of success for what remained of his company, he ordered the company sergeant-major to withdraw the survivors to their original line. The casualties of "C" Company were 69 out of the 100 who crossed the parapet.

The fate of "A" and "B" Companies was still harder. The two companies advanced rapidly behind our barrage and entered Snag Trench. They failed, however, to realize that they had reached their objective, and continued beyond it. The whole place was so battered by shell-fire that the trench outlines had become obscure. They saw about 600 yards on their right some of the Highlanders of the 26th Brigade, but they had now wholly lost touch with their flanks, and the enemy was filtering in between them and their old front. Lieutenant Stapleton with a few stragglers succeeded in returning, after killing ten Germans and taking nineteen prisoners; two officers and sixteen other ranks were captured; but with these exceptions all the men of "A" and "B" Companies were killed.

At daybreak a gallant attempt was made by Major Ormiston, commanding the troops on the Pimple, to bomb along the trench leading to the junction of the Tail and Snag Trenches, but it broke down under machine-gun fire from the German strong-point at the Nose. A block was established about 50 yards up the trench from the Pimple, but no further progress could be made, since the trench dipped into a hollow, and was wholly commanded by the Germans at the Nose.

During the night a company of the 3rd S.A.I., under Captain Langdale, had been moved forward to the front line and put at Lieut.-Colonel Dawson's disposal. They took up a position at the mill. A company of the 4th S.A.I. was sent to replace it in the support line. The key of the enemy position was clearly the Nose, and until this could be thoroughly bombarded progress was impossible. Communications, however, were so difficult

BUTTE DE WARLENCOURT.

that all day our guns were firing on the wrong point.

On the 18th Lieut.-Colonel Dawson was ordered to renew the attack at 5.45 p.m. He ordered "D" Company of the 1st S.A.I. to attack from the Pimple, while Captain Langdale's company of the 3rd advanced from Pearse's trench. Captain Langdale advanced with only one platoon and two Lewis gun teams. He entered Snag Trench without opposition, and moved along it to the right for some 200 yards, where he made a block and left a Lewis gun. He then moved westward to a point about 25 yards from the Nose, where he came upon three German machine-guns in action. He did not feel strong enough to attack them himself, and after remaining there about an hour withdrew his men to the original front line. The bombing attack from the Pimple had also failed. Lieut.-Colonel Dawson ordered Captain Langdale to return at once and reoccupy Snag Trench, and this was done between twelve and one on the morning of the 19th.

Meanwhile the G.O.C. South African Brigade had sent forward a company of the 4th S.A.I., under Captain Ross, with instructions to carry out a fresh attack at the junction of Snag and Tail Trenches and Captain Langdale was informed of this. Captain Ross reached the front line about 4 a.m. on the morning of the 19th. At about 5 o'clock the enemy launched an assault with bombs and *flammenwerfer* against Captain Langdale's and Captain Ross's men in Snag Trench, and drove them out, with heavy casualties to Captain Ross's company. The position now was that Snag and Tail Trenches were held in force by the enemy, and that we were everywhere back in our old line except on the extreme right, where some details of the 3rd and 4th S.A.I. remained on the left flank of the 26th Brigade.

On the morning of the 19th it was decided to make another attempt to clear Snag Trench, and for the purpose a company of the 3rd S.A.I., under Lieutenant Elliott, was ordered to report to Lieut.-Colonel Dawson. All that morning the two machine-guns at the Pimple, under Major Ormiston, had enfiladed the trench, and by the afternoon few of the enemy were left in Snag Trench; but the machine-guns were still at the Nose, and our artillery seemed unable to touch them.

At noon Lieutenant Elliott reported at Lieut.-Colonel Dawson's Headquarters, and was instructed to occupy Snag Trench, to get in touch with the 26th Brigade on his right, and then to work his way towards the Nose and drive out the enemy there. At five minutes to three Lieutenant Elliott entered Snag Trench without difficulty, but could not advance towards the Nose, beyond which Major Ormiston, at the Pimple, was waiting to attack as soon as there was a supporting movement from the east. The thing had now become hopeless. Lieut.-Colonel Dawson had not a single officer or man fit to make another journey to the front line. The mud was so thick that rifles, machine-guns, and Lewis guns were constantly jamming, and among the little party on the Pimple there was not one rifle which could be fired. In many of the trenches the mud was three feet deep, and the wounded had to be dug out at once before they suffocated. Every man was utterly exhausted.

That night the remnant under Lieut.-Colonel Dawson was relieved by the 6th K.O.S.B. from the 27th Brigade, and early on the morning of the 20th all were back in High Wood.

In the ten days from the 9th to the 19th October the South African casualties were approximately 1,150, including 45 officers, 16 of whom were killed.

On the 21st October the Brigade, with the exception of the 3rd S.A.I., which was in High Wood in reserve to the 27th Brigade, moved to Mametz Wood. On the 23rd orders were received that the Brigade would be in reserve in the attack to be carried out by the 9th Division on the 25th. Presently these orders were cancelled, and the entire division was taken out of the line. At the end of the month it moved north to an area south of the Doullens-Arras road, and became part of the VI Corps in the Third Army.

During November the 1st S.A.I. was in huts at Duisans, the 2nd at Lattre St. Quentin, the 3rd at Wanquetin, and the 4th billeted in Arras, where it was engaged in improving the defences of that city. The other battalions were occupied in training, in the construction of new roads and cable trenches, and in the other preliminary work necessary in the area of a coming battle. For it had already been decided that the great thrust of the spring would be from Arras eastward.

On 2nd December General Lukin was promoted to the command of the 9th Division with the rank of Major-General, on General Furse's appointment as Master-General of the Ordnance. He was succeeded in the command of the Brigade by Lieut.-Colonel Dawson, of the 1st S.A.I., who was succeeded in turn by Major F. H. Heal.

CHAPTER III.

THE BATTLE OF ARRAS.

(January—July, 1917.)

In November, 1916, a conference of representatives of all the Allied Powers was held at French General Headquarters, and a plan made for the campaign of the following year. Sir Douglas Haig desired to undertake in 1917 a great offensive in Flanders, with a view to clearing the Belgian coast, for in that area he believed that success would give the highest strategic reward. But before this movement began it was desirable to reap the fruits of the Battle of the Somme. In November the enemy was penned in an awkward salient between the valleys of the Ancre and the Scarpe. The British Commander-in-Chief proposed early in the spring to attack this salient simultaneously on two sides—the Fifth Army moving on the Ancre front, and the Third Army attacking from the north-west about Arras. At the same time the First Army was to carry the Vimy Ridge, the possession of which was necessary to secure the left flank of our operations farther south. So soon as this was completed, the Flanders campaign would begin with an assault on the Messines Ridge, to be followed by an attack eastward from the Ypres Salient.

This plan had to be wholly recast. The British and French Governments decided that Sir Douglas Haig must take over a longer front, and before the end of February, 1917, the British right was as far south as a point opposite the town of Roye. Again, the retreat of the Germans during February and March, 1917, destroyed the salient which Haig had proposed to attack. There now remained nothing of the preliminary movement as originally planned, except the carrying of the Vimy Ridge. But a fresh scheme had been proposed by the French and accepted by the British Government. Under the new French Commander-in-Chief, Nivelle, an ambitious operation was conceived on the heights of the Aisne, which, it was trusted, would open the way to Laon. In this action the old method of limited objectives was to be relinquished; and Nivelle hoped, by means of his new tactics and by an unexampled concentration of troops, to break through the enemy lines on a broad front and restore the war of movement. This attack was fixed for the middle of April. It would operate against the southern pivot of the Siegfried zone, and it was arranged that Sir Douglas Haig should use his forces against the northern pillar east of Arras, and should strike a week before.

In December, 1916, the 9th Division relieved the 35th Division, which was then holding the trenches in front of Arras. The front held by the South African Brigade extended now for 1,800 yards northwards from the River Scarpe. For three months they remained in this section, during the severest winter known in France for many years. For most of December it rained, and in January and February there came heavy snow and bitter frost. On 14th January the 9th Division passed from the VI Corps to the XVII Corps, commanded by Lieut.-General Sir Charles Fergusson, and this involved an alteration in the divisional boundaries. The 26th Brigade, which was holding a line of trenches south of the Scarpe, now relieved certain Canadian units; and the whole of the new corps front, since several of its divisions had not yet arrived, was held by the 9th Division, with all three brigades in line. Early in February the 51st (Highland Territorial) Division took over the ground held by the 26th Brigade, and the 34th Division relieved the 27th Brigade, when the 9th Division's front from St. Pancras Trench to the Scarpe was held by the South African Brigade.

These months were filled with preparations for the great spring attack. New trenches had to be made and old trenches diverted; headquarters had to be found for battalions and brigades, and emplacements constructed for artillery and trench mortars. In addition to this, patrols and wiring parties were busy every night. On January 3rd, 1917, a party from the 3rd S.A.I., commanded by Lieutenants B. W. Goodwin and W. F. G. Thomas, made a successful raid on the German trenches. After our barrage had drenched the enemy front line the raiders entered the German trenches, which were found to be very deep and magnificently constructed, though badly damaged by our gun-fire. Only one prisoner was brought in, but a number of dug-outs and concrete machine-gun emplacements were destroyed, and the enemy suffered many casualties.

On 4th March the South African Brigade was relieved by the 26th Brigade, and marched from Arras to the neighbourhood of Ostreville, where they began their intensive training for the coming offensive. Their casualties during the previous three months in the line had been 2 officers and 49 other ranks killed, and 5 officers and 166 other ranks wounded. The health of the men, considering the severity of the weather, had been extraordinarily good. On 5th March Sir Douglas Haig inspected the 1st and 4th S.A.I., and complimented them highly on their smartness.

While the South Africans were beginning their intensive training, the Germans were completing their retirement from the Bapaume Ridge to the Siegfried Line. At the hamlet of Tilloy-lez-Mofflaines, on the Arras-Cambrai road, this line branched off from the old front. Beaurains was now ours, and Arras was therefore free from its former encirclement in the south. The German position from the northern pivot of the new Siegfried Line to Lens was very strong, consisting of three main systems, each constructed on the familiar pattern of four parallel lines of trenches studded with redoubts, and linked up by numerous switches. A special and very powerful switch line ran for 5½ miles from the village of Feuchy northward across the Scarpe to beyond Thélus, and constituted what was virtually a fourth line of defence. The whole defensive belt was from two to five miles deep, but the German High Command were not content with it. They had designed an independent line running from Drocourt, south-east of Lens, to the Siegfried Line at Quéant as an alternative in case of an assault on the Arras salient. Towards the close of March this position, which was to become famous as the Drocourt-Quéant Switch, was not complete. It was intended as a protection to Douai and Cambrai, the loss of which would have made the whole Siegfried system untenable. But it was designed only as an extra precaution, for there was every confidence in the mighty ramified defences between Lens and Tilloy and in the resisting power of the northern Siegfried section. The country through which the German positions ran was peculiarly suited to their purpose. It represented the breakdown of the Picardy wolds into the flats of the Scheldt, the last foothills of the uplands of northern France. Long, low spurs reach out to the eastward, separating the valleys of the Scarpe, the Cojeul, and the Sensée, and their sides are scored with smaller valleys—an ideal terrain for a defensive battle.

It will be seen that Sir Douglas Haig had a formidable problem before him. The immediate key of the area was Vimy Ridge, the capture of which was necessary to protect the flank of any advance farther south. It was clear that no strategic result could be obtained unless the Drocourt-Quéant Switch were breached, and that meant an advance of well over six miles. A result so far-reaching demanded a combination of fortunate chances, which as yet had not been vouchsafed to us in any battle of the campaign.

The city of Arras, situated less than a mile inside the British lines, was, like Ypres, the neck of a bottle, and through it and its environs went most of the transport for the new battle front. A city makes a difficult base for a great attack. It must be the route of advancing infantry and their billeting area, and it is a mark which the enemy guns can scarcely miss. To minimize this danger the British generals had recourse to a bold plan. They resolved in this section to assemble their armies underground. After the fashion of old French towns, Arras had huge ancient sewers. A map of them was found, and the underground labyrinth was explored and enlarged. Moreover, the town had grown over the quarries from which the older part of it had been built, and these also were discovered. The result was that a second city was created below the first, where three divisions could be assembled in perfect security. Here it was arranged that the greater part of the VI Corps should assemble for the attack due east of the city.

During these days the British artillery was very busy. So great was the concentration of guns that they could have been placed wheel to wheel from end to end of the battle-front. Various "Chinese" attacks were organized, as rehearsals and to mislead the enemy. In the third week of March a systematic cutting of the German wire began, and our heavy artillery shelled their back areas and communications. On Thursday, the 5th of April, a steady bombardment opened against all the main German positions, more especially the great fortress of the Vimy Ridge. Wonderful counter-battery work was done, and battery after battery of the enemy was put out of action, located partly by direct observation from the air, and partly by our new device for sound-identification. These were for the most part days of clear, cold, spring weather, with the wind in the north-east; and from dawn to dark our airplanes fought on their own account a mighty battle. The history of that week must rank as an epoch in the campaign in the air. It was a time of heavy losses, for the British airmen kept up one continuous offensive. Forty-eight of our own planes failed to return, and forty-six of the enemy's were destroyed or driven down out of control.

The British front of attack was slightly over twelve miles long, from Givenchy-en-Gohelle in the north to a point just short of Croisilles in the south. On the left was the Canadian Corps under Sir Julian Byng, with one British brigade, directed against the Vimy Ridge. On their right lay the Third Army. Its northern Corps, next to the Canadians, was the XVII, with three divisions in line—from left to right the 51st, the 34th, and the 9th; and one, the 4th, in support. The central Corps was the VI, with, in line, the 15th, 12th, and the 3rd Divisions, and the 37th in support. On the right of the battle was the VII Corps, with the 14th, 56th, and 30th Divisions in line, and the 21st forming a pivot on the right.

On 13th March the 9th Division had received the plan of attack, and from 5th April onward its divisional guns—269 pieces in all—were busy with the preliminary bombardment. On Friday, 6th April, the South African Brigade—with the exception of the 1st S.A.I., which was in line—was inspected by Lieut.-General J. C. Smuts, but lately returned from his East African campaign.

On the following day the 1st S.A.I. was ordered to carry out a daylight raid. The attempt was originally timed for eleven in the morning, but it was subsequently postponed to three in the afternoon. At that hour, under cover of our barrage, a party of 5 officers and 50 other ranks, under Captain T. Roffe, crossed our parapets, and reached the German trenches without a casualty. A large dug-out was found, out of which three Germans of the 8th Bavarian Regiment were taken prisoner. Their object having been accomplished the party retired, and reached their own lines with the loss of one killed and three wounded.

That night the Brigade, less the 1st S.A.I., marched from its training area to Arras, and took up its quarters in the northern outskirts. The artillery preparation continued to be intense till the next day, Sunday, 8th April, the day originally fixed for the attack. That Sunday the weather was clear and calm, with a foretaste of spring. A lull seemed to fall upon the British front, and the ear-splitting din of the past week died away into sporadic bombardments. It is possible that this sudden quiet outwitted the enemy. He was perfectly aware of the coming attack, and he knew its area and objectives. He had expected it each day, and each day had been disappointed. On the Sunday he began to reply, and rained shells at intervals into the streets of Arras, but did little harm. The troops of attack there were waiting comfortably in cellars and underground assembly stations. In the late evening the weather changed, the wind shifted to the west, and blew up to rain and squalls of snow. During the night there were long spells of quiet, broken by feverish outbreaks of enemy fire from Vimy to Croisilles. Our own batteries were for the most part silent.

That night the South African Brigade began to assemble in the front and support lines preparatory to their attack. The 9th Division was holding some 1,800 yards of front from the river Scarpe to a point just north of the Bailleul road. It had the 26th Brigade on the right next the river, the South African Brigade in the centre, and the 27th Brigade on the left. Three objectives had been given to the Division, known as the Black, the Blue, and the Brown Lines. The Black Line, from the river Scarpe to Chantecler, including the village of Laurent-Blangy, represented the last line of the enemy's front system, and was approximately 800 yards away from our own front trenches. To reach this line two, and in places three, trench lines had to be taken and passed. The Blue Line was 900 yards east of the first objective, and represented the enemy's second trench system on the Arras-Lens railway. The Brown Line, from 800 to 1,000 yards farther east, was the German third system, running from the village of Athies to the Point du Jour. To reach the Brown Line a distance of some 2,700 yards had to be traversed. If the Brown Line were taken, the 4th Division was to pass through the 9th, and capture the Green Line, including the village of Fampoux—the last German system before the Drocourt-Quéant Switch.

The arrangements for the South African Brigade were that they should attack on a two-battalion front of 600 yards, with the 4th S.A.I. on the left and the 3rd on the right, each battalion attacking on a two-company front, supported by its two remaining companies, while each company in turn would be on a two-platoon front. The 2nd S.A.I. was in support on the left, and the 1st on the right. When the first two objectives were taken the two battalions in support were to become the attacking battalions for the third objective—the Brown Line—while the two original assaulting battalions remained in support. The 1st S.A.I. was under Lieut.-Colonel Heal, the 2nd under Lieut.-Colonel Tanner, the 3rd under Lieut.-Colonel Thackeray, and the 4th under Lieut.-Colonel Christian. Pontoons were thrown across the Scarpe during the night to facilitate the march of the men to the assembly area; and the Royal Engineers attached to the Brigade blew twenty-six craters in No Man's Land to accommodate the leading waves of the attack. By 2 a.m. on the morning of Easter Monday, 9th April, all four battalions of the Brigade were in position.

Zero hour was at 5.30 in the morning. At 4 a.m. a drizzle began, which changed presently to drifts of thin snow.

At zero hour our barrage opened fifty yards in front of the first German trenches, and under its cover the 3rd and 4th S.A.I. advanced to the attack. Close on their heels came the supporting companies of the 1st and 2nd S.A.I., and occupied some trenches just beyond the German front line, as the supporting point to the attack on the first objective. The battalions, as they crossed the parapet and moved over No Man's Land, met with heavy gun and machine-gun fire, and suffered many casualties. Our barrage, however, was perfect, and the skilful use of smoke shells blinded the enemy's vision. In thirty-four minutes the Black Line was reached. The "mopping-up" detachments, consisting of fifty men from the 4th S.A.I., two platoons from the 1st, and two platoons from the 2nd, reached the trenches with the first wave, and cleared out the dug-outs, taking many prisoners, and meeting with little resistance.

At 7.30 the advance was continued towards the Blue Line, supported not only by the artillery, but by a creeping barrage of twenty machine-guns. At first sight this was a far more formidable objective, for it included the cutting of the Arras-Lens railway, and the attackers had to descend a slope where were a number of wire entanglements not fully destroyed. It was at this point that most of the casualties occurred, for the passes through the wire were commanded by snipers on the edge of the railway cutting. Once down the slope some protection was given by the bank beside the railway. Mounting this, our men looked down into the cutting, where the enemy were sheltering from our guns in their dug-outs. Here there were many machine-gun posts, which, being visible to us, were engaged by our Lewis guns. There was one awkward incident. The South African attack had pushed slightly in advance of the 26th Brigade on its right, thus causing a gap; and the Germans were able to open machine-gun and rifle fire along the railway. Captain Vivian, however, of the 3rd S.A.I., pushed forward some details of the 26th Brigade who had joined him, and cleared out the German machine-gunners and snipers. The Blue Line, which lay on the eastern side of the cutting, was then consolidated. Part of it was a veritable fortress, and in the cutting itself concrete machine-gun posts had been built. By the time the whole Brigade had reached the second objective it was just on 10 o'clock.

The attack on the final objective, the Brown Line, was timed to start at 12.45. The 1st and 2nd S.A.I. took the place of the 3rd and 4th, who became the supporting battalions. The 1st S.A.I. was on the right, with a strength of 20 officers and 488 other ranks; on the left was the 2nd, with a strength of 20 officers and 480 other ranks. Punctual to time the final advance began under the same methodical barrage. The German wire in the valley

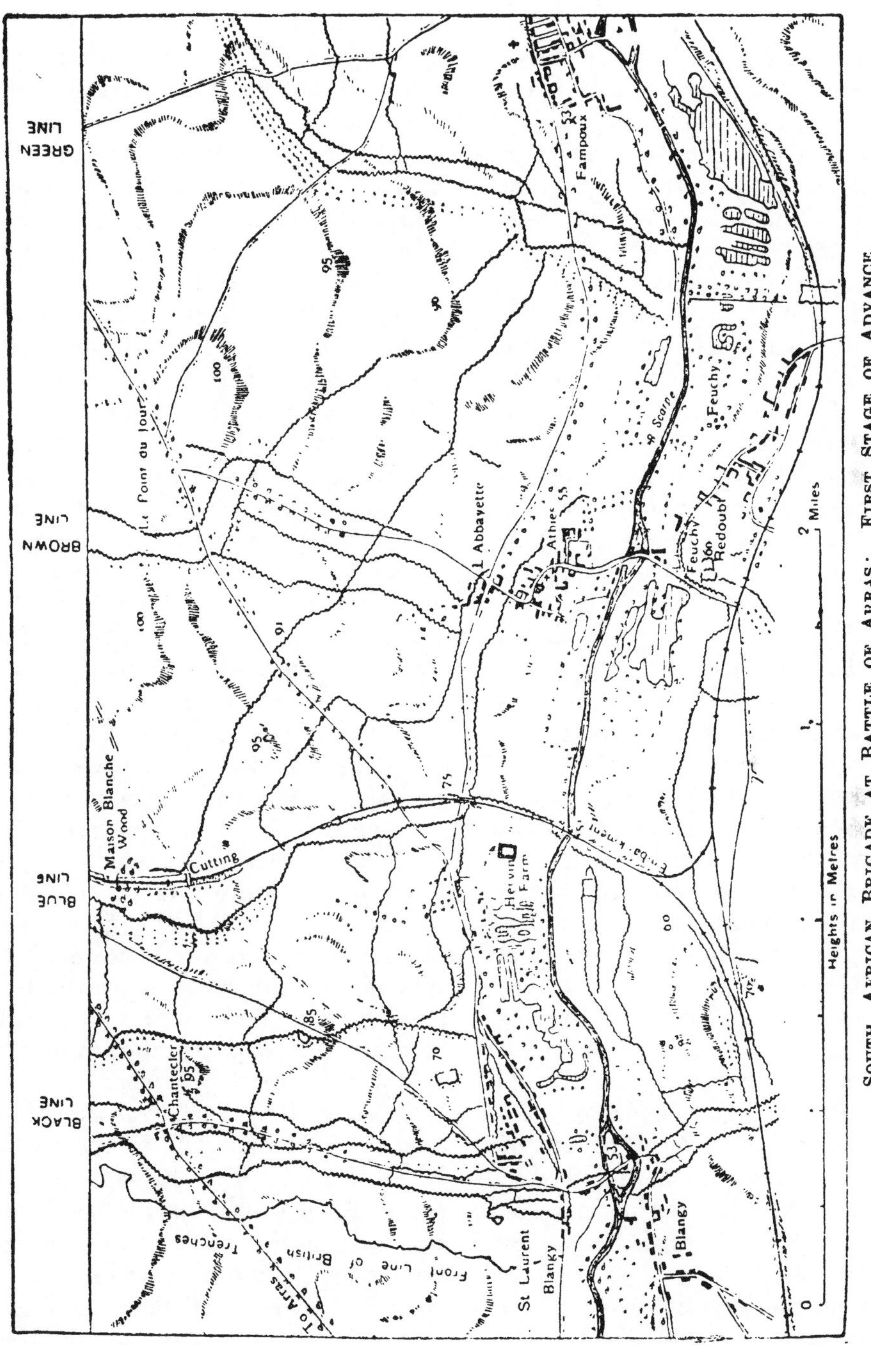

SOUTH AFRICAN BRIGADE AT BATTLE OF ARRAS: FIRST STAGE OF ADVANCE.

just west of the Brown Line was found to be very strong and untraversable, except through a passage cut by the enemy and a communication trench. Had there been serious resistance the attack might have been long delayed at this point, but already there were signs that the enemy was breaking. Few prisoners were found in the trenches, but groups were seen to advance from the Green Line and surrender. About 2 o'clock the Brown Line was occupied, where the trenches were found in almost perfect order, having suffered little from our bombardment.

The work of the South Africans was now accomplished. The 4th Division, about 3 o'clock, moved up and passed through the 9th Division to the assault of the final Green Line. Before dark the Green Line had fallen, the strong-post of the Hyderabad Redoubt was rushed, and the 4th Division was in Fampoux. This was the apex reached on the first day of the battle. The right of the XVII Corps and the left of the VI Corps formed a salient on both sides of the Scarpe, the point of which was facing no prepared position nearer than the Drocourt-Quéant Line.

The record of the 9th Division that day was not excelled by any other unit in the battle. All three brigades had performed to the full the tasks allotted to them. They had taken the strength of a brigade in prisoners—51 officers and 2,088 other ranks; they had taken 7 howitzers, 10 field-guns, and 84 machine-guns.

The total casualties were—in the 1st S.A.I., 15 killed and 69 wounded or missing; in the 2nd S.A.I., 20 killed and 68 wounded or missing; in the 3rd S.A.I., 53 killed and 226 wounded or missing; in the 4th S.A.I., 57 killed and 186 wounded or missing.

Throughout the day the work of the Field Ambulance was admirably performed. The advance was so rapid that the task of the stretcher-bearers was a heavy one, for the distance from the farthest objective to the nearest collecting post was more than 3,000 yards. Had the weather been fine, the difficulties would have been great enough, but the drizzle and sleet showers soon converted the battle area into a sea of mud. Nevertheless, by working without rest, under the brilliant direction of Captain Lawrie, before 6 o'clock that evening all the wounded of the Brigade had been collected and evacuated by the South African Field Ambulance, who had also dealt with casualties from the other two brigades of the 9th Division, and from the 34th and 4th Divisions.

The result of the first day of Arras was that all the enemy's front positions had gone, and his final position, short of the Drocourt-Quéant Line, had been breached on a front of 2½ miles. Unfortunately the weather became his ally. It changed to intense cold and wet, and with the sodden ground it took long to bring up our guns. He held us up with machine-guns in pockets of the ground, which prevented the use of our cavalry, and there was no chance of a dramatic *coup de grâce*. The infantry could only push forward slowly and methodically, and complete the capture of the remains of his position. We had made a breach, a genuine breach, on a broad front in his line, but we could not exploit our success owing to the nature of the ground and the weather. Our remarkable gains, won at small cost the first day, could only be increased by small daily additions, for the elaborate preliminaries of Arras could not be improvised, and the infantry must wait on the advance of the guns.

Tuesday, 10th April, was spent by the South African Brigade in the Blue and Black Lines. The Brigade was then placed at the disposal of the 4th Division, and early on Wednesday, the 11th, orders were received for it to relieve the 10th Brigade, which was then holding the Brown Line. That day the 4th Division was attacking at noon, and the 1st and 2nd S.A.I. moved up to a forward post under cover of a ridge 500 yards behind the Green Line to act in support. The

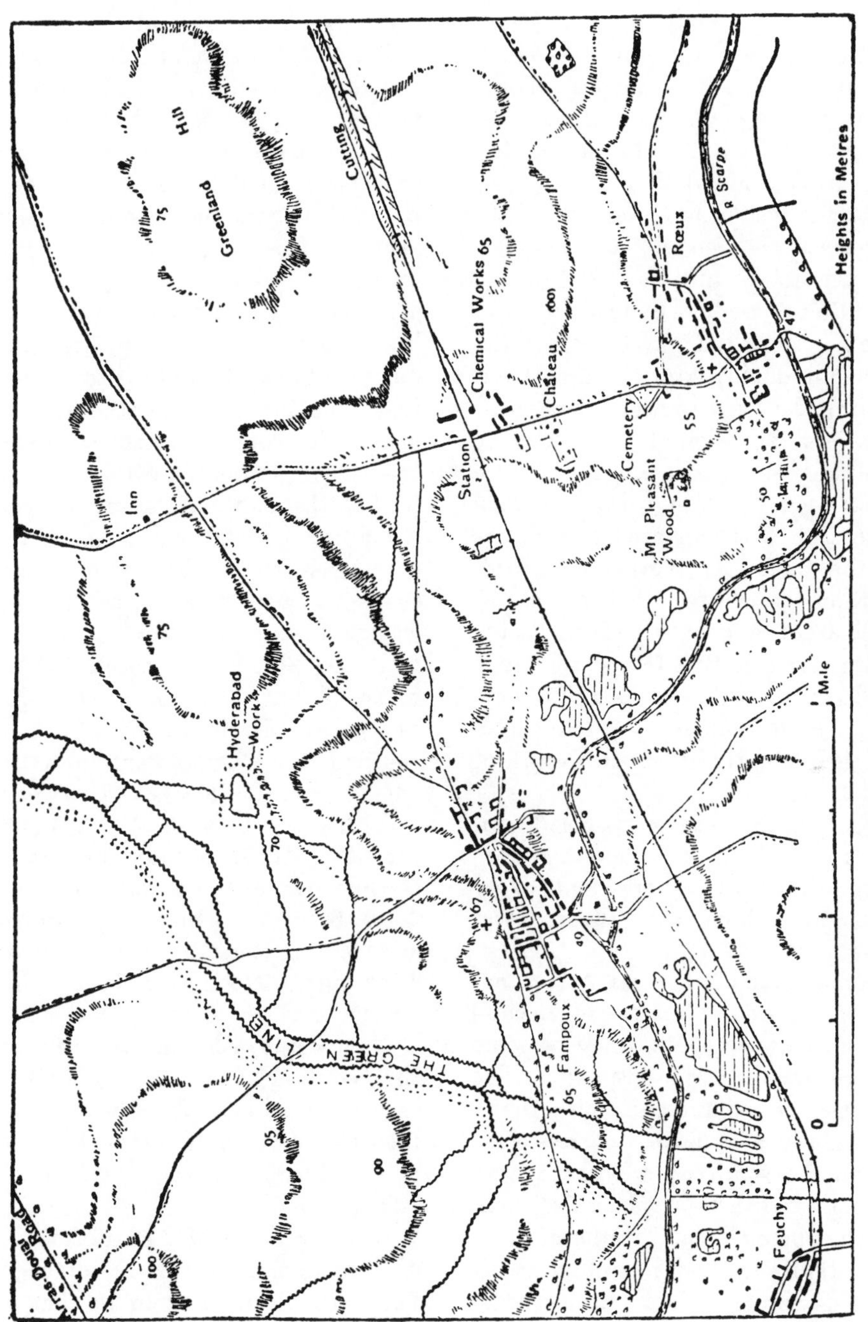

BATTLE OF ARRAS: FINAL STAGE OF ADVANCE.

attack of the 4th Division gained some ground, but failed in its main purpose; and after dark the 1st, 2nd, and 4th S.A.I. took up a position running north-west from Fampoux, with the 3rd S.A.I. in reserve. At that moment the enemy held a line running from south to north from Rœux through the Chemical Works and the railway station along the Gavrelle road. Behind it to the east lay the slopes of Greenland Hill.

An attack was ordered on the 12th April against this position. The 9th Division was to advance against the line between Rœux and the roadside inn which lay a thousand yards east of the Hyderabad Redoubt, with the 15th Division holding the front south of the Scarpe and the 4th Division to protect the northern flank of the attack. There were two objectives—the first being the road from the inn to the station; and the second, the Chemical Works and buildings south of the railway, the wood called Mount Pleasant, and the village of Rœux. The South African Brigade on the right and the 27th Brigade on their left were to capture the first objective, after which the 26th Brigade would advance south of the railway.

At 3 p.m. on the 12th the 1st, 2nd, and 4th S.A.I. assembled in Fampoux, where they were subjected to a heavy and steady bombardment, which cost them many casualties.

The prospects of success were not bright. There was no chance of an adequate bombardment, and there was no time to reconnoitre the ground. The country between Fampoux and Rœux Station was perfectly open, and was commanded in the south by a high railway embankment and three woods, all of them held by the enemy; while in the north it sloped gradually to the inn, around which the Germans had organized strong-points. It was impossible, therefore, to prevent the movement of troops being observed by the enemy. The South African dispositions were the 1st S.A.I. on the right and the 2nd on the left, with two companies of the 4th in support of each. The 3rd S.A.I. was held in brigade reserve. As the different companies began to deploy from the shelter of the houses in the east end of Fampoux they were met with heavy machine-gun and rifle fire.

The attack was timed for 5 p.m., when our guns opened fire. Unfortunately our barrage dropped some 500 yards east of the starting-point, and behind the first enemy line of defence, so that the South African Brigade had a long tract of open ground to cover before they could come up with it, and the enemy machine-gun fire from the railway embankment, combined with the flanking fire from the woods in the south and the south-east, and from the direction of the inn, played havoc with both the attacking brigades.

The result was a failure. A gallant few of the South Africans succeeded in reaching the station, a point in their objective, where their bodies were recovered a month later when the position was captured. For the rest, only one or two isolated parties reached points as much as 200 yards east of the line held by the 4th Division. The casualties of the 2nd S.A.I., who went in 400 strong, amounted to 16 officers and 285 men; the 1st S.A.I. lost 2 officers and 203 men; and the 4th, 6 officers and 200 men. Since the first part of the assault had failed, the 26th Brigade, which was waiting to advance on Rœux, was not called upon. That night it took over the line from the Scarpe to the Hyderabad Redoubt, where it linked up with the 4th Division, and the South African Brigade withdrew to the Green Line. They were finally relieved on the night of the 15th, having, in the three days since the 12th, suffered 720 casualties.

In the unsuccessful operations in front of Fampoux the Field Ambulance, which had a collecting station in that village, had a heavy task. Many of the stretcher-bearers had been working without rest for three days, but they continued to do their duty till they dropped from sheer exhaustion. The work of one man, Private

Remains of Chemical Works, Roeux.

R. W. Nelson, deserves special mention. He had carried continuously from the morning of the 9th, and was already worn out when the attack opened on the 12th. He worked on steadily, until he collapsed late in the evening. Nevertheless, he refused to be relieved, and after a short rest returned to his post, and carried seven cases before morning.

The Brigade was to have no further part in the long-drawn-out struggle lasting till far on in May, which the failure of the French attack on the Aisne compelled us to continue in the Arras area. It was in the Monchy-Breton District during the latter part of April. On 5th May a composite battalion, consisting of a company from each of the 1st, 2nd, 3rd and 4th S.A.I., was formed under the command of Major Webber, and moved to Arras, where it was placed at the disposal of the 27th Brigade. It took its share in holding the front line till 14th May, when it rejoined the Brigade. On the 13th of that month Sir Edmund Allenby inspected the Brigade, and congratulated the men on the distinguished part they had played in the late battle. In June it was in Arras as divisional reserve, and on 5th June two composite battalions were formed to assist in the attack on Greenland Hill. That attack, carried out by troops of the XVII Corps, was so successful that the supports were not called upon, and these battalions rejoined their Brigade on the 6th.

Its numbers had now grown sadly thin. To replace losses, drafts to the strength of 1,448 had been sent to France between the end of April and the end of June, but even with these it was gravely under strength. On 30th June the strength of the different battalions was as follows:—
1st S.A.I., 38 officers, 680 other ranks;
2nd S.A.I., 37 officers, 601 other ranks;
3rd S.A.I., 35 officers, 691 other ranks;
4th S.A.I., 39 officers, 818 other ranks.

In July the Brigade moved to the Somme area for training, and on the 27th of that month, along with the rest of the 9th Division, was transferred to the IV Corps. On the 28th it relieved the 174th Infantry Brigade in the Trescault section of the line, north of Havrincourt Wood and along the Canal du Nord. This was then a quiet region, and beyond a few minor raids there was no incident to record.

CHAPTER IV.

THE THIRD BATTLE OF YPRES.

(July—November, 1917.)

When, on the last day of July, 1917, Sir Douglas Haig launched his attack in the Ypres Salient, the nature of the war had dramatically changed. The great plan conceived for 1917, of which the Somme had been the logical preliminary, had proved impossible. This was not due wholly or mainly to the failure of the ambitious offensive in April at Arras and on the Aisne. The real cause was the defection of Russia, for, by the failure of one great partner, the old military coherence of the Alliance had gone. The war on two fronts, which had been Germany's chief handicap, looked as if it might change presently to a war on a single front. Whatever victories might be won during the remainder of 1917, it was now certain that a decisive blow could not be delivered. The Teutonic League, just when it was beginning to crumble, had been given a new tenure of life. Sir Douglas Haig was compelled to protract the fighting in the Arras area so long as the French on the Aisne required his aid; but by the end of May he was free to turn his attention to the plan which, as early as the previous November, had been his main preoccupation. This was an offensive against the enemy in

Flanders, with the aim of clearing the Belgian coast and turning the northern flank of the whole German defence system in the West. It was a scheme which, if successful, promised the most far-reaching results. It would destroy the worst of the submarine bases; it would restore to Belgium her lost territory, and thereby deprive Germany of one of her most cherished bargaining assets; it would cripple the enemy communications with the depots of the Lower Rhineland. But time was the essence of the business. The blow must be struck at the earliest possible hour, for each week's delay meant the aggrandisement of the enemy.

Sir Douglas Haig's first business was to clear his flanks for the coming attack, and on the 7th June, by one of the most perfect operations in the campaign, he won the Messines-Wytschaete ridge at a single bound. His next step was the advance east of Ypres. The famous Salient had during three years been gradually contracted till the enemy front was now less than two miles from the town. The Germans held all the half-moon of little hills to the east, which meant that any preparations for attack would be conducted under their watchful eyes. They were very conscious of the importance of the position, and the wary general who now commanded their Fourth Army was not likely to be taken by surprise. This was Sixt Von Armin, who had commanded the 4th Corps at the Somme, and had there shown himself one of the most original and fruitful tacticians on the enemy's side.

The Battle of Messines was over by the 12th June, but for various reasons it was not till late in July that the date of the main advance could be fixed. It was now more than ever a race against time, for the precarious weather of autumn was approaching; and, unless the advance proceeded strictly according to time-table, it ran a grave risk of failure. The high ground east of the Salient must be won in a fortnight to enable us to move against the enemy bases in West Flanders and clear the coast-line. The nature of the countryside made any offensive a gamble with the weather, for the Salient was, after Verdun, the most tortured of the Western battle-fields. Constant shelling of the low ground west of the ridges had blocked or diverted the streams and the natural drainage, and turned it into a sodden wilderness. Weather such as had been experienced on the Somme would make of it a morass where tanks could not be used, and transport could scarcely move, and troops would be exposed to the last degree of misery.

The coming attack was much canvassed in Germany beforehand, and Von Armin, having learned the lesson of his defeat at Messines, had prepared his defences. In Flanders the nature of the ground did not permit of a second Siegfried Line. Deep dug-outs and concreted trenches were impossible because of the water-logged soil, and he was compelled to find new tactics. His solution was the "pill-box." These were small concrete forts, sited among the ruins of a farm or in some derelict piece of woodland, often raised only a yard or two above the ground level, and bristling with machine-guns. The low entrance was at the rear, and the "pill-box" could hold from eight to forty men. It was easy to make, for the wooden or steel framework could be brought up on any dark night and filled with concrete. They were echeloned in depth with great skill, and, in the wiring, alleys were left so that an unwary advance would be trapped among them and exposed to enfilading fire. Their small size made them a difficult mark for heavy guns, and, since they were protected by concrete at least three feet thick, they were impregnable to the ordinary barrage of field artillery.

Von Armin's plan was to hold his first line—which was often a mere string of shell craters—with few men, who would fall back before an assault. He had his guns well behind, so that they should not be captured in the first rush, and would be available for a barrage if his opponents became entangled in the "pill-box" zone. Finally, he had his reserves in the second line, ready for the counter-stroke before the attack could secure its position. It will be seen that these tactics were admirably suited for the exposed and contorted ground of the Salient. Any attack would be allowed to make some advance; but if the German plan worked well, this advance would be short-lived and would be dearly paid for. Instead of the cast-iron front of the Siegfried area, the Flanders line would be highly elastic, but it would spring back into position after pressure with a deadly rebound.

The "preparation" for the battle lasted for the greater part of July, and every part of the Salient was drenched with our fire. On the last day of the month came the advance on a front of 15 miles—from the river Lys to a little north of Steenstraate, the main effort being that of the Fifth Army, on the 7½ miles between Boesinghe and the Zillebeke-Zandvoorde road. With the attack the weather broke. The purpose of the attack was to carry the enemy's first defences, situated on the forward slope of the rising ground, and his second position along the crest. The opening day saw a brilliant success, for everywhere we captured the first line, and in many parts the second. But the weather prevented the series of cumulative blows which we had planned. For a fortnight we were compelled to hold our hand, since, till the countryside grew dryer, advance was an impossibility.

The second stage of the Ypres struggle began on 16th August, when the Fifth Army attacked the German third position, the Gheluvelt-Langemarck line, which ran from the Menin road along the second of the tiers of ridges which rimmed the Salient on the east. These tiers, the highest and most easterly of which was the famous Passchendaele crest, had the common features that they all sprang from one southern boss or pillar, the point on the Menin road marked 64 metres, which we knew as Clapham Junction, and all, as they ran northward, lost elevation. The attack, which took place at dawn, made a considerable gap in the German third line, but it was very far from attaining its main objectives. That day, indeed, showed at its best Von Armin's new defensive method. The weather was in his favour, for the air was thick and damp, making airplane observation difficult, and therefore depriving us of timely notice of the enemy's counter-strokes. The ground was sloppy, and made tangled and difficult with broken woods; and the whole front was sown with "pill-boxes," against which we had not yet discovered the proper weapon. The result was a serious British check. The splendid courage of the Fifth Army had been largely fruitless. Fine brigades had been hurled in succession against a concrete wall, and had been sorely battered.

Sir Douglas Haig took time to reorganize his front and prepare a new plan. He extended the Second Army northward, so that it should take over the attack on the enemy front on the Menin road. Sorely tried divisions were taken out of the line, and our whole artillery tactics were revised. The "pill-box" problem was studied, and a solution was found, not by miraculous ingenuity, but by patient and meticulous care. Early in September the weather improved, and the sodden Salient began slowly to dry. But the process was slow, and it was not till the third week of the month that the third stage in the battle could begin.

For this third stage the 9th Division was brought up from the Somme. It arrived at Brandhoek on 14th September, where it became part of the V Corps of the Fifth Army. The next few days were spent in careful training for the impending attack. The objectives set before it had already been attacked fruitlessly more than once, and the reason of failure seemed to be clear. The enemy came out of holes and dug-outs behind the attacking wave, and held up the second wave and isolated the first one. Hence the men were trained to stop at every "pill-box," trench, or dug-out, and clear out all occupants, the troops behind them passing through them to a further attack. It was beyond doubt the only method which offered a reasonable chance of success. The "pill-boxes" in front of the 9th Division were carefully reconnoitred and located. In the attack it was arranged that the field-gun barrage should lengthen on both sides of a "pill-box," so that the advancing troops, hugging their barrage, might get round its unprotected rear. The barrage was to be high-explosive instead of shrapnel, for the path of the former could be more exactly noted and closely followed.

The front allotted to the 9th Division was some 2,000 yards north of the Ypres-Menin road. Through its centre ran the Ypres-Roulers railway. On its right was the 2nd Australian Division, and on its left the 55th Division of West Lancashire Territorials. The 9th Division formed the right of the Fifth Army. Its attack was to be on a two-brigade front, the South African Brigade on the left and the 27th Brigade on the right, while the 26th Brigade was held in reserve. The South African Brigade was disposed as follows:—The 3rd S.A.I., under Lieut.-Colonel Thackeray, on the right, and the 1st, under Lieut.-Colonel Heal, in support; on the left the 4th S.A.I., under Lieut.-Colonel MacLeod,* supported by the 2nd, temporarily under Major Cochran. When the first objective had been taken, the two supporting battalions were to pass through and attack the second and third objectives.

The British line at the moment lay on the east side of the Frezenberg Ridge. The first objective for the South African Brigade was roughly the line of the Steenbeek stream.† The second was a line running north and south a little west of the junction of the Ypres-Zonnebeke road and the Ypres-Roulers railway. This was now the main German position, part of the great Langemarck-Gheluvelt line. The final objective, known as the Green Line, was very slightly east of the second, and involved an advance mainly on the left wing of the attack. The purpose was to win the ridge which gave observation of Zonnebeke, and which, until it was captured, hindered all advance further north. The countryside was to the last degree blind and desperate. Not only was there a stream to cross, and many yards of swamp to struggle through, but the area included some of the most formidable "pill-boxes" on the German front, while in the main enemy line stood the Bremen Redoubt, and the stronghold made out of Zevenkote village.

The starting-point being what it was, a night assembly in such an area was the most intricate of problems. On 17th September the South African Brigade moved into the front line, relieving the 125th Brigade. Wednesday, the 19th, was a clear, blowing day; but about 10 o'clock in the evening the rain began, and fell heavily all that night. During the darkness the Brigade was getting into position for attack. The black night and the slippery ground made the whole operation extraordinarily difficult in a place devoid of communication trenches and honeycombed with shell-holes. The ground was so cut up that it was possible to move only by duck-board tracks, and it was hard to get reports back from the different units. Nevertheless, long before zero hour, the attacking battalions were in their place.

* MacLeod took over the 4th from Christian on 25th April when he returned from sick leave, Christian going to the XVII Corps School of Instruction as Commandant.

† On some maps this is given as the Hansbeek, or Hannebeek, but it is more convenient to keep this name for the larger stream which runs by St. Julien.

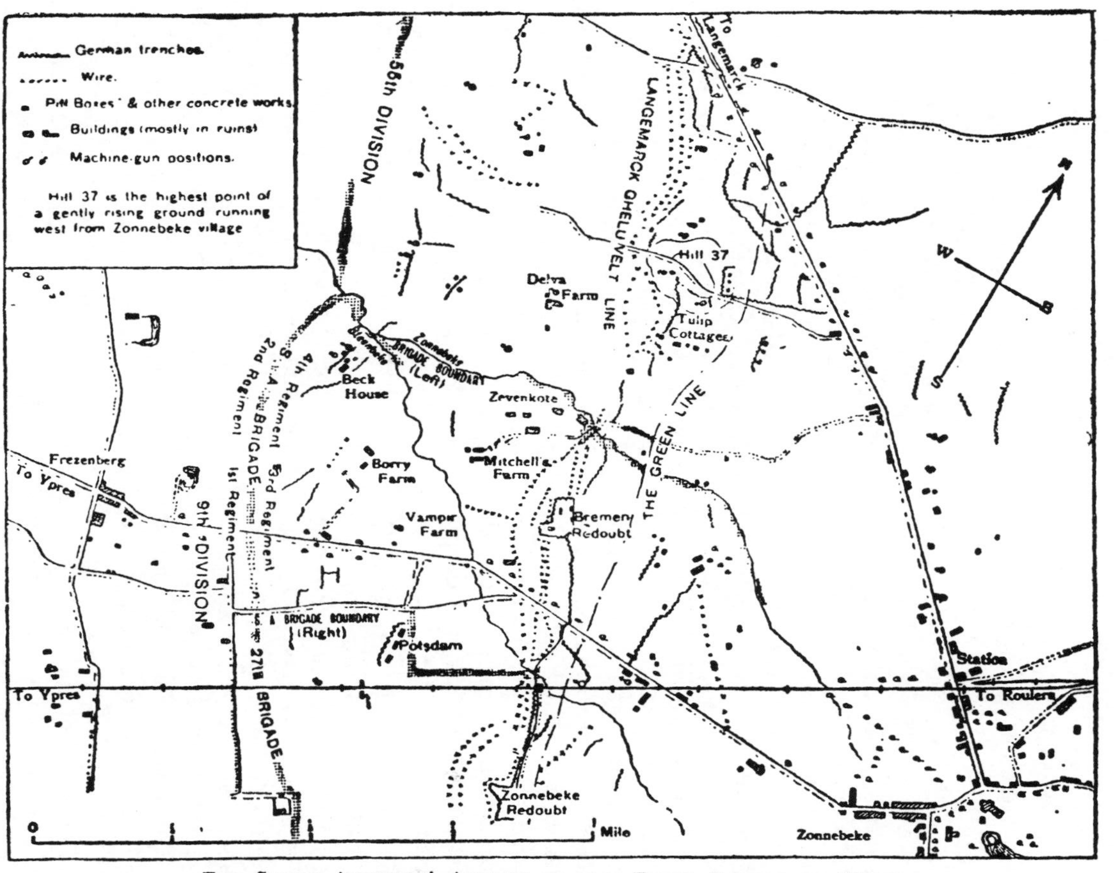

THE SOUTH AFRICANS' ATTACK AT THE THIRD BATTLE OF YPRES.

At dawn the drizzle stopped, but a wet mist remained, which blinded our air reconnaissance. At twenty minutes to six, preceded by a barrage of high explosives and smoke shells, the attacking troops moved into the desert of mud. In the dim light, obscured by smoke, it was impossible to see their objective. The advance had scarcely begun when the German barrage came down on our old front line, so that the supporting battalions had to close up as near as possible to the leading troops.

The right battalion, the 3rd S.A.I., had a strength of 20 officers and 617 other ranks. The left battalion, the 4th S.A.I., had a strength of 21 officers and 511 other ranks. The 4th S.A.I. took the strong-points known as Beck House and Borry Farm in their stride, and by half-past six had reached their first objective. Seeing the place called Mitchell's Farm in front of them, a party went through our own barrage and captured it, killing most of its garrison. A machine-gun across the brook on their left flank gave trouble, so a platoon, under Second Lieutenant Saphir, crossed the stream and took the German post there, bringing back the gun and twenty prisoners.

In the meantime the left wing of the 3rd S.A.I. had taken Vampir Farm and reached its objective. Its right, however, was held up by the position of the left battalion of the 27th Brigade, the 12th Royal Scots, who, in their area, had encountered the formidable redoubt known as Potsdam, which, in addition to other defences, included three "pill-boxes." When "A" Company and part of "B" Company of the 3rd S.A.I. reached their objective they were too far in advance of their neighbouring brigade, and were subjected to a heavy enfilading fire from Potsdam. Captain Vivian of "A" Company immediately organized an attack on that point, leading the assault in person, but he was killed. Captain Sprenger of "B" Company then collected all the men he could, both from the 3rd S.A.I. and the 1st, and with two Lewis guns and one machine-gun he advanced by rushes from shell-hole to shell-hole against the redoubt. This gallant attack, combined with the pressure of the 27th Brigade from the west, brought about the fall of the place. The enemy was seen bolting south towards the Ypres-Roulers railway line, and in a quarter of an hour the fort was in our hands.

A halt was called for an hour before the attack on the second objective. After passing Potsdam it had been arranged that the area of the South African Brigade would be extended to the right till it included the northern bank of the railway. This made it important to clear that northern bank. Second Lieutenant Lawrence of the 1st S.A.I. had accordingly been sent forward as soon as the attack began, and had met with no opposition till he came under machine-gun fire on the west side of Potsdam. Finding no troops near him, he retired till he fell in with some derelict tanks, when he turned south-east and reached the railway. Here he found some South Africans, who had become separated from the rest, clearing a dug-out on the south side of the line. Going eastward he found a large dug-out, where he took twenty German prisoners and captured three machine-guns. He then found touch with the 12th Royal Scots, which had been his main object, and rejoined his battalion before the second stage of the battle began.

Just previous to the opening of this stage some men of the 1st and 3rd S.A.I., headed by Sergeant Frohbus, advanced through our own barrage against a large "pill-box" immediately on their front. On calling on the inmates of the "pill-box" to surrender, some thirty or forty came out, but the remainder declined to move. All the loopholes and openings of the structure were closed, but "Mike" Fennessy, of the 3rd S.A.I., managed to get a bomb either through a ventilator in the roof or through a window which

Pill-Boxes, East of Zevenkote.

had been blown open by a grenade. This set fire to the wood lining, and the garrison broke out and were shot down. Four machine-guns were captured in the place.*

The 3rd and 4th S.A.I. now remained at the first objective and consolidated the ground, and the two supporting battalions at 7 a.m. moved against the second objective, the main Langemarck-Gheluvelt line. The 1st S.A.I. was on the right with a strength of 20 officers and 546 other ranks, and the 2nd on the left with a strength of 20 officers and 566 other ranks. The task of the 1st S.A.I. was easy, and it advanced smoothly towards its second objective. At 7.50 Colonel Heal was able to report that his section of the main German line had been taken. The 2nd S.A.I., however, on his left, had a heavier duty. Mitchell's Farm had been previously taken by the 4th, but the enemy was still holding Waterend Farm, and from beyond the stream was galling their flanks with machine-gun and rifle fire from the high ground at the place called Tulip Cottages and Hill 37—all in the area of the 55th Division. Before them, too, lay the strong Bremen Redoubt and the fortified village of Zevenkote. Nevertheless, the Bremen Redoubt and Zevenkote were carried, and with them the second German position. But the situation on his left made Major Cochran uneasy. The men of West Lancashire were held up by the enemy at Hill 37, and the South Africans had therefore an exposed flank. He extended his left, and captured Waterend Farm, together with three machine-guns and seventy prisoners, and thereby found touch with the 55th Division, and formed a defensive flank. It was not till the afternoon that the Lancashire troops gallantly stormed Hill 37, which enabled the South African left to advance to the Green Line, the final objective, where they held a position consisting mainly of a string of shell-holes.

Meantime there was no word of Von Armin's usual counter-stroke. The troops against us were some of the best in the German Army, part of the 2nd Guard Reserve. But the speed and fury of the advance of the 9th, the accuracy of their artillery barrage, and the skill with which they accounted for "pill-box" after "pill-box" had paralyzed the enemy. During the morning there seemed to be a concentration for a counter-attack near Bostin Farm, but this was dispersed by our guns. Only small parties moving from shell-hole to shell-hole advanced, and these never came nearer than 800 yards. By the evening of that day on nearly all the British front of attack the final objectives had been reached. The 9th Division had carried theirs in the record time of three hours.

Delville Wood was still for the Brigade the most heroic episode in the war. But its advance on 20th September must without doubt be reckoned its most successful achievement up to that date in the campaign. It carried one of the strongest parts of the enemy's position, and assisted the brigades both on its right and left to take two forts which blocked their way. The day was full of gallant individual exploits and Lance-Corporal W. H. Hewitt of the 2nd S.A.I. was awarded the Victoria Cross. He attacked a "pill-box" in his section, and tried to rush the doorway, but found a stubborn garrison within, and received a severe wound. Nevertheless he managed to reach the loophole, where, in his attempts to insert a bomb, he was again wounded. Ultimately he got a bomb inside, dislodged the occupants, and took the place.

On the 21st there was heavy shelling, but no serious counter-attack on the 9th Division, though the 55th, on their left, faced and defeated a strong enemy attempt. Early on the morning of the 22nd the Brigade was relieved from the

* Private C. E. Fennessy was awarded the Military Medal for this exploit.

front line. Its casualties were not light. The 1st S.A.I. had 58 killed and 291 wounded and missing; the 2nd S.A.I. had 61 killed and 224 wounded and missing; the 3rd S.A.I. had 88 killed and 283 wounded and missing; the 4th S.A.I. had 56 killed and 197 wounded and missing.

In recounting the doings of the Brigade in this battle the subsidiary services must not be forgotten. The Field Ambulance had the hardest task which they had yet faced. In getting back the walking wounded they were much helped by the Décauville trains, which were run by a section of the South African railwaymen. Owing to the impossibility of making dug-outs the wounded, as they became numerous, had to be dressed in the open, and it was no light task to attend fifty wounded men on stretchers with shells dropping around. In spite of every difficulty the arrangements worked with wonderful precision, and no casualties were ever better cared for than those of the Brigade.

The Brigade was not yet finished with Third Ypres. On 24th September it left the battle-front, and on 4th October it was in the Houlle area, where for five days it underwent general training. On 10th October the 9th Division began to concentrate in the forward area of the XVIII Corps with a view to relieving the 48th Division in line. It thus became again the right division of the Fifth Army. On 12th October it entered the support line, along the canal bank at Ypres. The battle, in the meantime, had moved slowly. By 25th September we had won all the interior ridges of the Salient and the southern pillar; but we were not yet within striking distance of the north part of the main Passchendaele Ridge. To attain this, we must lie east of Zonnebeke and the Polygon Wood, at the foot of the final slopes. Sir Douglas Haig struck on the 26th September in fine weather, and took the Polygon Wood and Zonnebeke village. On the 4th October, the very day fixed for a great German counter-attack, he struck again, and by a little after midday had gained all his objectives. He broke up forty German battalions, taking over 5,000 prisoners, and now held 9,000 yards of the crest of the ultimate ridge. On the night of the 13th the 2nd and 4th S.A.I. moved up to the front line, taking over trenches held by part of the 26th and 27th Brigades, which had been engaged in an attack on the 12th which was foiled by disastrous weather. The relief was very difficult, for the whole country had become an irreclaimable bog, and the mud was beyond all human description. There was intermittent shelling during the 14th and 15th, and much bombing from enemy planes. On the night of the 16th the 2nd and 4th S.A.I. were relieved by the 1st and 3rd. For five more days the Brigade remained in the front trenches, taking part in no action, but suffering heavily from the constant bombardment. Between the 13th and the 23rd of October, when it moved out of the Salient, it had no less than 261 casualties in killed and wounded. The 9th Division now relieved the 41st Division in the Nieuport area, and remained on the Belgian coast till 20th November, a period of welcome rest. On 15th October Lieut.-Colonel Tanner, who had commanded the 2nd S.A.I. since its formation, left the Brigade to take over the command of the 8th Brigade in the 3rd Division. He was succeeded by Lieut.-Colonel Christian.

In November the struggle at Ypres reached its close. On Tuesday, the 6th, the Canadians carried the last fragment of the Passchendaele Ridge, and wiped out the Salient, where for three years we had been at the mercy of the German guns. Sir Douglas Haig had not come within measurable distance of his major purpose, and that owing to no fault of plan, but through the maleficence of the weather in a terrain where weather was all in all.

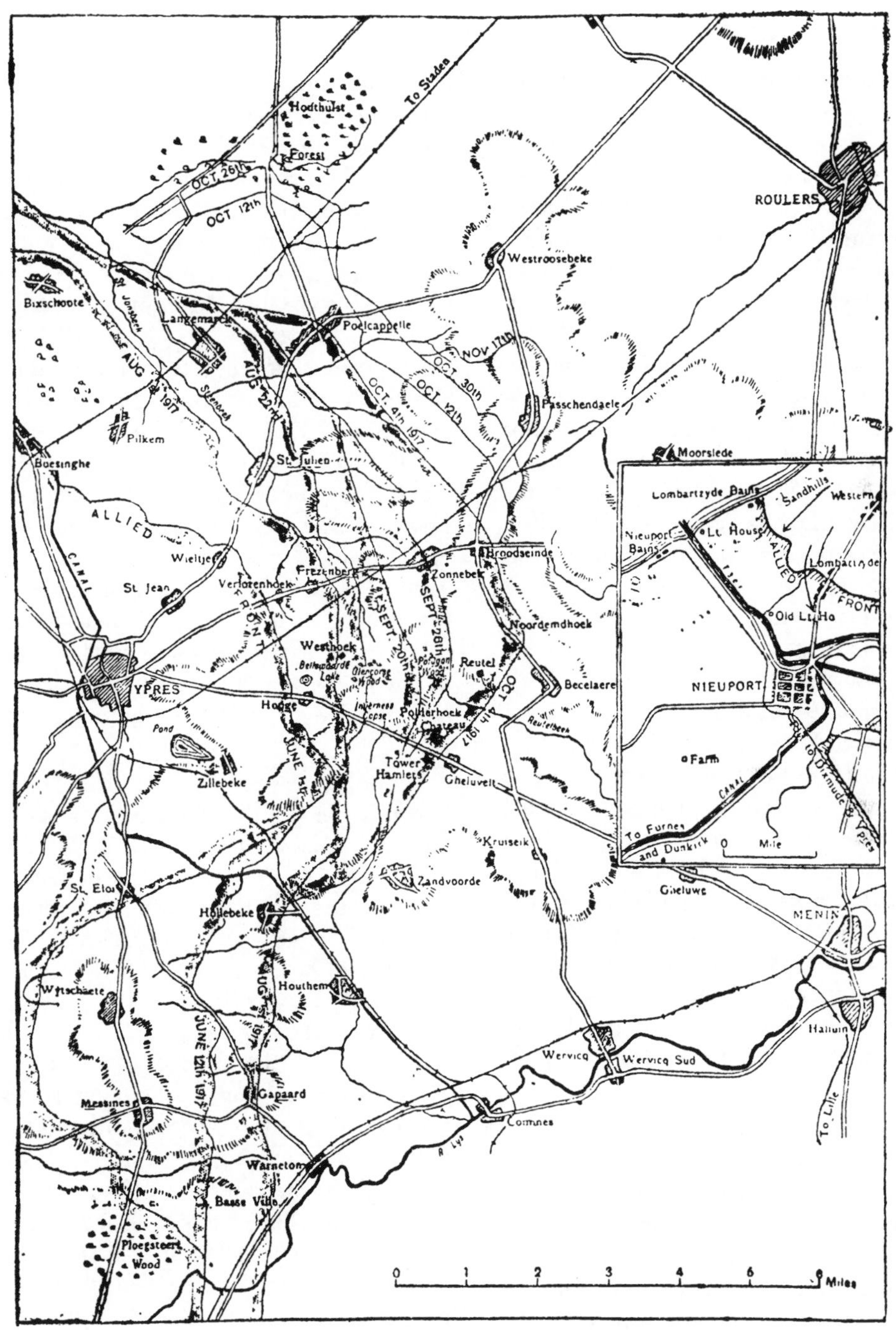

THE THIRD BATTLE OF YPRES.

CHAPTER V.

THE EVE OF THE GREAT GERMAN ATTACK.
(November, 1917—March, 1918.)

During the summer months there was a strange quiet on the Eastern front. The German armies did not advance, though the way seemed plain before them. But they were not idle. Ludendorff had seen the opportunity afforded by the downfall of Russia, and believed that long before America took the field in strength he could deal a decisive blow to the Allies in the West. He prepared most patiently for this final *coup*, and turned the whole of his Eastern front into one vast training camp, where picked divisions were practised in open fighting; for his scheme demanded a high perfection of discipline and individual stamina. He had seen that surprise was essential, and that therefore a laboured artillery "preparation" was out of the question. He realized, too, that in order to get the full cumulative effect of a blow, division must follow division to strike while the iron was hot. If these two things—surprise and an endless chain of troops of assault—could be found, then it might be possible to deal the decisive blow within the narrow limits of time still permitted to her. A break here and a break there meant only a restricted advance, behind which the enemy's front grew solid in time. He therefore aimed not at a break-through in the older sense, but at a general crumbling.

Ludendorff's plan was based upon the highly specialized training of certain units, and was a legitimate conclusion from the German use of "storm troops." The first point was the absence of any preliminary massing near the front of attack. Men were brought up by night marches just before zero hour, and secrecy was thus obtained for the assembly. Again, there was no long bombardment to alarm the enemy, and the guns began at the moment when the infantry advanced, the enemy's back areas being confused by a deluge of gas shells. The assault was made by picked troops in open order, or rather in small clusters, carrying light trench mortars and many machine-guns, with the field batteries close behind them in support. The picked troops made gaps through which others poured, till each section of the defence found itself outflanked and encircled. A system of flares and rockets enabled the following troops to learn where the picked troops had made the breach, and the artillery came close behind the infantry. The men had unlimited objectives, and carried iron rations for several days. When one division had reached the end of its strength, another took its place, so that the advance resembled a continuous game of leap-frog.

On 20th November the 9th Division moved from the Belgian coast. The South African Brigade spent some days in rest-billets in the Fruges area, engaged in training the recruits which had arrived to replace the casualties of Third Ypres. On the 30th news came of the counter-stroke at Cambrai, and the battalions were ordered to be ready to move at short notice. On the morning of the 1st December they began their long march southward to the accompaniment of a deluge of rain and a sharp east wind. Presently came snow, and then a binding frost, and when, on 3rd December, the Brigade arrived at Moislains, it was after three days of weary marches in the worst of weathers and a freezing night in the train.

During the night of the 3rd they were ordered to relieve the 2nd Brigade of Guards at Gouzeaucourt, nine miles off.

The 9th Division became part of the VII Corps, under Sir Walter Congreve. By the night of the 4th the 2nd and 4th S.A.I. had taken over a section of the front line, with the 1st in support and the 3rd in reserve. The line now held was that established by the Guards Division after their brilliant advance on 1st December. It consisted of a newly dug trench on the east slope of Quentin Ridge, extending from Gauche Wood, on the right, to a point near the head of Flag Ravine. No communication trenches existed, and in the right battalion section all approaches to the front line were under enemy observation. The trenches were neither fire-stepped nor revetted, and no dug-outs or shelters existed in the forward area. There was also very little wire, the whole position having been extemporized during the recent battle.

As attacks on this part of the front were daily expected, the forward battalions had to detail troops to occupy the immediate support trenches as "counter-attack forces," while the reserve battalion constituted a counter-attack force for the Brigade. The next few weeks were filled with strenuous work. Material had to be salved or brought up for the defence of the area, a large number of British and German dead had to be buried, trenches had to be broadened and deepened, and shelters constructed. All through December the Brigade was heavily shelled. On the night of the 8th the 2nd and 4th S.A.I. were relieved by the 1st and 3rd, the 4th becoming the Brigade reserve, while the 2nd formed the garrison of the support and reserve lines. During the first week the casualties averaged throughout the Brigade about thirty a day, which were severe for trench warfare. After that they slackened, but carrying parties at night continued to suffer heavily. The Brigade, by constant patrolling, maintained its ascendancy in No Man's Land, but the German outposts were exceptionally vigilant. The worst trial was the weather, which was first frost, then thaw, and then about the middle of the month a settled frost, which lasted until the New Year.

On 13th January the Brigade came out of the line, and for ten days was billeted in the villages of Moislains, Heudicourt, Fins, and Sorel-le-Grand. On the 23rd the 2nd and 3rd S.A.I. moved again into the line to relieve units of the 26th Brigade, and the 1st and 4th S.A.I. followed the next day. The relief was carried out without casualties. When the Brigade arrived at Heudicourt on 4th December it numbered 148 officers and 3,621 other ranks. By January 23rd its total strength had shrunk to 79 officers and 1,661 men. On the last day of January all four battalions came out of the front trenches, and were moved to a back area for a much-needed month's rest.

That month was spent in training for the great battle which was now believed to be due in early March. It had been resolved to reduce the British divisions from a thirteen-battalion to a ten-battalion basis, and this meant that one battalion must disappear from each Brigade. General Smuts and General Lukin, after consultation with General Dawson, decided to disband the 3rd (Transvaal and Rhodesia) S.A.I., which had received the smallest number of recruits during the past twelve months. On 8th February General Dawson visited the battalion to explain the decision. On 18th February the 3rd S.A.I. was finally disbanded.

In the beginning of March General Lukin returned to England on leave. While there he was compelled because of the grave illness of his wife to accept the offer of a tour of duty in England. The command of the 9th Division passed to Major-General Tudor, who up till then had commanded the Divisional Artillery.

But before these changes came about one great episode in the past record of the Brigade was commemorated. On the 17th February all its battalions, including the vanishing 3rd, took part in a memorial service at Delville Wood. On the south side of the place towards Longueval a tall wooden cross had been erected, bearing the inscription: "In Memory of the Officers and Men of the 1st South African Brigade who fell in Action in July, 1916, in the Battle of the Somme." Before this cross, among the shattered tree-stumps, the drumhead service was held, and around in a square stood details of the four battalions.

Early in March the Brigade moved up to the front area, and on the night of the 12th began to take over from the 116th Brigade of the 39th Division the sector east of Heudicourt. Ever since the close of 1917 the Allied Command in the West had been conscious that the situation had altered. The Germans were able now to resume the offensive at their will, and the next phase of the campaign must see the Allies on their defence. Sir Douglas Haig and General Pétain were aware that large reinforcements could be brought from the East, which would give Ludendorff a numerical superiority until such time as the Americans arrived to redress the balance. They knew that the German Staff would make a desperate effort to secure a decision while they still held their opponents at a disadvantage.

Early in January, 1918, the British Army had to take over the French line as far as Barisis, south of the Oise. For this new duty Sir Douglas Haig had not received proportionate reinforcements. He had now a front of 125 miles, and he did not dare to weaken his north and central sections, where, in the case of an attack, he had but little room to manœuvre. So he was compelled to leave the Fifth Army on his right in a condition of perilous weakness. The Fifth Army, with a front of 72,000 yards, had no more than eleven divisions in line, and three infantry and two cavalry divisions in reserve. The right three divisions were holding 30,000 yards—an average of one bayonet to the yard, while the German average was four.

The British Command attempted to atone for its weakness in numbers by devising defences of exceptional strength. In front, along the ground held by the Third and Fifth Armies, lay the "forward zone" organized in two sections—a line of outposts to give the alarm and fall back, and a well-wired line of resistance. In both were a number of skilfully placed redoubts armed with machine-guns, and so arranged that any enemy advance would be drawn on between them so as to come under cross-fire. The spaces between the redoubts were to be protected by a barrage of field-guns and corps heavy guns. The line of resistance and the redoubts were intended to hold out till the last, and to receive no support from the rear, except for such counter-attacks as might be necessary. The purpose of this "forward zone" was to break up an advancing enemy, and the principle of its organization was "blobs" rather than a continuous line.

Behind the "forward zone," at a distance of from half a mile to three miles or more, came the "battle zone," arranged on the same plan, except that it had no outposts. It was a defence in depth, elaborately wired, and studded with strong-points. A mile or two in its rear lay the third and final defensive zone, which in March was little more than a sketch. The theory of the system was that the "forward zone" would break up the cohesion of any assault, and that the "battle zone" would be impregnable against an attack thus weakened. Considering the small number of men available, it was not possible to provide any further safeguards in the time. On the "battle zone" rested the hope of resistance for the Third and Fifth Armies. If it failed to stand, the situation would be grave indeed, for there were no prepared defences to fall back upon, and no immediate hope of reserves.

The 9th Division formed the extreme left of the Fifth Army, with, on its right, the 21st Division; and on its left the 47th Division—the right flank of the Third Army. The 9th held its front with two brigades, the 26th on the left, and the

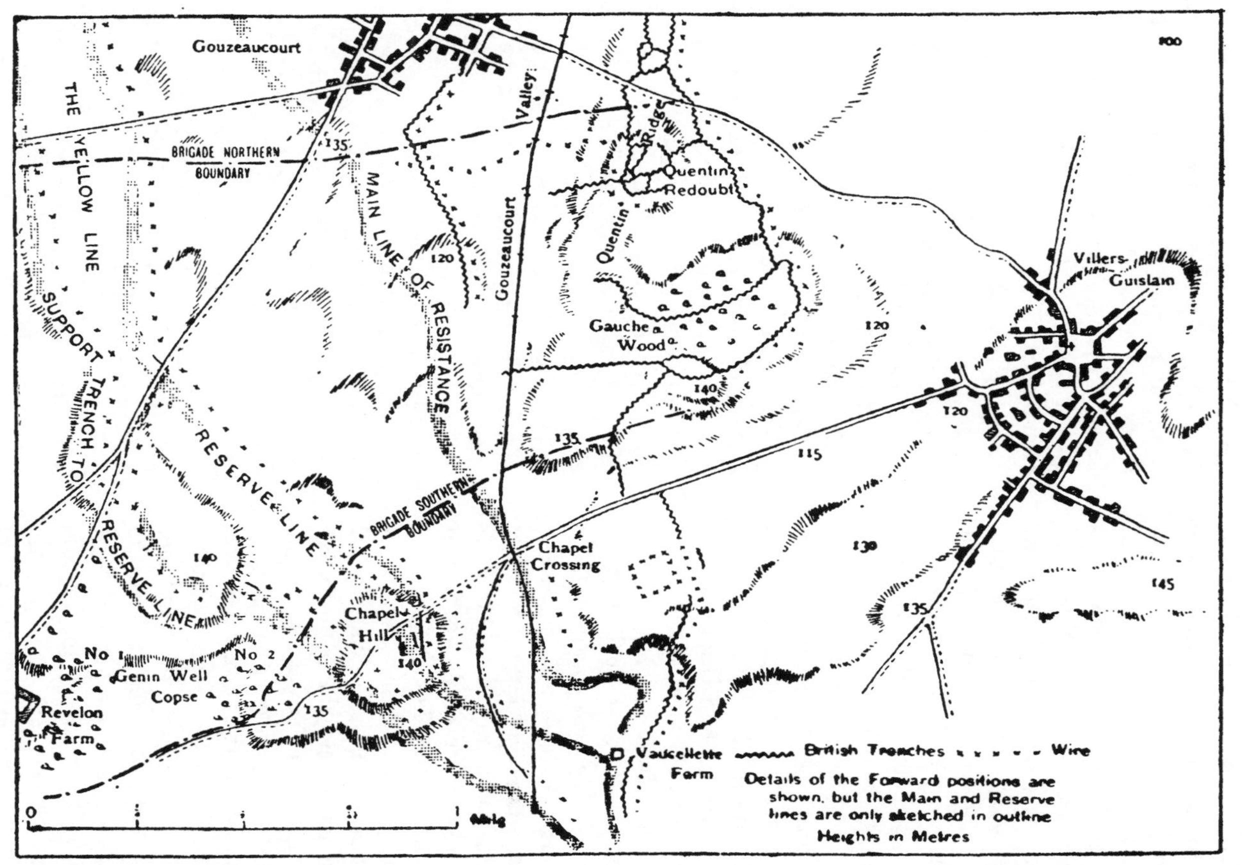

POSITIONS HELD BY THE SOUTH AFRICAN BRIGADE AT THE OUTSET OF THE GERMAN OFFENSIVE OF 1918.

South Africans on the right, with the 27th in reserve. The South African Brigade sector covered some 2,000 yards from just north of Quentin Redoubt to just south of Gauche Wood. The Brigade was distributed in depth—that is to say, it was responsible not only for the front line, but for all other trench lines to the depth of about a mile. This made it impossible for it to man the entire length of its trenches, so its front was held by a series of posts placed at key positions, and so arranged as to enable their occupants to cover the whole ground with their fire. As the hour of attack approached, the "forward zone" was held by the 2nd S.A.I. on the right and the 1st on the left, with the 4th S.A.I. in reserve in the "battle zone."

To understand the battle which followed, it is necessary to examine more closely the nature of the Brigade's position. The country around Gouzeaucourt is more deeply cut than most of the tableland, with small valleys and ravines running north by east. The South African "forward zone" lay west of the village of Villers-Guislain, and was separated from it by a well-defined hollow. The outpost line had two important points—Quentin Redoubt on the north, garrisoned by a company of the 1st S.A.I., and Gauche Wood on the south, held by a company of the 2nd S.A.I. The line of resistance ran from near the point called Chapel Crossing on the railway, along the west side of the Gouzeaucourt valley, and along the east side of the ruins of Gouzeaucourt. The "battle zone" began about the same point, and its first line, following the high ground west of the valley, curved round the western end of Gouzeaucourt. The reserve line of this zone lay some three-quarters of a mile farther west, from Chapel Hill along the eastern slope of the ridges north of Revelon Farm. This was known to the Brigade as the Yellow Line. A few hundred yards farther back, on the western slopes of the same ridges, lay the Brown Line, the final line of the "battle zone." Three miles in the rear lay what was known as the Green Line, the third zone of defence, which was still in embryo. Apart from the posts in the "forward zone," the specially fortified areas of resistance for the 9th Division were—for the 26th Brigade, Gouzeaucourt village and the place called Queen's Cross, south-east of Gouzeaucourt; and for the South Africans, Revelon Farm, and, should that fail, the village of Heudicourt.

The first weeks of March saw the dry, bright weather of a Picardy spring. As early as the 14th our airplanes reported a big concentration well back in the enemy's hinterland, and the Third and Fifth Armies were warned of an approaching battle. Many raids undertaken during these days established the arrival of fresh enemy divisions in line; but they gave us no notion of the real German strength. One fact, however, was learned—that Thursday, the 21st March, was the day appointed for the attack.

The last eight days were the quietest which the South African Brigade had ever known in the front line, and they had scarcely a casualty. On Tuesday, the 19th, the weather broke in a drizzle, but it cleared on the Wednesday, with the result that a thick mist was drawn out of the ground and muffled all the folds of the downs. There was no warning of any enemy movement, scarcely even a casual shell or the sputter of outpost fire.

About 2 a.m. on the morning of the 21st word was passed along our lines to expect an assault. The "forward zone" was always kept fully manned; but at half-past four the order went out to man the "battle zone." Then, precisely at a quarter to five, the whole weight of many thousand German guns was released on the British forward and battle zones, headquarters, communications, and artillery posts, the back areas specially being drenched with gas.

CHAPTER VI.

THE SOMME RETREAT: GAUCHE AND MARRIÈRES WOODS.
(MARCH 21–27, 1918.)

Our artillery replied to the German barrage as well as it might; but no gunner or machine-gunner or observer could see fifty yards before him. Under the cloak of the mist the vanguards of the enemy were everywhere cutting the wire and filtering between the Allied strongholds. The infantry attack was timed differently along the front, in parts beginning as early as 8 o'clock, but by 10 in the morning it was general. In the thick weather the enemy was beyond the places where the cross-fire of machine-guns might have checked him long before the redoubts were aware of his presence. The first thing which most of the outposts knew was that the Germans were in their rear, and they were overwhelmed before they could send back warning. Even when they had longer notice, the S.O.S. signals were everywhere blanketed by the fog. Presently the bulk of the outpost line was gone, and the enemy was well into our forward zone. There the line of resistance held on gallantly for hours; and long after the main battle had swept beyond it messages continued to be received from odd posts, until that silence came which meant destruction. The havoc wrought among our communications kept the battle zone in the dark as to what was happening in front. Often, too, in those hours of fog, our guns received their first news of the assault from the appearance of German infantry on flank and rear. A little after eleven the brume lightened, and it was possible to see something of the landscape to the east. With the lightening came the German airplanes, flying low to attack with machine-guns our troops and batteries.

The main outposts of the forward zone held by the South African Brigade were Quentin Redoubt and Gauche Wood. At the first, where a company of the 1st S.A.I. was stationed, there was no attack. The main enemy shock in that area fell upon the left brigade of the 21st Division, and "B" Company of the 2nd S.A.I. in Gauche Wood. This company was under the command of Captain Garnet Green. There were three strong-points inside the wood and one in the open on the south-west side; there were also in the wood two machine-guns and a detachment of the Brigade Trench Mortar Battery under Lieutenant Hadlow. Under cover of the fog the enemy worked his way into the wood from the east. Second Lieutenant Kennedy fought his machine-gun till all his team were killed or wounded, and he himself was wounded and taken. About 10.15 Captain Green reported that the Germans were in the wood, but that the strong-points were intact. Presently the enemy began to creep in from the north, and the two posts in the eastern half, under Lieutenant Bancroft and Lieutenant Beviss, were overpowered. Lieutenant Bancroft and most of his men fell, and the rest were wounded and captured, with the exception of one who rejoined company headquarters. Lieutenant Beviss, with nearly half his garrison, succeeded in cutting his way through and reaching Captain Green. The latter, finding that the enemy was on three sides of him in overpowering numbers, withdrew the garrison of the third post in the wood to join the fourth post in the open ground to the south-west. Every yard was fiercely contested, and, since the Germans exposed themselves recklessly, they lost heavily from the Lewis guns and rifles. They attempted to dig themselves in on the western edge of the wood, but our fire was too strong for them and they fell back in confusion into cover.

The situation was now clear to General Dawson. He directed the fire of all the guns at his disposal on Gauche Wood. Before midday the mist had lifted and the garrison of Quentin Redoubt on the north were able to open a heavy flanking fire on the advancing enemy. Throughout the rest of the day Captain Green, with his little band, was able to maintain his position on the western and south-western skirts of the wood. The situation, however, had become very serious farther south. At the first rush the Germans had forced back the left brigade of the 21st Division and taken the cluster of ruined buildings called Vaucellette Farm. This they used as an assembly position for extending their attacks. The right flank of the South African Brigade at Gauche Wood was therefore wholly exposed, and by the early afternoon the enemy had worked his way more than a mile westward, reaching the slopes of Chapel Hill.

The front had now a singular formation, running back sharply from the extreme point of Quentin Redoubt in the north-east, by the west side of Gauche Wood to the north side of Chapel Hill, which itself was in the area of the 21st Division. The two forward battalions of the South African Brigade, the 1st and the 2nd, were most gravely menaced. After midday came worse news, for the enemy was reported to be as far west as Genin Well Copse. It was necessary to recapture Chapel Hill, so "A" Company of the 2nd S.A.I., which had been reserved for a counter-attack, was sent early in the afternoon to strengthen the right flank. They found the Germans holding the trenches on the north ridge of the hill, and could make no further progress. Meantime the 4th S.A.I., which was manning the battle zone, was able to bring flanking fire to bear on the Germans at Genin Well Copse, and this, aided by a detachment of machine-gunners at Revelon Farm, stayed further enemy progress on the south.

At 3.30 the 2nd S.A.I. reported that the Germans were concentrating in large numbers south-west of Vaucellette Farm for a further attack. It was difficult to check them with artillery, for the guns of the Brigade at the time were covering not only their own front, but 600 yards of that of the 21st Division. At half-past five Lieut.-Colonel MacLeod, commanding the 4th S.A.I., was ordered to send a company to retake Chapel Hill. "A" Company, under Captain Bunce, was detailed for the purpose, and by a spirited counter-attack they took the crest as well as the trenches on the south and south-east slopes, and so enabled posts to be established linking up the ridge with Genin Well Copse.

During the afternoon orders arrived from the Division for a general retirement of all forward troops to the Yellow Line, and for Brigade Headquarters to fall back upon Sorel. The reason for this order lay in the general position of the battle. On the Fifth Army front the Germans had before midday broken into our battle zone at Ronssoy, Hargicourt, Templeux, and Le Verguier, and were threatening the valley of the Omignon. Later came news that the same thing had happened at Essigny and Maissemy. In the Third Army area the forward zone had gone at Lagnicourt and Bullecourt, and the fight was being waged in the battle zone northward from Doignies to the Sensée. Against 19 British divisions in line Ludendorff had hurled 37 divisions as the first wave, and before the dark fell not less than 64 German divisions had taken part in the battle—a number much exceeding the total strength of the British Army in France. In such a situation the Flesquières salient could not be maintained, though it had not been seriously attacked.

Accordingly during the evening and early night the South African Brigade fell back from the whole forward zone to the Yellow Line, the reserve position of the battle zone. The general line of the railway east of Gouzeaucourt was held up

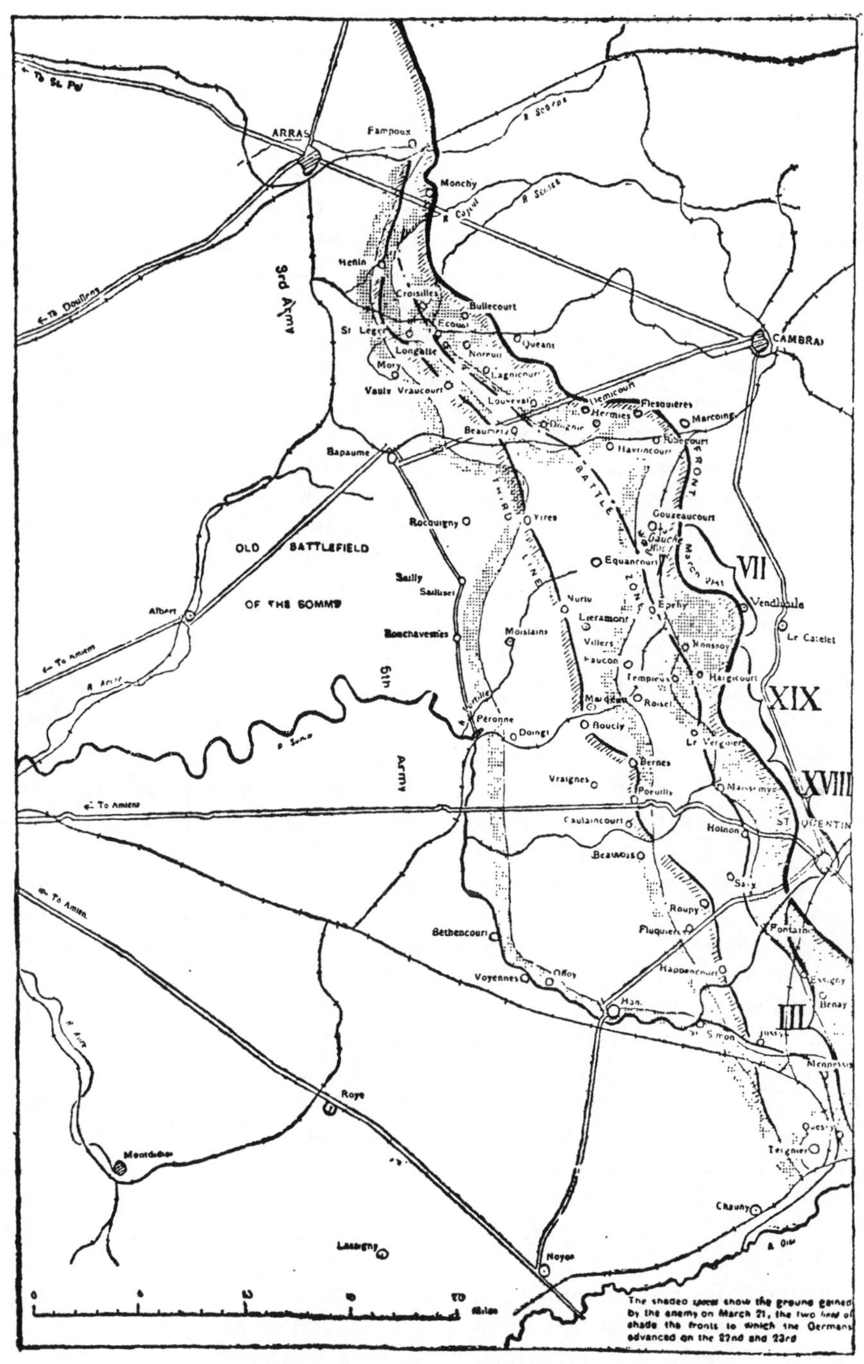

THE SOMME RETREAT.

till 2 a.m. on the 22nd, and by 5 a.m. the retirement was complete. During the night the left brigade of the 21st Division carried out a counter-attack, and re-established itself in the Yellow Line. By dawn on the 22nd the following was the disposition of the South African Brigade:—On the left the 1st S.A.I. held the Yellow Line with three companies, one platoon of each in the front line, and two in support. Its fourth company was in the Brown Line, the last line of the battle-zone system. On the right the 4th S.A.I. was in the Yellow Line and on Chapel Hill with three companies, and the remaining company at Revelon Farm. Two companies of the 2nd assisted the 4th in holding the advance position on Chapel Hill, and the remainder of that battalion was in the Brown Line. So closed the first day of the battle. The Brigade had not received the full shock of the German onrush, and its main concern had been its right flank, where, by the gallant defence of Gauche Wood and the rapid counter-attack on Chapel Hill, it had checked for the moment the dangerous enemy infiltration in the area of the 21st Division.

The fog thickened again in the night, and by the dawn of Friday, the 22nd, it was as dense as on the previous morning. The first day of the battle had by no means fulfilled Ludendorff's expectations; but he had time to spare, and had still the chance of complete victory. From the first light the enemy pressed heavily on the whole battle front, but notably at the danger spots which the previous day had revealed in the line of the Fifth Army. Once again he made no serious attack on the South African Brigade, except on its right flank, where he laboured to work his way through it and the left brigade of the 21st Division. He had brought up a number of light trench mortars, and opened a heavy bombardment on Chapel Hill, Genin Well Copse, Revelon Farm, and Railton. General Dawson had received during the night the 11th Royal Scots from the 27th Brigade, which he used in the Brown Line in front of Heudicourt.

Throughout the morning, under cover of a heavy bombardment from artillery and trench mortars, the Germans gradually closed round Chapel Hill and Revelon Farm, both of which fell in spite of a most gallant defence. Shortly after noon orders came from the Division to give up the Yellow Line and fall back upon the Brown, the retirement to be complete by 4.30, and to be ready to retire later to the Green Line, three miles in the rear. The Green Line was the third defence zone, a partly completed line of trenches between Nurlu and Equancourt. Each battalion in the Yellow Line was directed to leave one section per company as a rearguard on its retirement to the Brown Line. The first part was carried out successfully. But as soon as the enemy noticed the withdrawal he advanced in close formation, and presently had reached the Brown Line in the 21st Division's area, had outflanked Heudicourt, and was occupying the high ground south-west of that village. The retirement of the 4th S.A.I. was only made possible by an accurate supporting fire from the 2nd. General Dawson sent his Acting Brigade-Major, Captain Beverley, about 3.30, on horseback, to give the battalions the order to retire to the Green Line. This he succeeded in doing, after having his horse shot under him. All the troops had their instructions before 5 o'clock.

The disposition of the Brigade was now as follows:—On the right, at the quarry on the east of Heudicourt (the old Brigade Headquarters), was "B" Company of the 2nd S.A.I., with one company of the 11th Royal Scots and a few details of the 21st Division extending the line on the right. In the centre was the 4th S.A.I., and on the left the 1st S.A.I., both in the Brown Line. But the situation was full of peril, for the Brown Line was hopelessly outflanked on the right, and the enemy was moving northwards round the south end of Heudicourt. While the

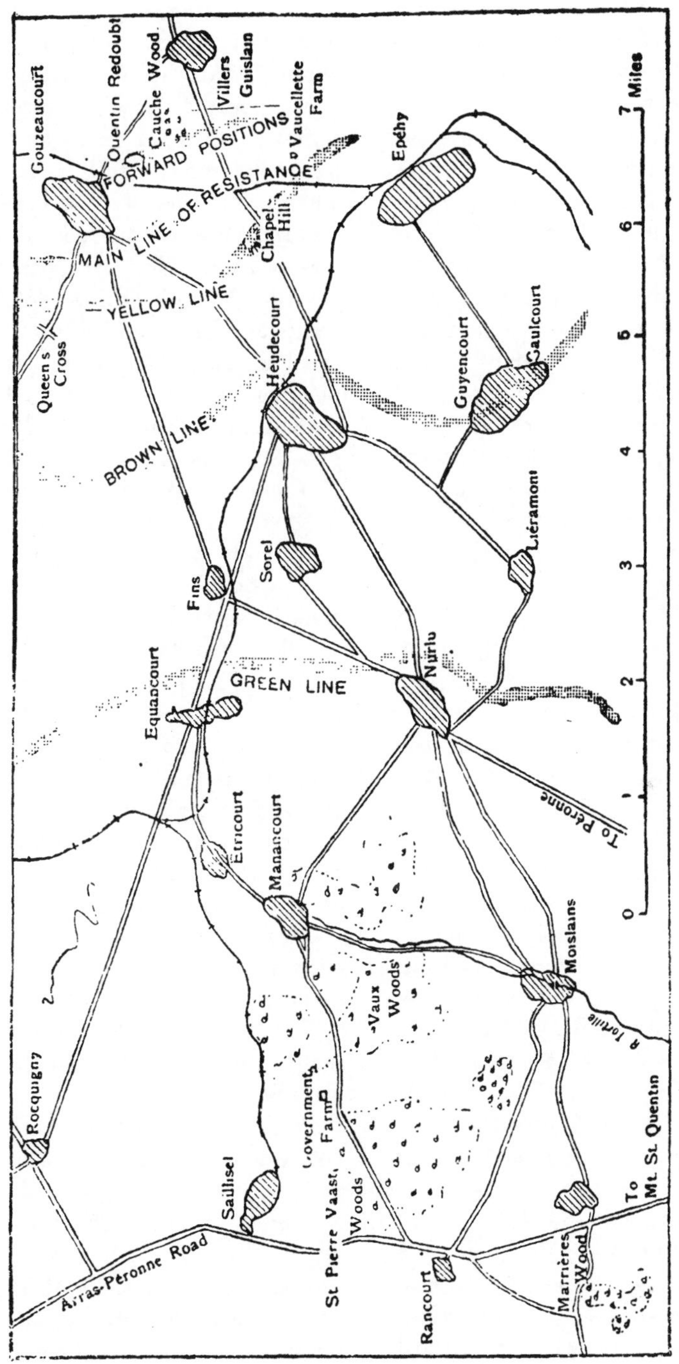

Retreat of South African Brigade.

guns were falling back, about thirty enemy airplanes, flying low, kept up a continual fire on the teams and also on the infantry in the trenches. Everything depended on whether the German advance could be stayed till darkness came, and under its cover the various units could reach the Green Line.

The Brigade Headquarters were at Sorel, and in the dusk the Germans could be seen in great strength moving westward south of the village. As our wounded and guns were passing through the place it was vital to defend it until the retirement was complete. The whole countryside seemed to be in flames; Heudicourt was spouting like a volcano, and everywhere was the glare of burning stores and bursting shells. The Brigade Headquarter Staff were formed up and put into the trenches east of Sorel, to give the guns and wounded time to get clear. About this time Major Cochran, the Brigade-Major, returned from leave and resumed his duties. The Headquarters details succeeded in arresting the enemy's advance, and, before he had time to reconnoitre or to organize an attack, the last guns had passed through Sorel, Brigade Headquarters withdrawing to Moislains.

The gravest danger was in the south, for any further enemy advance there would turn the Green Line. Owing to the Germans moving northward behind our front it was impossible to keep to the original route of retirement, and all three units had to withdraw in a northern direction before striking west. The task of the 1st S.A.I. on the left was the least difficult. Under Lieut.-Colonel Heal it fell back upon Fins. Lieut.-Colonel MacLeod, who commanded the 4th S.A.I., was wounded during the afternoon, and the remnant, under Captain Bunce, moved along the Brown Line to the Fins-Gouzeaucourt road, and then westward from Fins. The most difficult operation fell to Lieut.-Colonel Christian, of the 2nd S.A.I., but by a series of providential chances he extricated a large part of the regiment, following mainly the direction of the 4th. For "B" Company and its heroic commander, Captain Green, there was no chance of withdrawal. They were destroyed, fighting to the last. The details of the Brigade, to the strength of about 650 all ranks, had, on the 21st, been encamped at Heudicourt under Lieut.-Colonel Young. Early on the 22nd they were ordered to fall back upon Nurlu, where, together with other 9th Division details, they laboured to improve the Green Line. The Brigade in its retreat passed through these details, and by about two in the morning of the 23rd had reached the Green Line and taken up a position along the Nurlu-Péronne road south-east of Moislains. Two weak companies of the 1st S.A.I., under Captains Burgess and Ward, had become detached in the darkness, and for the next few days fought along with the 26th Brigade.

The South Africans were now in divisional reserve. Their casualties during the first two days of the battle had been about 900 all ranks. In the circumstances the withdrawal of the Brigade to the Green Line must be regarded as a very remarkable feat of arms. For two days they had fought with their flank turned, and only the tenacity and courage of the men and the extreme coolness and daring of the junior officers had prevented a wholesale disaster. At about five in the evening of the 22nd it might well have seemed that nothing could save them.

While we leave the South Africans secure for the moment in the Green Line, we must note what happened elsewhere that day on the battle front. The Third Army had been the less heavily engaged, and during the day yielded little ground. The enemy's main effort was against the Fifth Army, especially at the three critical points of the Cologne and Omignon valleys and the Crozat Canal. By midday the canal had been lost, and early in the afternoon the Fifth Army was almost everywhere in the third defensive zone. By the evening that zone had been broken around Vaux and Beauvois. Our last reserves had been thrown in, and. save for a French division and some French cavalry, now heavily engaged on the Crozat Canal, there was no help available for the hard-pressed Fifth Army. The gaps could not be stopped, so at all costs our front must withdraw. At 11 p.m. that night the Army Commander gave orders to fall back to the bridgehead position east of the Somme, a position which, as we have seen, was not yet completed. The XVIII Corps was to retire to the river line; the XIX Corps and VII Corps were to hold the Péronne bridgehead on a line running from Voyennes through Monchy-Lagache to Vraignes, and thence continue in the third zone to the junction with the Third Army at Equancourt. This compelled the Third Army to fall back to conform, and its front ran now in the third zone to Héninsur-Cojeul, whence the old battle zone was continued to Fampoux.

The third zone was nowhere a real defence, and presently it was clear that the Péronne bridgehead was little better. During the thick night, while the divisions of the Fifth Army, now in the last stages of fatigue, struggled westward, the Army Commander was faced with a momentous decision. He now knew the weight of the German attack; his right flank was in desperate peril; he had no hope of support for several days; and his men strung out on an immense front had been fighting without rest for forty-eight hours. If he faced a general engagement on the morrow he might suffer decisive defeat. There seemed no course open to him but to abandon the Péronne bridgehead, and fall back behind the river. It was a difficult decision, for it shortened our time for defending the river line and for clearing troops and material from the east bank. But the alternative was certain disaster, and beyond doubt in the circumstances General Gough's judgment was right. Accordingly, very early on the morning of Saturday, the 23rd March, instructions were given to the XIX Corps to withdraw gradually to the river line, while the VII Corps, on its left, was to take up a position between Doingt and Nurlu. The front of the VII Corps would now just cover Péronne on the north, and it would have behind it, flowing from north to south, the little river Tortille.

Saturday, 23rd March, dawned again in fog, and from an early hour it became clear that the position allotted to the VII Corps could not be held. That day Von der Marwitz began the most dangerous movement of all—the attempt to drive a wedge between the Third and Fifth Armies. Very early in the morning he attacked the Green Line, which was held by details of the 9th Division. The advance was checked; but the position was clearly untenable, and the South African details, under Lieut.-Colonel Young, fell back to Bouchavesnes, where they again came under General Dawson's orders.

That day the South African Brigade was nominally in reserve, holding a position in echelon on the right flank of the 27th Brigade. But a wavering front, faced by preposterous odds, called every man into the fight, and presently the Brigade was in the front line again on the right of the 27th, endeavouring to maintain touch with the 21st Division, which was compelled to retire by the withdrawal on its right from the Péronne bridgehead. During the morning the South African Brigade fell back from Moislains, and took up ground about midday on the ridge south-west of that village, overlooking the Tortille River, where, during the afternoon, it was heavily shelled. Once again came the old menace on the right wing. The 21st Division, itself outflanked by the withdrawal farther south, was again retiring, and presently the Brigade's flank was in the air, and the enemy in the immediate south was more than a mile behind its front. General Dawson had five tanks as a flank-guard, and he endeavoured to fling out posts as a defensive flank across the Péronne-Arras road. An officer and twenty men were sent to occupy the cutting on the summit of the ridge overlooking Mont St. Quentin. All afternoon the enemy poured down the slopes along the Péronne-Nurlu road, and before dark fell he had occupied Moislains and Haute-Allaines.

General Tudor visited General Dawson in the evening. The situation of the whole 9th Division under Von der Marwitz's thrust had grown desperate. It was holding an impossibly long line, and a gap had opened between its left and the V Corps in the Third Army, of which the enemy had promptly taken advantage, in spite of gallant attempts to fill the breach made by the 47th London Division and a brigade of the 2nd. On its right it was out of touch with the 2st Division; so that that evening it was holding a salient of high ground with both flanks hopelessly in the air. There was no other course but to fall back, especially as the retirement of the 21st Division was by no means at an end. The 1st S.A.I. had been moved from the left of the South African Brigade to strengthen the right flank, but it could not hope to fill the breach, the more as the enemy was pressing hard from Moislains against this weak spot.

General Tudor told General Dawson that instructions had come for the Division to withdraw after dark to a position on the line from Government Farm by the east of St. Pierre Vaast Wood to the road just west of Bouchavesnes which led to Cléry. He informed him that the Corps Commander had ordered that this line must be held " at all costs," and added that he presumed, if it was broken, it would be retaken by a counter-attack. These words of General Tudor's are of importance, for they were General Dawson's charter for the fighting of the next day. He was also bidden keep in close touch with the troops on his right—a counsel of perfection hard to follow, for the Army Commander's decision on the night of the 22nd involved an indefinite retreat westward, and in such circumstances a unit which had orders to stand at all costs must inevitably be left in the void. General Dawson saw his commanding officers, Heal and Christian (the remnants of the 4th had now been attached to the 2nd), and explained to them the gravity of the position. Whoever retired, the Brigade must stand.

The withdrawal started at 9.45 p.m., and the last troops had begun their retreat by 11 p.m. At 3 a.m. on the morning of the 24th all were in position in the new line. It was not the line which General Tudor had indicated, for by this time the left brigade of the 21st Division was more than a mile westward of that front, and if the South African Brigade was to stand it must find ground which, at any rate to begin with, was not hopelessly untenable. General Dawson decided to occupy a ridge some 1,500 yards west of General Tudor's line, so that by throwing back his right flank he might reduce the gap between the South African Brigade and the 21st Division to a less dangerous size. His Brigade-Major was sent to prospect the position while it was still light, and to get into touch with the neighbouring Brigadier of the 21st, from whom he learned that immediately after dark that brigade intended to make a further retirement. In the South African withdrawal some of the posts flung out on the right flank lost their way, and wandered back to the transport lines. During the night touch was obtained with the 21st Division, which, after retiring, had again advanced. The left flank of the Brigade was in touch with a company of the 6th K.O.S.B. of the 27th Brigade. The situation on that flank, however, was far from secure, for the K.O.S.B. did not know the whereabouts of the rest of their battalion or of their brigade. General Dawson sent out patrols to look for them, but there was no sign of them anywhere in the countryside.

By dawn on Sunday, the 24th, the South African Brigade was holding a patch of front which lay roughly behind the northern point of Marrières Wood,

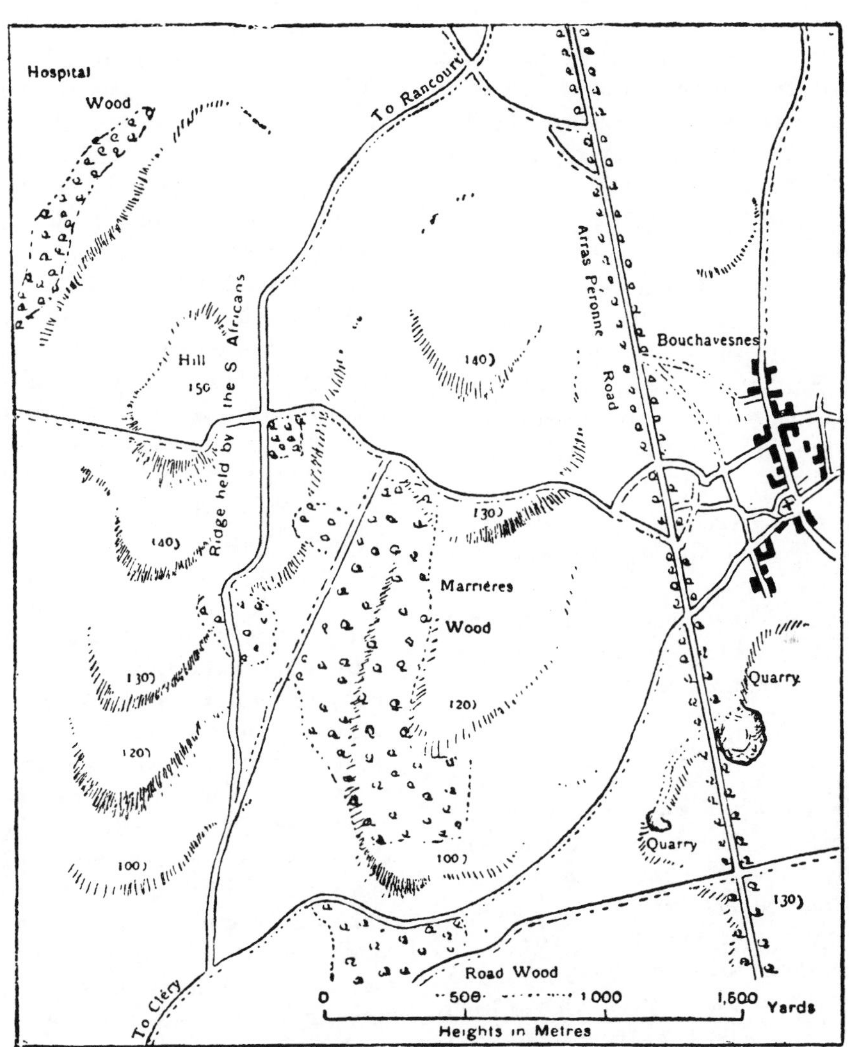

THE FIGHT AT MARRIÈRES WOOD.

running north-east in the direction of Rancourt, a little over two miles north-west of Bouchavesnes village. The ground sloped eastward, and then rose again to another ridge about 1,000 yards distant. There was one good trench and several bad ones, and the whole area was dotted with shell-holes. General Dawson took up his headquarters in a support trench some 300 yards in rear of the front line. The strength of the Brigade was about 500 in all, composed of 478 men from the infantry, one section of the 9th Machine-gun Battery, and a few men from Brigade Headquarters.

On the morning of the 24th each man of the Brigade had 200 rounds of ammunition and there was a fair supply of Lewis gun drums. One section, however, of the Machine-gun Battery had only four belts of ammunition, and three of the guns with their teams were therefore sent back to the transport lines at Savernake Wood.

Soon after daylight had struggled through the fog the enemy was seen massing his troops on the ridge to the east, and about 9 o'clock he deployed for the attack, opening with machine-gun fire, and afterwards with artillery. At 10 o'clock some British guns opened an accurate fire, not upon the enemy but upon the South African lines, especially on the trench where was situated Brigade Headquarters. Three runners were sent to tell the batteries what was happening, but the messengers do not seem to have reached their goal, and the fire continued for more than an hour, though happily with few casualties. After that it ceased, because the guns had retired. One of our heavies continued to fire on Bouchavesnes, and presently that, too, was silent.

It was the last the Brigade heard of the British artillery.

Meantime the enemy gun-fire had become intense, and the whole position was smothered in dust and fumes. Men could not keep their rifles clean because of the débris choking the air. The Germans were now some 750 yards from our front, but did not attempt for the moment to approach closer. The firing was mostly done at this time by Lewis guns, for ammunition had to be husbanded, and the men were ordered not to use their rifles till the enemy was within 400 yards. He attempted to bring a field gun into action at a range of 1,000 yards, but a Lewis gunner of the 1st S.A.I. knocked out the team before the gun could be fired. A little later another attempt was made, and a field gun was brought forward at a gallop. Once again the fire of the same Lewis gunner proved its undoing. The team got out of hand and men and horses went down in a struggling mass.

About noon General Tudor sent word that the 35th Division, which had arrived at Bray-sur-Somme, had been ordered to take up position 1,000 yards in rear of the Brigade. For a moment it seemed as if they still might make good their stand. But during that day the 35th Division was never within seven miles of the South African Brigade. General Dawson sent back a report on the situation to General Tudor. It was the last communication of the Brigade with the outer world.

By midday the frontal attack had been held, an attack on the south had been beaten off, and so had a very dangerous movement in the north. The grass in that parched week was as dry as tinder. The enemy set fire to it and, moving behind the smoke as a screen, managed to work his way to within 200 yards of our position in the north. There, however, he was again checked. But by this time the German thrust elsewhere on the front was bearing fruit. Already the enemy was in Combles on the north and at Péronne and Cléry on the south. The 21st Division had gone, and the other brigades of the 9th Division were being forced back on the South African left. At about half-past two on that flank an officer with some thirty men began to withdraw under the impression that a general retirement had been ordered. As they passed Headquarters, Major Cochran and Captain

Marrières Wood.

Beverley, with Regimental Sergeant-Major Keith of the 4th S.A.I., went out to stop them under a concentrated machine-gun fire. The party at once returned to the firing-line and were put into shell-holes on the north flank. Unhappily Cochran was hit in the neck by a machine-gun bullet and died within three minutes.

General Dawson, early in the afternoon, attempted to adjust his remnant. The enemy now was about 200 yards from his front and far in on his flank and rear. Major Ormiston, 1st S.A.I., took out some twenty-five men as a flank-guard for the left. All wounded who could possibly hold a rifle were stopped on their way to the dressing-station, and sent back to the front line. Ammunition was conserved with a noble parsimony, and the last round was collected from casualties. But it was now clear that the enemy was well to the west of the Brigade, for snipers' fire began to come from that direction. For the moment the most dangerous quarter seemed to be the north and Lieutenant Cooper of the 2nd S.A.I., with twenty men, was sent out to make a flank-guard in shell-holes 100 yards from Brigade Headquarters. The little detachment did excellent work, but their casualties were heavy, and frequent reinforcements had to be sent out to them.

As it drew towards 3 o'clock there came a last flicker of hope. The enemy in the north seemed to be retiring, and at the same time the enemy artillery lengthened and put down a heavy barrage 700 yards to the west of the Brigade. It looked as if the 35th Division had arrived. All that had happened was that the enemy machine-guns and snipers to the west of the Brigade were causing casualties to his troops to the east. He therefore assumed that they were British reinforcements.

About this time Lieut.-Colonel Heal, commanding the 1st S.A.I., was killed. He had already been twice wounded in the action, but insisted on remaining with his men.

All afternoon the shell-fire had been terrific. Batteries of 7.7 cm., 10.5 cm., and 15 cm. were in action, many of them in full view of our men. A number of light trench mortars were firing against the north-east corner of our front and causing heavy losses. The casualties had been so high that the whole line was now held only by a few isolated groups, and control was impossible. Every machine-gun and Lewis gun was out of action, the ammunition was nearly gone, the rifles were choked, and the breaking-point had been reached of human endurance.

Some time after 4.15 p.m. enemy masses appeared to the east-north-east of Brigade Headquarters. It was the final attack, for which three fresh battalions had been brought up, and the assault was delivered in close formation. There were now only 100 South Africans, some of them already wounded. There was not a cartridge left in the front line, and very few anywhere except in the pistols of the officers. The South African Brigade had resisted to the last moment when resistance was possible; and now they had no weapon. The Germans surged down upon a few knots of unarmed men.

The Brigade had ceased to be. Less than 100 unwounded prisoners fell to the enemy; the rest were killed or crippled or lost, all but the little group of details and stragglers now in the transport lines. The rest of the 9th Division, along with the remnants of the 21st, were now fighting desperately north of the Somme behind Cléry, struggling to the line from Ham through Trônes Wood to Longueval, where the 35th Division and the 1st Cavalry Division were to come to their aid. It will be remembered that two companies of the 1st S.A.I. had gone astray on the night of the 22nd and had since been fighting with other brigades. There were also the parties left behind in the Brown Line on that date, which had been unable to rejoin their units, and there were the posts flung out on the right flank on the 23rd, and which had lost their road in the last withdrawal.

These oddments, along with the details and the transport of the Brigade, collected that evening half-way between Bray and Maricourt, and on the following day were formed into a composite battalion of three companies under Lieut.-Colonel Young. Each company represented a regiment of the Brigade. The fighting strength was some 450 rifles. On the 26th they were ordered to Dernancourt to report to General Kennedy of the 26th Brigade. They there found the 9th Division holding a line from that village to south of Albert, and took up a position in trenches and along the railway embankment south-east of the former place. This ground they held in spite of furious enemy efforts to dislodge them, until they were relieved by the Australians on the night of the 27th, when the whole division was withdrawn from the line.

In all that amazing retreat, when our gossamer front refused to be broken by the most fantastic odds, no British division did more nobly than the 9th. It held a crucial position in the line, and only by its stubborn endurance was a breach between the Fifth and Third Armies prevented. Among the brigades of the 9th, the chief brunt was borne by the South African. A great achievement is best praised in the language of the commanders themselves. General Tudor wrote:—

"I think everybody should know how magnificently the South African Brigade fought. None but the best could have got through on the 22nd from the Yellow Line with Heudicourt in the hands of the enemy. They were sadly thinned then, only about 900 rifles all told when they got back, but they left their mark on the Hun. The story of the magnificent stand made by the Brigade when afterwards surrounded can only be told by those who were with it to the last; but this much is certain, that it was shortage of ammunition alone which made the survivors surrender. The division will not seem the same again without them, and it was they who bore the brunt of the fighting of the 9th on the 21st and 22nd."

Here are General Dawson's words:—

"It is impossible for me to do justice to the magnificent courage displayed by all ranks under my command during this action. For the two years I have been in France I have seen nothing better. Until the end they appeared to me quite perfect. The men were cool and alert, taking advantage of every opportunity, and, when required, moving forward over the open under the hottest machine-gun fire and within 100 yards of the enemy. They seemed not to know fear, and in my opinion they put forth the greatest effort of which human nature is capable. I myself witnessed several cases of great gallantry, but do not know the names of the men. *The majority, of course, will never be known.* It must be borne in mind that the Brigade was in an exhausted state before the action, and in the fighting of the three previous days it was reduced in numbers from a trench strength of over 1,800 to 500."

The stand of the South African Brigade was no piece of fruitless gallantry. General Dawson, as he was tramping eastwards, saw a sight which told him that his decision had been right, and that his work had not been in vain. The whole road for miles east of Bouchavesnes was blocked by a continuous double line of transport and guns, which proved that the South African Brigade had for over seven hours held up not only a mass of German infantry, but all the artillery and transport advancing on the Bouchavesnes-Combles highway. Indeed, it is not too much to say that on that Sabbath the stand of the Brigade saved the British front. It was the hour of Von der Marwitz's most deadly thrust. While the Fifth Army was struggling at the river crossings, the Third Army had been forced west of Morval and Bapaume, far over our old battle-ground of the Somme. The breach between the two armies was hourly widening. But for the self-sacrifice of the Brigade at Marrières

Wood and the delay in the German advance at its most critical point, it is doubtful whether the Third Army could ever have established that line on which, before the end of March, it held the enemy.

CHAPTER VII.

THE BATTLE OF THE LYS.

(MARCH 27—MAY 5, 1918.)

When the composite battalion, under Lieut.-Colonel Young, was withdrawn from the line on the night of 27th March it marched along with the rest of the 9th Division to Candas, arriving there on 1st April. It detrained at Abeele on the morning of the 2nd, and moved into the Ridgewood area. Every man who could be found was brought from England, and during the next few days drafts to the number of 17 officers and 945 other ranks arrived. The reorganization of the Brigade was immediately begun, and General Tanner, the former leader of the 2nd S.A.I., came from the 8th Brigade to its command. Presently the Brigade had a strength of 39 officers and 1,473 other ranks, and the old battalions were once more in being, the 1st under Lieut.-Colonel Young, the 2nd under Captain Jacobs, and the 4th under Captain Reid.

By the 6th of April the German thrust towards Amiens had failed, and for the moment the gate of the Somme was closed. Brought to a standstill, Ludendorff cast about for a diversion, for he could not permit the battle to decline into a stalemate, and so lose the initiative. His main purpose was the same, but he sought to achieve it by a new method. He would attack the British elsewhere on some part of the front where they were notoriously weak, and compel Foch to use up his reserves in its defence. Then, when the Allied "mass of manœuvre" had shrunk, he would strike again at the weakened door of Amiens. On Ludendorff's plan the operation was to be a strictly subsidiary one, designed to prepare the way for the accomplishment of his main task farther south. He proposed to allot only nine divisions for the initial stroke, and to choose a batle-ground where even a weak force might obtain surprising results.

That battle-ground was the area on both sides of the Lys between the La Bassée Canal and the Wytschaete Ridge. The German Staff were aware that it had already been thinned to supply ten divisions for the contest in the south, and that at the moment it was weakly held, mainly by troops exhausted in the Somme battle. Sir Douglas Haig, as we know from his dispatch, had drawn especially upon this section, since a retreat there would not imperil the whole front so gravely as would the loss of ground between La Bassée and Arras. Nevertheless, it was a very real danger-point. The enemy had the great city of Lille to screen his assembly. Certain key-points of communications, like Béthune and Hazebrouck, lay at no great distance behind the British front. The British communications were poor, and the German were all but perfect. Any advance threatened the Channel Ports, and might be expected to cause acute nervousness in the mind of British Headquarters. Reinforcements would be demanded from Foch, and the place was far enough from the Amiens battle-ground to put a heavy strain upon the Allied power of reinforcement. Ludendorff's aim was by a sharp, short thrust to confuse the Allied plans and absorb their reserves. If he could break through at once between La Bassée and Armentières and capture Béthune, he could swing north-westward and take Hazebrouck and the hills beyond Bailleul, and so compel a general retirement west of Dunkirk and the floods of the river Aa. But to succeed he must have a broad enough front. He must take Béthune at once and the Messines Ridge soon after, for, if the British pillars of the gate at Givenchy and Messines should stand, his advance would be squeezed into narrows where even a weak and tired force might hold it.

On the 8th of April the South African Brigade moved to hutments along the road between La Clytte and the little hill of Scherpenberg. On the morning of Tuesday, 9th April, Ludendorff struck between the Lys and La Bassée with Von Quast's Sixth Army. He broke that part of the line held by the Portuguese, and in the afternoon had swept over the Lys on a broad front. But at one vital point he failed. The 55th Division still held the gatepost at Givenchy, and throughout the whole battle that key-position was never yielded by British troops.

That night General Tudor instructed General Tanner that the South Africans would be placed at the disposal of the 19th Division, which, along with the 25th and 9th Divisions, was holding the Messines Ridge and the line just north of the Lys. The corps was the IX, under Lieut.-General Sir A. Hamilton Gordon. Next morning, 10th April, at 5.30, the Fourth German Army, under Sixt von Armin, attacked from Frelinghien to as far north as Hill 60. Under cover of the fog the enemy filtered into our positions from Ploegsteert Wood to Messines along the valleys of the Warnave and Douve streams. By noon he had taken Ploegsteert village and the south-east part of the wood, and had got Messines, while farther north he had driven in our line as far as Hollebeke, and was close on the Wytschaete crest.

At eight that morning the Brigade was ordered to move to a position of assembly just south of the village of Neuve Eglise, where they formed part of the reserve of the IX Corps. The march was accomplished during the morning.

At noon General Tanner saw the General Officer Commanding the 19th Division, and received his orders. The enemy had broken through between Messines and the place called Pick House on the Wytschaete road, and the situation at the moment was obscure. The South Africans were to counter-attack and retake that section of the crest of the ridge. The front established by the Messines victory of June, 1917, had been more than two miles east of the crest, but that morning's fighting had brought it back generally to the western slopes. The counter-attack, in which the 57th and 58th Brigades of the 19th Division were to co-operate, was aimed at recovering the ridge and its eastern slopes. The area of the South African Brigade was between Messines village and Lumm's Farm. Their first objective was the Messines-Wytschaete road; the second the original British third defence zone, bending round the village on the east from Bethlehem Farm in the south to Pick House in the north; and the third the original battle zone. The defence system in this area had not the elaboration of that of the Somme, and the second and third objectives may be best described as the old British third and second lines.

At 5.15 p.m. the South African Brigade moved from its position of assembly to the line of the Steenebeek stream, where, at 5.45, it deployed for the attack. The 1st S.A.I. was on the right, and directed against Messines village; the 2nd on the left against the front between the village and Pick House. The 4th was in support to both battalions, and one of its companies was allotted to the assistance of the attack of the 1st on Messines itself. The spring day had clouded over, and there was mist and a slight drizzle when the infantry advanced. The western slopes of the ridge were held at the time only by some units of the 19th Division. On the South African Brigade right was the 57th Brigade, and on its left, beyond Pick House, on the Wytschaete Ridge, the rest of the 9th Division.

Messines, from Trenches South of Village.

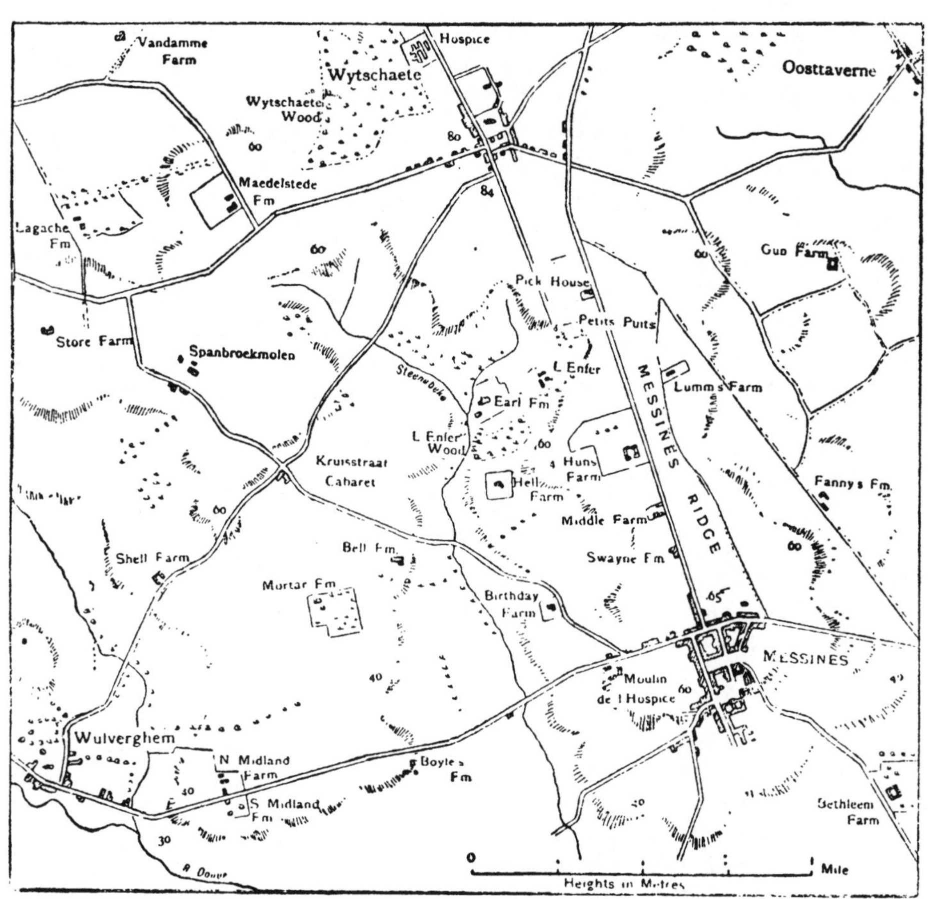

ACTION OF SOUTH AFRICAN BRIGADE ON MESSINES RIDGE.

In the mist it was not easy to keep close touch, and the 1st S.A.I. reached the western slopes ahead of the time, so that for a little its left flank was out of touch with the 2nd. As had been expected, our artillery support proved very weak, and in no way affected the German machine-gunners established in our old strong-points, and their snipers in shell-holes. As the South African Brigade approached the crest it was met by a heavy fire from the outskirts of the village, and from Middle Farm, Four Huns Farm, and Pick House. Nevertheless, by 6.30 the 2nd S.A.I. had won its first objective and crossed the Messines-Wytschaete road. Presently it had reached the second position, "D" Company, on the left, capturing Lumm's Farm with two machine-guns, much ammunition, and part of the garrison, while the right companies, reinforced by part of the 4th S.A.I., took Four Huns Farm, Middle Farm, and Swayne's Farm, together with four machine-guns and many prisoners. Pick House itself, however, which consisted of three concrete pill-boxes, was too strongly held, and Captain Jacobs, commanding the 2nd S.A.I., was compelled to swing back his left company to Earl Farm, where it formed a defensive flank in touch with the 5th South Wales Borderers in the 58th Brigade. Here it was heavily enfiladed from a strong-point north of Messines and from Pick House, and early in the night Captain Jacobs took up a crescent-shaped line astride the Messines-Wytschaete road, with his right resting on Middle Farm, his left on Petits Puits, and his own headquarters at Hell Farm. The casualties on the left had been slight, but the companies of the 2nd S.A.I. on the right had lost some 50 per cent. of their effectives.

In the meantime the 1st S.A.I. had met the enemy issuing from Messines, had charged him with the bayonet, and had driven him back well over the ridge. In the eastern outskirts of the village, however, they were held up by heavy machine-gun fire from the direction of Bethlehem Farm, and from various strong-points north of it. One of the latter was captured, and many prisoners were taken. For an hour there was severe hand-to-hand fighting, in which many casualties were sustained, all the officers in the vicinity being either killed or wounded. Owing to the shortage of men the position soon became untenable, and what was left of the 1st S.A.I. was compelled to withdraw to a line about 100 yards west of Messines. The headquarters of the 4th S.A.I. in support had been established at Birthday Farm.

The situation, therefore, on the evening of the 10th was as follows:—The new German line ran from Hollebeke, east of Wytschaete, which was held by the 9th Division; along the crest of the Messines Ridge, and just west of the village; through the south-east corner of Ploegsteert Wood, and west of Ploegsteert village. Farther south the advance was deeper, for the enemy were north of Steenwerck, north and west of Estaires, just east of Lestrem and the Lawe River, and then curving south-eastward in front of the unbroken position at Givenchy. It was a narrow front for a great advance, for the pillars at Givenchy and the Messines Ridge were still standing. The safety of the British front depended upon the 55th, the 19th, and the 9th Divisions.

Little happened during the night of the 10th. The South African Brigade retained its ground and endeavoured to gain touch with the troops of the 9th Division about Pick House, while the 4th S.A.I. took over part of the line of the depleted 1st. On the morning of the 11th the 108th Brigade was moved forward in support of the South Africans, and took up a line along the Steenebeek stream. The South African Brigade front at the time ran from the western skirts of Messines through the Moulin de l'Hospice, then to Middle Farm and Lumm's Farm northwards, and back to Petits Puits, with an outpost at Rommen's Farm.

Pill-Box, Messines Village.

Early in the afternoon Von Armin attacked with fresh troops, and the situation north of the Lys became very grave. On the British right the 40th Division was forced well north of Steenwerck. On its left the 34th Division was strongly attacked, and with difficulty succeeded in holding Nieppe, which, owing to the pressure on the 25th Division from Ploegsteert, had now become an ugly salient. That afternoon Hill 63 was lost. The enemy attacked in great force on the South African left on the line between Middle Farm and Petits Puits, and drove the 2nd S.A.I. back to a front parallel to and about 600 yards west of the Messines-Wytschaete road. Captain Jacobs having been wounded during the morning, Captain L. Greene assumed command, and, with Lieutenant Thompson of the 4th S.A.I., immediately counter-attacked and regained the lost ground. Presently, however, the enemy succeeded in working round the left flank, and the South Africans were compelled to retire to a line 200 yards east of Hell Farm, where they were in touch on their left with the 5th South Wales Borderers. In this position, in spite of repeated assaults, they were able to remain during the evening. There was also trouble on the right, where the 4th S.A.I. had relieved the 1st. Middle Farm had been strongly assaulted, and our counter-attack had sustained severe casualties. The 108th Brigade moved up in support, and for the moment the German advance was arrested.

The loss of Hill 63, though the 9th Division was still standing south of Hollebeke and at Wytschaete, compelled Plumer to rearrange his front. Early on the night of the 11th he relinquished Nieppe, retiring the 34th Division to the neighbourhood of Pont d'Echelles. This involved the falling back of the 25th and 19th Divisions to a front about 1,000 yards east of Neuve Eglise and Wulverghem, and the consequent abandonment of the important point Hill 63, just north of the western extremity of Ploegsteert Wood. South of the Lys there had been heavy fighting. The line of the Lawe had been lost, and by this time the enemy was in Merville. That night the British front ran from Givenchy to Locon, west of Merville, west of Neuf Berquin, north of Steenwerck and Nieppe, east of Neuve Eglise and Wulverghem, west of Messines, and along the ridge just covering Wytschaete.

About 2 p.m. on the 11th information had been received at Brigade Headquarters to the effect that in the event of the loss of Hill 63, which was on the right of the South African front, and was being strongly attacked, a general withdrawal would be necessary during the night, and about 4 p.m. orders were received from the 19th Division for this withdrawal, which was to take place in the early hours of the morning of the 12th April. The South African Brigade was to fall back to a line from North Midland Farm by Kruisstraat Cabaret and Spanbroekmolen to Maedelstaede Farm, with the 108th Brigade on their right and the 57th in reserve along the Neuve Eglise-Kemmel road. About 8 o'clock the Germans were found to be working round the left flank in the vicinity of L'Enfer. This flank had been continuously exposed throughout these operations, as touch with the troops attached to the 9th Division had not been established, accordingly two companies of the 1st Battalion Royal Irish Fusiliers from the 108th Infantry Brigade were sent to protect this flank and if possible obtain touch with these troops on the left. For the rest, the withdrawal was carried out without incident. By 5 a.m. on the 12th the South African Brigade was in its new front.

Up to now the enemy had not used more than sixteen divisions; but on the morning of Friday, the 12th, he began to throw in his reserves at a furious pace. Elated by his rapid success, he turned what was meant as a diversion into a major operation, and dreamed of Boulogne and Calais. It was Ludendorff's first blunder, and it was fatal. It saved the Allied front, but for the moment it all but destroyed the British Army. Our reinforcements were arriving from the south, but they could only gradually come into line. That day the enemy came very near to crossing the La Bassée Canal. He made an ugly gap in our line south-west of Bailleul, which let through detachments, who seized Merris and Oultersteene north of the railway. He was now close on Bailleul Station, pushing direct for Hazebrouck, and but for a gallant stand of a brigade of the 33rd Division would have been through the breach. In the section of the 9th and 19th Divisions nothing happened. The enemy, having gained the Messines Ridge, was apparently content to rest there for a time, and made no further attack.

The South African Brigade was to have been relieved during the night of the 12th, but the relief was cancelled, since the troops detailed to take its place had to be used to restore the situation farther south. During the night General Tanner established an outpost line along the Wulverghem-Wytschaete road. On the morning of Saturday, the 13th, his outposts reported that the Germans, under cover of the mist, were massing opposite Kruisstraat Cabaret. They were quickly dispersed by our artillery, which during the day dealt faithfully with similar concentrations. That night the Brigade was relieved in line by the 58th, and withdrew to hutments at La Clytte, where it came once more under the 9th Division.

The stand at Messines by the South Africans played a vital part in the Battle of the Lys. For thirty hours the Brigade delayed the enemy's advance, and took heavy toll of him. In the words of the special order of the IX Corps, "Its tenacity in the face of superior numbers and heavy firing undoubtedly relieved a serious situation, and obliged the enemy, when he was able to occupy the ridge, to be content to stay there during the whole of the 12th April without any further attempt to advance." Major-General Jeffreys, commanding the 19th Division, and Sir A. Hamilton Gordon, the Corps Commander, bore testimony to the quality of the exploit. The latter wrote: "I wish to express to the General of the South African Brigade, and to all his officers and men, my appreciation of their wonderful fighting spirit and most gallant doings in the great fight which we have been having in the last three days against heavy odds." Sir Herbert Plumer wrote that if any unit could be selected for exceptional praise it was the South African Brigade. Remember that the great majority of the men were new drafts, who had just arrived from home. Once again the Brigade had performed what seemed to be its predestined duty in an action—fighting outside its own area with its flank turned; and, as was inevitable, it paid a heavy price. For the three days its casualty list amounted to 639 all ranks; of these 89 were killed, 270 wounded, and 280 were missing, of whom the majority were afterwards proved to be dead. Yet, as the men marched back from the line, their spirits seemed to be as high as when they had entered it.

In the early hours of Tuesday, the 16th, the British front at Wytschaete and Spanbroekmolen was attacked in force, with the result that both places fell. At 8.30 came orders from the 9th Division that the South African Brigade was to move at once to a position in the Vierstraat line from Desinet Farm, in the north, to La Polka, just east of Kemmel village. General Tudor was about to attempt the recapture of Wytschaete. By noon the South African Brigade was in position, the 1st S.A.I. on the right, 250 strong, and the 4th S.A.I., with the same strength, on the left, while the 2nd S.A.I., 292 strong, was disposed in the second line along the whole front in the trenches, which were known as Sackville Street.

At 3.30 in the afternoon General Tanner was instructed to send 100 men of the 2nd S.A.I. to occupy an advanced position between Store Farm and Van Damme Farm, part of the line from

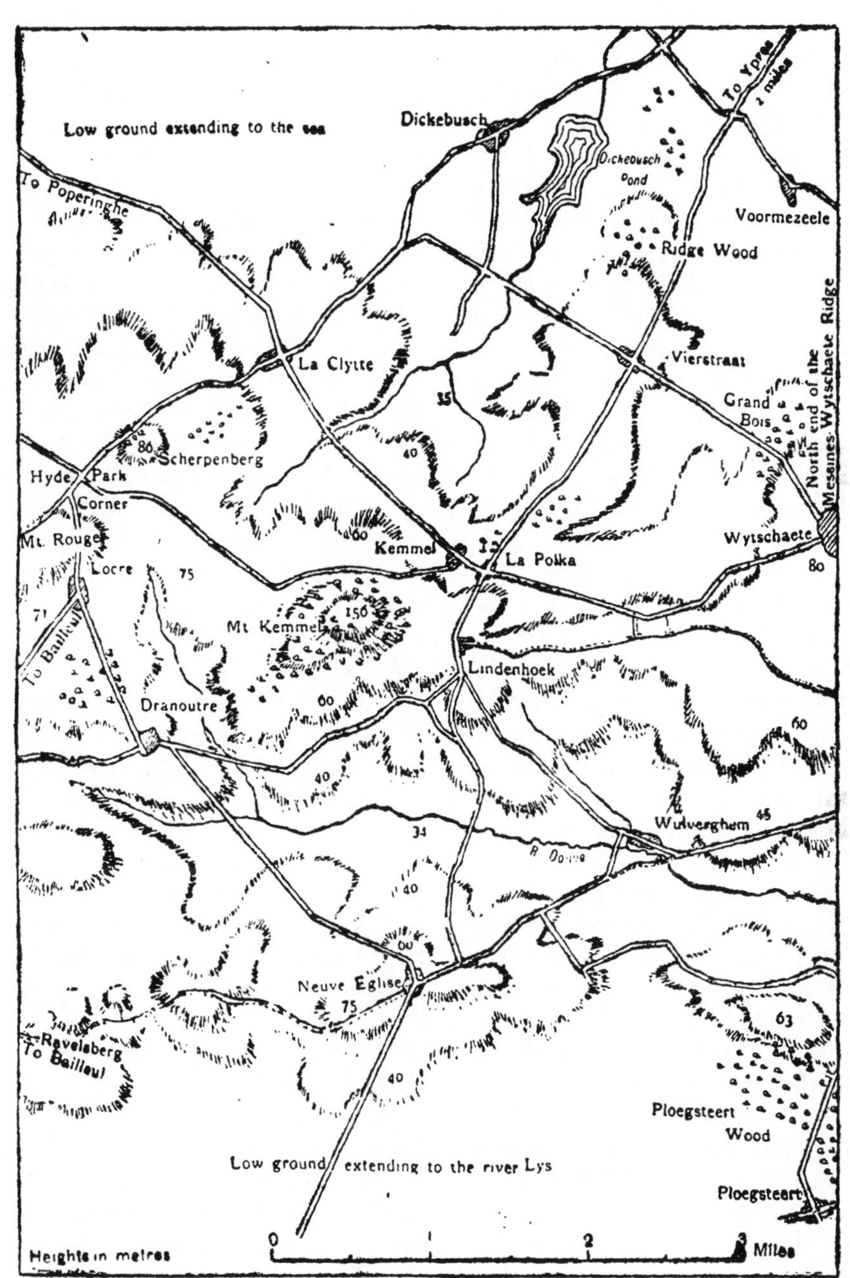

SCENE OF FIGHTING AROUND MONT KEMMEL.

which it was proposed to make a counterstroke. These men were required to form a garrison there, while the attack was delivered by the French. Meantime on the left the 26th Brigade of the 9th Division was to move on Wytschaete. The latter attack was launched at 7.30 in the evening, but was held up in the north-west of the village. A quarter of an hour before midnight the Divisional Commander ordered General Tanner to place the 4th S.A.I. under the orders of the officer commanding the 7th Seaforth Highlanders, in order to assist in clearing up the situation. At midnight the 1st S.A.I. and, two hours later, the 2nd S.A.I. (less the garrison on the Store Farm-Van Damme Farm line) were also despatched to the Seaforths. The 4th S.A.I. on its arrival was employed to fill a gap in the line on the north-west skirts of the village, while the 1st and 2nd S.A.I. were held in reserve. Some hours later Captain Farrell, who was now in command of the 4th S.A.I., reported that parties of his men had succeeded in entering Wytschaete, but on account of heavy machine-gun fire and the lack of touch with their flanks, had been compelled to fall back.

Such was the situation on the morning of the 17th. It was for the enemy the most critical moment, perhaps, in the whole Battle of the Lys. He had reached his greatest strength, and the British troops were not yet reinforced at any point. That morning Von Armin's right attacked in the Ypres Salient, and wholly failed to break the Belgian front. At the same time his left, now that the possession of the Wytschaete Ridge gave him observation over all the land to the west, assaulted the wooded slopes of Kemmel, the key of the countryside. After an intense bombardment the German infantry advanced with great resolution from their new positions at Neuve Eglise and Wulverghem, but were repulsed at all points with heavy losses by the 34th, 49th, and 19th Divisions. During the 17th the South African Brigade was temporarily placed under the 26th Brigade, and the 100 men of the 2nd S.A.I. in the Store Farm-Van Damme Farm line rejoined their battalion in front of Wytschaete. In that position during the night the 1st and 2nd S.A.I. relieved the 4th S.A.I. and the 7th Seaforth Highlanders, the 4th returning to the La Polka-Desinet Farm section, where it came once again under the South African Brigade.

Meantime General Tudor had received the 62nd and 64th Brigades from the 21st Division as reinforcements, and contemplated a further attack upon Wytschaete. The 64th Brigade relieved the 26th, while the 1st and 2nd S.A.I. remained in line under the orders of the former brigade. This plan, however, did not mature. During the morning of the 18th, under cover of mist, the enemy assaulted the position held by the 1st S.A.I., and captured its advanced posts, one officer being killed, and 48 other ranks missing. Save for this incident the situation remained unchanged that day. On the 19th 100 men of the 4th S.A.I. were detailed to relieve some troops of the 19th Division. On the night of the 20th, the 4th was relieved in the southern part of the Vierstraat line and moved into support, while the detachment lent to the 19th Division rejoined its unit. Early on the morning of the 22nd the 1st and 2nd S.A.I. were also relieved and moved to Dickebusch, and on the 23rd the whole Brigade reassembled in the Hopoutre area.

It was clear that the reconstructed Brigade could not continue. The drafts received after the 24th of March had been used up in the heavy fighting on the Messines-Wytschaete ridge, and further reinforcements were not forthcoming to build it up to some semblance of fighting strength. No other course was possible but to organize the remnants into one battalion. The history of the doings of the South Africans in France is now the history of this composite unit, which was commanded by Lieut.-Colonel H. W. M. Bamford, M.C., of the 2nd

S.A.I. Each of the four companies were made up of officers, N.C.O.'s, and men of the old battalions, and these, with the drafts arriving from England, brought the battalion to a total strength of 59 officers and 1,527 other ranks.

The name of the South African Brigade was still to be retained, and the unit was to include, in addition to the Composite Battalion, the 9th Scottish Rifles (formerly in the 27th Brigade) and the 2nd Royal Scots Fusiliers. General Tanner was the Brigadier.

Ludendorff had dipped too deeply in the north to withdraw easily. If he could seize Kemmel Hill, he would broaden his comfortless salient and win direct observation over the northern plain. In front of Kemmel was the junction of the British and French lines, which he regarded as the weakest spot in our front. Accordingly, on Thursday, the 25th April, he struck again for Kemmel.

In the early hours of that day a heavy enemy bombardment presaged the coming attack. At 3.35 a.m. the South African battalion, which had been taken over on the 24th by Lieut.-Colonel Bamford, was warned to be ready to move at fifteen minutes' notice. At 5 a.m. Von Armin attacked with nine divisions, five of which were fresh. In the British area the 9th and 49th Divisions were hotly engaged west of Wytschaete, and before midday the right of the 9th was forced back to Vierstraat. In the afternoon the 21st Division, farther north, was also attacked, and by the evening the British front had been compelled to withdraw to positions running from Hill 60 in the north by Voormezeele and Ridge Wood to the hamlet of La Clytte on the Poperinghe-Kemmel road, where it linked up with the French.

By the next morning supports had arrived, and General Plumer made a great effort to recapture the lost ground. The 25th Division, along with French troops and elements of the 21st and 49th Divisions, re-entered Kemmel Village, but found themselves unable to maintain it against flanking fire from the northern slopes of the hill. After midday came the second wave of the German assault. It failed to make ground owing to the gallant resistance of the 49th Division and of troops of the 21st, 30th, 39th, and 9th Divisions, all four of which had been fighting for five weeks without rest. That afternoon the French recaptured Locre, on the saddle between Kemmel Hill and the heights to the west, so that our line in that quarter now ran just below the eastern slopes of the Scherpenberg, east of Locre, and then south of St. Jans-Cappel to Méteren.

At 2.15 p.m. on 26th April General Tanner took over command of the sector held by the 26th Brigade. He had the 9th Scottish Rifles in line, and the 8th Black Watch and the 5th Camerons (both of the 26th Brigade) in support and reserve, for the South African battalion was still in divisional reserve at Hopoutre. Presently the Black Watch and the Camerons were relieved by the 2nd Royal Scots Fusiliers. The South African Brigade was for the moment under the command of the G.O.C. 49th Division. The Brigade line ran roughly from the cross-roads called Confusion Corner, west of Vierstraat, to the southern end of Ridge Wood. The 9th Division was now back in support, and the South African Brigade had on its right troops of the 49th, and on its left the 21st. The German attack came at 3 o'clock in the afternoon, and was repulsed with heavy losses; but the 9th Scottish Rifles suffered so gravely that they were relieved by the 2nd Royal Scots Fusiliers. The night passed quietly, and on the 27th the South African battalion, with a strength of 23 officers and 707 other ranks, moved forward and took up position in the La Clytte-Dickebusch support line. There it remained for two days under considerable shell-fire, which occasioned some 60 casualties.

On the 28th the fighting fell chiefly to the lot of the French at Locre, and there was no material change in the situation. But on the morning of Monday, the 29th, after one of the most intense German bombardments of the war, Von Armin attacked the whole front from west of Dranoutre to Voormezeele. The Allied line at the moment ran round the eastern base of Mont Rouge, just covering Locre, across the low saddle of the range to the meadows in front of La Clytte, and thence by Voormezeele to the Ypres-Comines Canal. The British right was in the neighbourhood of the cross-roads which we called Hyde Park Corner, on the saddle between the Scherpenberg and Mont Rouge. There lay the 25th Division as far as the little stream which runs from Kemmel to the Dickebusch Lake. On its left was the 49th Division as far as Voormezeele, and beyond it the 21st Division to the canal. Von Armin made three main assaults—the first against the French to carry Locre and Mont Rouge; the second, at the junction of the French and the 25th Division, aimed at turning the Scherpenberg; and the third, between the 49th and 21st Divisions, to turn the obstacle of Ridge Wood.

The infantry attack was launched at 5 a.m. in a dense mist by at least eleven divisions—six against the French and five against the British. It was delivered in mass formation, the density being from six to eight bayonets to the yard. On the British front no ground was gained at all. The three divisions in line, with the assistance of troops of the 30th and 39th Divisions, not only stood firm, but in some cases advanced to meet the Germans and drove them back with the bayonet. By the end of the day the single German gain was the village of Locre, which was retaken by the French the following morning.

The battle of the 29th was a complete and most costly German repulse. The enemy had attacked with some 80,000 men, and his casualties were at least a quarter of his strength. The Royal Scots Fusiliers in General Tanner's brigade had suffered heavily, and the South African battalion was ordered to relieve them. The work was complete by 4 o'clock on the morning of the 30th. For the next five days the situation was unchanged, for the fight on the 29th was the last great episode of the Battle of the Lys. On the night of the 5th the battalion was relieved.

CHAPTER VIII.

THE SUMMER OF 1918.
(May—September, 1918.)

The summer of 1918 may be regarded as an interlude in the history of the South African forces in France. The continuity was not broken, for there was still a titular South African Brigade, commanded by a South African general; but the old regiments had shrunk to companies, and only one battalion was South African in its composition.

The Brigade during the summer was with the 9th Division in the area of the Second Army.

From the 10th to the 23rd May the Brigade was busy training in the Heuringhem area. On the latter date, with the 5th Cameron Highlanders in place of the 9th Scottish Rifles, it marched to Hondeghem, and next day relieved the 26th Brigade in the support line, the South African battalion, on the left, being available as a counter-attack battalion. On the 25th, since a German attack seemed to be imminent, it was decided to hold the 9th Division sector with a two-brigade front: on the left the 26th Brigade, with two battalions in line and one in support; on the right the South African Brigade, with one

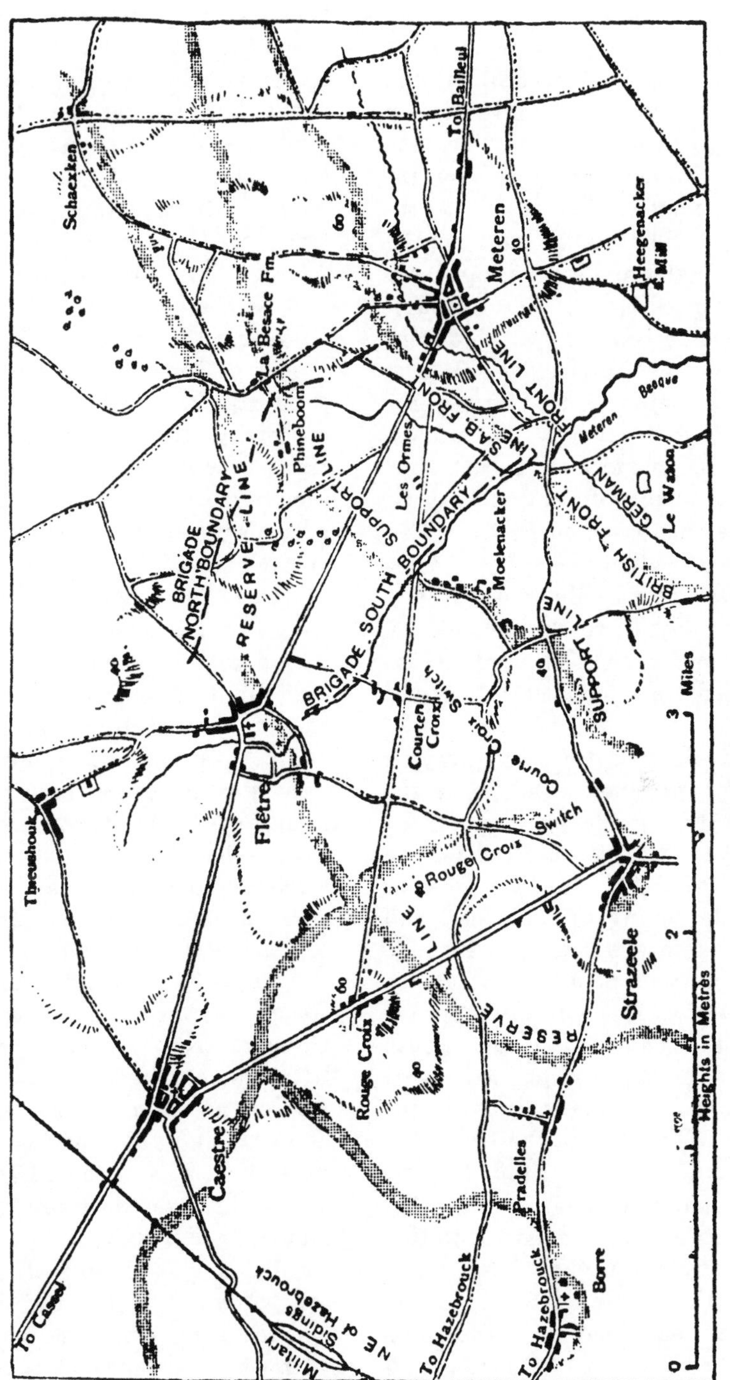

THE FIGHTING ABOUT METEREN.

battalion in line, one in support, and the South African Composite Battalion in divisional reserve in the village of Thieushoek. The 27th Brigade was at Hondeghem in corps reserve.

At that time our front ran in this area from Locre by the north of Bailleul and just west of the village of Méteren to a point half-way between Strazeele and Merris. The sector taken over by the Brigade lay facing Méteren from the Méteren-Cassel road to the tiny water-course called Méteren Becque, which ran south-east from Flêtre. The defences were organized in two zones. The front line consisted of sections of trenches covered by an outpost line between 150 and 200 yards in front of them, in close touch with the enemy; a support line, with the strong-point of Princboom in it; and a reserve line based on Flêtre. This forward zone was almost completely over-looked by the enemy in Méteren, and any movement by day there was impossible. The second zone, some 2,000 yards in the rear, included the fortified village of Caestre.

During these days patrols were busy on the quest for prisoners, and from the intelligence thus gathered it appeared that the German attack was fixed for the morning of the 29th. Much work was done in strengthening the defences, and a special battalion was formed of Brigade details, which was held at Caestre in divisional reserve. But nothing happened on the 29th. That night the South African battalion moved into the support line, and on the 1st June it relieved the 2nd Royal Scots Fusiliers in the front line.

On the South African right lay the Australians, and on the night of 2nd June they carried out a minor operation in order to straighten their line; while the South Africans co-operated by a pretended attack on Méteren. The Australians reached their goal without serious opposition. A German relief was in progress, and in consequence 5 officers and 250 other ranks, besides many machine-guns and trench mortars, were captured. For the next few days the enemy front was stagnant, and on the night of the 5th the Brigade was relieved in the front line by the 26th, and moved back to the Hondeghem area for further training.

On the 11th June the Composite Battalion marched to Thieushoek, and that night relieved the 7th Seaforth Highlanders in divisional reserve. Once again a German attack threatened. The South African Brigade front was now held by two battalions, and on the 17th the South African battalion relieved the 9th Scottish Rifles, on the right of the front adjoining Méteren Becque.

The position at Méteren was far from comfortable, and General Tanner, after conferring with the Australians on his right, submitted to the Divisional Commander a proposal for a further adjustment of the line, which involved an advance of some 425 yards on a front of 750. The scheme was approved, but, since full artillery support was necessary, it had to be postponed till the night of 23rd June. The attack was to be delivered by the 1st Australian Brigade and by the South African Composite Battalion. Zero was fixed for half an hour after midnight on the 24th, in order that the troops should have sufficient time after nightfall to form up, and the remainder of the short midsummer dark for the consolidation of their gains.

At zero hour an accurate artillery and trench mortar barrage opened on the German front trenches, and presently lifted a hundred yards. The attack, moving close to the barrage, succeeded at once, and the German machine-guns were rushed and silenced as soon as they opened fire. Many small parties of Germans were found in the hedges and cornfields, who either fled or were quickly overpowered. The objective was soon reached, and consolidation began, and, with the assistance of a section of the 63rd Field Company R.E., by dawn the new line had been wired across its whole front. As a result of the operation 29 prisoners and 6 machine-guns were taken, while 36 dead of the enemy were counted. The losses of the Composite Battalion were 5 men killed, and 2 officers and 21 other ranks wounded. The following night the battalion was relieved by the 5th Camerons, and next day moved back to Hondeghem.

There the South African Brigade remained till the last day of June, when they came again into the front line to relieve one of the units of the 26th Brigade. It had been resolved to attempt the capture of Méteren village in the near future, and the task had been entrusted to the 26th and South African Brigades.

The 10th of July was at first chosen as the day; but the weather grew bad, and the operation was postponed. On the night of the 12th the South African Brigade had been relieved by the 27th, and had returned to Hondeghem, with orders to be in readiness to move up at short notice. The two battalions of the Brigade selected for the assault—the South African Composite Battalion and the 2nd Royal Scots Fusiliers—rehearsed the business in complete detail. By the 17th the weather had improved, and on the night of the 18th the Brigade relieved the 27th in the right sector of the divisional front, and took up positions of assembly ready to move on the following day.

Zero was fixed for five minutes to eight on the morning of the 19th. At that hour the troops of assault left the trenches in artillery formation, and under cover of a smoke and high-explosive barrage rapidly over-ran the enemy front-line posts and prevented the use of his machine-guns. One or two strong-points held out till they were enveloped on the flanks. The main attack, admirably led by the section commanders, bore down all resistance, and both battalions reached their objectives by the appointed time. One company of the Composite Battalion, which held the line on the extreme right, south of the point on which the operation hinged, had been ordered to watch for opportunities to harass the enemy while the main attack was proceeding, and, when the barrage ceased, to push up patrols along the front, and, if possible, capture the German trench between Méteren Becque and the road from Brahmin Bridge to Alwyn Farm. This they did with complete success, and took many prisoners and seven machine-guns.

The main attack, having reached its goal, sent out patrols, who managed to establish themselves on a point some 200 yards north of the line between the Gaza cross-roads and the Brahmin Bridge road. There was some stubborn fighting at Alwyn Farm and among the hedges north of it; but in the afternoon the divisional artillery cleared the place. Under cover of this outpost line a position in Méteren village and on the ridge was rapidly established, and one of the most awkward corners of the British front made secure. During the latter part of the day our advance lines were heavily shelled, but no counter-attack developed. It appeared that the Germans had been taken by surprise. They expected only a gas discharge, and had in many cases put on gas masks, and were wholly unprepared to resist the rush of our infantry.

The night passed in comparative quiet. On the morning of the 20th the Composite Battalion was ordered to test the enemy front on the right of the division, which seemed to have retired. Fighting patrols were pushed out, and a line was established some 400 yards farther south. The Brigade held their sector until the 24th, when they moved to the left of the divisional front, where for some days they were busy in restoring and draining the dilapidated trenches. On the night of the 30th the Composite Battalion was relieved by the 5th Camerons, and marched back to a rest area.

The capture of Méteren was a good example of a perfectly planned and perfectly executed minor action. The captured material consisted of 1 field gun, 13 trench mortars, and 30 machine-guns, of which the Composite Battalion's share was 10 trench mortars and 23 machine-guns. Between 200 and 300 prisoners fell to the Brigade. The casualties of the Composite Battalion were 130, of whom 27 were killed and 2 died of wounds.

On 5th August the Composite Battalion was again in the line on the right of the division, which by now extended beyond Méteren Becque, and included Le Waton. Little happened for the better part of a fortnight except patrol work along the Becque. On the 18th the 27th Brigade, with the 9th Scottish Rifles, attacked and captured the mill of Hoegenacker, taking 10 officers and 230 men prisoners. By way of retaliation the Germans heavily shelled the South African front, in spite of which Sergeant Thompson of the 4th Company of the Composite Battalion, with five men, raided and captured an enemy post during the morning. That night the battalion was relieved by the 8th Black Watch, and withdrew from the front.

On the day before the capture of Méteren, Foch on the Marne had delivered the great counter-stroke which decided the issue of the campaign.

During August 1,000 reserves arrived at Lumbres from England, and it was now possible to consider the reorganization of the Brigade. On the 28th the Composite Battalion marched to Lumbres and prepared for disbandment. Since its formation on 24th April it had been almost continually in the line. Seventy-five officers had served with it at one time or another, and of these 7 had been killed and 11 wounded. Of the men, 84 had been killed, 27 had died of wounds, 329 had been wounded, and one was missing. For the operations in which it had taken part it had won two bars to the Military Cross, three Military Crosses, one Distinguished Conduct Medal, one bar to the Military Medal, and thirty Military Medals.

On 11th September the Brigade, now re-formed, was withdrawn from the 9th Division, with which the South Africans had served since their arrival in France. For the purpose of administration it was transferred to the VII Corps, with which it trained till 22nd September. On that day it joined the 66th Division, which was then attached to the First Army. It was commanded, as before, by General Tanner, and in addition to the three infantry battalions contained the Signal Section, the South African Light Trench Mortar Battery, and the 1st South African Field Ambulance. The 1st S.A.I. was under the command of Major H. H. Jenkins, and 2nd under Lieut.-Colonel H. W. M. Bamford, and the 4th under Lieut.-Colonel D. M. MacLeod.

It was not easy for the South Africans to leave the 9th Division, or for the 9th Division to part with them. Together they had fought in the bitterest actions of the campaign, and their glory was eternally intertwined. I quote General Tudor's farewell letter:

"I wish to express to you and to your officers, warrant officers, N.C.O.'s, and men of the Brigade under your command my great regret that the exigencies of the service prevented me seeing you all personally before you were transferred from the 9th Division, in order to say good-bye. For two and a half years your Brigade has shared the fortunes of the 9th Division. At Delville Wood, at Arras, at Ypres, in the Somme retreat, and finally at Méteren, it has fully contributed in establishing and maintaining the glorious record of this division. The South African Brigade bore the brunt of the attack on the divisional front on March 21, 1918, and its final stand at Bouchavesnes on 24th March, when it held out all day until all ammunition was exhausted, will live as one of the bravest feats of arms in the War. The cheery keenness and comradeship with which the South African Brigade has always worked and fought will be very much missed by me personally, and by all the 9th Division. We wish you and your Brigade the best of fortune, and know that you will always fully maintain the splendid name you have earned."

CHAPTER IX.

THE ADVANCE TO VICTORY.
(SEPTEMBER 28—NOVEMBER 11, 1918.)

As the last stage in this record approaches, it is necessary to gather up the threads of the campaign and observe the position of the great Allied movement at the time when the South Africans appeared again on the main front of battle. During the summer months Foch had warded off Ludendorff's successive assaults, and had accumulated a reserve which, at the end of July, by the accession of the American troops, gave him a final superiority both in men and material over anything which the enemy could compass. He had also devised a system of tactics which embraced all that was best in the German plan, and avoided its defects. By his counter-stroke on 18th July against Von Boehn's exposed flank he had given the *coup de grâce* to Germany's offensive, wrested from her the initiative, and forced her back in some confusion on her defences.

By the 24th Ludendorff was everywhere back in his last lines—the "granite wall" which the German army chiefs had told their countrymen could never be pierced. There he hoped to stand till such time as winter took the edge from the Allies' ardour, and disposed them to compromise.

He had not reckoned with Foch—nor with Haig—for on the 26th there began on the Meuse the *arpeggio* of attack which broke through the defences prepared during four years, and in six weeks brought Germany to surrender. On the 27th Sir Douglas Haig struck at the main Siegfried zone from Cambria to St. Quentin, and his blow was meant to shatter. It is no secret that the opinion of his Allies and of his own Government was not favourable to his boldness: even Foch, while he agreed that the plan was the right one, doubted its feasibility. The British Commander-in-Chief took upon himself the responsibility of one of the most audacious operations of the war, and, daring greatly, greatly succeeded. That day the Third and First British Armies crossed the Canal du Nord, and next day reached the Scheldt Canal. On the 28th, too, the Belgians and the Second Army swept east from Ypres, and Mangin and Guillaumat opened a new battle between the Ailette and the Vesle. On the 29th came the main blow at the Siegfried citadel, when the Fourth Army, in conjunction with the Third Army and Débeney, crossed the Scheldt Canal and stormed their way far into the fortified zone. In days of wind and cloud they enlarged this gap till St. Quentin fell, and Cambrai was utterly outflanked. On 30th October the Australians broke through the northern part of the Beaurevoir-Fonsommes line, the last of the Siegfried works, and looked into open country. Between the 27th September and the 7th October Sir Douglas Haig had crossed the two great canals, and destroyed all but the final line of the Siegfried zone, while this final line in one part had been passed. The time had come for an advance on a broad front which should obliterate the remnants of the Siegfried works, and with them Germany's last hope of a safe winter position. Her nearest refuge would be the Meuse, and, shepherded by Foch's unrelenting hand, it was very certain that her armies would never reach the banks of that fateful river.

On 28th September the 66th Division had been transferred to the Fourth Army, and by the 5th October it had moved south to the old Somme area, and was in the neighbourhood of Ronssoy. It was now part of the XIII Corps, which contained also the 18th, 25th, and 50th Divisions.

On 6th October the 66th Division was warned that it would be used presently in a major operation in which the Fourth and Third Armies would co-operate. The object was to destroy the remnants of the Beurevoir line, and with it the Siegfried zone. The country was the last slopes of the Picardy uplands, where they break down to the flats of the Scheldt—wide undulations enclosing broad, shallow valleys. There was little cover save the orchards and plantations around the farms and hamlets, but there were many sunken roads, and these, combined with the perfect field afforded everywhere for machine-gun fire, made it a good land for rear-guard fighting. The XIII Corps was now the right flank of the Fourth Army, with the II United States Corps on its right, and the British V Corps on its left. The 66th Division was in the centre of the corps, and the task specially committed to it was the capture of Serain. The Divisional Commander attacked with two brigades—The South African on the right and the 198th on the left, each on a two-battalion front. The starting-point was a line running north-west and south-east through the eastern outskirts of Beaurevoir village. In the South African Brigade the 2nd S.A.I. was on the right and the 4th on the left, with the 1st S.A.I. in support.

It was a wild, wet autumn morning when the Third and Fourth Armies advanced on the 17-mile front, from south of Cambrai to Sequehart, while Débeney extended the battle four miles farther south. Zero hour for the Fourth Army was 5.10; for the Third Army, 4.30. The South African Brigade had moved on the 7th into the Siegfried lines at Bony, and by 3.30 a.m. on the 8th it had occupied its battle position. Lieut.-Colonel Bamford, the commanding officer of the 2nd S.A.I. was wounded here. His place was taken by Major Sprenger.

The attack at 5.10, covered by a creeping barrage, moved swiftly towards its goal, and by 7 o'clock the South Africans had their first objective. The enemy resisted stoutly, and made full use of the sunken roads, especially at the Usigny ravine, which was in the ground of the 2nd S.A.I. There he disputed every yard with machine-guns and snipers, and did not yield till all his posts had been killed or captured. The whippet tanks, moving in front of the infantry, were mostly put out of action by shell-fire at the start, but one arrived opportunely at the Usigny ravine and helped to break down the last resistance there. The 2nd S.AI. took at this stage nearly 500 prisoners, two anti-tank guns, seventeen machine-guns, and four field-pieces. These last were captured by a few men under Lieutenant E. J. Brook and Sergeant Hinwood, who pushed forward and rushed the guns 400 yards south-east of Petite Folie Farm, and then turned them on the retreating enemy. The 4th S.A.I. on the left had also to face heavy machine-gun fire, but it swept through the German position at La Sablonnière and Hamage Farm, taking no less than thirty-five machine-guns.

As soon as the first objective was won the ground was consolidated. Covering posts were pushed out, and the two battalions were reorganized. The supporting battalion, the 1st S.A.I., had been caught in the early morning barrage on the railway embankment north of Beaurevoir, and had suffered 23 casualties. Later it moved east of Beaurevoir, and provided a platoon to reinforce the 2nd before retiring to Brigade reserve. The losses so far in the assaulting battalions had not been unduly heavy. The 2nd had suffered most in its commissioned ranks. The 4th had 45 men killed and 4 officers and 194 men wounded.

The first objective having been taken, the 199th Brigade, according to plan, took up the attack, leap-frogging the South African and 198th Brigades, and by 11 a.m. had taken Serain and reached the final line. For a little its left flank was exposed, for Villers-Outréaux was still in German hands. By three in the afternoon, however, the V Corps had

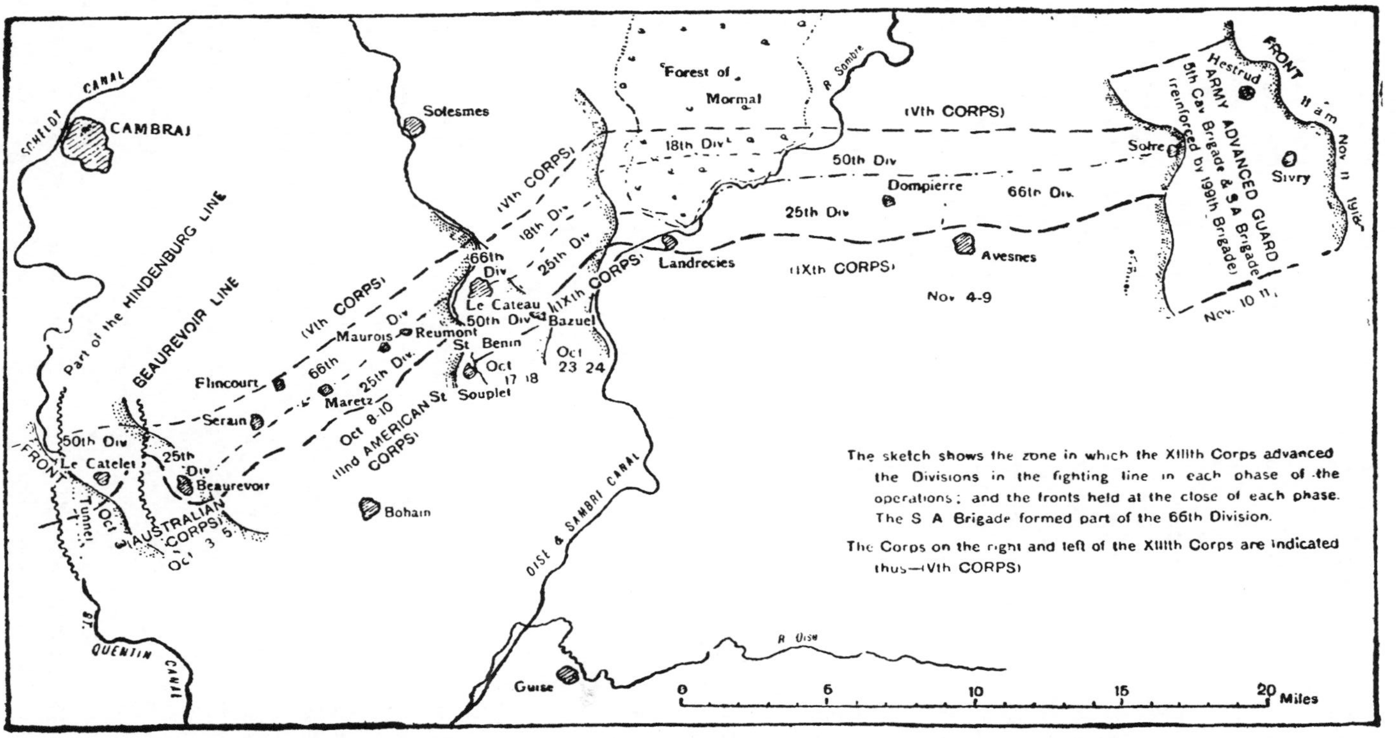

THE VICTORIOUS ADVANCE—OPERATIONS OF THE XIII CORPS UP TO 11TH NOVEMBER, 1918.

succeeded in carrying that village, and the XIII Corps was able to establish itself securely east of Prémont and Serain. It had been a day of unblemished success. Sir Douglas Haig and Débeney had advanced between three and four miles, and the Siegfried zone had disappeared in a cataclysm. The enemy was falling back to the Oise and the Selle, and for the moment was in dire confusion. Every road converging upon Le Cateau was blocked with troops and transport, and our cavalry were galloping eastward to harass the retreat. Next day Cambrai fell, and the Germans retired behind the line of the Selle. The war of positions had ceased, and the combatants were now in open country.

On the 9th the Third and Fourth Armies pressed their advantage against the stricken enemy, who had no position on which he could stand, short of the Selle river. The South African Brigade began the day in reserve, the attack on Maretz being conducted by the 198th and 199th Brigades. By 10 o'clock Maretz, Avelu, and Elincourt had fallen, and half an hour later the South African Brigade passed through the two brigades and moved against the second objective, a line east of Maurois and Honnechy and Gattignies Wood. There was some hope that before nightfall the crossings of the Selle might be seized and the ridge to the east, which, it was clear, were the immediate objects of the German retreat. But though the enemy was disordered he was not in rout, and his machine-gunners fought stubborn rear-guard actions. The 2nd S.A.I. on the right, now under Major Sprenger, came under heavy fire as soon as it emerged from the eastern skirts of Maretz. As its left approached Gattignies Wood it was strongly opposed by machine-guns and snipers, but by the assistance of two armoured-cars the southern part of the wood was cleared. On the right the advance was held up for half an hour by enemy posts along the Le Cateau railway. To add to Major Sprenger's difficulties, the 4th S.A.I. on his left was compelled to veer north towards Bertry, since the troops on its left had fallen slightly behind and got out of touch. He was compelled to bring up one of his supporting companies, and presently established his line on the Cambrai railway, where many machine-guns and prisoners were taken. Before him lay the villages of Maurois and Honnechy, which appeared to be lightly held, since some of the houses were flying white flags. The 2nd S.A.I., with three companies in line and one in support, moved through the village with little opposition, and was received with wild enthusiasm by the French inhabitants. A little after 1 p.m. Major Sprenger reached his final objective, where he found his flanks exposed, since he had outrun the general advance.

Meantime Lieut.-Colonel MacLeod, with the 4th S.A.I., had had severe fighting. His task was simple till he reached the northern edge of Gattignies Wood, which was held in strength by the enemy. By a flanking movement he overcame the resistance and pushed on to the south-west skirts of Bertry. This village was not in the Brigade's area, but the delay in the advance of the division on its left made any further movement by the 4th S.A.I. impossible till Bertry had been taken. Accordingly the left company swung northwards and occupied the village. By 4.30 p.m. Lieut.-Colonel MacLeod had reached his objective and pushed outposts to link up with the 2nd S.A.I. The Brigade was now established on a line east of Maurois and Honnechy.

The day had gone so well that it seemed as if more might be accomplished than had been forecast in the original plan. The cavalry was ordered to go through and ride for Le Cateau and beyond, in the hope of cutting the main enemy communications through Valenciennes. By 2 p.m. the Canadian Cavalry Brigade had gone forward, encircled Reumont, and formed a picket line beyond it. The South African Brigade was instructed to make good that village, and for the purpose

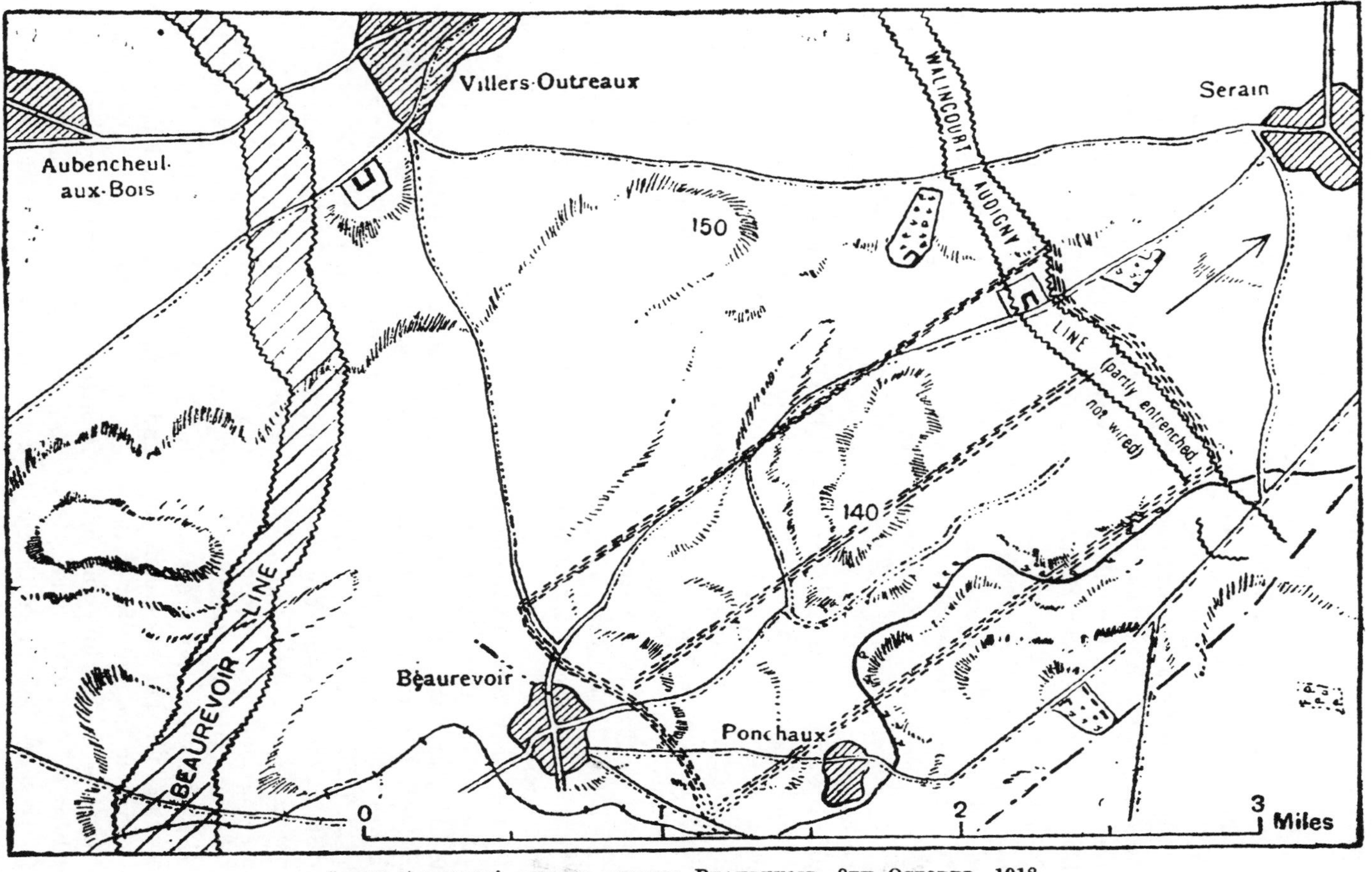

SOUTH AFRICANS' ATTACK BEYOND BEAUREVOIR, 8TH OCTOBER, 1918.

General Tanner brought up the 1st S.A.I. under Lieut.-Colonel Jenkins. By dusk the work was accomplished, and the 1st S.A.I. took over from the Canadian cavalry, occupying a line covering Reumont on the north and east. The more distant objective had proved impracticable. It was not possible to push through large bodies of cavalry owing to the many strongly held machine-gun posts. That night the front of the 66th Division ran from the western skirts of Escaufourt, east of Reumont, to the east of Bertry Station. For the South African Brigade it had been a day of distinguished achievement. The two battalions of assault had taken 150 prisoners, more than twenty machine-guns, several anti-tank guns, and, at Bertry, a motor-car containing a German officer. Their losses had been light.

On the 10th the Brigade was in reserve at Reumont and Maurois, where it was continuously shelled, the 1st S.A.I. sustaining some twenty casualties. That day the divisional advance was conducted by the 198th and 199th Brigades, who pressed forward to the slopes above the Selle. By noon they held the spurs overlooking Le Cateau from the west, and had patrols in the environs of the town itself. But Le Cateau was not to fall at the first summons. The 66th Division found itself much harassed by artillery fire from the high ground towards Forest in the north-east, which overlooked its position. On its right the 25th Division could do little so long as St. Benin was untaken, and St. Benin was in the area of the II United States Corps, whose left division had been checked. The 25th Division attacked St. Benin in the afternoon and drove the enemy across the Selle, but was unable to follow him owing to the difficulty of the river crossings and the machine-gun fire from the railway on the eastern bank. In the evening General Bethell, with the 199th Brigade, attempted to carry the high ground east of Le Cateau and north-east of Montay. The 5th Connaught Rangers reached the railway east of the town; the 18th King's Liverpool Regiment reached Montay, but found the banks of the Selle heavily wired and could not cross. The Divisional Commander accordingly withdrew the Connaught Rangers to the west side of Le Cateau, where they held the line of the Selle as it passed through the town.

That night the II United States Corps took over St. Benin, and the XIII Corps lay north from it for the most part along the western shore of the Selle. The German 17th Reserve Division had arrived to reinforce the enemy, and his front along the east bank of the river was very strong.

It was now the eve of the last great fight of the Brigade—the last, indeed of the campaign in the West. To understand it we must note the configuration of the battle-ground. The valley of the Selle at Le Cateau has on each side slopes rising to plateau country some 200 feet above the bed of the river. On the west these slopes mount gently in bare undulations, but to the east they rise more abruptly, and the country in that direction is intersected with many orchards and hedges. A spur running north-east from Montay to Forest gives direct observation up the valley and over the eastern uplands. The Selle at Le Cateau is from fifteen to twenty feet wide, and usually about four feet deep, but with the recent heavy rains it was now rising fast. South of the town it flows through marshy meadows; in the town itself the banks are bricked up, and it is spanned by two bridges; farther north towards Montay it runs through firm pasture land. Le Cateau is a town normally of some 10,000 inhabitants, full of solidly built houses and factories, the greater part of which are on the slopes east of the river. On its eastern side runs the railway to Solesmes, which, with its embankments and cuttings, gave the enemy a position of exceptional strength. A formidable strong-point was the railway station and yard, which were bounded on the east by a bank thirty feet high, while a mound

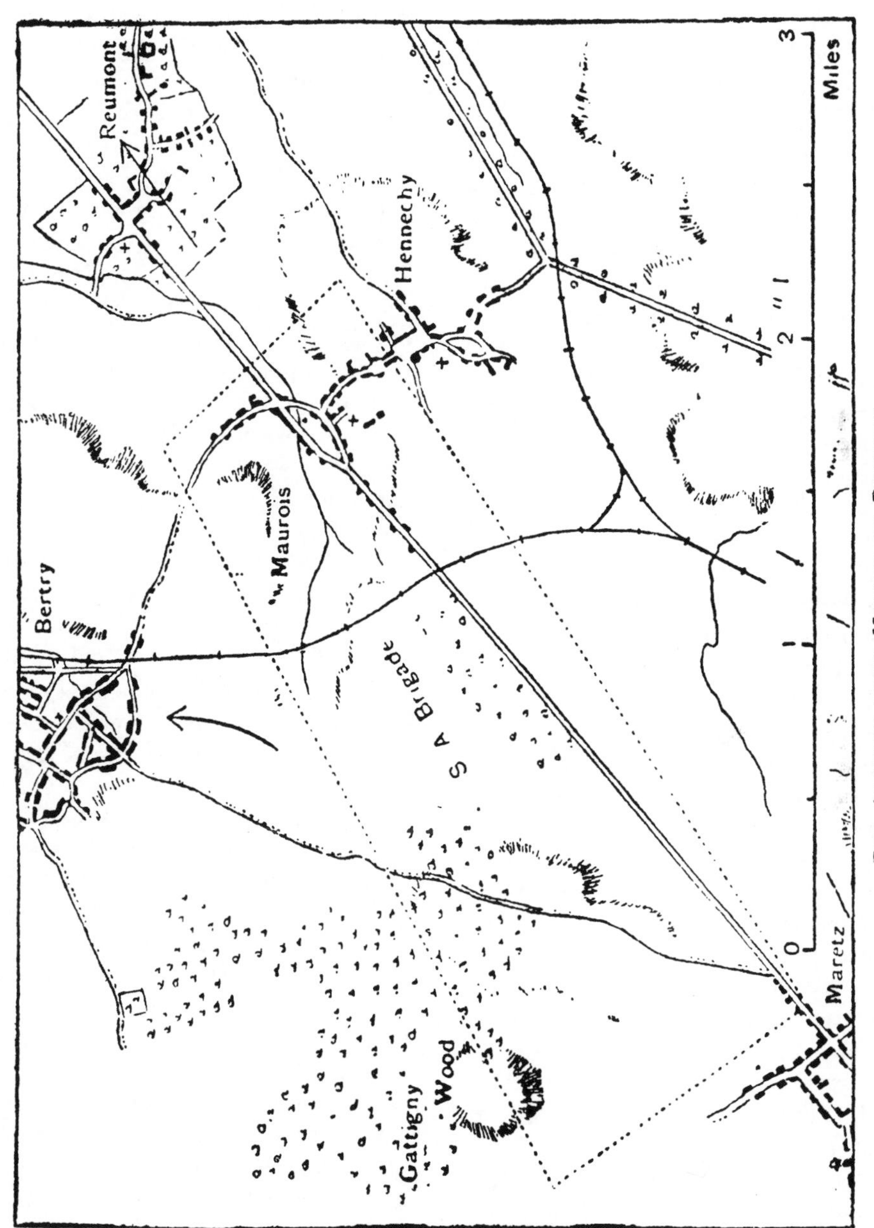

THE ADVANCE FROM MARETZ TO REUMONT.

farther east, which could not be seen from the west bank of the Selle, gave good observation southwards.

The position from the point of view of the defence was all but perfect. The wiring was everywhere elaborate, the machine-gun posts had been prepared on a lavish scale, and the buildings and cellars were admirably adapted for a prolonged resistance. Four enemy divisions held the place, and two of them were fresh from reserve. The importance which the German High Command laid upon a stand on the Selle—which they knew as the "Hermann Line"—was shown by orders captured during our attack. One, issued by General Von Larisch, commanding the 54th Corps, announced that the army would accept a decisive battle on that line, which must be held at all costs. An order of an artillery group declared that the possibility of an armistice being arranged depended on the battle coming to a standstill on the Selle. Still another artillery order warned the troops that if the Hermann Line were held a favourable peace could be arranged; otherwise there was no prospect of an end to the war. If the position was vital to the enemy it was no less vital to the Allies. By 10th September the two main German salients (between the Lys and the Somme and between the Selle and the Argonne) had become precarious. Ludendorff had now but the one object, to protect the main lateral railway, from Lille by Valenciennes and Hirson to Mézières, long enough to permit of an orderly retreat. If it fell too soon, large parts of his front would be cut off. It was Haig's aim to cut that railway as soon as possible by forcing the Selle and pressing on to Maubeuge across the many rivulets which drain to the Scheldt from the Forest of Mormal.

On 11th October the position was that the XIII Corps held ground in the skirts of Le Cateau, west of the Selle and along the river line. A frontal attack was impossible, and the town must be enveloped by its flanks. On the south the floods were extending, and a crossing place must be sought well upstream, so the Corps extended its right wing to St. Souplet. Simultaneously with any advance in the south there must be a movement on the north to capture the ridge north-east of the town. The immediate objective was the Solesmes-Le Cateau railway and the easterly ridge; the ultimate goal the village of Bazuel.

Several days had to be spent in preliminary work. On the night of the 11th the South African Brigade moved up from Reumont and relieved the 198th and 199th Brigades. The 1st S.A.I. held the line opposite Le Cateau, with the 2nd and 4th S.A.I. in support on right and left. Between the 12th and the 15th the 1st pushed forward north of the town to the edge of the Selle. It was no easy task, for the western outskirts were not yet cleared of the enemy, and our positions were dominated by the high ground on the eastern bank and by the houses in the northern suburbs. In these days the 1st S.A.I. suffered some twenty casualties in officers and men, while a post of one N.C.O. and seven men was reported as missing. The next task was to establish bridgeheads in the area of the town itself, and in particular to hold the two ruined bridges. The capture of one of these was assigned to the 2nd S.A.I., and Major Sprenger on the 15th ordered Second Lieutenant R. D. Hewat, with one Lewis gun section and one rifle section, to establish posts east of the bridge on both sides of the road. Owing to the constant machine-gun fire the débris of the bridge could not be used, so Lieutenant Hewat and his men waded across the stream, heavily bombed all the while by the enemy, and carried out their instructions. During the 16th he was frequently attacked, but with seven survivors he held his ground, and when the general advance began next morning he was found engaged against three machine-guns. Later that day he rejoined the Brigade after a most gallant feat of arms, having held out for over thirty-six hours.

The main attack of the XIII Corps was fixed for the morning of the 17th. On the right the 50th Division, under Major-General Jackson, was to cross at St. Souplet and St. Benin, capture the railway embankment opposite them and the railway triangle, and then swing north and take the railway station. Their supporting troops were then to move on Bazuel. The South African Brigade was to cross the Selle north of the town, seize the railway, and link up with the 50th north of the railway triangle; and, in the final stage, swing forward its right and establish itself on the spur east of Le Cateau. Since the V Corps on the left was not attacking, arrangements were made to obscure the enemy observation from the high ground north-east of Montay by a smoke barrage.

Meantime, on the evening of the 16th, the 1st S.A.I. had attacked at 5.45 p.m. in order to win positions on the eastern bank, which would enable eight bridges to be thrown across the river, since it was necessary that the assaulting position should be on that bank. This work was successfully accomplished by "A" and "B" Companies. It was found that strong wire entanglements had been constructed on the east shore, through which openings had to be cut to permit of the assembly of the assaulting battalions.

At 8 p.m. that evening the 4th S.A.I. on the right and the 2nd on the left—together with "D" Company of the 1st, which had been detailed to follow the 2nd—began to move forwards. The crossing of the river was slow work, owing to the slender footbridges and the narrow gaps in the wire. The South Africans, when they reached the east bank, found themselves in places not fifty yards from the enemy, who held the railway embankment, and had pushed forward machine-gun outposts to the river-side road. By 4.30 on the morning of Tuesday, the 17th, the assembly was complete, and the South Africans laboured to make their position secure. They had little time for the work, for zero hour was approaching and their situation would have been perilous indeed but for the merciful interposition of the weather. Just before dawn a heavy mist rose from the valley, blinding the enemy's eyes, so that most of his artillery and machine-gun fire passed harmlessly over their heads.

Zero hour for the 50th Division was 5.20 a.m., for it had much ground to cover before it could come into line with the 66th, and in order to permit of the 50th Division coming into line the zero hour for the South African Brigade was timed for 8.5 a.m. The 151st Brigade crossed the river with ease, but met with a stubborn resistance at the station. The 149th Brigade followed for the attack on the second objective, and found like difficulties at the railway triangle. The South African Brigade had taken immense risks in its assembly and in the exposed nature of the position during the daylight hours preceding the zero hour of 8.5 a.m.

The heavy fog which settled down along the valley of the Selle was a merciful act of Providence, as it entirely concealed the presence of our men and saved them from the effects of the enemy barrages which, in replying to those of our own guns at both 5.20 a.m. and 8.5. a.m., fell well in rear of them along the line of the position held the previous day. It was a welcome relief to all ranks when the appointed hour for the attack arrived.

The mist was still thick, and no man could see ten yards before him. From the outset the attack had to face great belts of single and double apron wire and heavy machine-gun fire from both flanks. After a hundred yards had been covered the South Africans came upon a sunken road protected by a palisade, where the 4th S.A.I. was held up for some time, and suffered many losses. As they approached the railway they encountered another and more formidable obstacle—a belt of wire entanglements sixty yards deep. The railway at this point ran in a deep cutting, the sides of which were studded with machine-gun posts and rifle-pits. The South Africans rose to the emergency. They found a shallow trench used by the Germans as a route from the railway cutting to an outpost; they found a tortuous path through the wire made for the use of German patrols.

Along the shallow trench Captain Jacobs, 2nd S.A.I., with a party of men, rapidly made his way into the enemy position in the railway cutting, where, owing to the dense nature of the fog, a number of the enemy riflemen and machine-gunners were taken unawares and dealt with in detail by enfilade fire along the railway cutting.

Other entrances were cut through the difficult wire entanglements. Soon, after stern fighting, the cutting was in our hands.

It was a magnificent feat of cool resolution, and it was performed under the most galling fire. It was Ludendorff's old device of "infiltration" in miniature, and at 9.15 Captain Jacobs, of the 2nd S.A.I., reported to Major Sprenger that the first objective had been reached.

The situation, however, was still full of danger. The first objective was beyond the railway line; but, since our troops could not dig themselves in in the open because of machine-gun fire, they were compelled to fall back to the railway itself, where they had some kind of cover, though the German field-guns were accurately registered on it. Slowly they cleared the line, and by midday General Tanner was able to inform the Divisional Commander that he held the railway from a point 500 yards north of the railway triangle to the northern boundary of the XIII Corps. Meanwhile "D" Company of the 1st S.A.I., which had followed the 2nd, succeeded under great difficulties in its appointed task of establishing a defensive flank on the left between the railway and the Selle. Every officer of the company was wounded during the course of the day. The losses of the assaulting battalions had been high, and the 1st S.A.I. was now called upon to reinforce each with a company, while a little later the remaining company was sent forward to strengthen the left flank. One battalion of the 198th Brigade was busy clearing up in Le Cateau.

There could be no advance to the second objective yet awhile, for the 50th Division was in difficulties. It had not succeeded in carrying the railway triangle, and was involved in intricate fighting among the station buildings, much galled by machine-gun fire from the mound to the east.

The South African Brigade spent an uneasy night of "standing to." The enemy's bombing patrols were busy, his machine-gun and trench-mortar fire was accurate and intense, and his artillery fire, with light, heavy, and gas shells, was unceasing. At 5.30 a.m. on the 18th the 50th Division again attacked and carried all its objectives, establishing itself on the Le Cateau-Catillon road, with outposts east and north-east of Bazuel. During the afternoon the 66th Division swung forward its right, and the task originally allotted to the XIII Corps was completed. At 5 p.m. orders had been issued for a relief of the South African Brigade by the 199th, but owing to the lateness of the hour the relief was cancelled. Unfortunately this cancelling order did not reach "B" Company of the 1st S.A.I. till it had withdrawn, and in returning to the line it lost thirteen killed. The final objective of the Brigade was established about 4.30 a.m. on the 19th.

Such was the part of the South African Brigade in the forcing of the Selle, the last of their great battles. Between the night of 7th October and the night of 19th October they had taken prisoner 4 officers and 1,238 other ranks, and had captured 367 machine-guns, 19 trench-mortars, 22 field-guns, 4 anti-tank guns, and a mass of other equipment. Their casualties were 47 officers and 1,229 men, of whom 6 officers and 184 other ranks were dead.

The achievement on the 17th is worthy to rank with their advance at Third Ypres

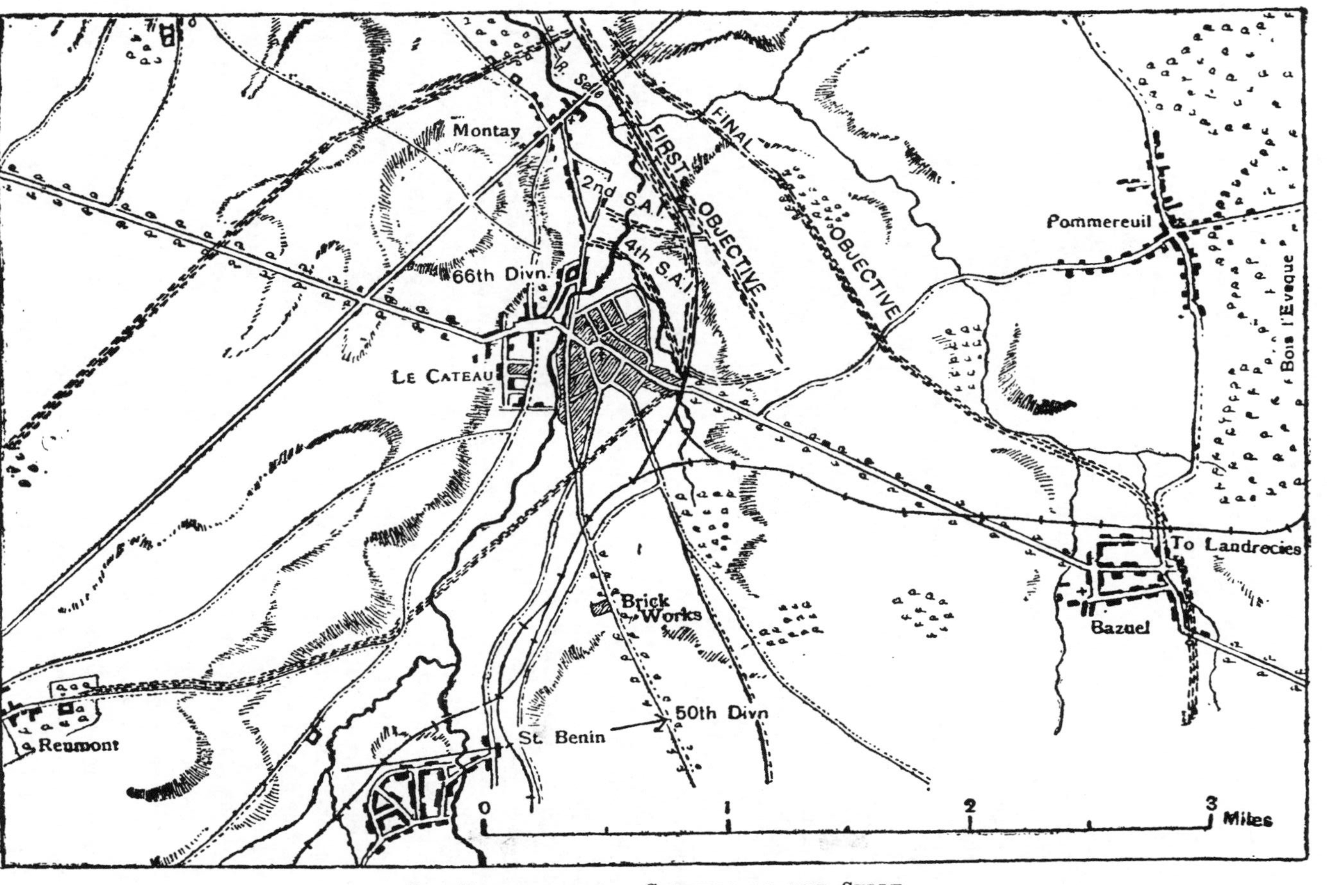

THE FIGHT FOR THE CROSSING OF THE SELLE.

as a brilliant feat of offensive warfare, and as such it was praised by their comrades in arms. Brigadier-General Ian Stewart, of the XIII Corps Headquarters Staff, wrote to General Tanner: "I shall always look on the capture of the railway embankment north of Le Cateau as one of the most astounding feats of the War. It will be good for South Africa to know what a brave part her contingent played in the closing chapter of the Great War, and it is no little honour to have been the foremost troops of the British Armies in France when the curtain fell on the greatest tragedy the world has seen." And when the war was over and the Brigade about to leave the 66th Division, Major-General Bethell wrote in his special order of the day: "In after life, if any of you are up against what you imagine to be an impossible task of any description, call to mind the Boche position on the east bank of the Selle River north of Le Cateau, or ask some one who was there to depict it to you. Then remember that the South African Brigade crossed that stream and took that position, which the enemy thought impregnable to attack from that direction, and that, on looking back at it from the enemy's side, it was hard to understand how the apparently impossible had been done by you."

The fighting front of the XIII Corps was now occupied by the 25th and 18th Divisions, and the 50th and 66th Divisions fell back into reserve. The South African Brigade was in rest billets at Serain till the 2nd November.

On 27th October Berlin accepted President Wilson's terms, which were that the only armistice to be considered must be one that made impossible the renewal of hostilities on the part of Germany, and was negotiated by a people's Government and not by the Great General Staff. The acceptance of such conditions was tantamount to an admission of defeat in the field. On Saturday, the 26th, Ludendorff resigned his command.

By now the condition of the German armies was in the last degree desperate. On 21st March they had had a reserve of eighty fresh divisions, and during the summer no division was returned to the line without at least a month of rest and training. By 30th October they had but one fresh division, and the intervals of rest had shrunk to nine days. There were divisions on their front which mustered less than 1,000 rifles, and the total shortage of rifles to establishment was not less than 500,000. Their casualties since March had been some 2,500,000, of which at least 1,000,000 represented permanent losses. Of the 18,000 pieces of artillery on their front on 15th July, a third had since been captured or destroyed. Worse still, they had been manœuvred into a position from which retreat was in the long run impossible. Pershing and Gouraud were about to cut their main trunk line in the south, and Haig's deadly pressure was shepherding them northward into the gap of Liége.

The South African Field Ambulance, which, under Lieut.-Colonel Pringle and Major M. B. Power, did magnificent work at that stage, had a difficult task because of the steady German shell-fire, which searched out all the back areas. As the advance grew faster, it became hard to keep up with the infantry and to bring back the wounded expeditiously by ruined roads and broken bridges over distances unknown in the previous history of the campaign.

On 2nd November the South African Brigade moved forward from Serain. That day Valenciennes fell to the Canadians under Horne, and next day the German retreat increased its pace. By Monday, the 4th, Pershing, who in three days had advanced 12 miles, had the southern railway at Montmédy and Longuyon under his fire. On the 4th Sir Douglas Haig attacked on the thirty-mile front between Valenciennes and the Sambre, and by the next day the Forest of Mormal was behind him. The enemy's resistance was finally broken and his armies were not in retreat, but in flight, with their two wings for ever separated. Through the fifty-mile pocket between Avesnes and Mézières the whole German forces in the south must squeeze if they would make good their escape, and the gap was hourly narrowing. Mangin and Guillaumat were close on Hirson, Gouraud and Pershing were approaching Mézières, and Haig had the Sambre valley as an avenue to Namur. Moreover, Foch had still his trump card to play, the encircling swing of a new American army north of Metz to cut off the enemy from his home bases. On the 7th Byng was in Bavai, and on the 8th in front of Maubeuge. That day Rawlinson took Avesnes, and on the 9th the Guards entered Maubeuge, while farther north Condé and Tournai were in our hands. On the 6th Gouraud was in Rethel, and on the 7th Pershing was in the western skirts of Sedan. On the 6th the German delegates, Erzberger and his colleagues, left Berlin on their embarrassed journey to Foch's headquarters. On the 9th came the revolution in Berlin, and the formation of a Council of National Plenipotentiaries under Ebert. Next day the Emperor fled from Main Headquarters to seek sanctuary in Holland.

On the morning of the 8th the South African Brigade was in reserve to the 66th Division at Dompierre, just west of Avesnes. Next day it marched by Beugnies to Solre-le-Château—an arduous journey, largely over field tracks, since most roads and bridges had been destroyed by the enemy. General Tanner had been informed by his divisional commander that, owing to the new situation, it had been resolved to create a mobile column under his command. This column was to be part of an advanced guard to cover the Fourth Army front, which guard was to be under General Bethell, and was to include the 5th Cavalry Brigade. General Tanner's force was made up of his infantry brigade, "B" Battery 331st Brigade R.F.A. with six 18-pounders, "D" Battery of the same brigade with one section of 4.5 howitzers, the 430th Field Company R.E., "C" Company 100th Machine-gun Battery, two armoured-cars, and two platoons of the XIII Corps Cyclists. The general scheme was that the column should move on Beaumont and cross the stream there, preceded by the 12th Lancers, while the remainder of the 5th Cavalry Brigade operated on its southern flank.

At 7 a.m. on the morning of Sunday, 10th November—about the time when the courier of the German delegates was reaching Spa with Foch's terms in his pocket—the column moved out from Solre-le-Château on the Beaumont road, the 1st S.A.I. forming the advanced guard. A culvert a mile to the east had been blown up, and took some time to repair, so it was 9.30 before the head of the column reached Hestrud. The 12th Lancers, who were in possession, reported that the enemy was in considerable force on the high ground north and south of Grandrieu. General Tanner accordingly halted the main body under cover at the Bois de Madame, and ordered the 1st S.A.I., after a brief reconnaissance, to deploy for attack in order to clear the way for the column. The attack of the 1st on a three-company front began at 10.30 with the fording of the Thure River, the road-bridge having been destroyed. The enemy, part of the Guard Reserve Corps, opened the sluices of a reservoir upstream. with the result that the assaulting troops were cut off till the flood subsided. Presently it became clear that they were facing an organized rearguard position, strongly held by machine-guns and supported by artillery.

The flanks of the advance were exposed, and since the bulk of the 5th Cavalry Brigade had not come up, the Divisional Commander moved forward the 199th Brigade on the right of the South Africans in the direction of Sivry, where they were in touch with the 20th Hussars. The instructions of the advanced guard were to keep close to the enemy, but not to attack if he was found in a strong position. Accordingly General Tanner did not force the advance, and in the afternoon the 1st S.A.I. was ordered to dig in. It was thought likely that the Germans might retreat during the night, so vigilant patrolling was carried out; but at dawn on the 11th the situation had not altered. In the meantime the bridge at Hestrud had been rebuilt by the Engineers.

The morning of Monday, 11th November, was cold and foggy, such weather as a year before had been seen at Cambrai. Very early, while the Canadians of the First Army were entering Mons, the 1st S.A.I. attacked, but could make little progress, though a patrol managed to gain some ground on the left flank. By 8 o'clock a considerable advance was made on the right, where the 20th Hussars were feeling their way through Sivry. At 10 a.m. General Tanner received by telephone the news that an armistice had been signed. "Hostilities," so ran the divisional order, "will cease at 11 o'clock to-day, 11th November. Troops will stand fast on the line reached at that hour, which will be immediately reported by wire to Headquarters, Fourth Army Advance Guard. Defensive precautions will be maintained. There will be no intercourse of any description with the enemy until receipt of instructions." The news must have reached the enemy lines earlier, and he signalized its arrival by increasing his bombardment, as if he had resolved to have no surplus ammunition left when the hour of truce arrived.

Punctually at 11 o'clock the firing on both sides ceased. There came a moment of dramatic silence, and then a sound as of a light wind blowing down the lines—the echo of men cheering on the long battle-front. The final "gesture" fell to the arm which from the beginning of the campaign had been the most efficient in the enemy service. At two minutes to eleven a machine-gun opened about two hundred yards from our leading troops at Grandrieu, and fired off a whole belt without a pause. A German machine-gunner was then seen to stand up beside his weapon, take off his helmet, bow, and, turning about, walk slowly to the rear.

At the hour of armistice the line reached by the advanced guard ran from Montbliart in the south, west of Sautain, through the Bois de Martinsart, round the eastern edge of Grandrieu to the western skirts of Cousolre. It represented the easternmost point gained by any troops of the British Armies in France. The South Africans had the honour of finishing the war as the spear-point of the advance to victory.

PART VII.

PAGE.

I.—The South African Heavy Artillery 185

II.—The South African Signal Company 189

III.—The South African Medical Corps in France 200

IV.—The Railway Companies and Miscellaneous Trades Company 206

V.—The Cape Auxiliary Horse Transport Companies ... 207

I.

THE SOUTH AFRICAN HEAVY ARTILLERY.

THE five batteries of the old South African Heavy Artillery Brigade were armed, on arriving in England, with 6-inch howitzers and affiliated to the Royal Garrison Artillery, becoming the 71st, 72nd, 73rd, 74th, and 75th Siege Batteries, R.G.A. In April, 1916, a sixth battery, the 125th, was formed. Early in 1918 a seventh battery, the 542nd, and an eighth, the 496th, were created, but when they arrived in France they were broken up, and their guns and personnel distributed, the 542nd between the 75th and the 125th, and the 496th between the 72nd and 74th. A ninth battery, the 52nd, armed with 8-inch howitzers, was formed in the autumn of 1918, but the war ended before it could be brought into action. We have therefore to deal with six siege batteries, which were engaged in France from the summer of 1916 to the date of the armistice. At first the batteries were independent units, being allotted to widely separated corps and heavy artillery groups. It was not till the beginning of 1918 that they were brought together, and two South African Brigades formed, the 44th and the 50th—the 44th including the 73rd (S.A.), 71st (S.A.), 125th (S.A.), and 20th Batteries; and the 50th, the 74th (S.A.), 72nd (S.A.), 75th (S.A.), and 275th. It will be convenient to take the doings of each battery separately up to January, 1918, and thereafter to deal with the record of the two brigades.

THE 71ST SIEGE BATTERY, R.G.A.

The 71st Battery arrived at Havre on 16th April, 1916, under the command of Major H. C. Harrison. It was destined for the impending operations on the Somme, and its first position was at Mailly-Maillet in the VIII Corps area. On 2nd June, however, it was ordered north to Ypres, where the Canadians at the moment were heavily engaged. On the 18th it returned to Mailly-Maillet, where it participated in the opening days of the First Battle of the Somme. On 5th July it moved to Bécordel, and supported the attack on Mametz Wood, Ovillers, and Contalmaison, and the September attack on Martinpuich and Flers. On 20th September it moved forward to Bazentin, where till the close of the year it was engaged in battling with the problem of the Somme mud. After a short period of rest it was at Ovillers on 2nd January, 1917, and during February and March moved slowly eastward, following the German retreat. In April it was engaged against the Hindenburg Line, and had a share in the fierce fighting around Bullecourt. In July and August it had a position at Croisilles, some 2,000 yards from the enemy front. One sector moved north on 31st August to a position just outside the Menin gate at Ypres, and the rest of the battery followed on 15th September. There it took part in the Third Battle of Ypres, supporting the attack of the South African Brigade on 20th September, the first occasion when it was in action along with its own infantry. Its position was badly exposed, and it suffered many casualties from enemy shell-fire and air-bombing, till it was relieved on 22nd October.

Much worn out it now moved to Liévin in the Lens area, where for a little it had a quieter life. On 8th November it handed over its guns to the 73rd (S.A.) Siege Battery, and with the guns of the latter went south to Bapaume. Its new position was in the outskirts of Gouzeaucourt, where, on 20th November, it shared in the Battle of Cambrai. The German counter-attack of the 30th came very near its position, and during those stormy days the battery, under the command of Major P. N. G. Fitzpatrick, did brillant work under great difficulties. Unhappily, on 14th December, at Beaumetz, Major Fitzpatrick was killed by a chance shell. On the 18th the guns were withdrawn to Beaumetz, and by the end of the month the battery was on the front between Béthune and Lens, one section going to La Bourse, and the other to Beuvry. Here it became part of the 44th (S.A.) Brigade.

THE 73RD SIEGE BATTERY, R.G.A.

This battery, after its period of training in England, landed at Havre on 1st May, 1916, under the command of Major Walter Brydon.

On 9th May it reached Bienvillers-au-Bois, in the Somme area, where it took up a battle position under the command of the 19th Artillery Group. On 15th May it fired its first round for sighting purposes. On 1st July, when the First Battle of the Somme began, it covered the infantry advance on Gommecourt, attaining the record of thirty-two rounds in eight minutes with each gun. On 17th July it moved to the village of Berles-au-Bois, and was engaged in smashing enemy trenches and counter-battery work in the neighbourhood of Monchy-au-Bois and Ransart. On 25th August it moved back to Doullens, and thence to Albert, where it took up position in the ruins of La Boisselle. Here it supported the attack on Pozières, Courcelette, and Thiepval; and Major Brydon was wounded while observing for the battery in the front trenches. In October it advanced its position to Pozières, where it suffered considerably from enemy fire, and had its fill of discomforts from the weather of that appalling winter. In February, 1917, Major Brydon returned to duty.

In March, in a heavy snowfall, the battery left the Somme and went north to the Arras area, where, in the Battle of Arras on 9th April, it supported the attack of the Canadians on Vimy Ridge. By noon the advance had progressed so far that the battery was out of range, and moved forward first to Ecurie and then to Thélus. Thélus proved a hot corner, and the battery had many casualties, notably on 1st May, Major Brydon being wounded for the second time. Soon after it was relieved and retired to Houdain, its first spell out of the line since its arrival in France. It returned to Thélus on 28th May, Captain P. A. M. Hands being temporarily in command, and remained there till the last day of June, when it was transferred to Flanders. Its new position was in the Ypres Salient, at the village of Zillebeke, close to Hill 60, where it was much exposed to the enemy's fire, and within 1,000 yards of his front lines. The guns were in position by the 17th July, and on the 25th Major Brydon came back from hospital. The battery was bombed night and day by enemy aircraft, and had no means of making shell-proof cover, for the water was only two feet below the surface of the ground. On 29th August it was relieved for a short space, but it was not till 1st November that it finally left Zillebeke and the Second Battle of Ypres. During the four months there it had nine guns put out of action by hostile fire. On 7th October Major Brydon was gassed, and went to hospital for the third time.

The battery returned to its old ground at Thélus, which had now become a quiet area, and on 11th November moved to Liévin, west of Lens. Here it had comfortable quarters, and was busy preparing positions in anticipation of an attack. It pulled out for Christmas to Béthune, and on 5th January, 1918, took up position at Loisne, where it received news of its inclusion in the new 44th (S.A.) Brigade, R.G.A.

The 125th Siege Battery, R.G.A.

The 125th Battery was first organized on 4th April, 1916, under the command of Major R. P. G. Begbie. It arrived at Havre on 21st July, and reached the Third Army area on 26th July, during the fourth week of the First Battle of the Somme. Its position was at Sailly-au-Bois, on the extreme left of the battle-ground, where its principal targets were the German batteries at Puisieux, Bucquoy, and Grandcourt. On 19th October it moved to the eastern edge of Englebelmer Wood, where it was attached to the Fifth Army. Here it "prepared" and participated in the attack on Beaumont-Hamel on 13th November. It was a difficult task, for its gun positions were remote from the road, and every 100 lb. shell had to be carried some 400 yards through a swamp, until eventually a line of rails was laid. On 20th January, 1917, the battery moved to a new position on the Auchonvillers road, half a mile north of Mailly-Maillet, where for the next few weeks it was engaged by enemy batteries and a heavy calibre naval gun, and suffered many losses. On 22nd February it moved into Beaumont-Hamel, where it had better quarters.

On 22nd March, over impossible roads, the battery moved north to Arras, where its first position was beside the Faubourg d'Amiens. On the second day of the Battle of Arras it moved east to St. Sauveur, and on 16th April it went forward a mile east of Tilloy-lès-Mofflaines, on the Arras-Cambrai road. Here it was much exposed, and three days later it moved back to the wood of Tilloy. For the next month its guns were constantly in action by day and night. On 11th May it pulled out for a much-needed rest, during which time it received reinforcements which brought it up to strength. On 18th June it moved to Roclincourt, in the Oppy section. On 21st July it took up position at Vermelles-lès-Béthune, in the Lens area. Here it came under the First Army, and from the 15th to the 23rd August was heavily engaged in supporting the attack of the Canadians on Hill 70, east of Loos. On the evening of the latter day it moved forward into the ruins of Loos, and rendered brilliant service in the action of the 24th. Its cables were constantly cut by shell-fire, and on 5th September it had 28 casualties from a deluge of German gas shells. The personnel of the battery was withdrawn to rest between the 9th and 21st of September, but from the latter date till 8th October it resumed its work in that section. When the four guns were brought back to Béthune, it was found that not one was fit for further action.

The battery was now attached to the Belgian Army as one of the thirteen siege batteries constituting the XIV Corps Heavy Artillery. Its position was in the swampy country in the neighbourhood of Steenvoorde and Oostkerke. On 3rd December it moved to the La Bassée area, and rejoined the First Army, taking up position at Annequin. On 9th January, 1918, there came a short space of rest near Lillers. Major Begbie handed over the command to Major J. G. Stewart, and the battery became part of the 44th (S.A.) Brigade.

The 44th (South African) Battery, R.G.A.

On 29th January, 1918, Lieut.-Colonel T. H. Blew, D.S.O., of the South African Permanent Force, took command of the Brigade, with headquarters at Beuvry Château. The four batteries were in position east and south of Béthune. During February and March this was a quiet sector, but the batteries were busy preparing reserve positions in depth in view of a possible German attack. From the first day of April the guns were actively engaged in counter-battery work.

The German assault came on 9th April, and one of its main objectives was the right pillar of the British front at Givenchy, held by the 55th Division. All the battery positions of the Brigade, except that of the 125th, had been located by the enemy, who from the early morning drenched them with high explosives and gas shells. For a time all communications with Brigade Headquarters were cut. The falling back of the Division on their left allowed the enemy to advance almost up to their gun positions. The 73rd Battery was in the most hazardous case, and owing to the shelling it was impossible to bring up motor transport to evacuate its guns. Major Brydon, who had returned the month before from hospital to the command of the battery, was ordered to blow up his guns, but instead he served out rifles and a couple of machine guns to his men, and bade them stand to. At one time he had to send the breech-blocks to the rear for safety, but the attack was stayed before it reached the guns, and the breech-blocks were brought back. Though wounded and gassed, he refused to leave his battery. Finally he was compelled to retire. The men dragged the guns for nearly a mile under cover of darkness, and by 2 a.m. on the morning of the 10th a new position had been found, and the battery was again in action. The casualties of the Brigade that day were 13 men killed, and 6 officers and 29 men wounded.

The stand on the 9th checked the enemy for a time, and all batteries were able to take up less exposed positions. They suffered, however, from a continuous bombardment, and on the 12th the heroic commander of the 73rd was killed by a shell.

The 18th of April saw another severe bombardment, when five officers of the 73rd Battery were gassed. The expenditure of ammunition during that period had been enormous: the 71st Battery, for example, fired 11,000 rounds. The Brigade remained on the same front till the 27th June, when it was brought out to rest. On the 27th July Lieut.-Colonel Blew relinquished his command, being succeeded temporarily by Major E. H. Tamplin, who, on 17th August, handed over to Lieut.-Colonel C. M. Bennett, formerly commanding the 74th Battery.

On returning to the line on 2nd August, the Brigade took up positions farther south in the neighbourhood of Hulluch. On the 22nd its Headquarters were heavily shelled. During August and September the batteries supported the steady pressure maintained along this sector in anticipation of the German retirement, all moving to forward positions. On the 2nd October the enemy fell back three miles to the line of the Haute-Deule Canal, and the advance of the Fifth Army began. As soon as roads were repaired, the guns moved up to Douvrin, Hulluch, and Wingles, and on the 12th October assisted in the capture of Vendin by the 15th Division. Owing to the difficulty of bridging the many canals, siege batteries could only follow very slowly, and the Germans were on the line of the Scheldt before they came again into action. The enemy kept up a heavy bombardment during the first week of November, and on the night of the 6th the Brigade suffered its last casualties in the war. The bridging of the Scheldt was in rapid progress, and the batteries were preparing to advance across the river, when on the 11th hostilities ceased.

The 72nd Siege Battery, R.G.A.

The 72nd Battery landed in France on 21st April, 1916, under the command of Major C. W. Alston. Its first position was at Mailly-Maillet, where with a very short allowance of ammunition it entered upon its field experience. It was sent to Ypres on 3rd June along with the 71st to assist the Canadians, where it had some hard fighting, Major Alston being severely wounded, and Captain A. G. Mullins taking over the command. Returning to Mailly, it took part in the opening days of the First

Somme, and then moved first to Englebelmer, and then to Authuille. This last was an excellent position, with a steep bank in front of the guns and the Ancre in the rear. The battery remained there for eight months, until the retirement of the enemy enabled it to advance to Thiepval and Grandcourt.

On 22nd March, 1917, it moved to the Arras neighbourhood, taking up ground near Berthonval Wood, a few miles east of Mont St. Eloi. From this position the battery shared in the battle for Vimy, after the fall of which it moved forward to Souchez, under the northern end of the ridge. On 30th April it retired to Houdain for its first spell of rest since it arrived in France. On 12th May it was at Thélus, and four days later it was transferred to the 1st Canadian Heavy Artillery Group, and took up position at Zouave Valley, near Givenchy, in the Vimy area. There it remained for three months, supporting the Canadian attack at Lens.

On 25th October the battery went north with the Canadian Corps to Ypres, where it relieved the 73rd (S.A.) Siege Battery in a peculiarly unhealthy spot between Zillebeke and Observatory Ridge. There, during the first twenty-four hours, it had twelve casualties. On 17th October the command was taken over by Captain C. P. Ward. On 11th January, 1918, after a period of rest, the battery took up position behind the Damm Strasse, near Wytschaete. It was now brigaded with the 50th (S.A.) Brigade.

The 74th Siege Battery, R.G.A.

The 74th Battery landed at Havre on 30th April, 1916, under the command of Major Pickburn. It proceeded to Authuille, and on the 4th May took up position at Bienvillers-au-Bois. On the first day of the First Battle of the Somme its four guns fired 1,733 rounds, supporting the unsuccessful attack of the infantry at Gommecourt. It then took over the position of the 73rd Battery, and later, on 27th August, moved to the Martinsart-Aveluy road for the operations against Thiepval. On 7th October it was in the orchard at Colincamp, a place without cover and a favourite target for the enemy. On 7th November the battery commander, Major Pickburn, was killed. On the 20th November the enemy kept up a severe bombardment all day, and four gunners lost their lives. It was the same on the 29th, when an armour-piercing shell penetrated to a cellar protected by seven feet of earth and bricks, and killed the three occupants. The position was really untenable for the battery, but it was held till early in December, when a move was made to Auchonvillers. It presently moved to Gouy-en-Artois, and then to Arras and the Faubourg d'Amiens. In the early weeks of the year it was at Rivière, opposite Ficheux, and then again in a suburb of Arras.

In the Battle of Arras the battery supported the advance of the South African Infantry Brigade, and on the 12th its right section was in the old German line at Point de Jour, supporting the fighting in the Oppy, Gavrelle, and Rœux area. At that time they were the farthest forward siege guns on the British front. There the battery continued till the battle died away. Major Tamplin was gassed and returned to England, Major Murray-MacGregor taking over the command. By 5th July the whole battery had moved to the Ypres neighbourhood, where it took up ground on the canal bank near "Shrapnel Corner." There, during the first stages of Third Ypres, it suffered the usual fate of combatants in the Salient. Major Murray-MacGregor was succeeded in the command by Major G. M. Bennett. Presently it moved to a position on the Verbranden-Molen road, and a little later to Hooge. This was its station during the remainder of the battle. It had many casualties from shell-fire and gas, and the reliefs coming by the Menin road had to face an incessant enemy barrage. The total men available on each shift were only seventeen for all four guns, and had not three of the guns been knocked out the task would have been impossible. When at last the battery was withdrawn, it was reduced to 1 gun and 70 men.

On 21st December the battery, now brought up to strength, went back to the line as part of the 50th (S.A.) Brigade, R.G.A.

The 75th Siege Battery, R.G.A.

The 75th Battery reached France on 24th April, 1916, under the command of Major W. H. L. Tripp. It took up its position on the outskirts of the town of Albert, near the hospital, being attached to the III Corps. It participated in the "preparation" for the First Battle of the Somme, and on 1st July fired 1,312 rounds before noon. On 14th July it moved to Bécourt Wood, and on the 29th to a position north of Fricourt Wood. Here it supported the attack of 15th September. On the 21st of that month it moved to the wood of Bazentin-le-Grand, where it was in touch with the South African Infantry Brigade during its fight at the Butte de Warlencourt. On 29th January, 1917, it moved back to Albert, and early in February went south of the Somme into the old French area. There it advanced as the Germans fell back, crossing the Somme at Péronne on 25th March, and occupying ground successively at Templeux-la-Fosse and Longavesnes. On 6th April, at St. Emilie, it fired its first shot against the

Hindenburg Line, and remained in that area till the end of June, when it moved north to Flanders.

By 13th July all four guns were in position on the Vlamertinghe-Elverdinghe road, where, owing to the flat country, the battery had great difficulty in finding suitable O.P.'s. On the night of 30th July it moved forward to the bank of the Ypres Canal, where it supported the opening of the Third Battle of Ypres. Later it advanced to the Pilckem Ridge, where in a much exposed position it supported the attack on Houthulst Forest and Passchendaele. In the middle of December it went south to the Zillebeke Lake, and on 11th January, 1918, it moved to the Damm Strasse, near Wytschaete. It was now part of the 50th Brigade.

The 50th (South African) Brigade, R.G.A.

This Brigade was formed during January, 1918, under the command of Lieut.-Colonel W. H. L. Tripp, D.S.O., M.C., formerly of the 75th Battery. On 28th January it was attached to the Australian Corps, occupying positions between Zillebeke and Wytschaete. On 26th February it went into General Headquarters Reserve, being encamped near Bailleul. On 6th March the 496th (S.A.) Siege Battery arrived, and was split up between the 72nd and 74th Batteries, making these six-gun batteries. On 10th March the Brigade was ordered to prepare positions behind the Portuguese divisions, but the orders were cancelled. On 13th March it was attached to the Second Army. On the 24th, after the great German attack had been launched at St. Quentin, it began to move southwards, and on the 28th was at Neuville St. Vaast during the German assault on Arras. On the 30th it was attached to the Canadian Corps.

During April the batteries were in position at Roclincourt, to the north-east of Arras, and settled down to the familiar type of trench warfare. Since the whole military situation was uncertain at the moment, much time had to be spent on the preparation of reserve battery positions. Five series were selected, varying from three to fifteen miles behind those in use. On 1st May the Brigade was ordered north, the 72nd and 74th Batteries joining the I Corps near Mazingarbe, and the others going to the XIII Corps, in the vicinity of Hinges. By the 3rd these orders were changed, and the whole Brigade was sent to Arras to the XVII Corps. There it remained till the end of August, engaged in normal trench warfare. On 7th August Captain E. G. Ridley, M.C., was promoted major in command of the 74th Battery, to replace Major Bennett, who had gone to command the 44th Brigade.

On 26th August the Brigade supported the advance of the Canadian Corps and the 51st Division, which resulted in the capture of Monchy. The batteries now began to move forward along the Arras-Cambrai road, where they were engaged in cutting the wire of the Drocourt-Quéant switch. On the 2nd September the Canadians carried the Drocourt-Quéant switch, all the guns in the Brigade assisting in the preliminary bombardment and the subsequent barrage. Next day the Brigade passed under the XXII Corps, which held the line of the Sensée, in order to protect the flank of the Canadian thrust towards Cambrai. No serious operations took place for more than three weeks; but on the 27th came the great advance of the Canadian and XVII Corps towards and beyond Cambrai, and it became clear that a general enemy retirement was a matter of days. On 3rd October Major Ridley left for England to form a new 8-inch S.A. battery, and his place in command of the 74th was taken by Major C. J. Forder. On the 11th the Brigade came under the Canadian Corps.

On the 12th the batteries advanced, first to Tortequesne, and then to Estrées and Noyelle. On the 19th they were at Lewarde. On the 20th October a section of the 74th Battery moved to Wallers to support the Canadian attack. This was the last engagement of the Brigade in the war, for on the 24th it was placed in army reserve, and remained there till the armistice on 11th November.

II.

THE SOUTH AFRICAN SIGNAL COMPANY (R.E.).

Inception and Organization—August-October, 1915.

When, towards the close of the campaign in German South-West Africa, the composition of the Union Oversea Contingent was decided, the offer of a Divisional Signal Company was willingly accepted by the Imperial authorities.

The raising of this company was entrusted to Major N. Harrison, Engineer-in-Chief of the Union Post Office, who had acted as Director of Signals to the Union Forces during the Rebellion and the German South-West African Campaign. The personnel were drawn from all four Provinces of the Union and Rhodesia.

The backbone of the company consisted of skilled telegraphists and linemen from the Union Post Office. The drivers were recruited mainly from the farming population.

By the beginning of October all the officers, who had been selected from officials of the engineering branch of the Post Office and electrical engineers of the Witwatersrand, had joined, and on the 17th October the unit, in company with the S.A.M.C. and details of the South African Brigade and S.A.H.A., sailed for England on the " Kenilworth Castle," with a strength of six officers and 229 other ranks. The company arrived at Bordon Camp, Hants, on 4th November.

Reorganization and Training of the Company in England—November, 1915–April, 1916.

As the South African Brigade would constitute only one-third of the infantry of some Imperial Division, the company could not serve with the Infantry Brigade in the capacity of a divisional signal company. On the other hand, new army corps were in course of formation, and corps signal companies had to be raised and trained for them. A corps signal company requires a high proportion of skilled technicians in the ranks, and as the company possessed such a proportion, the War Office decided that it should be reorganized in order to form a Corps Signal Company, and proceed to the Signal Service Training Centre in Bedford for the necessary specialized training. The company accordingly entrained for Hitchin on the 23rd November, and during the next few days was reorganized.

The following months were spent in continuous training. Early in April, 1916, the company received orders to proceed to France. It embarked at Southampton on the 10th April, in the s.s. " Investigator " and landed at Havre on the 21st.

In France: The Fricourt Sector—April, 1916.

After a day at Havre the move was continued —motor transport sections by road and cable sections by train—to Vignacourt. At this village in the Somme Valley, between Abbevillle and Amiens, the headquarters of the newly constituted XV Corps was concentrating under Lieut.-General Horne, and Major Harrison, on the 23rd April, was appointed Assistant Director of Army Signals. The company now became the XV Corps Signal Company, and served continuously with that Corps throughout the remainder of the war. A few days later the Corps moved into line between the III and XIII Corps becoming a part of the Fourth Army, and took over the sector fronting Fricourt and Mametz, between Bécourt and Carnoy. On the 30th April the company took over from the XIII Corps Signal Company at Heilly, a village on the Ancre, near Corbie. B.F. and B.G. sections were sent to join the headquarters of the two divisions in line—the 7th and 21st respectively—and B.F. section proceeded to Ville-sur-Ancre, and took charge of the Corps heavy artillery's communications on the 27th April.

As soon as the area could be thoroughly surveyed, a programme of work was drawn up covering—

(*a*) reconstruction of and additions to the inadequate open wire routes in the back area, from Corps Headquarters up to behind Méaulte, Morlancourt, and the Bois des Tailles, sufficient to cope with the number of units and formations to be thrown in for the battle, and suitably designed and located for rapid extension along the probable roads of the anticipated advance;

(*b*) a complete network of cable trenches extending from the heads of the open wire routes to the front line, providing telephone communication down to the company and battery command posts and artillery observation posts.

Labour for the heavy artillery cable trenches was not secured till June, when four battalions were placed under the direction of Lieutenant Ross for this work. Digging the trenches and laying cable were then pressed forward continuously night and day. Much of the work was only possible at night, as the ground was under direct observation, and the few skilled sappers available, after working most of the night with infantry digging parties, had to be turned out again at dawn, day after day, to take charge of scratch cable-laying parties made up from the signallers of batteries. The heavy artillery allotment for the XV Corps in the coming battle was twenty-three batteries, organized in five groups, and an independent railway battery. The tactical conditions made the communication problem one of peculiar difficulty, because they enforced the siting of the batteries in two main clusters—one in the valley of the Ancre and the other in Happy Valley—both on the extreme flanks of the Corps' frontage. Further, owing to the enemy's tenure of the Fricourt salient, many batteries, to carry out their work, had to establish communication with observation posts sited on the opposite flank of the Corps area to the position of the batteries, and the most favourable O.P. positions lay far outside the Corps boundaries. The fact that many of the batteries only took position and settled on their

O.P.'s in the last few days was an additional complication.

By much strenuous effort the programme was completed, and when the preparatory bombardment opened, 500 miles of cable had been laid and joined up in over twenty miles of cable trench, and every battery had excellent and reliable communication forward to its observation posts and back to its group commander. Two dug-outs had been constructed on each flank, into which all O.P. lines were led and terminated on special switchboards, designed and made up at the company headquarters.

Through these O.P. exchanges any battery could be connected to any O.P. for control of fire, which proved most valuable in the changing circumstances of the fighting. At that date the establishment of neither groups nor batteries included switchboards for metallic circuit lines. The necessary number—over thirty—were improvised in a few days at the company workshops out of electric light fittings purchased in Amiens.

Meanwhile the other sections working at similar high pressure had completed the main communications from Corps Headquarters to the battle headquarters of the Divisions, the 7th in dug-outs near Groveton, and the 21st in dug-outs on the edge of the plateau above Méaulte, and B.F. section had established and staffed a Corps Advanced Exchange at Morlancourt. The Carrier Pigeon Service had been organized, and arrangements made for the systematic distribution of pigeons to the assaulting brigades from the main lofts in Heilly, Albert, and Méaulte, and the most rapid circulation from the pigeon lofts to all staffs concerned of information contained in messages brought by the birds returning from the front line.

A wireless detachment was supplied from Fourth Army Signals, and the personnel completed by skilled operators selected from the company. The headquarters station was fixed on the high ground near the Bray-Albert Road on the cable trench between the two O.P. exchanges, and provided with direct communication to Corps through the underground system, and mobile stations were attached to the Signals of the attacking divisions. The Corps Staff Observation Posts in Péronne Avenue trench and the Grand Stand above Bonte Redoubt were connected by direct lines to the General Staff at Headquarters in Heilly, about ten miles off, and the special linemen provided to look after these lines kept them through without interruption during the attack.

The Somme Battle—July-November, 1916.

In the early morning of the 1st July, after a continuous bombardment from the 25th June, the XV Corps attacked with the 7th Division on the right, the 21st on the left, and the 17th in support. All signal arrangements for a rapid advance were in readiness, including the lines necessary to divert communications to Vivier Mill, outside Méaulte, which was to be the first bound of the Corps Headquarters, while the cable sections stood by with wagons packed during the morning. In spite of the gallantry of the infantry assault, by the evening it was clear that no great depth would be attained.

The village of Fricourt was still holding out, and had repulsed a frontal attack with heavy loss, while the converging attacks of the 7th and 21st Divisions on the flanks of the salient, which were to have pinched it out, had carried Mametz, but just failed to link up behind Fricourt. The III Corps on our left had taken La Boisselle and entered Ovillers, but had been driven out again; Montauban had fallen to the XIII Corps on the right, but heavy fighting continued. Fricourt was bombarded all night by heavy howitzers, and deluged with a new gas shell by a brigade of French 75's, which, together with an additional brigade of heavies, had been attached to the Corps Heavy Artillery shortly before the battle. When the infantry advanced next morning the village was found evacuated, and a party from B.E. section were able to make a preliminary reconnaissance for pushing forward the artillery routes. Our tenure of the high ground between Mametz and Montauban was now sufficiently secured, and the roads Méaulte-Fricourt and Carnoy-Mametz repaired to such an extent as to permit the advance of the heavy batteries to positions about our old front line.

It was evident from the map that while the fighting for Mametz Wood continued, the new centre of observation would be about Pommiers Redoubt—the highest point of the Mametz-Montauban ridge—and after a hasty reconnaissance which located our advanced line down the forward slope about Caterpillar Wood, it was decided to lay a few pairs of armoured cable up to the old German trenches from the new battery positions about Carnoy and Fricourt. The only armoured cable to be obtained was a portion of that already laid in the trench between the two O.P. exchanges. A few signallers having been collected from the batteries, this heavy armoured cable was recovered from the trench, conveyed forward by wagon, and again laid out up to Pommiers Redoubt. 51 Air Line Section was engaged in following up the advance with a light open wire route up to Fricourt, and B.G. and B.F. Sections were worked with the 21st Division Signals and the Corps observers respectively.

The commencement of active operations brought the work of the operators and the dispatch riders at headquarters and with the Heavy Artillery to a point of extreme pressure, which was maintained with little variation throughout the following months. Up to two thousand telegrams, and a larger number still of D.R.L.S. packets, were received or dispatched daily. The telephone exchanges at Corps and Heavy Artillery Headquarters, with over sixty and thirty connections respectively, worked hard day and night, handling urgent priority calls. The destruction of lines by hostile shelling and traffic was met by the skilful use of alternative routes and by the quickness and energy of the maintenance linemen.

On the 10th July, B.G. Section, under the command of Lieutenant Covernton, did a notably fine performance in laying and maintaining lines through the intense barrages surrounding Mametz Wood. One of the first valve amplifying listening sets supplied to the British forces for use in intercepting enemy messages, by picking up weak leakage or induced currents through earth or along parallel conductors, had been issued to the company for trial. As a large number of enemy cables ran through Mametz Wood, and some extended to enemy territory behind it, favourable results seemed probable. Lieutenant Collins took up the set, and tracing the cables into No Man's Land, tapped in there. Owing to the excellent discipline of the enemy in obeying the limitations prescribed for use of wire communication in the front line, no tactical messages were obtained.

On the 14th July another general assault secured the line along the ridge between Bazentin-le-Petit and Longueval. Accordingly, heavy batteries were moved up as far as Caterpillar Wood in the valley in front of Montauban, and on the 15th a party of B.E. Section reconnoitred for lines to Bazentin-le Petit, in which village it was proposed to establish H.A. Headquarters. The German reaction had, however, already begun, and the party found the conditions in the village highly unsuited for a headquarters, so much so that a warm infantry combat was proceeding in the outskirts. Nevertheless, over a mile of ground had been gained, and the corresponding extension of communications necessarily taxed all sections to their limit. The advanced headquarters of divisions moved up to the dug-outs in the chalk under the ruins of Fricourt Château, in which, thirty feet underground, the German Staff had dwelt during the bombardment of the village. A twenty-four wire heavy route was rapidly constructed by the 4th Army Signals from Méaulte to this point, and thence to Mametz, in readiness for the advance, and the wire light route built by the company was extended by the Air Line Section past Fricourt, up Death Valley, to Mametz Wood. The next deep advance was not, however, to occur till two months later, as the Corps front was now becoming a salient, and it was necessary to clear the flanks and broaden the base of the attack. Therefore, while the Anzac Corps and III Corps on the left, and the XIII Corps succeeded by the XIV Corps on the right, hammered away round Pozières and Ginchy respectively, the XV Corps was engaged in continuous auxiliary attacks, and its heavy artillery co-operated largely with the operations of the flanking corps.

This situation did not bring any relaxation to the Signal Company. The German artillery, whose work behind the front line had been feeble immediately after the 1st July, had now been heavily reinforced, and the salient position of the Corps inevitably drew much enfilade fire. One of the effects was the continuous destruction of lines back to points thousands of yards from the front. In moving up after the 14th July, all units had finally passed beyond the buried cables laid down for the battle. Forward lines were now entirely overground, and if not blown up by direct hits, were cut by the smallest splinters.

As the month of July wore on the demand for additional forward communication and the strength of the hostile fire increased. It was obvious that no satisfactory communication could be secured beyond Fricourt except by burying. It was decided to commence by burying sixteen pairs of armoured cable from the head of the open route at Mametz to Pommiers Redoubt dug-outs, where there were now Brigade Headquarters and Divisional Report Centres. The work was entrusted to B.G. Section, and proved difficult, not only because of the maze of old trenches, barbed wire, and shell-holes through which the cable trench had to go, but also because of the frequent shelling of Mametz and along the ridge. The trench was completed, and subsequently the cables were extended to Caterpillar Trench. At the same time, 51 Air Line Section diverted the open wire route between Fricourt and Mametz by constructing a substantial pole route skirting both villages, which carried eight pairs of twisted D5 cables hung in slotted boards. This cable route was not only much less frequently shelled down, but could be quickly repaired, as the cable when cut could be rejointed and worked, even if lying on the ground.

During the comparative lull towards the end of July the shelling of the Fricourt area became so pronounced that, pending the next general attack, the headquarters of the Divisions in line were moved back to Bellevue Farm—between Méaulte and Albert—and the opportunity was at once taken to transfer the Corps Exchange in Fricourt into the dug-outs so vacated. A new route was built by 51 Air Line Section from Bellevue Farm to link up this new position with the main forward route at Vivier Mill, and was calculated on a scale sufficient to meet requirements in the event of the headquarters of the Corps moving to Bellevue Farm when the advance resumed.

Long before the Somme Battle, the exigencies of trench warfare had altered the original organization of army corps. The corps had ceased to be a unit composed of specific divisions, and divisions were no longer affiliated permanently to one corps, but moved at frequent intervals from quiet sectors to active ones to take part in an offensive, and after a short period of heavy losses and extreme exertion would be again withdrawn to another quiet sector or a training area for rest, recruitment, and refit. Therefore, on a front like the Somme, a continuous stream of divisions passed through the corps, each taking its share of the fighting and being in turn relieved. The Corps Signal Company had to fit each fresh Division into the frame of the existing communications as they chanced to stand at the moment, and assist the divisional signals to pick up and utilize the available lines. The organization had, also, to be elastic enough to meet the requirements of administering anything from two to seven divisions simultaneously. During the Somme, nineteen different Divisions passed through the XV Corps, and many of them went through the furnace more than once. There were altogether fifty-three divisional changes.

The excellence of the work of the B.E. Section with the Heavy Artillery was recognized in a communication addressed to Major Harrison, in which the Corps commander stated that he much appreciated the work done by Lieutenant Ross and his party, and considered that the work of this section was typical of the whole South African Signal Company. When General Horne himself left the Corps at a later date to take command of the First Army, he congratulated the A.D.A.S. on commanding a unit "second to none in France."

By the beginning of September the flanking Corps had made the necessary progress, and everything was in readiness for the great attack of 15th September. The vital importance of secure communication being fully appreciated by the Staff, the necessary labour was made available for a considerable buried scheme. The first section of the new bury consisted of a six-foot deep cable trench, extending from Pommiers Redoubt via the famous Cosy Corner, where the Carnoy and Mametz Roads join outside Montauban, and thence to York Trench on the left of Longueval. This trench had nine framed test points let into the walls every four hundred and forty yards, and contained forty-five pairs of cable. The accumulation of the necessary quantities of cable suitable for the work presented great difficulty, and the trench probably set up a record for the number of different varieties it contained—from nineteen pair V.I.R., as thick and heavy as a hawser and supplied on drums weighing over half a ton each, to one pair G.P. Twin, about as stout as a double bootlace. The actual digging was done by a battalion of the 7th Division, the work being under the charge of Lieutenant Collins, assisted by Lieutenant Baker, with B.G. Section and most of the sappers of B.E. and W.W. Sections. The jointing, terminating, and testing of the wires had to be completed against time, and with a limited number of expert men, as the maintenance of the widespread network for which the company was responsible had absorbed many of the best men out of all sections. The lines were, however, ready in time for the Divisions who had moved headquarters up again to Fricourt and Pommiers Redoubt, with advanced headquarters at York Trench, and also for the Heavy Artillery, most of whose batteries took positions along the Mametz-Montauban ridge and in folds of the forward slope towards Caterpillar Wood and Longueval. To cope with the steady forward drift of the Corps units, and to provide another advance maintenance point, a new Corps Forward Exchange was established in a dug-out at Pommiers, and after the attack B.E. Section staffed this exchange and maintained the area.

The attack on 15th September proved highly successful, a depth of over a mile being made good, including the villages of Courcelette, Martinpuich, and Flers. Communications held well throughout the day, and the good liaison between infantry and artillery so secured played an important part in the result. The recently introduced power buzzers for transmitting high-power buzzer signals through earth to be picked up by valve amplifying receivers at distances up to three thousand yards, were used with fair success in the advance. These sets were controlled by the Wireless Section, but the forward stations were manned by signallers of the attacking battalions.

The advance rendered a further extension of the cable trench urgent, but for the moment suitable cable for a permanent bury was not available. Another section of trench, however, was dug immediately in order that units might have the benefit of its protection in running temporary field cables forward. This section extended from York Trench through the corner of Delville Wood to Switch Trench. To prevent confusion and facilitate maintenance, the left-hand side of the new trench was assigned to divisions and the right to the Heavy Artillery, the Headquarters Signals of which prepared and erected along the trench fixtures for cables in the shape of angle-iron high-wire entanglement pickets, each having a piece of two-inch by two-inch wood screwed to it with a dozen diagonal slots cut in it for the cable.

Liaison lines had grown formidably in numbers. Direct lines were now demanded not only between Heavy Artillery Headquarters and the Artillery Headquarters of all Divisions in line, but between the divisional artilleries and the majority of the heavy artillery groups. There had been a great development of the service of observation in the shape of artillery aeroplanes, kite balloons, of which there were now three sections attached to the Corps and Observation Groups of the R.E. Survey battalion. Whenever possible lines were now required from these units, not only to the artillery groups, but to the batteries specially assigned for counter-battery work. To co-ordinate and render fully effective this work of the systematic location and destruction of neutralization of hostile batteries, a special staff, commanded by a colonel, had been added to the H.A. Headquarters, and this staff, in its turn, required additional direct lines and communication facilities to enable it to function promptly and effectively.

On the 25th September the intermediate German line, including Morval, Lesboeufs, and Gueudecourt, succumbed, and the Corps front again advanced over a mile. On the 26th the victory was completed by the Fifth Army's capture of Thiepval. The weather, however, intervened on the side of the Germans, and breaking decisively on the 26th, remained miserably cold and wet thenceforward, and largely stultified the heroic efforts repeatedly made throughout October.

During this period, the heavy batteries of some of the H.A. Group Headquarters moved up to and in front of Longueval, necessitating the running of many new cable lines. Permanent cable was laid in the second section of the main cable trench up to Longueval, and a third section of trench was dug forwards to the sugar works at Factory Corner in front of Flers.

At the end of October the Anzac Corps, under General Birdwood, relieved the XV Corps, commanded by Sir John Ducane since the departure of General Horne, and "K" Corps Signal Company took over the signal system.

In view of the extensive system to be taken over, the relief by "K" Corps Signal Company was conducted gradually, and B.E., the last section to leave the line, did not reach the new headquarters at Long until the middle of November.

On Major Harrison's promotion, Captain Dingwall now assumed the executive control of the company, but scarcely had the sections completed their refit when orders were suddenly received for the Corps to take over a portion of the French front in the Péronne sector, with the 4th, 8th, 33rd, and 40th Divisions then in rest.

The Winter Campaign on the Somme—16th December–17th March.

The move into line commenced on the 3rd December, and was completed on the 6th. The cable sections moved with the Divisional Signal Companies, and were directed—B.E. and B.G. on Bray, and B.F. on Maricourt.

Headquarters and the Air Line Section joined the Corps Headquarters at Etinehem, a village on the right bank of the Somme, a mile or so west of Bray. The Corps front extended from the XIV Corps boundary on the north at Combles, previously the extreme right of the British line, to near Bouchavesnes, and ran in front of St. Pierre Vaast Wood, where the most desperate French attacks in the autumn had, like our own in the north, been stifled in the mud. The terrain as a whole was of similar nature and condition to that in the Longueval sector, but the roads were better, Décauville tramways existed, and, best of all, from a signal point of view, a very fair network of deep cable trenches had been dug in the forward area. Though the cable used in these "buries"—mainly one pair lead covered with impregnated paper insulation — proved unreliable in insulation, and much trouble was caused and many circuits lost thereby, yet the "buries" proved very useful, and, supplemented by the construction system of several new open routes in rear, enabled a communication system to be rapidly completed, sufficient for the needs of the defensive winter campaign. Corps forward exchanges were established with the Heavy Artillery Headquarters in excellent French dug-outs at Bois Louage in front of Maurepas, as at Maricourt, in charge of B.F. Section, and with B.G. Section at Bray, where the horse lines of all cable sections were shortly concentrated. The sappers of B.E. Section remained with H.A. Headquarters under Lieutenant Collins, who replaced Captain Ross as H.A. Signal Officer, while the latter did duty at Headquarters.

During December it was understood that the French contemplated launching an attack against Mont St. Quentin and Péronne, and to this end they retained a frontage on both banks of the Somme. However, early in January, 1917, the project was abandoned, and orders were received for the XV Corps to extend its front to the right, taking over to the river by Cléry, and simultaneously handing over a divisional frontage on the left to the XIV Corps. The divisional sectors were taken over successively, and the move completed by the 22nd January without interference by the enemy, the headquarters of Divisions in line being established at P.C. Chapeau and P.C. Jean, ex-French divisional command posts judiciously and inconspicuously sited under the high bank running parallel to the Somme bank. H.A. Headquarters with B.E. Section moved also to P.C. Chapeau, and the Corps Forward Exchange at Maricourt was transferred with B.F. Section to Suzanne. The weather, that had been cold and wet from the beginning of December, now turned to snow and hard frost. The latter penetrated the ground to such an extent that by the end of the month all digging became impossible, and work on a buried cable trench between Ouvrages and Oursel, to provide forward communications for the 33rd Division, had to be suspended. The ex-French bury forward of P.C. Jean proved very faulty, and a section of twelve pair open-wire heavy route was put in hand early in February, running forward to Monac, partly to supplement the bury and partly to carry forward the head of the main route in anticipation of the advance next spring. As the forward end of this route came under direct observation, the last few hundred yards were run in cables hung on short stakes, each cable from a small bobbin insulator nailed to the side of the stake. This method was copied from the French, who had used it extensively in the area, and proved very satisfactory in this instance.

In the meantime, aeroplane night-bombing and the shelling of back areas by long-range guns, initiated in the latter stages of the Somme Battle, had developed.

This hostile aeroplane activity caused a rapid increase of anti-aircraft units. Batteries and searchlights were now dotted over the area, and the installation and maintenance of a separate and complete system of communication for the anti-aircraft defence of the Corps area was now added to the company's duties, and the H.A. Signal Officer found himself occupied with communications for the survey groups and the installation of lines to their O.P.'s, and to the microphone positions of the sound ranging section now added to the H.A. counter-battery organization.

Though the duties of the H.A. Signal Officer were somewhat reduced by the appointment in January of a R.E. Signal Officer to each H.A. group, the commencement by the enemy of systematic counter-battery work, in imitation of the British methods initiated in the previous year, made it more than ever difficult to keep the forward lines in continuous operation. A scheme for the forward extension of the buried system, till recently used by the French, was prepared. But the deep crust of frozen ground prevented digging, and the important local attack of the 8th Division on the 4th March on Fritz Trench above Bouchavesnes had to be carried through without the assistance of the new buried communication, and as most of the above-ground cables were cut, the first news of the assaulting troops was brought by pigeon to the Corps left at Etinehem. The attack was fully successful, and the effective use made by the artillery of the excellent observation secured by it, no doubt expedited the general retirement of the enemy in this sector.

The general withdrawal began on the 15th March, the enemy falling back on the Corps front across the Canal du Nord. The advance of the XV Corps was conducted methodically, touch with the enemy rearguards being maintained by the Wiltshire Yeomanry and the Corps Cyclist Battalion until a Cavalry Division could come up.

The Signal Company's share in the work was first to maintain direct touch between the Corps Staff and the advanced troops, for which purpose D.R.'s were attached to the cavalry, but by a special effort of B.E. Section direct telephone communication was soon secured and maintained. Secondly, the main communication network had to be extended forward at the same rate as the advance, and, as a counter-attack was very possible, the full organization for position warfare accompanied the Corps. The signal difficulties were doubled on the 25th March by the sudden withdrawal from line of the XIV Corps on the right and the consequent extension of the already wide Corps frontage which then stretched from Péronne to Le Transloy.

Early in April the advance reached its limit, and was definitely held up in front of La Vacquerie and Havrincourt—outlying strong points of the Hindenburg Line. On the 17th, Corps Headquarters was established in hutments and tents near Haute-Allaines, after a short interval at P.C. Chapeau.

Little relaxation of effort was possible however. The Germans in their retreat had demolished all signal communications. Every pole was sawn through when not bodily removed. Scarcely a yard of usable line—

cables or open wire—existed in the new area, and the whole of the immense network of communications for stationary warfare had to be reconstituted under continuing supply and transport difficulties, while the hasty work done in the advance had to be overhauled and made permanent.

Scarcely was this task well under way when orders were received to prepare signal plans for an offensive and commence the necessary works as early as possible. The position in regard to materials was alleviated in May by the organization of a temporary Corps Signal Salvage Unit, composed of B.F. Section, a platoon of a Labour Company, and the necessary horse and motor transport under Lieutenant Jack. This made it possible to push forward work on two heavy open-wire routes, running from Corps Headquarters, through Nurlu and Fins, and through Sèvo Wood, Liéramont, and Heudicourt respectively with the necessary spur and lateral routes. To economize cable, which remained very short in supply, the subsidiary routes were run as far as possible in light iron wire (60 lb. to the mile), on air line or light hop poles, and considerable use was made of a light type of French cable with all copper conductors salvaged in the back area. This use of low resistance conductors, and the maintaining of good line conditions, made clear speech possible between O.P.'s and H.A. Headquarters, and on special occasions Corps Headquarters, a point of great value in securing rapid and effective counter-battery work. Up to this time all the British field cables, except D5, had steel conductors, and were, therefore, of high resistance, and good speech could only be obtained on short lines. Plans were also elaborated for a buried cable scheme covering the area between the front line and heads of open wire behind Gouzeacourt and Gonnelieu respectively. The permanent routes had progressed beyond Fins and Heudicourt, when, towards the end of May, orders arrived for the XV Corps to hand over to the III Corps and proceed to Villiers-Bretonneux. The cable sections of the company joined various Divisions, and, at the end of May, accompanied them out of the area to unknown destinations.

The remainder of the company reached Villiers-Bretonneux on the 3rd June.

The great and continuing growth in the demands on the Signal Service, particularly in connection with the Heavy Artillery, had for long unduly taxed the available personnel, and increase in establishments was overdue. To the Corps Signal Company was, therefore, now added a Heavy Artillery Headquarters Signal Section, with a strength of one officer and thirty-seven other ranks. The personnel for this section was obtained from drafts built up on a nucleus of experienced men, mainly from R.E. Section. At the same time, a signal sub-section of one officer and twenty-seven other ranks was formed for each H.A. Group, but as H.A. Groups were frequently moved from Corps to Corps, these sub-sections were organized from Imperial R.E. personnel. The Company Headquarters Section was also strengthened by the withdrawal of four telegraphists from each cable section, the vacancies being filled with additional pioneers. The Signal Section forming part of the Headquarters of S.A. Infantry Brigade was now affiliated to the Company, and thenceforward drew its reinforcements therefrom.

The interlude at Villers was abruptly cut short by orders to move on the 10th June for a secret destination. The secret was extremely well kept, and not until the convoy actually entered Dunkirk on the 11th was it realized that the Corps was to take over the Nieuport sector—the important bit of line running from the sea along the Yser, which had been held by the French since the momentous days of the First Battle of Ypres. Corps Headquarters were established on the 11th in the Casino of Malo-les-Bains, a suburb of Dunkirk, and arrangements for the relief of the 36th French Corps at once put in hand.

The Belgian Coast and the Battle of the Dunes—November, 1917.

Though this sector had been for a long period a quiet one, the German artillery concentration opposite it was already great, especially in heavy long-range guns. Normal trenches in this terrain were impossible, and both sides stood behind breastworks that in the dunes were merely gabions filled with sand; but here, as on the Ypres front, the liberal use of concrete by the enemy had given his front-line troops, as well as his batteries and command posts, the protection of many "pill-boxes" and concrete shelters of various forms. For a long period the French had held the sector comparatively lightly; consequently the whole of the titanic task of mounting a trench warfare offensive fell on the incoming corps. On such terrain the preparations presented extreme and unique difficulties, and those of Signals were enhanced by the fact that not only did the nature of the ground forbid deep cable buries, but very few shallow ones existed; while the existing communications were almost entirely open wire to within four thousand yards of the front line, and sited along roads certain to be heavily shelled.

British divisions began to arrive in the area on the 15th June, bringing the absent cable sections of the Company with them, and between the 20th and 23rd the French divisions in line were relieved by the 1st and 32nd Divisions. Thereafter the Corps Heavy Artillery commenced to move in, the H.A. Signal Section and B.E. Section proceeding to the late French Heavy Artillery Headquarters, D.C.A.L. to a small copse about two miles south of Nieuport, and B.G. Section to Coxyde to prepare for the establishment of a forward exchange.

After a rapid survey of the area, a communication scheme to meet the needs of Corps, Divisions, and the Heavy Artillery on a hitherto unprecedented scale was prepared. Meanwhile the various sections toiled at the familiar task of connecting up the units that were streaming into the area daily, and preparing the new Corps Headquarters at Bray-Dunes Plage. The H.A. Section had, even with the assistance of B.E. Section, a particularly strenuous task in coping with the concentration of eleven groups of " heavies," and found it necessary to endeavour to bring into use at once the incomplete French buries.

The movement of Corps Headquarters to Bray-Dunes was effected on the 29th June. A few days later the Heavy Artillery quarters moved back to the village of Oost Dunkirk, about six thousand yards from the line, and occupied the Villa Rosarie. During the first week in July a considerable increase in hostile shelling was noted, but not to an alarming extent, and no immediate operations were anticipated.

The enemy, however, had decided to nip our attack in the bud by taking the initiative himself, and had only delayed to complete a crushing artillery concentration. Thus about 9.30 a.m. on the 10th July, when many batteries were not yet in position and many others not yet ready for action, an intense bombardment dropped over the whole Corps area up to nine thousand yards behind the front line. With the most admirable accuracy and thoroughness, every village and battery position was searched, and every road of approach swept by heavy shell-fire. Forward communications failed almost at once, the bridges across the Yser below Nieuport were destroyed, the breastwork trenches melted away before the storm of high explosive, and when the infantry assault was delivered about 7 p.m. few survivors of the Brigade of the 1st Division that held the trenches across the Yser in front of Nieuport Bain remained to resist, and the German front line was established on the Yser bank in this sector. On the other flank, at Lombartzyde, the 32nd Division managed by desperate fighting to retain most of the ground in front of Nieuport, but the main German object was achieved; the approaches to the bridgehead were now limited to the single entry of Nieuport, and the bridgehead itself was so reduced in area as to make a serious attack in force a very desperate venture.

This day was naturally a most trying one for the Signal personnel. Nearly all wire communication was lost in the first two hours, and all formations from Corps downwards had to fall back on dispatch riders and runners. Very fine work was done by the company's dispatch runners on the shell-swept roads, while the sections strove to patch up and keep going the vital command lines. Thanks to cool and quick repair work by the sappers, and to the use of a short piece of cable trench completed on the previous day, touch was kept with most of the Heavy Artillery Groups continually throughout the day. The observation lines could not, however, be kept going, and thus the batteries not put out of action were blinded, and could not effectively support the infantry across the river. Oost Dunkirk village suffered heavily, and after nightfall the H.A. Staff were forced to move into the sand dunes half a mile to the flank, when temporary cables were run back to the signal office at the Villa Rosarie, which enjoyed protection in a sand-bagged shelter behind the house.

The attack was not resumed on the following day, and while every nerve was strained to get the existing lines restored, work on the new communications began and was pressed forward night and day. The buried scheme originally planned provided for four forward trenches, one along the sea coast, one through the dunes, one partly French and already dug through the polder area, and one consisting of cable laid in the bed of the Nieuport Canal—all to be connected by a lateral trench running through H.A. Headquarters, which was to become the chief maintenance and test point. Lieutenant Collins, with B.E. Section and a rapidly increasing number of Imperial sections, loaned from Army Signals, was entrusted with this work. In view of the experiences of the 10th, two additional trenches were added to the plan, one from a main open route junction point behind Coxyde, forward along the fringe of the dunes to H.A. Headquarters, and the other along the sea-beach above highwater mark from Corps Headquarters at Bray-Dunes to the same point.

This latter trench, which contained twenty-five pair dry core cable, was completed by Lieutenant Hill with skilled cable jointers from 51 Air Line. Labour was made freely available by the Corps Staff, and as material now came forward rapidly, up to two thousand men a day were employed on these works. The forward portion of the scheme presented great difficulty, as the area was now so sown with batteries that it was almost impossible to trace the trenches so as to avoid battery positions and the shelling which they attracted. The greater part of the work could only be done by night because of enemy observation; and, further, time did not admit of the usual detailed preparation for the working parties. Nevertheless, all works were completed for the attack.

The experiment made on the Somme of using a kite balloon to maintain communication with the front line, was now repeated, and the result was satisfactory.

Though all other preparations were well advanced, the attack was postponed from date to date, until it finally became evident by the transfer of a large proportion of the heavy batteries to the Ypres front, that the slow progress made there was likely to postpone the Nieuport offensive indefinitely.

During the interval the forward buried system, unavoidably shallow from the nature of the ground, was continuously broken by shell fire. During September the cable trenches were blown up by direct hits on the average nearly twice a day. The repairs were most difficult and laborious owing both to the persistent shelling and the rise of the water-level everywhere after the wet weather of August. Even with the sappers of three cable sections—B.F., B.E., and A.U. Imperial Cable Section, and two area Signal Detachments from the Fourth Army, it became impossible to keep going satisfactorily the network of forty miles of trenches containing 1,200 miles of cable; and finally the assistance of the Corps Cyclist Battalion was obtained to dig diversion trenches in the worst shell areas, and a new trench in the Belgian area in substitution of the cable laid in the Nieuport Canal, the insulation of which began to fail soon after laying.

Corps Headquarters moved to La Panne at the beginning of September and transferred to Bray-Dunes. The relief of the Corps by the XXXVI French Corps commenced on the 19th November. On the 20th the headquarters of the company, under Captain Dingwall, who had been acting as A.W. Signals since September during Lieut.-Colonel Harrison's absence on sick leave, moved to Hinges near Béthune, and commenced to take over from the XI Corps a sector between Béthune and Armentières.

The Lys Area.

After some readjustments of frontage in December, the XV Corps settled down to hold the sector in front of the Lys, from Houplines to Laventie, with the Portuguese Corps on the right and the Aanzac Corps on the left. In January, 1918, Corps Headquarters were shifted from Hinges to La Motte-aux-Bois, in front of the Forest of Nieppe, and Heavy Artillery, with the H.A. and B.E. sections, to Estaires, where 51 Air Line was already established. A further reorganization of the company now took place. The decision was reached to disband one cable section in each Corps, to reduce the strength of the Corps Air Line Section to 42 all ranks with one heavy and two light lorries, and with the surplus personnel so accruing form an additional Air Line Section for each Corps. B.G. Section was, accordingly, converted into the nucleus of the new 91 Air Line Section, to which Lieutenant Dobson was appointed. At the same time "Q" Wireless Section became an integral portion of the Signal Company, and was taken over by Lieutenant McArthur, with Second Lieutenant Fitzgeorge as second officer, the Imperial personnel being rapidly replaced by South Africans. A second officer was also authorized for the Heavy Artillery Section, and Lieutenant M. Cohen was appointed.

The communications here were such as would serve on a thinly held and lightly shelled front. Buries were few and becoming inefficient with age; the light open-wire routes which formed the bulk of the communication were run close up to the front line. Ample and secure communications were a first necessity, and a complete scheme was prepared on a scale of magnitude and thoroughness which surpassed any previous performance. All trenches were to be seven feet deep and carry no less than thirty pairs of wires.

Work could not be commenced before the 25th January, owing to the whole Lys Valley, which is very low lying, becoming water-logged by heavy rain. By unremitting effort the Corps section of the trenches was completed by the beginning of March, and a portion of the work originally assigned to Divisions taken over.

While the other sections were so engaged, B.F. was employed on another section of the scheme in and around Armentières itself. In this town a considerable underground sewer system existed, and though not comparable with the underways of Arras, yet these sewers proved extremely valuable as affording ready-made covered ways for cable. B.F. accordingly spent two months in laying securely many miles of cable. The new 91 Air Line Section meanwhile pushed on the necessary additions to the open-wire routes forward from Corps Headquarters. Hostile artillery activity began to increase considerably in March, and about the middle of the month became so marked that from this and other symptoms an immediate attack was expected.

This alarm proved for the time false, the offensive commencing instead on the Third and

Fifth Army fronts on the 21st March. The immediate effect was the withdrawal of all the divisions in the Corps and their replacement with exhausted divisions from the south the 34th and 40th—who naturally could provide no labour. The greatest anxiety was now felt lest the communication should not be finished in time, and work was rushed day and night. With the assistance of the Corps Cyclists temporary sandbagged test points were erected where the concrete work was still lacking, and when the storm finally broke on the 9th April practically all cable laid had been joined up and was working, and three-quarters of the original scheme had been completed.

The attack began at 4.30 a.m. with an intense bombardment extending back to and beyond the river, followed by an infantry assault about 7 a.m., which immediately broke through the Portuguese on the Corps right. There were no reserves available to man effectively the new line dug on the northern bank, and during the afternoon the enemy crossed at Bac St. Maur, and by 7 p.m. had forced our firing line back behind the signal test point at Croix de Bac. Communications had held well so far; the 34th Division was still maintaining its ground on the left around Armentières, and there was hope of an immediate restoration of the situation by counter-attack. The lineman at this point—Corporal Shepherd, of the H.A. Section—was, therefore, instructed not to destroy the lines, but to leave them all through, and fall back on the next test point. He did so, but omitted to put through one of the lines. On ascertaining this when he reached H.A. Headquarters, he voluntarily returned and managed to re-enter the dug-out, which was now in No Man's Land, and put the line through. Though this dug-out passed into the enemy's hands during the night, and after a temporary reversal of fortune again next morning, direct communication from Corps Headquarters to troops in Armentières was maintained over the cables passing through it till afternoon on the following day, when the evacuation of the town began.

By next morning the Germans had forced the river to Estaires. This town had been intensely shelled all day; nevertheless, the Corps Exchange was kept going till a late hour that night by Lieutenant Hill with 51 Air Line Section and a party of operators from the Headquarters Section.

During the 10th, 11th, and 12th, the Corps was steadily driven back by the heavy thrust made by the enemy for Hazebrouck. The 29th and 31st Divisions and the 4th Guards Brigade were successively thrown in, but their desperate fighting only succeeded in slowing the German advance, until the entry into line of the 1st Australian Division on the night of the 12th, when the enemy was finally brought to a stop on the edge of the Nieppe Forest.

The effort to keep up communications during these days tested every one to the limit. Units were changing location like figures in a kaleidoscope, and nearly the whole of the existing system of lines had passed into the enemy's hands. However, by the most strenuous efforts, touch was maintained throughout the retreat, and the good work done was recognized by the Corps commander, for in a letter addressed to Colonel Harrison he conveyed his appreciation of the work carried out by all ranks of the company during the recent operations. He added that he realized that, owing to the untiring energy and devotion to duty shown by all ranks, a very high standard of communication was maintained, and thanked all for the efforts made and the results achieved.

On the 11th Corps Headquarters fell back to Wardrecques, between St. Omer and Hazebrouck, leaving an advanced signal office at La Motte until the evening of the 12th. During the next few days it became evident that the front was established again, and the work of restoring the normal network of communication at once commenced, at first with great shortage of material, as all forward signal dumps had been captured.

Captain Dingwall now left the company to join L Signal Battalion, and was replaced by Captain Ross, who was relieved of the Heavy Artillery Section by Lieutenant Collins. Lieutenant Hill took up duty at Headquarters, and Lieutenant McArthur left the Wireless Section for 51 Air Line Section.

At this time also Lieut.-General Sir J. P. Ducane was summoned to replace Sir Henry Rawlinson on the Versailles Council, and the XV Corps was henceforward commanded by Lieut.-General Sir B. de Lisle.

On leaving the Corps, General Ducane sent the following message:—

"In the many bright spots of the XV Corps, I have always maintained, and always will maintain, that the Signal Service was far away the best Signal Service of any other organization in France. Not only was there a very thorough grasp of the work—but always—what was so pleasant to find—there was a desire to go out of your way to help. It is with the greatest pleasure that I write to say how much I always appreciate having the South African Signal Company in the XV Corps. They were not only highly efficient in all departments of this work, but I can honestly say they were the most energetic, hard-working, well-disciplined, and courteous body of men that I have come across in my experience of the Army.

"I always felt in dealing with you that nothing was ever too much trouble for you or your men, and that no matter how exacting the demands made upon you—and they were often very heavy indeed—no effort would be spared to carry them through successfully. Never were we let down during the most trying times—on the Somme, on the coast, or on the Lys. During the enemy's attack on the Lys in April, 1918, the truly remarkable way in which all our communications held out for three days, till we were compelled to abandon La Motte, greatly facilitated the exercise of the command of the Corps during those difficult days, and was an eloquent testimony of the thoroughness and skill with which the work of preparation had been carried out."

The final holding up of the Germans at Kemmel on the 28th April made it possible to commence effective work on the defences at Hazebrouck, and during the next few months successive lines of trenches and belts of wire came into existence, and seamed the country as far back as St. Omer. The company's share in these preparations was work on a buried cable scheme which started early in May, and gradually developed as labour and material were obtainable, until, when the advance began, a network of trenches extended across the whole Corps area for 13,000 yards in depth and 7,000 in breadth, embodying thirty miles of seven-foot deep trench and nearly 1,200 miles of pair cable. This work, though never tested by another offensive, was of great value during the prolonged artillery duel which followed the Battle of the Lys.

The German evacuation commenced at the end of August, and thenceforward all ranks were occupied in the rapid restoration of communications through the devastated area. An attempt was made to utilize the old buries laid down by the XV and other Corps before the retreat; but these were too effectively destroyed by the enemy to admit of rapid restoration.

After the successful attack of the Belgian and Second British Armies at the end of September, in which the XV co-operated on the right flank, Headquarters were moved to St. Jans-Cappel on the 4th October, and on the 21st to Mouvaux, near Tourcoing, following the rapid retreat of the enemy to the Scheldt. On this occasion a fast piece of work was done by 91 Air Line and B.E. Cable Sections, two lines being completed across the Lys to the new Headquarters—a distance of nearly twenty miles—in one day.

The signal portion of the preparations for forcing the passage of the Scheldt filled the period up to the 10th November; but as the enemy retired during the night, and the armistice was proclaimed the following day, they proved unnecessary.

III.

THE SOUTH AFRICAN MEDICAL SERVICES IN FRANCE.

When the South African Expeditionary Force was organized on the termination of the campaign in German South-West Africa arrangements were made for the mobilization of one Field Ambulance and one General Hospital. The former, under the command of Lieut.-Colonel G. H. Usmar, S.A.M.C., assembled at Potchefstroom with the 1st South African Infantry Brigade; while the General Hospital was formed at Wynberg, the personnel being largely composed of volunteers from the staffs of No. 1 General Hospital, Wynberg, and No. 2 General Hospital, Maitland, and included representatives from each of the four Provinces of the Union. It subsequently provided the personnel for the depot in England, and the South African Military Hospital at Richmond, which was afterwards built and organized.

No hospital equipment was available in South Africa, but the Official Advisory Committee on Voluntary Aid, of which Sir Thomas Smartt was chairman, met the difficulty by voting £15,000 to purchase it on arrival in England, and a further £1,500 to augment the equipment taken by the Field Ambulance.

Both units accompanied the Infantry Brigade to England, and on arrival there they proceeded to the R.A.M.C. Depot at Twezeldown, near Aldershot. At the depot the training of the Field Ambulance proceeded under its own officers. On 29th December the unit proceeded by route march to Farnham, there entraining for Devonport, where it embarked on H.M.T. "Corsican" for Egypt, Alexandria being reached on 13th January, 1916.

In the meantime, the personnel of No. 1 General Hospital—which had been particularly fortunate in securing the services of some of the leading surgeons and physicians and most experienced nurses in South Africa—was temporarily detailed to strengthen the staffs of various Imperial hospitals in England. On 20th December, however, the unit was reassembled at Bournemouth, where it took over and staffed the Mont Dore Military Hospital, which, under an Imperial officer as commandant, had just been equipped for 520 patients.

In February, 1916, the control of the "Grata Quies" Auxiliary Hospital was transferred to the Mont Dore, which became a "Central Hospital," and on 1st April, 1916, seventeen additional auxiliary hospitals, situated in the districts of Poole, Wimbourne, Swanage, Sherbourne, and Yeovil, were affiliated, increasing the number of beds controlled to over 1,200.

The first patients from oversea were admitted on 8th January, the majority being medical cases, and few wounded were received up to the time the unit left on 3rd July, 1916, when it proceeded to Aldershot preparatory to joining the British Expeditionary Force in France.

When the decision to send South African troops to England became known, a number of prominent South Africans in London formed a committee under the chairmanship of Lord Gladstone—until recently the Governor-General—to start a fund for the establishment of a hospital and for the general comfort of the troops. On the arrival of the contingent in England this movement received renewed attention, a proposal then being under consideration to erect huts to accommodate some three hundred patients, as a South African wing to the Royal Victoria Hospital at Netley. On further investigation, however, it was found that the site, although in many respects an ideal one in the summer, would not have been suitable for South African troops during the winter, and further search had to be made. Many places and buildings were inspected, and finally a site in Richmond Park, for which His Majesty the King was graciously pleased to grant the necessary permission, was selected, and no more beautiful, convenient, and healthy spot could possibly have been obtained.

Much of the success of this hospital was due to the time and care spent over the plans, and Mr. Allison, the chief architect of the Office of Works, was always ready to adopt any recommendations made. The desire was to provide 500 beds, but for financial reasons it was decided to start with 300, on the basis of plans which provided for future necessary extensions.

The construction was begun early in March, and on 16th June, 1916, the hospital was formally opened by its patroness, H.R.H. Princess Christian, being then taken over fully equipped as a gift from South Africans by the D.D.M.S., London District, on behalf of the Army Council.

On the opening of the hospital, the S.A.M.C. Depot in England was transferred to Richmond, and a redistribution of the personnel of No. 1 S.A. General Hospital carried out, which enabled a South African staff to be placed in charge of Richmond without interfering with the efficiency of the former unit. Major Thornton, the adjutant and registrar of No. 1 South African General Hospital, succeeded Lieut.-Colonel Stock in command at Richmond, and Captain Basil Brooke was appointed adjutant and registrar. Before, however, proceeding further with the history of the South African Hospital at Richmond, it will be convenient to follow the fortunes of the units which left England.

On 13th January, 1916, No. 1 South African Field Ambulance arrived at Alexandria, and marched the following day to Mex Camp, where the Infantry Brigade was encamped. Its history is included in that of the South African Infantry Brigade, with which it was associated from this date until the cessation of hostilities.

On the arrival of No. 1 South African General Hospital at Aldershot, the final touches were given to the unit, and about 400 shipping tons of stores and equipment drawn, which, by a special arrangement with the Army Council, had been paid for out of the £15,000 voted by Sir Thomas Smartt's committee in Capetown.

On 12th July the unit entrained for Southampton, there to embark on H.M.T. "Huntcraft." The ship berthed at Havre about 10.30 a.m. on the 13th, and on the following day the unit—together with its stores and equipment—left for Abbeville, which was reached on 15th July.

Here it was found that the Hospital would be established next to No. 2 Stationary Hospital, an Imperial unit which had been there for some time. The necessity for not interfering with the ripening harvest considerably curtailed the choice of a site, the ground allotted being a ploughed field on the slope of the hills overlooking the valley of the Somme. Abbeville itself lay about a mile away in the valley, but the railway station and "triage" were on the far side of the town nearly three miles from the Hospital.

Some hospital marquees had already been erected, but the lay-out of the Hospital was greatly handicapped by the cramped area of ground then available. As the corn was reaped more ground became vacant, and, later on, by frequent striking and repitching of tents, the hospital gradually took a more symmetrical and workable shape.

When the unit arrived in France the First Battle of the Somme had begun, and hospital accommodation was urgently required for the large number of casualties. So, in the absence of any kind of building, a store tent was converted into an operating tent; an improvised sterilizing shelter erected; and within forty-eight hours of arrival patients were admitted and every available surgeon hard at work.

The initial difficulties were many: buildings and engineering services were almost impossible to obtain, and it was not until the end of November that the operating block—the first building to be erected—was completed. All, however, were willing workers, and it was not long before additional tentage was pitched and the kitchens, stores, and a hundred and one odd things appertaining to the Quartermaster's Department had been organized.

Until early in August the hospital was without its own nursing sisters—these services being performed by members of the Q.A.I.M.N.S., the Canadian Military Nursing Service, and English V.A.D.'s, who did all that hard work and devotion to duty could do to make up for the shortage in number. On 5th August, however, Matron Creagh and twenty-one members of the S.A.M.N.S. arrived from England, and the greatest difficulties in this respect were over. The nurses' camp had to be pitched in the wooded ground of a château some little distance off; but when the winter rains set in, they had perforce to be billeted in the town until the huts which were contemplated for them were completed.

Situated as it was at the advanced base in a convenient position for their reception, the hospital, during the autumn of 1916, received a large number of wounded direct from the Somme battlefield. Amongst the earliest admissions in July, 1916, were South Africans wounded at Delville Wood.

The most severely wounded journeyed by specially-fitted hospital barges, which, from the casualty clearing stations around Corbie, floated down the Somme to Abbeville, where the patients were disembarked and taken by motor ambulances to the hospital. The use of barges was restricted to those cases who were unable to stand the strain of a journey by train. Usually they travelled in pairs, but on more than one occasion during the autumn of 1916 patients from six barges were admitted during the twenty-four hours. Towards the end of 1916 the barges ceased running, as the winter rains had rendered the passage down the Somme too dangerous, and they were not again employed, as the advance in the spring of 1917 carried the fighting away from the river.

Progress was gradually made in the erection of temporary buildings, and by the end of 1916 there was accommodation in huts for 120 patients. It was obvious, however, that for that winter at least the majority of beds would be under canvas, and a particularly successful form of sliding door with windows at the top was designed and with the funds available a local contractor was engaged, who quickly fitted them at each end of the tented wards. At the same time the Royal Engineers undertook the installation of stoves and wood flooring, and with doors closed and the sides of the tents fastened down the tented wards were really most comfortable.

During the period 23rd July, 1916, to 31st December, 1916, the total admissions were 6,436, of whom 3,032 were "battle casualties" and 3,404 "sick." During the same period 5,719 were "discharged hospital." Of these 673 were returned to duty, 548 transferred to convalescent depots, 3,306 evacuated to the United Kingdom, and 1,192 transferred to hospitals at other bases in France. Five hundred and eighty-eight major operations were performed; and there were in all, for the same period, 236 deaths, or—calculated on the number of admissions—a percentage of 3.68. This comparatively high mortality is explained by the fact that practically every case admitted to this Hospital was seriously wounded. The mortality was further increased owing to the fact that this Hospital was the nearest General Hospital to the Somme front, and many moribund patients were taken off ambulance trains on account of their being too ill to travel to more distant bases. By the end of the year, in addition to the operation block, hutted accommodation for 120 patients was erected, and in the early part of 1917 hutted quarters for the nursing staff and rooms for officers', sergeants', and men's messes were added, as well as buildings for part of the quartermaster's stores.

Early in the year instructions were received from General Headquarters that the hospital was to be enlarged from 520 beds to a normal capacity of 1,120 beds, with a "crisis expansion" to 1,500 beds. The hospital remained on this basis, and during the latter part of 1917, and not infrequently during 1916, as many as 1,600 to 1,700 patients were accommodated at one time.

The total admissions for the year 1917 were 19,109, of which 7,613 were battle casualties and 11,496 were sick. During the same period there were 18,277 discharges. Of this number 2,638 were returned to duty, 4,253 were transferred to convalescent depots, 8,749 were evacuated to the United Kingdom, and 2,637 were transferred to hospitals at other bases in France. 1,210 major operations were performed during the year 1917. For the same period, including 11 cases brought in for burial, there were 181 deaths in the hospital. Of these 128 were due to wounds—a percentage of 1.68; and 53 were due to sickness—a percentage of .46. The death rate from all causes for this year worked out at .94 per cent.

In October, 1917, it was decided to erect such huts as was possible with labour supplied by the staff of the hospital. A start was made, with the idea of housing the men of the company who were over forty years of age, and a hut was built, using discarded telegraph poles as the principals, covered with corrugated iron and lined with wood—the lining being bought from funds provided by the South African Hospital and Comforts Fund at a cost of, approximately, £120.

Stimulated by the success of the first, the building of the second hut was then taken in hand, and eventually, with the assistance of the engineer services, comfortable quarters for all the personnel were erected. In January, 1918, six hospital " Adrian " huts were erected, but were not completed until the end of March, chiefly owing to the lack of labour and uncertainty as to whether the hospital would have to be evacuated. Three double " Nissen " hospital huts were subsequently added—the last not being quite finished when the armistice was signed. The erection of a further eight, which would have completed the building programme of the hospital, was cancelled.

A church was erected within the precincts of the hospital, the cost of which was defrayed partly by subscriptions received from the patients and personnel, and partly by a donation of £75 from the South African Hospital and Comforts Fund, London. It was dedicated in the name of St. Winifred to the memory of the late staff nurse—Miss Winifred Munro, South African Military Nursing Service—and as a tribute to her devotion to duty.

In December, 1917, the hospital was specially selected for the reception and treatment of cases of fracture of the femur. Beds for the accommodation of 200 such cases were provided —50 being reserved for officers, and 150 for other ranks. The special bed and technique devised at the hospital were afterwards adopted as the standard for the British Army.

During the German offensive of 1918 the hospital passed through what was its period of most intense activity. The medical staff was depleted to replace casualties in the South African Field Ambulance and other units in the forward areas, while reinforcements from the male personnel were sent to the Field Ambulance. Practically all the female nursing staffs from this district were withdrawn on account of the enemy advance and the frequent bombing at night by hostile aeroplanes of the back areas. Thus the number of medical officers in charge of wards was reduced to 8 instead of the normal 22; the male personnel fell to 188—the normal establishment being 212; while the female nursing staff, with a normal establishment of 88, was reduced to 8.

With this depleted staff it would have appeared almost impossible to look after a normal number of patients, but many more than normal had to be dealt with during the last week of March, 1,820 being admitted and 2,365 discharged.

Many of these received at the hospital their first medical attention since leaving the battlefield, and a very large number had to be operated upon immediately.

This involved teams working in the operating theatre day and night.

The huts recently erected for accommodating the personnel had to be evacuated by them to make room for patients, of whom as many as ninety slightly wounded were packed into one hut on stretchers. The men were crowded into the remaining three huts, and the overflow slept on the football field.

Nor did the work end here, for, owing to the threat of hostile air attacks, it became urgently necessary to dig protective trenches for patients, sisters, officers, and other ranks, and also to erect sandbagged revetments around the wards which contained the helpless patients. Outside assistance at this time was unprocurable, and the task therefore fell on all ranks of the personnel. Soon after this air alarms became an almost nightly occurrence. Though no definite attack was made by hostile aircraft on the hospital, bombs on several occasions fell uncomfortably near.

The approach of the enemy and the frequency of bombing raids made the retention of cases of fracture of the femur in this hospital inadvisable, and on that account as many as possible were evacuated to the United Kingdom, together with the greater portion of the special equipment used for these cases.

Not long after the last consignment was dispatched the Allied offensive began, and the heavy influx of fractured femur cases—amounting to more than 150 in the hospital at one time—made it necessary to use improvised apparatus for dealing with a number increased to this extent, in spite of the fact that as many of these cases as possible were at once evacuated to the United Kingdom.

During the months of June and July, 1918, the admissions of sick to the hospital were large, owing to an epidemic of influenza. Since then admissions steadily increased, both of sick and wounded, due to the offensive which began in the latter part of July and which continued up to the signing of the armistice.

During September the admissions reached the figure of 3,276, while in October they numbered 3,214, and the discharges 3,318. For the period of 1st January to 30th November, 1918, the total admissions were 20,089. Of these 8,716 were battle casualties and 11,373 were sick; discharges for the same period amounted to 19,921. Of these, 4,196 were returned to duty, 4,229 were transferred to convalescent depots, 9,028 were evacuated to the United Kingdom, and 2,468 were transferred to other hospitals in France.

In June, 1917, a surgical team for duty at a casualty clearing station was provided by the unit, and performed continuous duty in the forward areas until December of that year. Since then a surgical team performed duty in the front areas on eight occasions. In addition, nursing sisters from time to time were detailed for duty on ambulance trains and for nursing duties and as anaesthetists at casualty clearing stations.

On 10th July, 1917, the hospital was honoured by a visit from Her Majesty the Queen and His Royal Highness the Prince of Wales.

To return to the South African Military Hospital at Richmond. In September, 1916, the Army Council, on its own account, proposed to add to the accommodation; the Committee, however, considered that, in view of the fact that the provision of 500 beds had been originally contemplated, the additional accommodation proposed should be undertaken by the Committee. This necessitated a further appeal for funds; but, to avoid delay, Mr. Otto Beit generously gave a very substantial contribution. Eventually the total donations received from the issue of the second appeal assured the extension being carried through. The work was pressed forward, and the extension was opened for patients in February, 1917. It was, however, hardly in use when a demand was made for further beds. This was met by the Committee converting into wards the quarters originally built for orderlies, and by renting a neighbouring house as an annex, so that in April, 1917, the total accommodation for patients had increased to 620 beds.

Early in 1918 the War Office, seeing that the Richmond Military Hospital was almost entirely filled with South African patients, proposed to the Committee that the South African and the Richmond hospitals should be amalgamated, the combined hospitals to be known as the South African Military Hospital. The Committee readily agreed, and the two hospitals were completely amalgamated on 1st July, 1918.

The enlarged hospital provided 1,098 beds; but even this was not sufficient, and 250 emergency beds were added by billeting patients in the neighbourhood. In addition, four auxiliary hospitals were attached, bringing the total number of beds to 1,321, or, including billets, 1,571.

The Park section of the combined hospitals stood on an enclosed site of about twelve acres, the actual area of the building being about two and one-third acres. The construction throughout was of timber with felt and weather-board linings on the outside, and asbestos board-sheeting on the inside of the walls and ceilings of all wards and principal rooms. A special feature of this section was the bath ward, with six fire-clay continuous baths for the treatment of patients suffering from severe wounds.

The Grove Road extension was a brick building, and consisted for the most part of modern infirmary wards supplemented by additional wards in old buildings.

The equipment of the Park section was entirely provided by the Committee, while that of the Grove Road section was found by the Board of Guardians and the War Office, and was only where necessary supplemented by the Committee.

Towards the end of 1916 the Committee offered the privilege of naming a bed in the hospital to any persons or institutions making a gift of £25, and of naming a ward for a donation of £600. The appeal resulted in 99 beds and 8 wards being thus named, approximately 265 of the beds being the gifts of schools in South Africa, the organization for these being initiated and carried out by Mr. Maskew Miller, of Capetown.

The Committee expended approximately £45,000 on building the hospital and its extensions, and £19,000 on equipment. The former figure, however, includes a sum of approximately £2,000 expended in erecting a concert hall and certain workshops, while the latter figure includes considerable sums spent on replacements.

The medical personnel consisted of 13 officers of the South African Medical Corps, and 11 civilian practitioners, who for various causes were not eligible for commissions in the S.A.M.C.

The nursing staff under the matron—Miss Jackson, R.R.C., Q.A.I.M.N.S.—consisted of 2 assistant matrons, 23 nursing sisters, 55 staff nurses, and 88 probationers, the larger proportion of whom were South Africans. The trained members of the staff mostly belonged to the Q.A.I.M.N.S. (Res.), or to the S.A.M.N.S. The subordinate personnel consisted, with a few exceptions, of N.C.O.'s and men who, having been invalided owing to wounds or sickness in the field, did duty at the hospital while regaining health and strength.

The hospital also served as the depot for the S.A.M.C. subordinate personnel; and 18 drafts, comprising 423 men, were sent to France as reinforcements for the First South African General Hospital and the First South African Field Ambulance.

The number of patients admitted up to 31st October, 1918, was 274 officers and 9,412 other ranks—a total of 9,686. This does not include any patients admitted to the Richmond Military Hospital prior to the date of amalgamation. Of the 9,686 patients, 2,628 belonged to Imperial units, but included a good many South Africans, and 7,058 were members of the South African Contingent; 8,260 patients were discharged, including 6,230 members of the Contingent.

The total number of operations performed under a general anaesthetic was 2,125, and the number of medical boards held was 1,559.

Most of the swabs and bandages used in the hospital were manufactured in the South African workrooms, organized by a group of ladies attached to the South African Comforts Committee. The ladies responsible for these workrooms made most of the curtains and other similar articles required to equip the hospital, and undertook most of the mending.

Shortly after the hospital was opened the problem of dealing with the permanently disabled men of the Contingent had to be faced. After negotiations with the War Office, it was arranged that a Vocational Training School should be established in connection with the hospital. A commencement was made in November, 1916, and the school was finally opened in February, 1917. The scheme involved awakening the men while still in bed to interest in their future, so that when well enough they might go to the classrooms and undertake extensive courses of training. The South African Military Hospital was the first primary hospital in the United Kingdom in which permanently disabled men, while being restored to the best possible physical condition, were trained, with due regard to their disabilities, for a civil career to enable them on discharge from the army to become self-supporting members of the community.

The South African Vocational Training Scheme was carried on side by side with the work of the hospital, and was successful both in improving the mental attitude—especially of limbless men—and in training many disabled men of the Contingent who would otherwise have been unproductive to the community.

The cost of the erection of the workshops—amounting to £2,335—was borne by the South African Hospital and Comforts Fund and the Governor-General's Fund.

Much of the equipment was either given or lent, but about £1,200 had to be expended to obtain such tools and appliances as could not otherwise be obtained. The latter expenditure was defrayed by the Governor-General's Fund. The scheme also necessitated the hiring of four houses in the vicinity of the hospital for housing students who had been discharged from hospital; the cost of the equipment of these, amounting approximately to £1,400, was also met by the two funds.

These hostels were managed by a small committee appointed by the General Committee. The expenditure on rents, rates, and taxes for the hostels was shared by the local fund and the Governor-General's Fund, but all other expenditure was met by the sub-committee which received through the High Commissioner the sum of £1 per week for each inmate. This sum represented a ration allowance of 1s. 9d. per head per diem received from Defence Votes, the balance being made up by the Governor-General's Fund. The Union Government also made itself responsible for the pay and allowances of the inmates, and entirely relieved the Imperial Government of all financial responsibility for the period during which the men were undergoing training after discharge from hospital. The number of crippled men who attended classes since their commencement was 393. Of these 167 remained on 31st October, 1918, and 226 had left. Of those remaining, 112 were out-students—that is, men discharged from hospital—and 55 were patients still in hospital. The number of out-students dealt with was 215, of whom 103 have left.

The school was at first under the direction of Mr. Charles Bray, but on his resignation owing to ill-health, Staff-Sergeant Newell, B.Sc., of the S.A.M.C., and in civil life on the staff of the Natal Education Department, was appointed as educational organizer. He was subsequently granted honorary commissioned rank in the Union Defence Force. The propaganda work in the wards and the ward teaching were in the hands of Miss Edith Hill, also of the Natal Education Department.

The hostels for housing out-students were managed by a matron—Mrs. Lennox, of Lovedale—and a staff of ladies, whose efforts were attended with every success.

But the success of the school, in spite of many initial difficulties, was due to the keenness of the men themselves and to the excellent co-operative work of the whole staff of the hospital, with the result that in a number of cases of limbless men the earning capacity was undoubtedly increased as a result of the training they received at Richmond.

IV.

THE RAILWAY COMPANIES AND MISCELLANEOUS TRADES COMPANY.

IN 1916 the railways, roads, canals, and docks in the British zone in France were brought under the control of "Transportation," which was under the command of Sir Eric Geddes. The War Office appealed to the Dominions for railway operating sections, or companies, each consisting of three officers and 266 men. In South Africa the position was such that the railways could, at the time, only spare sufficient men to form one company, but it was arranged to form a second from those not actually in the railway service, but who had railway experience, or were in other ways fitted for the particular work required of them.

The first company assembled at Potchefstroom in November, 1916, under Captain H. L. Pybus, and the second at Roberts Heights, Pretoria, under Captain W. McI. Robinson. Fifty locomotive drivers and a similar number of firemen and guards formed the backbone of each company, the balance being composed of traffic controllers, blockmen, signalmen, with the necessary mechanics and clerical staff to enable each company to operate as a separate and a complete unit.

Lieut.-Colonel F. R. Collins—a mechanical superintendent in the South African Railways—was appointed in command, and left for England in December, 1916, the companies following later under the command of Captain (Acting Major) Robinson, and arriving at Bordon, Hampshire, in March, 1917, at which place the depot was formed.

Both companies arrived in France at the end of March, 1917, and were detailed for light railway work, which was then in its initial stage. The first section was renumbered "No. 7 South African Light Railway Operating Company," and the second, "No. 8 South African Light Railway Operating Company," the former being sent to Romarin on the Belgian border, while the latter proceeded to Savy, in the Arras district. Twenty-five drivers and a like number of firemen from each company were transferred to the broad gauge, and remained on that work throughout the war. No. 7 Company stayed at Romarin until the operations in connection with the taking of Messines Village and Ridge were completed in June, 1917, during which time the Ploegsteert Light Railway system was built, over which the company was responsible for all traffic, the bulk being ammunition with delivery points at the different batteries. The 8th Company took over the light railway work from Maroeuil to the north and north-east of Arras, whence lines were extended after the Vimy Ridge operations. In June, 1917, both companies proceeded to Audruicq preparatory to taking up broad gauge work, and were designated No. 92 and No. 93 Companies respectively.

During most of this period Lieut.-Colonel Collins was attached to Transportation Headquarters, and in May, 1917, was appointed Assistant Director of Light Railways, Fifth Army, which was then operating in the Bapaume Sector. On the transfer of this army to Belgium to take part in the series of operations known as the Third Battle of Ypres, light railways, in addition to serving batteries and Royal Engineers, were now required to prepare to follow up any advance. For this purpose the services of the 92nd and 93rd South African Companies were loaned to light railways, and took their place with five Imperial operating companies in the Fifth Army area. They took part in the operations up to November, 1917, when the offensive ceased.

During this time the 92nd Company was employed on the system north-east of Ypres. The 93rd Company worked from Elverdinghe through Boesinghe to Langemarck, and among other duties was responsible for the placing of field gun ammunition in position in front of the field guns on the eastern slopes of the Pilckem Ridge and in the Steenbecque Valley prior to the attacks during September and October, 1917, which led to the front being advanced to the edge of the Houthulst Forest.

In January, 1918, the Fifth Army took over the sector of forty-five miles on the extreme south of the British front, and, in anticipation of an enemy offensive, light railway construction on a considerable scale was undertaken under Lieut.-Colonel F. Newell. Later, on the division of this system, Lieut.-Colonel Collins took over the northern area—the 92nd and 93rd Companies being ordered south from Belgium. The 93rd arrived early in March and was sent to Noyon, where it remained until the 23rd, when, retirement being forced by the enemy advance, the company proceeded by route march to Flexicourt, west of Amiens, and was employed on the construction of defence works in company with many other transportation units whose usual employment had been suspended for a like reason. Later, they were employed on railway construction necessitated by the altered conditions. In July, 1918, the company headquarters were established at Ligny, east of St. Pol, and the operation of the main trunk lines to Arras was undertaken. The German retreat caused a forward move, and the company, since November, operated over the section Douai to Mons inclusive, with headquarters at Somain.

The 92nd Company, after concentrating in Belgium in March for its projected move south, subsequently cancelled owing to the enemy's advance, went to Crombeke, and from there assisted in railway construction and other duties, until in September, when, with Berguette as headquarters, the operation of the newly-constructed line towards Merville and later towards Armentières was undertaken. In November the company moved forward to Lille, and with headquarters at Tourcoing worked the section from Tourcoing to Tournai.

In 1917 the South African Union Government consented to the formation of a Miscellaneous Trades Company for service in France. This company began to assemble at Potchefstroom in June, and, as recruiting was brisk, it was able to embark fully organized at Capetown as early as 25th July, under the command of Captain C. E. Mason, S.A.E.

Arriving at Bordon on 28th August, the company was given a short course of training at the Royal Engineers' Depot there, and sent to France on 14th October. Here the company was renumbered the 84th Miscellaneous Trades Company, R.E. (South African), and sent to the Director-General of Transportation, Chief Mechanical Engineer Department, Locomotive Workshops, situated at St. Etienne-du-Rouvray, near Rouen, where five companies of the Royal Engineers, under the command of Lieut.-Colonel Cole, R.E., were already stationed.

These were the largest locomotive workshops attached to the British Armies in France, and, by reason of its large percentage of skilled personnel, the 84th Company was enabled to take a very considerable share in the activities of the shops, Captain Mason being appointed Erecting Works Manager, and the N.C.O.'s of the company in many instances being entrusted with positions of responsibility. On the recall of Captain Mason to South Africa, Captain N. S. Weatherley, S.A.E., succeeded to the command of the company. When the armistice was signed in November, 1918, Lieut.-Colonel Cole ordered a special parade of the company, in order to express to all ranks his high appreciation of their services, which he characterized in the most complimentary terms.

A depot for the companies in France was originally established at Bordon, and was temporarily under the charge of Lieutenant Arthur, of the 1st Section. Advantage was taken of the instructional establishment at Longmoor to train as many men as possible in the operation of petrol tractors, which were largely used in place of steam locomotives in the forward areas on light railways. In June, 1917, the depot was taken over by Captain M. J. Byrne, who, on his transfer to France in July, 1918, to command the 93rd Company, was succeeded by Captain H. E. Greaves, M.C., R.E., the depot about the same time being transferred from Bordon to Longmoor.

V.

THE CAPE AUXILIARY HORSE TRANSPORT COMPANIES.

IN February, 1917, the Government of the Union of South Africa was asked by the War Office to raise eight companies of Cape coloured drivers for service with the Army Service Corps in France. The personnel originally required was:—

Officers	50
Warrant officers	6
Non-commissioned officers	60
Artificers	131
Drivers	2,316

but this was eventually increased to—

Officers	67
Warrant officers	23
Non-commissioned officers	92
Artificers and drivers	3,482

Towards the end of February Lieut.-Colonel J. D. Anderson took command, and arranged for the recruiting and organization of the eight companies. Kimberley was selected as the most convenient centre for mobilization, and De Beers Corporation gave the use of its Nos. 1 and 3 Compounds. Lieut.-Colonel Wynne was appointed camp commandant, with Captain MacKeurton as paymaster, and Captain Cooper as officer in charge of the records, and by the 12th March everything was in readiness for recruiting to begin.

The results were at first disappointing, as recruiting for the Cape coloured battalions for service in German East Africa was at this time being undertaken, and recruiting committes for this purpose were at work at all the principal centres in South Africa. However, these difficulties were soon overcome, and recruiting proceeded with great rapidity. Johannesburg,

Capetown, and Knysna each produced five hundred recruits in a short time.

On the arrival of the first detachment in France on 23rd May, the Director of Transport decided that the contingent should release for other service and take the place of the Army Service Corps personnel forming the following companies: —

No. 22 Auxiliary Horse Transport Company, A.S.C., stationed at Dunkirk and Calais.

No. 5 Auxiliary Horse Transport Company, A.S.C., stationed at Boulogne.

No. 2 Auxiliary Horse Transport Company, A.S.C., stationed at Havre.

No. 8 Auxiliary Horse Transport Company, A.S.C., stationed at Rouen.

No. 10 Auxiliary Horse Transport Company, A.S.C., stationed at Rouen.

No. 11 Auxiliary Horse Transport Company, A.S.C., stationed at Rouen.

Arrangements were also made for a base depot to be established at Havre.

The reorganization was commenced at once, one company of the first draft going to Calais and the two others to Rouen. As other drafts arrived they were sent to the base depot for three weeks, where they were equipped, and went through a course of training before being distributed to the various A.S.C. companies. Thus by the 31st August the Cape Auxiliary Horse Transport detachments had released the whole of the white personnel of six companies of the Army Service Corps, with the exception of five officers and a certain number of warrant officers and N.C.O.'s, whose services it was proposed permanently to retain, while after a few months in France the reorganized companies were all commanded by officers of the detachment.

The men did very excellent work at the base posts, but it was a great disappointment to all that the companies were not at once employed in the army areas. This was eventually done, and the 1st, 3rd, and 5th Army Auxiliary Horse Companies were taken over, the experiment proving an unmitigated success. The work of these companies consisted in conveying ammunition and supplies to the fighting troops, and transporting metal for the new roads which had to be constructed as the armies advanced.

Of the other companies which were employed on the lines of communication, Nos. 2, 5, 8, and 22 Companies were employed at the docks, the bulk of the work consisting in conveying munitions and supplies from the docks to the different distributing centres. The work was hard, the hours long, and the drivers much exposed to weather conditions.

Nos. 10 and 11 Companies were designated as "forest companies," and were employed almost entirely in hauling logs from the place where they were felled to dumping centres. In a report on the work in the forests in France, Lord Lovat, the Director of Forests, wrote that, without prejudice to other units, he wished to remark on the work done by the Horse Transport Companies manned by South African (Cape coloured) personnel, who had shown throughout both practical knowledge of the work and patriotic devotion to duty.

During their stay in France the health of the officers, N.C.O.'s, and men was much better than could reasonably have been expected. Casualties were estimated at 1 per cent. per month, but this figure was reduced by half.

PART VIII

ADMINISTRATION.

WORK DONE IN THE UNION INCIDENTAL TO ALL THE MILITARY ENTERPRISES ALREADY DESCRIBED.

THE multifarious duties in connection with the provision, equipment, and maintenance of the forces raised in the Union of South Africa for the various campaigns in which representative bodies of Union troops took part were carried out under the direction of the several sections of Defence Headquarters.

The Secretarial Section was concerned with the general policy of the Government in respect of the military aid extended to the different theatres of war, and with the supervision and solution of the complicated financial problems which called for settlement with the Imperial authorities. A heavy task, which called for great expansion on the financial side of the section and some considerable devolution of responsibility as compared with normal peace arrangements.

The military sections, charged with carrying out in detail the general military plans of the Government, were those of the General Staff, Adjutant-General, Quartermaster-General, and Medical Services.

With the decision to replace to the necessary extent the Imperial Military Garrison in South Africa, and to undertake a campaign against the enemy in German South-West Africa, at once arose the necessity for the mobilization of the Active Citizen Force and the raising of additional special units to consist of persons above the age limit for compulsory military training, but who, by reason of previous experience, were of the highest military value.

In the rebellion, the Government relied as a point of honour almost entirely on the loyal Dutch population for the suppression of the revolt, and its confidence was amply justified.

A.—The Provision of Forces and Furnishing of Reinforcements.

For the campaign in German South-West Africa, which was the first military enterprise in the war for which troops were furnished by the Union Government, the forces were obtained by a mobilization of the Active Citizen Force and the recruitment of volunteers who were above the age for compulsory service in that force.

In the first instance voluntary enlistment was restricted to recognized units, but on the 2nd October, 1914, instructions to recruit volunteer war commandos were issued. The rebellion, however, when it had reached its height, presented features of such gravity that commandeering "for the defence of the Union" was resorted to on the 11th October, 1914, as an immediate consequence of Maritz's defection.

At the conclusion of the rebellion the commandos were sent to their homes with orders to reassemble on various given dates at different centres, and the period between temporary dispersal and reassembly was occupied by the commandants in reorganizing their commandos and readjusting the personnel by a process of selecting those who could go into the field with least hardship to themselves or their dependents.

In July, 1915, the Imperial Government accepted the offer of the Union Government to form units for active service in other theatres of operations, and a Director of War Recruiting was appointed. Recruiting commenced, and was continued until the armistice in 1918.

In January, 1916, it was found desirable to appoint the officer who controlled the recruiting to the command of all the staffs and depots maintained for the purpose of collecting recruits. He was responsible for their elementary training, the dispatch of reinforcements as they were called for, and for the proper control of all the troops engaged for service in Union-Imperial service contingents.

This command was retained in the above form until the war came to an end.

Recruiting was conducted on a strictly voluntary basis.

War Recruiting Committees, consisting of Mayors, Town Councillors, and other leading citizens, were formed in all towns.

One hundred and forty-four such committees were formed and rendered most effective help throughout the period of their existence.

At intervals recruiting conferences were held to review the position and consider the best methods to adopt.

Special recruiting campaigns were constantly conducted under the direction of carefully chosen recruiting officers.

The following is a statement of all the forces raised throughout the war for the different campaigns and theatres in which the Union military forces were represented.

(a) *European.*

Theatre or Campaign.	Strength Raised.
Rebellion	30,000
German South-West Africa	67,237
Overseas (France)	30,880
German East Africa and Central Africa ...	47,521
Service in the Union	5,180
German East Africa (Road and Military Labour Corps)	1,044

(b) *Native.*

Theatre or Campaign.	Strength Raised.
German South-West Africa (non-combatant)	35,000
Overseas (mainly non-combatant)	5,823
East and Central Africa	18,000

The above figures include all units which may be regarded as military, whether combatant or departmental. In addition, the Union Native Affairs Department enlisted a Native Labour Corps for service in France, and enrolled natives for this purpose to the number of 25,090.

Details of the Labour units appear later in sub-section (x).

The strengths recorded in aggregate in the above tables A and B are made up of such separate units and formations as the conditions of the different theatres demanded.

An Infantry Brigade with a Field Ambulance, Heavy Artillery, a Signal Company, two sections from the South African Railways, Royal Flying Corps details, a Miscellaneous Trades Company, and a General Hospital were dispatched oversea for service in France and Flanders.

For East and Central Africa the Union supplied a strong brigade of field artillery; two mounted brigades and two separate mounted regiments; two infantry brigades and two separate rifle regiments; a motor-cycle corps; engineers and a water-supply corps; a strong signal unit; pioneers; and a large number of medical, service corps, and veterinary details, including, in the medical unit, many nurses. A variety of smaller units of special kinds completed the strength.

It should be mentioned that 1,969 of the Second Rhodesian Regiment are included in the figures shown in Table A under "Overseas," and 200 from the same unit under "East and Central Africa."

The whole of the 25,090 natives of the Labour Corps served in France.

The majority of the personnel recruited "for service within the Union" did duty in the South African Medical Corps in the several hospitals which were organized to cope with the return of thousands of men from East and Central Africa in a state of health so shattered by the deadly tropical diseases to which they had fallen victims as to require long months of careful hospital treatment.

The rest of the Union personnel served at the depots on the different establishments incidental to the recruiting, training, and maintenance of the troops.

B.—Bases and Depots.

(i) *Bases.*

For the purpose of the expedition against German South-West Africa the "Union Expeditionary Base" was formed at Capetown on the 19th September, 1914.

Large temporary camps were formed in the Peninsula for troops passing through and a general depot for details was established at Rosebank.

After the successful conclusion of hostilities in German South-West Africa the machinery at Capetown base was recast and adapted for the dispatch of reinforcements to Europe and the reception of troops and details returning from Great Britain and France.

The general depot was removed to Wynberg after the troops from German West Africa had been demobilized.

A base was formed at Durban in October, 1915, after it had been decided to comply with the request of the Imperial Government to assist in the prosecution of the war in East Africa.

Through this base passed all troops furnished by the Union for the East African campaign, together with very large consignments of animals, supplies, and material of varied kinds.

A general depot was established at Congella on reclaimed foreshore, and extensive hutments of excellent type and material were erected to deal with the large numbers of troops passing through.

In compliance with Admiralty requirements, an Imperial rest camp was established for the reception of Imperial troops compelled to remain at Durban in consequence of transhipment.

Special depots were also formed for the reception and maintenance of natives.

(ii) *Depots.*

The largest and most important depot maintained in the Union was opened at Potchefstroom on the 5th August, 1915, originally for the purpose of the 1st Infantry Brigade, which, at the end of the campaign in German South-West Africa, was raised for service in France.

This centre, which was the scene of continuous training, was maintained until the armistice, shortly after which the dispatch of reinforcements ceased.

In addition to infantry training, which was carried out on the most modern lines by instructors who had seen service on the Western European front, the Union schools of musketry and signalling were employed for war purposes at Potchefstroom, and training in both subjects was continuously afforded—900 signallers were trained and sent to Europe, and 1,501 were dispatched, after training, to East and Central Africa.

At the school of musketry, 844 machine-gunners and 47 Lewis gunners were trained. The Lewis gun training was undertaken late in the war. 6,620 details of the oversea infantry and other units were put through an elementary preliminary musketry course.

A training corps for combatant officers and N.C. officers, and a medical training school, were also established.

After the initial mobilization and organization of the Field Artillery Brigade the depot of the latter was transferred to Potchefstroom and attached to the Field Artillery Brigade of the South African Mounted Riflemen, the commanding officer of which was placed in command of the artillery depot and supervised the training of recruits. At the last stage of the war the S.A.M.R. artillery, with the artillery depot, was transferred to Roberts Heights, Pretoria.

The depot of the S.A. Heavy Artillery Brigade was established at the Castle, Capetown, where the training of recruits was carried out under the supervision of the Imperial General Officer Commanding, South African Military Command. This depot also was subsequently transferred to Potchefstroom.

The mounted brigades, drawn, as they were, almost entirely from the country districts and requiring training of a special nature, were dealt with at their own depot, which was located at Roberts Heights.

The Cape Corps was mobilized and its reinforcements were trained at a depot in the Cape Peninsula under the same supervision as the heavy artillery, i.e. the General Officer Commanding the Cape Peninsula. Later this depot was moved to Kimberley.

The depot of the Cape Auxiliary Horse Transport Corps was established at Kimberley for the collection, training, and forwarding of personnel. This unit served on the Western European front.

The very heavy demands from East Africa for motor transport and personnel (mechanics and drivers), combined with the adverse local climatic conditions, which caused great wastage of personnel and material alike, necessitated special efforts to cope with the unceasing requirements. A mechanical transport depot was accordingly formed at Roberts Heights.

Motor-cars were first used on a definite recognized scale in the capture of De Wet during the rebellion, and the practical proof of the capabilities of this form of transport then demonstrated resulted in increased stocks of vehicles being procured. 1,010 motor vehicles of various kinds were used in the German West African campaign, and approximately 2,000 men were enlisted for the motor services.

Approximately 4,000 motor vehicles were sent to East Africa and Nyasaland, and between 6,000 and 7,000 men were enrolled for mechanical transport units.

Different sub-depots and smaller establishments were organized from time to time subsidiary to the main depots described above.

(iii) *Ordnance.*

In common with all other military departments and services of the Union, the Ordnance Department was suddenly faced on the outbreak of war with a situation which it had not had time to prepare for, even if the tremendous nature of the world struggle had been anticipated.

Much ingenuity had to be applied to obtain the production of material and clothing locally, seeing that the usual source of supply from outside had been cut off.

In addition to a large amount of issue work incidental to the rebellion, approximately 67,000 European and 43,000 natives were equipped and maintained in equipment during the campaign in South-West Africa.

The value of the purchases of equipment and clothing made from September, 1914, to July, 1915, was £2,564,000, and the value of the issues made over the same period was £2,240,000. In addition, issues of clothing and equipments were made to Union-Imperial service contingents to the following extent:—

(1) Europe, 22,400 men equipped.
(2) East Africa, 37,099 men equipped.
(3) Nyasaland-Rhodesian Forces, 5,676 men equipped.
(4) Egypt, 4,286 men equipped.
Natives equipped, 24,113.

The duties undertaken by the Union Ordnance Department on behalf of the Imperial Military Authorities included (in addition to those incidental to equipping and clothing troops) the establishment of a conditioning depot with necessary personnel at Durban to receive, condition, and finally dispose of stores returned by Union-Imperial service contingents; the provision and shipment of stores for the campaign in East and Central Africa; and the issue of stores to Imperial troops passing through Durban and Capetown.

(iv) *Supplies.*

The rebellion and German West African campaign threw very heavy work on the Supply Branch of the Quartermaster-General's Section. This branch was organized only just prior to the outbreak of the war, and its main function was the provision and issue of rations at Citizen Force training camps, the requirements of which were known in detail well in advance.

The kaleidoscopic developments of the rebellion, and the extraordinary mobility of the troops, together with the rapid changes and counter-orders in connection with plans, produced an abnormally difficult series of supply problems. These were, however, all effectually solved.

In the campaign in German West Africa, when General Botha's rapid and wide encircling movements began, the food problem was for some weeks extremely grave. Supplies of excellent quality were in hand, but owing to inadequate transport facilities they could not be placed in sufficient quantity nor quickly enough with the troops. This difficulty did not occur in the final advance from Karibib.

The duties of the Union Supply Branch of the Quartermaster-General's Section in connection with the Imperial service contingents were confined to their supply whilst in Union depots, and were not unduly heavy.

The work done for the East and Central African campaigns, however, was consistently heavy during the continuance of hostilities.

Heavy purchases were made and the duties of checking, passing, handling, and forwarding of vast amounts of supplies were undertaken on behalf of the Imperial Government.

As in the case of other branches, such as that of the Ordnance, considerable assistance was afforded to the Rhodesian and Mozambique Governments.

Shipments of supplies were also made to Mauritius and Sierra Leone.

Personnel for Service Corps duties for the East and Central African theatres was also recruited under the supervision of the Director of Supplies.

(v) *Transport and Remounts.*

The Transport and Remounts portion of the Quartermaster-General's Section was not organized prior to the outbreak of war on a scale calculated to deal with any military undertaking in war.

The staff of the branch consisted of one officer and three clerical assistants at Headquarters.

At the end of the campaign in German South-West Africa the Headquarter Staff comprised 4 officers, 4 warrant officers, and a number of civilian assistants, while at depots and in the field 132 officers, 175 warrant officers, 1,721 non-commissioned officers, and 950 white drivers, in addition to thousands of natives, were employed.

No provision had been made in peace for a permanent nucleus either for depots or field establishments, or for sudden expansion in time of war.

The above figures are recorded as of interest for the purpose of showing the position generally as regards preparation for administrative services in time of war. While the actual figures vary in detail, generally speaking most branches of the military administrative services found themselves similarly situated on the outbreak of hostilities.

Except during the last few weeks shortage of transport was a serious drawback throughout the campaign in South-West Africa.

Animals and vehicles of all classes were purchased for the rebellion and German South-West African campaign to the value of £3,311,404.

In connection with the campaign in East Africa, six transport and remount depots were maintained in the Union for the reception and conditioning of all animals purchased, and large numbers of vehicles were overhauled for shipment to East African ports.

Purchasing Boards were formed and operated in the Union, and sales of all animals remaining on charge at the end of hostilities were arranged and put through on behalf of the Imperial Government.

(vi) *Veterinary.*

At the outbreak of war the military veterinary establishment consisted of one veterinary officer, one non-commissioned officer, and one civilian storeman, and there was no veterinary corps, either Permanent or Citizen Force.

Immediate expansion was essential on the outbreak of hostilities, and a Director of Veterinary Services was appointed, with four Assistant Directors.

A base veterinary depot was established at Booysens, Johannesburg, where enlistment and training of subordinate personnel were taken in hand.

Units were formed as trained personnel became available and professional officers were appointed.

Ultimately for the campaign in German South-West Africa eight veterinary hospitals and fifteen mobile veterinary sections were formed, and veterinary personnel was provided for attachment to all mounted formations, as well as to Transport and Remount depots, Purchasing Boards, and animal ships.

The establishment of personnel reached 47 officers, 450 N.C.O.'s and men, and 750 natives.

A base veterinary store was established at the South Arm, Docks, Capetown.

In the end, veterinary services had to be found for 160,000 animals. 60,000 horses, 12,168 mules, and 2,968 donkeys passed through the veterinary hospitals during the course of the rebellion and German South-West African campaign.

On the conclusion of the operations in German South-West Africa the Veterinary Branch was called upon for services in connection with the East African campaign.

Two base veterinary hospitals were formed, equipped, and dispatched to East Africa, as well as one advanced base veterinary hospital. Four mobile veterinary sections went forward from the Union, and a veterinary detachment was found for each of ten mounted regiments. Veterinary parties, under professional supervision, were formed for all animal boats plying between Durban and East African ports.

Veterinary hospitals were established at remount depots in the Union at Kimberley, Roberts Heights, Potchefstroom, Pietermaritzburg, and Durban.

In these hospitals 19,835 animals underwent treatment.

All veterinary personnel was recruited under the supervision of the Director of Veterinary Services; 47 officers were appointed and 1,079 N.C.O.'s and men were enlisted.

The Portuguese Government also received assistance from this branch of administrative services.

(vii) *Medical.*

When the call for active service came, the Medical Section was the only one with some degree of war organization.

Still the need for expansion here was also very great, and though a considerable number of field units were organized in the Active Citizen Force, provision for large hospitals had not been made and a nursing service was non-existent.

Private practitioners were asked to volunteer, and did so with striking goodwill and a patriotism no less remarkable than that which animated the thousands who went to the combatant units.

A Nursing Service was organized and performed splendid service in German South-West Africa, East Africa, oversea, and in the Union. The nursing service in East Africa suffered very severely in regard to malaria.

One general hospital and one field ambulance were dispatched to Europe, in addition to medical corps personnel who volunteered for regimental duties.

To East Africa went one general hospital, three field ambulances, five mounted brigade field ambulances, two sanitation sections, two Indian bearer corps, an advanced depot of medical stores, and a dental unit.

For this campaign regimental officers and medical personnel were provided for eight infantry battalions, one battalion Cape Corps, nine mounted regiments, and one Field Artillery Brigade.

The diseases encountered in the trying campaign in East Africa threw a very severe strain upon medical resources in the Union, where were treated thousands of men in varying stages of exhaustion, ravaged by tropical disease, emaciated by illness and want of proper food, and generally in a condition which made hospital treatment, in some cases literally for years, essential.

Hospitals and convalescent camps were formed as follows:—

Large general hospitals at Wynberg, Maitland, and Roberts Heights.

Each of these was capable of accommodating 1,500 patients.

Smaller general hospitals with accommodation ranging from 400 to 600 beds were established at Durban, Kimberley, and Potchefstroom.

Hospitals for special purposes (including the treatment of natives) were formed at Woodstock (Cape), Jacobs (Durban), Tempe (Bloemfontein), Johannesburg, and Pietermaritzburg.

Seven auxiliary hospitals (mainly for convalescents) were maintained, and convalescent camps were formed at Roberts Heights, Pietermaritzburg, Durban, and Kimberley.

(viiii) *Records*.

On the 1st October, 1914, an Information Bureau was established to deal with all inquiries regarding members of the Union forces on service, and for the purpose of conveying to relatives all information which it was possible and permissible to communicate.

Other of the more important duties allotted to the bureau were:—

The relief of distress among families and dependents of soldiers on active service. The record of casualties. Investigation of claims for and award of gratitudes and pensions to relatives of soldiers killed, and to those wounded or disabled.

In September, 1915, in view of the large numbers of Union soldiers on service, the Information Bureau was changed into the Record Office, and assumed, as its chief rôle, the duties indicated by the new title.

The office was established to obtain and keep a record of every citizen who volunteered and enrolled in the Union for active service with a Union-Imperial service contingent, or an Imperial or East African Protectorate unit.

Attesting and record officers were appointed and posted to all camps of mobilization as the latter were established.

The Record Office in the Union at Pretoria was known as the Main Record Office, the Branch Record Office being established at the Office of the High Commissioner in London.

Some of the sub-divisions of the Main Record Office were the casualty section; the estates of deceased personnel section; the document section; and the King's certificates, silver war badges, medals, and other decorations section. From these titles the general scope of the activity of the office may be gauged.

The work which occupied the attention of this office was found to be excessive, and with a view to relieving the congestion all pension matters in connection with the campaign in German South-West Africa which had been allotted to the Officer in Charge of Records were in January, 1916, transferred to the Military Pensions Commissioner.

The office dealt with some 90,000 attested men, handled all record details connected with 12,577 casualties (killed, died, missing, wounded, prisoners of war, excluding cases of sickness), and dealt with 3,159 deceased soldiers' estates, representing £59,629. 4s. 10d., in addition to a variety of other matters personally affecting the soldier.

The maintenance of the Record Office was necessary for long after the termination of the war.

(ix) *Coloured Troops.*

The strongly expressed desire of the coloured community in the Cape Province to render assistance, if possible in a combatant capacity, led to the formation of a battalion of the Cape Corps, organized on an ordinary infantry basis. Later a second battalion of the corps was raised.

This regiment, which was first sent to East and Central Africa, rendered most valuable service in the East African campaign, where it gradually gained the fighting experience which was to bring it to its highest pitch of military value.

Upon its return from the East African theatre the regiment was carefully reorganized, and as one battalion sent to Egypt, from which base it took part in the campaign in Palestine, where it saw heavy fighting, and bore itself with the utmost gallantry and achieved a high reputation for good conduct and military efficiency.

The Cape Auxiliary Horse Transport Corps was also raised and sent to the Western front in Europe, where it performed valuable and efficient service.

(x) *Natives.*

In the early stages of the campaign in German South-West Africa the Department of Defence undertook the supply of native labour for military purposes.

The demand for such labour was heavy and insistent, and soon difficulties were experienced by the Department in obtaining all the labour needed.

These difficulties were later surmounted when the Native Affairs Department took over the duties of procuring native labourers.

Depots were established at Capetown and De Aar, and arrangements were made for the effective protection of the interests of natives in the field.

The exceptional demands made from time to time for native labourers were met expeditiously, largely as a consequence of assistance from magistrates and labour organizations.

Thirty-five thousand natives were sent forward from the Union in connection with the German West African campaign, and 18,000 were dispatched to East Africa.

Though the Native Labour Contingent was not raised under the supervision of the Union Military Authorities—the Department of Native Affairs being responsible for the organization—any record of the services performed by natives of the Union during the war would be incomplete without a reference to this large body of labourers.

Early in September, 1916, the Imperial Government asked the Government of the Union to provide a force of 10,000 natives under a military organization for labour duties in France, and the duty of raising this force was entrusted to the Department of Native Affairs.

A depot was established at Rosebank Show Ground, Capetown, on the 8th October, 1916.

Within a month of the opening of the depot nearly 4,000 men were equipped, vaccinated, and inoculated, and, after some military training, dispatched to Europe.

A request from Europe for more men led to a resumption of recruiting and the dispatch of reinforcements, 10,600 men being sent forward between the 23rd March, 1917, and the 30th November, 1917.

In November, 1917, the cessation of recruiting was considered in correspondence between the two Governments, as it had become difficult, in consequence of shortage of shipping, to repatriate the personnel within the period stipulated in their contract of service. Eventually it was decided, in January, 1918, that recruiting should be discontinued.

The total strength engaged during the existence of the contingent was 292 officers, 1,204 European warrant and non-commissioned officers, and 25,090 natives.

On the occasion of the repatriation of the contingent and the termination of its service a farewell message was sent from the Commander-in-Chief in France which referred appreciatively to the excellent service performed. The Secretary of State for the Colonies also expressed pleasure at "the high commendation earned by the contingent."

In addition to the Native Labour Contingent, and before the request for the latter was received, the Union had raised a battalion of Cape (coloured) boys for labour purposes in France. The duty of raising this personnel was also allotted to the Department of Native Affairs.

(xi) *Demobilization.*

An account of the activities of the Department of Defence and of the military forces of the Union would fall short of an adequate record if reference to the work undertaken for the soldier during and after the war was omitted.

Though considerable work of the nature indicated was undertaken before the end of hostilities, and before demobilization began, this same work continued long after the armistice and conclusion of peace.

On the cessation of hostilities in November, 1918, steps were taken immediately to organize an efficient system of demobilization of the returning troops, which, from the different theatres, were estimated as likely to amount to 36,000.

A Demobilization Board, under the presidency of the Chief of the General Staff, was formed at Defence Headquarters for the purpose of settling the details of demobilization in agreement with the Imperial system as far as was necessary, and at the same time with due regard to local conditions.

The plan eventually adopted had as its main considerations the expeditious release of the soldier; his quick transport to his home or to the destination to which he elected to be sent; full opportunity to the soldier to avail himself of the machinery which had been devised for the purpose of resettling him in civil life; and proper care of and attention to the immediate needs of any soldier's wife, children, or dependents who might be repatriated to South Africa.

The troops to be demobilized were divided into four classes, viz.:—

(i) Union-Imperial service contingent troops arriving from oversea by the West Coast route and troops of the same contingent stationed or serving at Capetown at the time of demobilization.

(ii) Union-Imperial service contingent troops arriving from East Africa, Egypt, and oversea by the East Coast route and troops of the same contingent stationed or serving at Durban at the time of demobilization.

(iii) Union-Imperial service troops returning from Central Africa and troops of the same contingent stationed or serving at Roberts Heights at the time of demobilization.

(iv) Union-Imperial service contingent troops stationed or serving at Potchefstroom at the time of demobilization.

Dispersal camps for the demobilization of the troops shown under the above categories were established as follows:

(i) At Capetown.
(ii) At Durban.
(iii) At Roberts Heights.
(iv) At Potchefstroom.

With the object of ensuring control of the demobilization and avoiding overcrowding and delay in releasing troops, the Imperial Authorities were asked to return the troops in batches of not exceeding 2,000 in strength, and to ensure that at least one week should elapse between the arrival of batches.

It may be stated here that the whole process of demobilization worked without a hitch, and that no case of delay in clearing the dispersal camps occurred.

At Capetown the premises of the newly erected hospital at Maitland were available, having just been vacated by the

Union Military Medical Authorities. This made an ideal dispersal camp, the close proximity of the main railway line being a factor of importance.

At Durban the hutments and other accommodation were ample for all requirements, and here, as at Roberts Heights and Potchefstroom, dispersal camps were formed without any additional expense for structural alterations.

Railway transport officers were obtained from the Railway Administration, and their help in controlling and expediting railway movements of demobilized troops was of the greatest possible assistance.

In view of possible unemployment and hardship it was considered to be of the utmost importance that close touch between the returned soldier and the office of the Commissioner for Returned Soldiers should be established before the soldier was "dispersed." To secure this object a Staff Officer for Returned Soldiers was appointed at each dispersal camp as a representative of the Commissioner, and the responsibility for seeing that each soldier interviewed the Staff Officer for Returned Soldiers before leaving the dispersal camp was definitely placed upon the Dispersal Commandant of the camp.

The Staff Officer for Returned Soldiers at each camp, as well as being generally concerned with all difficulties or grievances which might be causing inconvenience to the returned soldier, was specially charged with the duty of ascertaining if employment was available in each case, and advising the local body dealing with returned soldiers' interests of the return and time of arrival of the returned soldier at his home.

The number of soldiers to be demobilized in the Union from the different theatres was approximately as follows:—

In Europe	22,000
In East and Central Africa...	8,200
In South-West Africa	2,300
In the Union	3,500

In addition to the soldiers, there were some 5,500 women and children (families of men with the oversea contingent) for whom accommodation had to be provided at the port of disembarkation until such time as their husbands had passed through the dispersal camp and could accompany them home.

The work to be done in respect of each soldier in his passage through the dispersal camp included settlement of his pay accounts (he received twenty-eight days' leave on full pay after demobilization), the issue of free railway and meal tickets, and careful medical inspection, including, if necessary, hospital treatment. Each soldier was allowed to retain his uniform, greatcoat, and two blankets, and was given £4 towards the purchase of civilian clothes.

Demobilization of troops from the various theatres was completed on the following dates:—

From Central Africa, end of February, 1919.

From East Africa and Egypt, middle of July, 1919.

Troops from Europe began to arrive in large numbers early in 1919, and repatriation was at its height in April. The bulk of the troops from Europe had been disposed of by August, 1919. Those returning after that date consisted of men who had been employed on special duties or who were hospital cases.

At Capetown some 6,500 non-continventers (i.e. men who had joined Imperial units singly and had not served with any South African formation) were dealt with in the dispersal camp on behalf of the local Imperial Military Authorities.

Under the supervision of the Demobilization Board regulations were drawn up for the proper control of the process of settling up with the soldier and bridging the gap between the termination of his military status and return to civil occupation.

Space will not admit of a full account of all the steps which were taken in detail, but the information may be gathered from "Demobilization Regulations" (Union of South Africa).

The women and children, to whom reference has been made earlier, were attended to by a committee of ladies at Capetown, headed by the Mayoress and the wife of the Archbishop. Lady Buxton took a specially keen interest in the work, and placed "Westbrook," Capetown, at the disposal of the committee as a hostel. The Government extended the necessary financial assistance.

(xii) *Returned Soldiers.*

Up to August, 1918, a considerable amount of work had been undertaken by the Government on behalf of the returned soldier, but on that date a conference was held to decide upon the best method of amalgamating and co-ordinating the work of the various small departments which had come into existence as their need from time to time became apparent. It was realized that central control and better organization would eliminate avoidable friction and tend to far better results.

On the 1st September, 1918, the department and office of the Commissioner for Returned Soldiers was established, and, as has been explained in the account of demobilization, a representative of the Commissioner was placed in each dispersal camp.

In November and December, 1918, a Returned Soldiers' Advisory Board was appointed at Capetown, Durban, and Johannesburg, as it was anticipated that at these three places the question of re-employment would, in view of the comparatively large numbers of returned soldiers involved, call for special attention.

The Boards consisted of representatives from various local organizations and public bodies, together with the local Chief Magistrate and District Staff Officer, and were provided with staffs paid at the public expense.

These Boards were originally intended to assist the Military Pensions Commissioner in connection with the investigation of pension cases. But, as in the case of the Returned Soldiers Department, so in these sub-divisions of it, co-ordination of all activities on behalf of the returned soldier quickly suggested itself as essential, and the Advisory Boards eventually assumed responsibility for all work, of whatever nature, in the interest of the returned soldiers in their areas.

The Boards were divided into different sections, from each of which information and assistance in respect of its special sphere were available to the returned soldier.

Fifty-four Returned Soldiers Employment Committees were established in the larger towns throughout the Union. Of these, fourteen were assisted by Government-paid clerical assistants, the work of the remainder being entirely voluntary. The provision of employment was the primary function of these committees, but to some extent they helped with the investigation of grievances and pension questions.

The War Recruiting Committees, having ceased activity in connection with recruiting, continued to afford assistance in connection with the problem of the returned soldier. These committees amalgamated with the Advisory Boards and Returned Soldiers Employment Committees where the latter existed, and continued their existence in forty-three centres, doing the work of the Advisory Boards and Employment Committees where these had not been established.

In centres where neither Advisory Boards, Employment Committees, nor Recruiting Committees existed, twenty-eight local committees of the Governor-General's Fund took the place of the first-mentioned bodies.

At eighty-one smaller centres the Magistrates acted in the place of the Boards and Committees.

The post offices rendered valuable help in connection with the Returned Soldiers Department, particularly in the very small centres where neither Boards, Committees, nor Magistrates were available.

The most important steps taken in connection with the re-settlement of returned soldiers were:—

(*a*) Training farms established at Vlakfontein, Riversdale, Oakdale, Indwe, Hartebeestpoort, and Beginsel.

(*b*) Returned soldiers admitted at Government expense to the Agricultural Colleges at Cedara, Elsenburg, Glen, Grootfontein, and Potchefstroom.

(*c*) Arrangements made for placing returned soldiers with private farmers for a two-year's course of practical training, the farmer providing board and accommodation and giving tuition, and the Government paying the returned soldier an allowance of 3s. a day during training, and an additional £2. 10s. a month for a man married or with dependents.

(*d*) Large numbers of returned soldiers settled on the land under a scheme which provided generous Government assistance.

(*e*) Government assistance extended to returned soldiers who had served a term of apprenticeship before going on active service, or who had enlisted immediately on leaving school. In such cases an allowance was paid from public funds to bring up the earnings of the apprentice to £10 a month.

(*f*) Money was voted to enable returned soldiers, whose studies had been interrupted by the war, to undergo a course of higher education.

(*g*) Returned soldiers battalions were formed for the temporary re-enlistment of ex-soldiers who had failed to find employment within a certain time.

Vocational training was carried out at Richmond (England) and at Maitland, Durban, and Roberts Heights in the Union, under the supervision of the authorities administering the Governor-General's Fund, the Government contributing a proportion of the expenditure.

Disabled soldiers undergoing a course of vocational training on the recommendation of the Pensions Board received the highest rate of disablement pension during the period of training.

(xiii) *South African Red Cross Society.*

The South African Red Cross Society is not a military organization, but the outbreak of war induced the military authorities of the Union to turn for assistance to the medical profession and the organized body which existed "to carry out works of relief for the sick and wounded in war."

This assistance was forthcoming at once and without stint.

The work of the S.A. Red Cross Society may be best described in the words of a "Brief Summary of its War Work," issued by the Society, from which the following extracts are taken:—

"On the 21st August, 1914, this Society appealed to the public through the Press for assistance to enable it to comply with one of its objects, 'to carry out works of relief for the sick and wounded in war.'

"About the same time the Central Good Hope Red Cross Committee, an organization for war purposes only, was resuscitated and made a similar appeal to the public at the Cape. Somewhat later the Women's Patriotic League in Natal and the Victoria League at Bloemfontein issued similar appeals, and South Africa was soon busily engaged in providing comforts and funds, not only for our own South African troops who were early in the field, but in assisting those oversea engaged in the great fight for liberty.

"The assistance of the Government was invoked and facilities were granted the several bodies for the free transport of comforts, etc., by rail and post.

"The rebellion caused a number of temporary hospitals to be established, and the demands upon the Red Cross became exceedingly numerous, but in every single instance the requests for assistance from any hospital or ambulance were immediately complied with. As far as can be gathered, the hospitals and ambulances established and operating in South-West Africa and in the rebellion were well and generously provided with everything necessary for the comfort of the patients. The cases and parcels dispatched during this period weighed many tons.

" When South Africa was called upon to assist in the East African campaign, steps were being taken for Red Cross South Africa to be represented, when the British Red Cross Society decided to send out a Commissioner and Staff with over £10,000 worth of stores to organize and supervise the distribution of comforts to the hospitals and ambulances. It was therefore decided to work in full co-operation with the Commissioner, Colonel Montgomery, who undertook to act as our agent, and who was advised that all requisitions he forwarded would be honoured in full.

" Many thousands of pounds worth of comforts were thereafter dispatched to East Africa, and anything asked for obtainable in the country was always promptly dispatched.

The Second South African Hospital, raised and organized by Colonel R. P. Mackenzie, was very fully supplied by this Society, so much so that Colonel Mackenzie stated that the hospital as established at Nairobi was one of the best equipped hospitals south of the line. The Second, Third, and Fourth Field Ambulances were also well supplied with stores and equipment before leaving Potchefstroom.

Central Africa was also not forgotten, and, despite difficulties of transport, a constant stream of supplies were sent forward until the hospitals in Nyasaland were closed, and money was remitted for the provision of ' rest houses.'

" The Society was also responsible for the provision of comforts to the Military Hospitals at Roberts Heights, Potchefstroom, and Kimberley, the Wanderers (both as a Military and V.A.D. Hospital), at the German Club, the military patients at the General Hospital, and, on the closing of the Wanderers, to the Gracedale Sanatorium."

(xiv) *South Africa Gifts and Comforts Organization Committee.*

The South Africa Gifts and Comforts Organization Committee was appointed by the Prime Minister " to co-ordinate, assist, and direct all public efforts in South Africa which are not covered by the work performed by the Governor-General's Fund and the Red Cross Society—

(1) for the supplying of gifts and comforts for the use of the South African forces, whether in Europe or in Africa;

(2) for the rendering of such similar assistance as may be possible to His Majesty's Government for the forces of the Empire."

A branch of the organization was established in each Province, with a Central Committee as a co-ordinating body at Capetown under the chairmanship of the Chief Justice of the Union.

In Natal the Women's Patriotic League, with headquarters at Pietermaritzburg and Durban, agreed to act as a branch of the Gifts and Comforts in Natal, and the Provincial War Relief and Victoria League Committee at Bloemfontein undertook similar responsibility as regards the Orange Free State.

The Central Committee, already mentioned, assumed charge of provincial operations in the Cape Province, and thus provincial representation was assured.

The varied and constant efforts of this organization were the cause of alleviating materially and most effectively the hardships of active service sustained by the troops.

A fund, amounting to £6,423, was raised for the provision of aeroplanes, of which four were purchased and presented to the British authorities. 4,700 sheep-skin coats were dispatched to Europe for the winter of 1915-1916. Further efforts in this direction ceased when, after the first insistent demand, complete arrangements for supply had been made by the War Office.

The issue of comforts was carefully systematized and responsibility definitely allocated as between provincial branches.

To the oversea contingent monthly supplies of tobacco and cigarettes were sent, together with large consignments of socks, mufflers, handkerchiefs, woollen waistcoats, mitts, etc., and a certain quantity of matches, dried fruit, sweets, and other articles.

Co-operation at the other end by the South African Hospital and Comforts Fund Committee in London very materially aided forwarding and distribution.

In the case of the East Africa and Nyasaland theatre the constant and great difficulties of transport, and the need for granting priority for war essentials, militated seriously against distribution to the troops, distant hundreds of miles in the interior remote from the seaports, on the scale and with the regularity possible on other fronts.

APPENDIX I.

VICTORIA CROSSES WON BY SOUTH AFRICANS DURING THE WAR.

LIEUTENANT (ACTING CAPTAIN) ANDREW WEATHERBY BEAUCHAMP-PROCTOR, D.S.O., M.C., D.F.C., No. 84 Squadron, Royal Air Force.

Between 8th August, 1918, and 8th October, 1918, this officer proved himself victor in twenty-six decisive combats, destroying twelve enemy kite balloons, ten enemy aircraft, and driving down four other enemy aircraft completely out of control.

Between 1st October, 1918, and 5th October, 1918, he destroyed two enemy scouts, burned three enemy kite balloons, and drove down one enemy scout completely out of control.

On 1st October, 1918, in a general engagement with about twenty-eight machines, he crashed one Fokker biplane near Fontaine and a second near Ramicourt; on 2nd October he burnt a hostile balloon near Selvigny; on 3rd October he drove down completely out of control an enemy scout near Mont d'Origny, and burned a hostile balloon; on 5th October, the third hostile balloon near Bohain.

On 8th October, 1918, while flying home at a low altitude after destroying an enemy two-seater near Maretz, he was painfully wounded in the arm by machine-gun fire; but, continuing, he landed safely at his aerodrome, and after making his report was admitted to hospital.

In all, he has proved himself conqueror over fifty-four foes, destroying twenty-two enemy machines, sixteen enemy kite balloons, and driving down sixteen enemy aircraft completely out of control.

Captain Beauchamp-Proctor's work in attacking enemy troops on the ground and in reconnaissance during the withdrawal following on the Battle of St. Quentin, from 21st March, 1918, and during the victorious advance of our armies commencing on 8th August, has been almost unsurpassed in its brilliancy, and as such has made an impression on those serving in his squadron and those around him that will not be easily forgotten.

Captain Beauchamp-Proctor was awarded the Military Cross on 22nd June, 1918; the Distinguished Flying Cross on 2nd July, 1918; a bar to the Military Cross on 16th September, 1918; and the Distinguished Service Order on 2nd November, 1918.

CAPTAIN WILLIAM ANDERSON BLOOMFIELD, Scout Corps, South African Mounted Brigade.

At Mlali, East Africa, on 24th August, 1916. For most conspicuous bravery. Finding that, after being heavily attacked in an advanced and isolated position, the enemy were working round his flanks, Captain Bloomfield evacuated his wounded and subsequently withdrew his command to a new position, he himself being among the last to retire. On arrival at the new position, he found that one of the wounded—No. 2475 Corporal D. M. P. Bowker—had been left behind. Owing to very heavy fire he experienced difficulties in having the wounded corporal brought in. Rescue meant passing over some four hundred yards of open ground, swept by heavy fire, in full view of the enemy. This task Captain Bloomfield determined to face himself, and unmindful of personal danger, he succeeded in reaching Corporal Bowker and carrying him back, subjected throughout the double journey to heavy machine-gun and rifle fire. This act showed the highest degree of valour and endurance.

No. 1630 SERGEANT FREDERICK CHARLES BOOTH, South African Forces, attached Rhodesia Native Regiment.

At Johannesbruck, near Songea, East Africa, on 12th February, 1917. For most conspicuous bravery during an attack, in thick bush, on the enemy position. Under very heavy rifle fire, Sergeant Booth went forward alone and brought in a man who was dangerously wounded. Later, he rallied native troops who were badly disorganized, and brought them to the firing line. This N.C.O. has, on many previous occasions, displayed the greatest bravery, coolness, and resource in action, and has set a splendid example of pluck, endurance, and determination.

No. 4073 PRIVATE WILLIAM FREDERICK FAULDS, 1st Regiment, South African Infantry.

At Delville Wood, France, on 18th July, 1916. For most conspicuous bravery and devotion to duty. A bombing party under Lieutenant Craig attempted to rush across forty yards of ground which lay between the British and enemy trenches. Coming under very heavy rifle and machine-gun fire, the officer and the majority of the party were killed or wounded. Unable to move, Lieutenant Craig lay midway between the two lines of trenches, the ground being quite open. In full daylight Private Faulds, accompanied by two other men, climbed the parapet, ran out, picked up the officer and carried him back, one man being severely wounded in so doing.

Two days later Private Faulds again showed most conspicuous bravery in going out alone to bring in a wounded man and carrying him nearly half a mile to a dressing station, subsequently rejoining his platoon. The artillery fire was at the time so intense that stretcher bearers and others considered that any attempt to bring in the wounded man meant certain death. This risk Private Faulds faced unflinchingly, and his bravery was crowned with success.

LIEUTENANT ROBERT VAUGHAN GORLE, "A" Battery, 50th Brigade, Royal Field Artillery.

For most conspicuous bravery, initiative, and devotion to duty during the attack at Ledeghem on 1st October, 1918, when in command of an eighteen-pounder gun working in close conjunction with infantry. He brought his gun into action in the most exposed positions on four separate occasions, and disposed of enemy machine-guns by firing over open sights under direct machine-gun fire at five hundred to six hundred yards range.

Later, seeing that the infantry were being driven back by intense hostile fire, he without hesitation galloped his gun in front of the leading infantry, and on two occasions knocked out enemy machine-guns which were causing the trouble. His disregard of personal safety and dash were a magnificent example to the wavering line, which rallied and retook the northern end of the village.

MAJOR (ACTING LIEUT.-COLONEL) HARRY GREENWOOD, D.S.O., M.C., 9th Battalion, King's Own Yorkshire Light Infantry.

For most conspicuous bravery, devotion to duty, and fine leadership on 23rd-24th October, 1918. When the advance of his battalion on the 23rd October was checked, and many casualties caused by an enemy machine-gun post, Lieut.-Colonel Greenwood, single-handed, rushed the post and killed the crew. At the entrance to the village of Ovillers, accompanied by two battalion runners, he again rushed a machine-gun post and killed the occupants.

On reaching the objective west of Duke's Wood, his command was almost surrounded by hostile machine-gun posts, and the enemy at once attacked his isolated force. The attack was repulsed, and led by Lieut.-Colonel Greenwood, his troops swept forward and captured the last objective with one hundred and fifty prisoners, eight machine-guns, and one field gun.

During the attack on the "Green Line," south of Poix du Nord, on 24th October, he again displayed the greatest gallantry in rushing a machine-gun post, and he showed conspicuously good leadership in the handling of his command in the face of heavy fire. He inspired his men in the highest degree, with the result that the objective was captured, and in spite of heavy casualties the line was held.

During the advance on Grand Gay Farm Road, on the afternoon of 24th October, the skilful and bold handling of his battalion was productive of most important results, not only in securing the flank of his brigade but also in safeguarding the flank of the division.

His valour and leading during two days of fighting were beyond all praise.

CAPTAIN PERCY HOWARD HANSEN, ADJUTANT, 6th (Service) Battalion, the Lincolnshire Regiment.

For most conspicuous bravery on 9th August, 1915, at Yilghin Burnu, Gallipoli, Peninsula. After the second capture of the "Green Knoll" his battalion was forced to retire, leaving some wounded behind, owing to the intense heat from the scrub which had been set on fire. When the retirement was effected, Captain Hansen, with three or four volunteers, on his own initiative, dashed forward several times some three hundred to four hundred yards over open ground into the scrub, under a terrific fire, and succeeded in rescuing from inevitable death by burning no less than six wounded men.

LIEUTENANT (ACTING CAPTAIN) REGINALD FREDERICK JOHNSON HAYWARD, M.C., Wiltshire Regiment.

Near Fremicourt, France, on 21st-22nd March, 1918. For most conspicuous bravery in action. This officer, while in command of a company, displayed almost superhuman powers of endurance and consistent courage of the rarest nature. In spite of the fact that he was buried, wounded in the head, and rendered deaf on the first day of operations, and had his arm shattered two days later, he refused to leave his men (even though he received a third serious injury to his head), until he collapsed from sheer physical exhaustion.

Throughout the whole of this period the enemy were attacking his company front without cessation, but Captain Hayward continued to move across the open from one trench to another with absolute disregard of his own personal safety, concentrating entirely on reorganizing his defences and encouraging his men. It was almost entirely due to the magnificent example of ceaseless energy of this officer that many most determined attacks upon his portion of the trench system failed entirely.

No. 8162 Lance-Corporal William Henry Hewitt, 2nd Regiment, South African Infantry.

At east of Ypres on 20th September, 1917. For most conspicuous bravery during operations. Lance-Corporal Hewitt attacked a "pill-box" with his section and tried to rush the doorway. The garrison, however, proved very stubborn, and in the attempt this non-commissioned officer received a severe wound. Nevertheless, he proceeded to the loophole of the "pill-box," where, in his attempts to put a bomb into it, he was again wounded in the arm. Undeterred, however, he eventually managed to get a bomb inside, which caused the occupants to dislodge, and they were successfully and speedily dealt with by the remainder of the section.

Second-Lieutenant (Acting Captain) Arthur Moore Lascelles, 3rd (attached 14th) Battalion, Durham Light Infantry.

At Masnières, France, on 3rd December, 1917. For most conspicuous bravery, initiative, and devotion to duty when in command of his company in a very exposed position. After a very heavy bombardment, during which Captain Lascelles was wounded, the enemy attacked in strong force, but was driven off, success being due in a great degree to the fine example set by this officer, who, refusing to allow his wound to be dressed, continued to encourage his men and organize the defence.

Shortly afterwards the enemy again attacked and captured the trench, taking several of his men prisoners. Captain Lascelles at once jumped on the parapet, and followed by the remainder of his company, twelve men only, rushed across under very heavy machine-gun fire and drove over sixty of the enemy back, thereby saving a most critical situation.

He was untiring in reorganizing the position, but shortly afterwards the enemy again attacked and captured the trench and Captain Lascelles, who escaped later. The remarkable determination and gallantry of this officer in the course of operations, during which he received two further wounds, afforded an inspiring example to all.

Captain Oswald Austin Reid, 2nd Battalion, Liverpool Regiment, attached 6th Battalion, Loyal North Lancashire Regiment.

At Dialah River, Mesopotamia, on 8th-10th March, 1917. For most conspicuous bravery in the face of desperate circumstances. By his dauntless courage and gallant leadership he was able to consolidate a small post with the advanced troops, on the opposite side of a river to the main body, after his lines of communication had been cut by the sinking of the pontoons.

He maintained this position for thirty hours against constant attacks by bombs, machine-gun and shell fire, with the full knowledge that repeated attempts at relief had failed, and that his ammunition was all but exhausted. It was greatly due to his tenacity that the passage of the river was effected on the following night. During the operations he was wounded.

Major (Acting Lieut.-Colonel) John Sherwood-Kelly, C.M.G., D.S.O., Norfolk Regiment, Commanding 1st Battalion, Royal Inniskilling Fusiliers.

At Marcoing, France, on 20th November, 1917. For most conspicuous bravery and fearless leading, when a party of men of another unit detailed to cover the passage of the canal by his battalion were held up on the near side of the canal by heavy rifle fire directed on the bridge. Lieut.-Colonel Sherwood-Kelly at once ordered covering fire, personally led the leading company of his battalion across the canal, and, after crossing, reconnoitred under heavy rifle and machine-gun fire the high ground held by the enemy.

The left flank of his battalion, advancing to the assault of this objective, was held up by a thick belt of wire, whereupon he crossed to that flank and with a Lewis-gun team forced his way under heavy fire through obstacles, got the gun into position on the far side, and covered the advance of his battalion through the wire, thereby enabling them to capture the position.

Later, he personally led a charge against some pits from which a heavy fire was being directed on his men, captured the pits, together with five machine-guns and forty-six prisoners, and killed a large number of the enemy.

The great gallantry displayed by this officer throughout the day inspired the greatest confidence in his men, and it was mainly due to his example and devotion to duty that his battalion was enabled to capture and hold their objective.

Captain (Acting Lieut.-Colonel) Richard Annesley West, D.S.O., M.C., late North Irish Horse (Cavalry Special Reserve) and Tank Corps.

At Courcelles and Vaulx-Vraucourt, France, on 21st August, 1918, and 2nd September, 1918. For most conspicuous bravery, leadership, and self-sacrifice. During an attack, the infantry having lost their bearings in the dense fog, this officer at once collected and reorganized any men he could find and led them to their objective in face of heavy machine-gun fire. Throughout the whole action he displayed the most utter disregard of danger, and the capture of the objective was in a great part due to his initiative and gallantry.

On a subsequent occasion it was intended that a battalion of light tanks, under the command of this officer, should exploit the initial infantry and heavy tank attack. He therefore went forward in order to keep in touch with the progress of the battle, and arrived at the front line when the enemy were in process of delivering a local counter-attack. The infantry battalion had suffered heavy officer casualties and its flanks were exposed. Realizing that there was a danger of the battalion giving way, he at once rode out in front of them under extremely heavy machine-gun and rifle fire and rallied the men.

In spite of the fact that the enemy were close upon him, he took charge of the situation and detailed non-commissioned officers to replace officer casualties. He then rode up and down in front of them in face of certain death, encouraging the men and calling to them "Stick it, men! Show them fight! and for God's sake put up a good fight!" He fell riddled by machine-gun bullets.

The magnificent bravery of this very gallant officer at the critical moment inspired the infantry to redoubled efforts, and the hostile attack was defeated.

APPENDIX II.

NUMBER OF SOUTH AFRICANS WHO WERE KILLED IN ACTION OR DIED AS THE RESULT OF ACTIVE SERVICE.

Union of South Africa.	
1st Permanent Batty. (S.A. Mtd. Riflemen)	1
5th Permanent Batty. (S.A. Mtd. Riflemen)	7
A.C.F. Artillery	5
S.A. Field Artillery	66
S.A. Heavy Artillery	176
S.A. Mtd. Riflemen	39
1st Mtd. Rifles (Natal Carbineers)	7
4th Mtd. Rifles (Umvoti Mtd. Rifles)	2
5th Mtd. Rifles (Imperial Light Horse)	17
6th Mtd. Rifles (Cape Light Horse)	1
8th Mtd. Rifles (Midlandse Ruiters)	8
9th Mtd. Rifles (Hogeveld Ruiters)	4
11th Mtd. Rifles (Potchefstroom Ruiters)	2
17th Mtd. Rifles (Western Province Mtd. Rifles)	1
18th Mtd. Rifles (Griqualand West Ruiters)	4
Natal Light Horse	27
Northern Transvaal Rifles	1
1st S.A. Horse	34
2nd S.A. Horse	30
3rd S.A. Horse	39
4th S.A. Horse	47
5th S.A. Horse	23
6th S.A. Horse	14
7th S.A. Horse	23
8th S.A. Horse	18
9th S.A. Horse	19
10th S.A. Horse	15
1st Mtd. Brigade Scouts	9
2nd Mtd. Brigade Scouts	3
1st Mtd. Brigade	12
2nd Mtd. Brigade	4
5th Mtd. Brigade	8
Mounted Commandoes	85
1st Infantry (Durban Light Infantry)	1
2nd Infantry (D.E. Own Rifles)	2
3rd Infantry (Prince Alfred's Guard)	1
4th Infantry (1st Eastern Rifles)	3
5th Infantry (Kaffrarian Rifles)	6
6th Infantry (D.C. and S. Own Capetown Hldrs.)	1
7th Infantry (Kimberley Regt.)	8
8th Infantry (Transvaal Scottish)	6
9th Infantry (P.W.O. Regt. C.P. Rifles)	1
10th Infantry (Wit. Rifles)	1
11th Infantry (Rand Light Infty.)	2
12th Infantry (Pretoria Regt.)	1
S.A. Irish	2
Rand Rifles	3
Southern Rifles	2
1st Dismounted Rifles	1
1st S.A. Infantry	1,156
2nd S.A. Infantry	1,262
3rd S.A. Infantry	658
4th S.A. Infantry	1,164
5th S.A. Infantry	94
6th S.A. Infantry	82
7th S.A. Infantry	133
8th S.A. Infantry	168
9th S.A. Infantry	34
10th S.A. Infantry	79
11th S.A. Infantry	41
12th S.A. Infantry	51
2nd S.A. Infantry Brigade	7
3rd S.A. Infantry Brigade	5
1st S.A. Rifles	19
2nd S.A. Rifles	45
S.A. Sharpshooters	6
Stokes Mortar Batty.	6
S.A. Pioneers	55
S.A. Motor Cycle Corps	34
S.A. Engineers	16
S.A. Signal Service	98
S.A. Railway Services	33
Miscellaneous Trades Coy.	11
S.A. Special Service Corps	6
S.A. Air Force	2
S.A. Service Corps	305
S.A. Medical Corps	203
S.A. Ordnance Corps	5
S.A. Veterinary Corps	17
S.A. Pay Corps	17
S.A. Water Supply Corps	4
S.A. Road Corps	12
S.A. Military Police	4
S.A. Military Constabulary	3
S.A. Intelligence Corps	5
General and Base Depots	18

Hdqrs., Record Office, and Camp Staffs	26
S.A. Vet. Reserve and Vet. Rgt.	12
Returned Soldiers' Battn.	1
Cape Corps	33
C.A.H. Transport Corps	6
S.A. Native Lab. Contingent	27
Mil. Labour Corps	39
S.A. Military Nursing Service	9
	6,803

RHODESIAN UNITS.

B.S.A. Police	71
Northern Rhod. Police	5
1st Rhod. Regt.	5
2nd Rhod. Regt.	89
Rhod. Native Regt	10
	180

SOUTH AFRICANS SERVING WITH IMPERIAL UNITS.

Royal Navy	35
Royal Air Force	260
Other Units	1,273
	1,568

NON-EUROPEANS.

Coloured	709
Natives	3,192

SUMMARY.

Europeans	8,551
Coloured	709
Natives	3,192
Total	12,452